SPLEEN
AND
NOSTALGIA

SPLEEN AND NOSTALGIA

A LIFE AND WORK IN PSYCHOANALYSIS

JOHN E. GEDO

JASON ARONSON INC.
Northvale, New Jersey
London

This book was set in 11 pt. Weiss by Alpha Graphics of Pittsfield, New Hampshire and printed and bound by Book-mart Press of North Bergen, New Jersey.

10 9 8 7 6 5 4 3 2 1

Library of Congress Cataloging-in-Publication Data

Gedo, John E.
Spleen and nostalgia : a life and work in psychoanalysis / John E. Gedo.
p. cm.
Includes bibliographical references and index.
ISBN 0-7657-0082-4 (alk. paper)
1. Gedo, John E. 2. Psychoanalysts—United States—Biography.
I. Title.
BF109.G48A3 1997
150.19'5'092—dc21 97-9834
[B]

Printed in the United States of America on acid-free paper. Jason Aronson Inc. offers books and cassettes. For information and catalog write to Jason Aronson Inc., 230 Livingston Street, Northvale, New Jersey 07647-1731. Or visit our website: http://www.aronson.com

What's gone and what's past help
Should be past grief

Shakespeare:
The Winter's Tale
(Act III, Scene 2)

CONTENTS

ACKNOWLEDGMENTS

The difficult birth of this book could not have taken place without substantial assistance from an unusually large number of persons who generously agreed to comment on several earlier versions of its manuscript. Among these midwives, I owe special debts of gratitude to Mary, Nicholas, and Paul Gedo, Meyer Gunther, Douglas Kirsner, Ernest and Julia Mond, George Moraitis, Leo Sadow, Paul Stepansky, and Charles Strozier. In addition, I received invaluable feedback from Eva Sandberg, who not only assisted me in preparing successive drafts of the manuscript but also provided much needed literary advice. Carol Johnson Nishiura has been extraordinarily kind in providing much of the photographic material for this volume.

I owe thanks to the staff of the MacLean Library of the Chicago Institute for Psychoanalysis, Nancy Harvey and Bill Kelly, for extensive help with the documentation of my text, and to Jerome Kavka, the Institute Archivist, who arranged my survey of the Kohut Archive and personally assisted my search for relevant documents in its files.

Finally, I wish to thank Michael Moskowitz, Publisher, and his staff at Jason Aronson Inc. for unfailing courtesy and efficiency in seeing this volume through to publication, as well as for crucial direction about the proper focus of a professional memoir.

WHAT MAKES A MEMOIR PSYCHOANALYTIC? (AN INTRODUCTION)

Although this volume reviews a career in psychoanalysis, that subject matter would not suffice to make it an analytic memoir. Rather, I think this effort is psychoanalytic for two reasons: first, because I attempt to convey the truth (as I see it, of course)—even when this puts me in a bad light; second, because my narrative is largely organized in an associative manner: it echoes the inner organization of the subject matter of psychoanalytic sessions. I often start chapters with an event in the recent past; what follows in every instance is a chain of associated thoughts that eventually lead me back to the present.

I have arranged the resultant units in a more or less chronological sequence that covers my professional life, but this framework does not add up to a chronicle. In other words, this memoir does not pretend to be a true autobiography; what it aims for, instead, is an overview of my emotional and intellectual odyssey within the profession—an overview organized in accord with categories relevant not merely to one participant's personal life but also to the manner in which that professional domain itself is structured.

In determining the final form of my text, I have reluctantly decided to depart in one respect from the basic rule of free association: in instances where I relate events that place individuals who played only an incidental role in my life in an unfavorable light, I have suppressed their names. As the title of this book indicates, it is principally focused on my subjective reactions to various people and events. I have tried hard to document my recollections through independent sources of information; most of this supporting material is to be found in the Notes that follow the text of the memoir. I have also made every effort to differentiate between my emotions and opinions, on one hand, and some kind of "objective" reality, on the other. I have striven to be as truthful as one needs to be in any analytic effort; I trust my readers will understand, however, that I do not regard my perception of the world as immune to error or injustice. I also nourish the hope that my text will convey the fact that the passage of time has moderated the intensity of the emotions I try to recollect in this book.

For the most part, I have omitted from this volume associative sequences with no bearing on my professional life, although numerous references to my family background and childhood are included as prime determinants of my characteristics as a psychoanalyst. Readers will note my failure to describe my wife, my children, and the colleagues who appear in my narrative but have been just as important to me as cherished friends as they were qua professional allies. All that belongs in a different memoir, lacking in spleen! To compensate for these missing tributes, I have supplied a limited number of personal photographs, each of which will, I hope, illustrate a suppressed chain of associations and fill in the lacunae in my story caused by the necessary limits of a book such as this.

PART ONE

THE FOLLIES OF YOUTH

❖ CHAPTER 1 ❖

METAMORPHOSIS

My life in America has followed a course so unexpected that I have never even had fantasies anticipating such developments. I associate these strange events with my very first experience of the New World, one that prefigured everything that was to come. On the last day of March 1941, my family was among a small group of passengers on the Spanish freighter *Navemar*, carrying a cargo of cork from Tangier to New York. It was a stormy crossing, although we felt secure in the illusion that a neutral vessel was in no danger from any of the World War II belligerents. Later that summer, the *Navemar* was sunk by an unidentified submarine. We were scheduled to dock in Brooklyn on the first of April. As night fell, the weather cleared, and an eerie light illuminated the entire sky. I was convinced that I was seeing the lights of the great American metropolis, and years passed before I realized that my adopted home is not quite that dazzling. It was my only exposure to the phenomenon of aurora borealis—an astonishing introduction to America.

I have continued to be astonished by the evolution of my subsequent fortunes—not only in sharing the prosperity of the entire country over the last fifty years, but in the professional arena as well, as a scientific contributor and a participant in the affairs of psychoanalytic organizations. Of course, from a conventional biographical viewpoint, my life has been rather uneventful: a professional education much like any other, marriage at 25, three sons raised without notable vicissitudes, and a prosperous private practice through the fat years of American psychoanalysis. I cannot imagine that I could ever have been made into a subject of interesting gossip. The most picaresque adventure I have had was that of performing a blood count on Hideki Tojo, the former Prime Minister of Japan, when he was awaiting his trial for war crimes. (It gave me the opportunity to boast to my children that I was the only Allied soldier to have bloodied one of the Axis leaders!)

According to Montaigne, it is ordinary lives that are most beautiful. Perhaps so—but it interests no one that I have lived for more than four decades with one wife and four poodles, or that Mary is a person of substance and I am a fan of the Chicago Bears. About all that, what is there to say beyond the poet's sardonic line, "The olive dries up . . ."?[1] I *could* say, of course, that such good fortune is astonishing in itself, but I do not really believe that chance played any part in my fate for, before I entered analysis in 1953, I was surely headed in a different direction. It is true that earlier in 1953 I had also married, but since I was seldom able to sustain meaningful relationships (trivial incidents sometimes caused me to change course in my dealings with people), the analysis was required to forestall expectable difficulties in marriage. I am truly one of those who owe whatever success they have had in life to an effective psychoanalytic experience.

When the Chicago Institute referred me to him for a training analysis, I had never heard of Maxwell Gitelson and was greatly surprised to discover that he was shortly to become president of the American Psychoanalytic Association. When he learned that I lived only a few blocks from his home, he offered me an early morning hour in his study there. I knew that the fee of fifteen dollars a session was below the going rate; when Max (my second Max; my paternal grandfather was named Maximilian) learned that I could not even pay that without relying on my parents—a necessity I contemplated with great distaste—he thoughtfully suggested that I could defer payment on any part of the bill I could not settle from my own current resources. It was understood that this arrangement was justified by the desirability of keeping third parties out of the analysis, but I was never unmindful of its generosity. (I still believe that, whenever there is a choice, analysts do well to be generous.) Of course, I also felt that Max was a grand seigneur; in those days, the entire Institute faculty carried an aura of being larger than life. In Max's case, this impression was reinforced by the splendor of the Gitelsons' lakefront apartment.

They lived on the corner of 55th Street and South Shore Drive, on the periphery of the University of Chicago neighborhood, in an immense, vintage 1925 apartment block later made famous in a Saul Bellow novel wherein title to one of the units is a bone of contention in a bitter divorce. In recent years, I have grown used to the building, because our friends Regina and Gerhard Casper bought that disputed unit.[2] (Of course, Gerhard, now that he has become president of Stanford University, could also pass for a lord, but even as university provost at Chicago he remained very much my junior, and Regina had been my supervisee at the Institute.) When I was 25, I found the setting somewhat overwhelming. It was also disturbing frequently to encounter Mrs. Gitelson, the psychoanalyst professionally known as Frances Hannett, who practiced only at home. I was particularly upset because Hannett, a handsome woman of around 50, was grossly overweight, and I had to tell her husband dreams about fat swine wallowing in mud. I do not know which of us was more reluctant to acknowledge that this was my venomous perception of a very nice lady.

Of course, any self-respecting candidate with an oedipal neurosis is bound to show hostility focused on the analyst's spouse sooner or later. Max must have realized that this issue had been stirred up a little too soon; I suspect this is why he eventually arranged to transfer our sessions to his downtown office. This large, paneled room was also unusually well appointed—a fitting inner sanctum for the president of the American Psychoanalytic Association. At any rate, the analysis went decidedly better in the less evocative atmosphere on the seventeenth floor of the Pittsfield Building. In retrospect, I can see that the entire process ran its course quite rapidly, for we reached a reasonable termination after some six hundred sessions in the course of three years.

In 1953, when we started, Gitelson had just assumed leadership of the conservative faction in Chicago psychoanalysis, those opposed to the radical therapeutic claims made by Franz Alexander and his many followers at the Chicago Institute. (Thus, entering analysis with Max had weighty political implications that I did not then understand. I shall come back to them presently.) At this stage of his career, Alexander was convinced that the brief therapies he had developed, based on "corrective emotional experiences" consciously devised by the analyst, were superior to traditional psychoanalysis. He was particularly concerned about the inability of the prevalent analytic techniques to deal with the regressive manifestations often evoked by the treatment—a concern that certainly had some justification. His group tried to modify analytic technique by introducing variations in the frequency of sessions as a means of counteracting regressive developments. These parallel departures from the analytic goal of elucidating whatever the method of free association brought to light had great appeal to the multitude of "psychodynamic psychotherapists" then active, but it did threaten to submerge psychoanalysis proper in this watered-down substitute.

Those of us who, as beginners, were taught to apply Alexander's therapeutic prescriptions found that this was easier said than done; one had to know what to say without very much evidence to guide one. Many of us did not have Alexander's charisma, and our "dynamic diagnoses" often seemed to fall flat. Moreover, at this time much of our work was with hospitalized patients, and with that population it was the examples of Harry Stack Sullivan and Frieda Fromm-Reichmann that were held up to us. *These* authorities certainly did not believe that in therapy "less is more." It was a confusing situation.

Far from looking for shortcuts, Gitelson firmly believed that analysis should be as intense an experience as possible, based on a schedule of daily appointments. (After some years of doing it both ways, I also concluded that five sessions per week yield much better results than do treatments conducted on a less intense basis. As I like to put it, I am not smart enough to understand patients I see less frequently.) At any rate, my analytic experience was very stirring—Mary still claims that for a couple of years I walked around like a zombie. Unless otherwise occupied, I became focused on my inner life, so that the process of its investigation became essentially continuous. The mental contents explicitly interpreted in the sessions were the familiar intrapsychic conflicts stressed in the era of ego psychology. In this sense, Gitelson lived up to his conservative reputation, and I was left to deal with some problems stemming from more archaic issues in my subsequent self-analysis.[3] For example, in our very last session, Max inquired whether there was anything I then wanted to ask him. Still free associating, I said, "How did I do?" Laughing good-naturedly, Max answered, "Well, one can't make a sow's ear out of a silk purse. . . ." I knew I was receiving a sardonic compliment, but I also came to feel that something had been missed. It took me about twenty years to figure out that one proper response to my association might have been, "It is for the analyst to ask the patient whether the treatment has been good enough." In other words, I was overly prone to accept that any flaw in a joint enterprise was my responsibility alone. This was one legacy of my close early relationship with a self-righteous mother.

As this anecdote illustrates, Gitelson's behavior in the consulting room was far from traditional. I am sure he had learned his technique, calculated to arouse as much affect as possible, in his own analysis with Lionel Blitzsten, his predecessor as Alexander's nemesis within the Chicago psychoanalytic community. Blitzsten was the first analyst to practice west of the Alleghenies; he once had a period of treatment in Berlin with Alexander. I do not know how they turned into enemies, but Blitzsten gradually collected around himself a loyal band of colleagues skeptical of Alexander's boundless therapeutic optimism and personal charisma.

By the time I arrived in Chicago, Blitzsten was mortally ill, more of a legend than an actual participant in the analytic community. One heard stories to the effect that he had a series of placards attached to the foot of his couch that he could manipulate by means of strings; one of these allegedly sported the inscription, "THAT IS THE *SADDEST* STORY I HAVE EVER HEARD!" In Chicago, such were the conservatives of the heroic age of psychoanalysis in America; I can only conjecture how wild the procedures of the radicals might have been.

Gitelson was a small, grizzled, feisty person whose demeanor reminded me of a Scottish terrier. The most valuable service he rendered me was to teach me how to fight, and to do it with appropriate feeling. Today, most of us would not approve of his puffing on stinky cigars while he worked, but (in contrast to my European elders) he did not look upon my disapproval of his vicious habit as a piece of impudence. (In his place, my father would have said, "Son, why are you trying to teach your father how to make babies?") Had I known that Max had already had a heart attack, I might have been deflected into trying to save him from the consequences of his lack of prudence—the poor man was to die before his time, of heart disease—but, in the anonymity of his analytic role, he merely became the target of my indignation. There was no hiding behind good manners in the analytic setting, and Max was wont to reply with something like, "Why do you think you want to knock the cigar out of my mouth?" It took me some time to learn to respond in kind—but I never did say, "Because it is there!"

At first such pugnacious inquiries tended to leave me speechless, but eventually Max's excellent example did teach me to articulate passionate answers to them, ones that did not let him attribute my objections to an infantile stereotype. After a couple of years of such sparring, I had the concrete sensation that a steel plate that had cut off my head from the rest of my body was being extracted, and thereafter I have always had full access to my emotions. People who have met me in recent years are incredulous when I tell them that, as a young man, I had been excessively timid.

Of course, by the time I was discharged from the Army at the age of 19, I *had* learned outwardly to impersonate an uninhibited person, but I did this without affect, by going through the motions. (Privately, I called this "pseudomanic schizophobia.")

If Gitelson's characteristic combativeness proved useful to me in treatment, his propensity to get embroiled in the political feuds of the analytic community certainly complicated the lives of his candidate-analysands. Fortunately, I did not get as enmeshed in these thickets as one of my fellow patients, whom I knew when we were both psychiatric residents at the University of Illinois. Late in his analysis, this very capable man managed to get himself rejected when he applied for matriculation at the Institute—according to all the rumors by bringing Gitelson's fight against Alexander into the matriculation interview.

I was immune to such temptations, first of all, because I have always been able to fall back on the Central European bourgeois manners I had been trained to follow as a child; more to the point, my experience with a mother who was often in the wrong in her dealings with people had taught me to give her opponents the benefit of every doubt. As a resident at the University of Illinois, I was in contact with Alexander (who taught a regular course there), and I admired his erudition and his charisma. Besides, I had reason to believe that he had a soft spot for Hungarians—when we first met, he greeted me by stating, "You are Hungarian, of course!?" "Of course!" I replied, triumphantly *refraining* from spelling out the obvious. Alexander moved to Los Angeles in 1956, just as I was matriculating at the Institute, so that I never had the opportunity to test out whether the Budapest connection would have been as valuable as I imagined. But I have never been tempted to enlist in any analytic condottiere's Sacred Band.

In the mid-1950s, the Chicago analytic community was fractured into a number of such competing cliques. As soon as I left Illinois to do my last year of residency at Michael Reese Hospital, I fell from the Gitelson-Alexander frying pan into the fire of a Gitelson-Grinker feud. I still do not know about the personal origins of these hostilities, which began in the 1930s, but in my time Roy Grinker (who was chairman of psychiatry at Reese) fought for the incorporation of psychoanalysis into psychiatry, whereas Max stood for its independent existence. When Gitelson was president of the American Psychoanalytic Association, Grinker was helping to organize a rival Academy of Psychoanalysis. The situation was quite confusing, because Max had some kind of power base at Michael Reese, and it was *his* clinical seminar that constituted the superstar attraction on the residents' agenda. Grinker was slow to accept me as one of his "boys," but he was enormously helpful when, upon completing the residency, I opened a full-time private practice.[4]

In 1955 it was not difficult to get started as an independent psychiatric practitioner in Chicago, although a beginner could not earn much more than ten dollars per therapy session. There were comparatively few trained psychotherapists in the area, almost all of them psychiatrists happy to make referrals to junior colleagues. By virtue of having had some residency in each of the three analytically oriented programs in the city (the University of Chicago, the University of Illinois, and Michael Reese), I had unusually good sources of referral, especially from faculty members who had supervised me. I should probably explain that, in the early 1950s, these psychiatric institutions ran a combined educational program, which was coordinated by the Institute for Psychoanalysis. Successful applicants began with a psychiatric residency and, if all went well, later matriculated for analytic training at the Institute. The entire consortium was known as the Associated Psychiatric Faculties of Chicago (APFC). It was understood that residents would start a training analysis as early as possible. We certainly felt ourselves to be members of the psychoanalytic community as soon as we were accepted.

Despite these advantages, when I went into private practice it would have taken some months to fill my available time without being sent patients in need of hospitalization. Everyone understood this state of affairs, and most would-be practitioners tried to join the medical staff (and thereby get hospital privileges) at Michael Reese, the only private hospital among the analytic trio in the city. Roy Grinker made sure that his former residents got the lion's share of the walk-in trade; as a result, my practice was full before the end of the first month. (From the summer of 1955 until I stopped clinical work in the fall of 1994, I literally never had open time in my schedule—nor was this happy condition unusual for the Chicago scene.)

At any rate, Grinker's evident good will and reliability made it impossible for me to join Max's campaigns against him. I do not believe that my insistence on neutrality in these analytic civil wars affected Gitelson's performance as my analyst, but it may have accounted for the fact that, unlike some of his other former patients, I never became socially friendly with him. Regrettably, these crucial issues of political loyalty did not occupy much of our time or attention in the analysis. Insofar as they were derivatives of the loyalty conflicts of my early childhood, these problems were not adequately dealt with—nor could they be—within an interpretive framework confined to the complex of oedipal hostility, anxiety, and inhibition. It may be adaptively useful to be able to remain neutral when caught in a cross fire, but it is exceedingly costly to be unable to tell people that they have no right to put one in that dilemma.[5]

In my case, it was all the more difficult to get beyond conventional formulations about oedipal inhibitions because they happened to be valid and their application relieved me not only of the constraint of being too tame but also of the tendency to deflect action into Hamlet's "pale cast of thought." If I was all too tempted into hostile-competitive possibilities vis-à-vis male authorities, this propensity served as a screen for my need to keep people at a distance if, like both of my parents, they demanded from me a loyalty I found stifling. I do not think Max ever understood why I did not become more involved with him, and I suspect in his psychoanalytic disputes he craved my support.

After Max's death, Frances Hannett reproached me for writing a review of his collected papers that was entirely objective in tone.[6] Such are the more or less covert pressures pulling psychoanalysts into clique formation. By that time, I was book review editor of the *Journal of the American Psychoanalytic Association* and would certainly have asked someone else to write the review had I had any doubt about my ability to remain "objective."[7] Gitelson had been my analyst, and I thought he had done a good job on my behalf, but thereafter I preferred that we keep out of each other's hair.

Of course, in a relatively small professional community, that is easier said than done. The Chicago analytic world was mainly divided into a smaller group whose offices were on the premises of the Institute (then located on the best part of Michigan Avenue, at Erie Street), and a more numerous Loop contingent that worked in a cluster of buildings around the central public library, on Washington Street. (That is where the 1968 protesters were chanting "The whole world is watching!" right under our windows.) I often ran into Gitelson in the restaurant where most of us had lunch and where colleagues would join each other on the spur of the moment. After we terminated the analysis, Max did not hesitate to sit with me if there was an empty chair at my table, and, after he established this precedent, I would naturally do likewise. In such a setting, Gitelson never talked about his personal life, and we soon discovered that, beyond psychoanalysis, we had few interests in common. Thus, the conversation remained focused on professional matters—often on the concern we shared about the low standards set for the education of psychoanalysts. In these discussions, Max always treated me as an intellectual equal, as he had all through the analysis. He did not think that there were many "silk purses" among the psychoanalysts he knew. In retrospect, the lax criteria of selection Max was decrying have in part determined the recent decline of American psychoanalysis; untalented practitioners have brought the discipline into disrepute by performing inadequately in our "impossible profession" (as Janet Malcolm called it[8]).

Because I waited to apply for enrollment in the Institute course work until I was ready to terminate my analysis, I did not come into contact with Gitelson as a faculty member until several years after we stopped working together. He was then conducting an advanced clinical seminar on termination, a course I found extremely useful—as did all the students, I believe.[9] It so happened that, when it was my turn to present a completed analysis, site visitors from the Committee on Institutes of the American Psychoanalytic Association sat in on this four-hour exercise. It proved to be my most harmonious encounter with Max. We were both at our best, and one of the site visitors blurted out at the end that this had been the best seminar he had ever attended. It was of some moment that the patient whose treatment I described was a fundamentalist minister who dreamt of defending a mountaintop against the besieging armies of the Inquisition, led by his mother. In an effort to teach the class to moderate therapeutic ambitions, Max stated that such a dream was in itself a marker of a satisfactory result. Turning to me, he said, "What more do you want?" The temptation was irresistible; I replied, "If you don't know, nobody does . . ." I thought it was necessary to end institutions established to "defend" a faith. He probably did not know, at that.

I believe the clearest indicator of the changes my analysis brought about occurred a year or so before this, when I got into a very rancorous dispute with a supervisor and requested reassignment to someone else—not a routine matter in those days. The administrator in charge of such negotiations was Joan Fleming, a schoolmarmish spinster (I use the term advisedly, to distinguish the type from liberated single women of a later vintage) who did not favor independence of mind but responded generously when someone needed help. She apparently decided to be very helpful to me, granted my request, but recommended nonetheless that I get more analysis. (She had supervised me when I was a resident at Michael Reese and had formed some prejudices about my character because I tried to use my time with her to discuss certain questions of theory. Of course, by doing that, I betrayed my own misunderstanding of Fleming's assets and limitations.) This was the first of a handful of occasions when an emotional challenge triggered a ceaseless self-analytic process in me—an involuntary, continuous, and profuse stream of associations that led me to certain conclusions.[10]

I made an appointment with Gitelson to discuss Fleming's recommendation and, in our initial meeting, told him the complex story of my dispute with the supervisor. Before my next appointment, a week later, I decided that the problem was that I had been excessively tolerant of unwarranted abuse, that I had finally mastered this propensity by taking the initiative to end the supervision, and that accepting Fleming's judgment (or Gitelson's, for that matter) about this sequence of events would be tantamount to allowing myself to be subjugated once again. And so I told everyone concerned. Before my analysis, such courage would have been beyond me; I would have been more likely to emigrate somewhere, like Southern California, while feeling like a victim.

What had made this transaction particularly painful was the fact that the abusive instructor had been an analysand of Gitelson's who for some time had a session with him immediately preceding mine. I had been hesitant to accept him as a supervisor out of concern about joining the Gitelson clique, for it was widely known that this man had become Max's close personal friend. I need not have been uneasy: far from offering to convoy me to graduation, the supervisor was unremittingly critical of everything I did. After some months, I challenged him about never having made one approving statement about my conduct of the analysis, and he grudgingly allowed that he did believe that my summaries of the treatment were reliable. The implication was clear: according to him, my analytic work was worthless.

I then had a traumatic dream of a supervisory session with a "Dr. Rip Slamming," a transparent anagram on the aggressor's name. In our next meeting, I asked him whether he remembered where he had seen me before. He did not. When I told him it was in Max's waiting room, he laughed and said he would no more have noticed me there than he would have noticed a cockroach. But I *knew* he had noticed me, for a couple of weeks before this interchange he had phoned me to ask whether I had taken his galoshes (and left him a pair that were ripped. "Rip!"). He was a smallish man, and his galoshes would not have fit over my shoes, as one moment's thought could have shown him. As cockroaches go, I am rather large.

When I told Gitelson all this, he made a great effort not to prejudge the issue—he clearly indicated that he grasped my view that Dr. Galoshes (so Mary and I were to call him thereafter) had enacted a complex transference schema of sibling rivalry involving all three of us. Max did add, however, that through the years he had never had any reason to suspect that any such transference residue was in existence, and I sensed that such a possibility caused him real distress. No doubt this perception helped me to decide that I had best rely on my self-inquiry: I suspected that no Institute faculty member would credit my story that the supervisor had been sadistically destructive with me. That judgment about Rip's personality only gained credence after Gitelson's death, because his unhappy epigone gradually slipped into overt misanthropy. By the time he committed suicide, at the threshold of old age, hardly anyone in the local analytic community was greatly surprised.

My pessimism about the fair-mindedness of Institute faculty was in all probability unjustified; the supervision of my (third) analytic case was kindly taken over by the late Fred Robbins, a very generous person who found my work more than adequate, even though my analysand chose not to resume treatment after giving birth to a boy whom she expected to console her for life's miseries. And I never heard one word of criticism, either about the supervisory mess or about my rejection of the advice to resume analysis. I was able to graduate in the minimum time contemplated by the Chicago program, and faculty members started to send me prospective analysands a year or two before that.

By the age of 33, I had the luxury of restricting my practice to patients who needed psychoanalysis proper. For Chicago, this was an unusual choice; when, a few years later, the Psychoanalytic Society surveyed its membership, only three respondents (including Heinz Kohut and me) reported that they did not accept patients for psychotherapy. Of course, with a full practice, such a policy entails little risk: in the natural course of events, one can barely start with two new analytic patients in an average year. Moreover, I was already convinced that our ability to predict analyzability is very poor, so that I decided to accept for analysis anyone interested in self-understanding, provided there was no obvious risk of adaptive decompensation. And circa 1960, all sorts of people could afford analysis who would not be able to do so today: social workers, nurses, teachers, young college faculty, civil servants. We have, in the interval, priced ourselves out of our best market. Moreover, in the good old days, analysts were by and large content to live on a relatively modest scale; I enjoyed the Chicago Symphony from the upper balcony just as much as I now do, sitting in the center of Row G of the orchestra section; until recently there was no admission charge at the Art Institute, and great Burgundies then cost less than table wines do today.

❖ CHAPTER 2 ❖

ORIGINS

In the summer of 1993, just one year away from full retirement, I seemed to have entered the ranks of the elders of psychoanalysis. Almost four decades of controversial activity were succeeded, more abruptly than might have been imagined, by an era of tolerant, even affectionate acceptance. I could not help but feel that I was now regarded as an aged Falstaff (*vecchio* [old] *John*, as Verdi puts it), no longer a threat to most colleagues. I suppose the change occurred in large part because, some five years before, I had closed my practice to new analysands and this information had slowly reached much of the analytic community. (At first, certain colleagues in Chicago actually thought that I was only pretending that I would retire, in order to bring off some political coup at the Institute!) One of the ways in which this change in my professional status was brought home to me was through participation in the celebration of the one hundred and twentieth anniversary of the birth of Sándor Ferenczi, the founder of the Hungarian Psychoanalytic Society—an organization triumphantly reborn in the wake of the defeat of totalitarianism in Central Europe.

More than fifty years before, the totalitarian right had exiled my father from Hungary, so that I experienced the reorganization of psychoanalysis in his homeland in personal terms, as the victory of justice and honor. It was an event I did not want to miss, and I expected that most analysts of Hungarian origin would return for the occasion. This fantasy proved to be a manifestation of my incorrigible naïveté about group behavior; Hungarian analysts, like all others, are divided into factions, many of which so disapprove of Ferenczi that his name sufficed to keep them away from Budapest! (There are others who cannot forget Hungarian complicity with the Nazis.) Those of us who did attend tended to belong to an ecumenical minority, with a sprinkling of fierce partisans espousing Ferenczi's viewpoints of the early 1930s.

It was Ferenczi's Budapest followers who had organized the meeting, and from their point of view my ecumenical position, stated over the years in a number of publications (1968b, 1986a [chap. 3], 1993h) was scarcely satisfactory. Hence, I did not leave the matter of an invitation to present my views entirely to chance; through a special friend in the Budapest circle, I let it be known that I considered an invitation to be my due as the senior Ferenczi scholar in America. And for the first time in my career, such an appeal actually worked! I was given carte blanche for a plenary talk on a subject of my choosing. I was planning to wish a plague on the houses of all factionalists who perseverate in arguing the issues that divided Freud and Ferenczi sixty years in the past.

My wife could not accompany me that summer, because she faced a pressing deadline in preparing for publication a volume of her papers in art history (M. Gedo 1993). When he heard about this circumstance, our old friend Mike Gunther, a Chicago colleague with a passionate interest in the culture of former Hapsburg lands, proposed to join me at the Budapest meeting; together we planned to proceed to Prague. My father got his medical degree from the now-suppressed German university there, and as newlyweds my parents lived in the Czech capital for several years—in fact, until a few weeks before my birth, when my father opened a practice in obstetrics and gynecology in his native town in Slovakia, just an hour's drive north of Budapest. The proposed journey could thus become an occasion to review what my life might have been if the fortunes of war and politics had left me in place on the borders of Hungary and Czechoslovakia.

I had never been back to my place of birth since we left it in the winter of 1938–39. It is a dusty little town of no conceivable interest to outsiders, and I had not chosen to drag my wife there when we had visited Budapest together. I decided to go on such a pilgrimage before the Ferenczi conference, with a cousin who had offered to act as guide because she was also born in the same locality. Éva Czecze is now in her middle sixties and has had a fine career in Hungary as a neurologist, reaching the position of a *Hauptarzt* (roughly, the head of a division) at the principal neuropsychiatric hospital of the Hungarian capital. She invited me to stay with her for a few days, and we arranged to go to Losoncz together. (To bring the story up to date: the town now officially belongs to Slovakia, and its current name is Lučenec.) We even planned to look for the hamlet in the Slovak hills where, before the First World War, our mothers had been raised.

I rented a car at the Budapest airport, probably to Éva's disappointment, for she had come out to meet me in a limousine commandeered from the mayor's office, where her son-in-law is something of a factotum. Her gesture was the first of many stunning details that showed me how drastically my life had changed as a result of migrating westward; although by American standards Éva is a pauper, she knows everyone who counts for anything in Hungary—at least she knows someone who knows anyone of that sort. She looks careworn and dresses like a woman of the people (hardly the fashion in post-Communist Hungary!), but she is a self-conscious member of a small intellectual elite, partly through her prestige in medical circles, partly because she had married a literary man. She is proud of having made a career without joining the Communist party, but she is a progressive in politics, contemptuous both of the materialism of the West and of the Hungarian nostalgia for a feudal past; she is content to have devoted her life to caring for the afflicted. There but for the grace of God go I (except that, unlike Éva, I cannot trace my family tree back to 1377).

The trip from Budapest to Losoncz now takes twice as long as it did in the 1930s; few border crossing points have been kept open, so that one must drive to Slovakia in a roundabout way. The countryside presents a mix of verdant pine forests and fields of sunflowers or grain. Individual farms have been wiped out; there are now no people and no animals to be seen in these collectivized agricultural enterprises. Everything looked eerily unfamiliar until we reached the outskirts of town. As I turned a corner, I suddenly became oriented, and I recalled every detail of the streets I had frequented for eleven years. Everything bourgeois has, of course, been obliterated: fine shops have been replaced by convenience stores, the nameplates of professionals have disappeared from the main streets, the old cafés are boarded up. My grandmother's gracious nineteenth century house has been replaced by an enormous barracks-like apartment building, the Communist Bloc's version of our public housing; a bus depot stands in place of the house where I was born. My uncle George Gedö's elegant villa still exists, half derelict, half occupied now by whole families housed in every room. It was an experience beyond grief, unassimilable. To make contact with my memories, I had to find my grandparents' graves; the cemeteries and the railroad station remain unaltered. Up in the hills, Éva and I found an old tavern that is all that remains, I believe, of our great-grandfather's legendary establishment to distill *borovička*.[1]

A week later, during the conference, János Harmatta, the new fiftyish president of the Hungarian Psychoanalytic Society, invited me to a dinner party. (He later told me it was the first dinner he and his wife had ever been able to give in their home. Under the Communist regime, mental health professionals were kept on a short leash!) Most of the other guests were Hungarian colleagues now practicing in Germany or analysts Harmatta had befriended on his own study trips there. (In fact, Harmatta had attended a seminar I gave in Stuttgart a year or so before.) I was most impressed by the opportunity to meet Harmatta's parents, lovely gentlefolk in their late seventies, who spoke to me in a refined Hungarian I was barely able to follow under the impact of strong positive emotion. They brought back to me the atmosphere of my childhood, although in the more sophisticated version that befits academic circles in the capital. The old lady was wearing a gown purchased in Paris, where her husband had worked for UNESCO. In our family, only my Aunt Bertha had moved in such company; Uncle George was attorney for a number of Budapest aristocrats with estates around our town, and Bertha was beautiful and seductive enough to enter their milieu. (It is also true that my mother virulently disapproved of all that and chose to live frugally: only two servants, no *Kinderfrau* from the Sudetenland; she even did her own shopping! Of course, this was Mother's brand of snobbism, as was her decision to engage a tutor to teach me English when I was barely 5. Yet in the late 1930s my father's income amounted to about a thousand dollars per year, which sufficed for a living standard decidedly superior to those of his American grandchildren today.) The dressmakers of Losoncz had not been up to Paris standards, but my mother did not look frumpy on a café terrace in Vienna or the *corso* in Abbazia.[2]

Harmatta's father reminded me of my paternal grandfather Max (Miksa)—the same little white mustache, just like the one I have these days, the same academic attitudes. Grandfather was the professor of mathematics and physics at the Losoncz gymnasium. I met his present-day successor when I explored the old school that both of my parents attended for eight years and I for barely two. (The building looked like it had not been repaired since its erection around 1860.) Miksa had been the most erudite person in town, educated at the University of Vienna around 1880; he was a classicist in addition to his expertise in his dual specialties. I remember watching his funeral cortege, in January 1932, from my sickroom window;

to a 4-year-old, the procession seemed endless. Not that Losoncz had been lacking in greater luminaries; the famous violin virtuoso Jenö Hubay owned a small manor house only a mile or so out of town. (This landmark I was unable to find. Who knows what the Czech Communist regime did with the home of a *ci-devant* Hungarian nobleman? The building of the Hungarian Reformed Church had barely survived as a community center.)

The elder Harmatta drew me aside to say that he knew how difficult it was for an exile to return and come to terms with everything that had caused the loss of his past. It was the most empathic statement anyone had ever made to me about the difficulties of living between disparate cultures. One may now read a certain genre of literature focused on such matters, elegiac works such as Czeslaw Milosz's *The Issa Valley* (about the lost world of the Polish/Lithuanian gentry) or Gregor von Rezzori's *The Snows of Yesteryear* (about that of the aristocrats of Bukovina, some two hundred miles east of my native town), but the only person I know who shares my interest in these books is my Lithuanian daughter-in-law, Ginta Remeikis. From a different perspective, a recently deceased Budapest cousin, Gábor Antal, who had a successful career as a journalist under the Communists, told me that only a psychoanalyst could write with appropriate empathy about the conflict of ideals that beset those who had never chosen exile.

Most people I meet, including the current generation of psychoanalysts, know little about exile and take me at my cavalier word that, after fifty-six years in this country, I am as American as any of my fellow citizens. (When I am offended by some whiff of nativism, I am likely to say that I am one of those essential Americans who still manage to maintain some vestige of our country's Eurocentric heritage!) In other words, I have generally chosen to keep my loyalty to my Central European past as private as I could. If someone was discerning enough to understand that the very choice of a psychoanalytic career should compel recruits to the discipline to adhere to the culture of the Central Europe of our grandparents, so much the better. Freud was the very model of the Central European intellectual, and we might do well briefly to recall some of the cultural characteristics that he transmitted to psychoanalysis.

Freud was closer to philosophical pessimism than to optimism, if not as despairing on that score as his great countryman (and mine!), his contemporary, Franz Kafka. He was committed to the search for knowledge, although he was willing to make some concessions in order to gain a public hearing—unlike his immediate predecessor in the introspective tradition, Friedrich Nietzsche. Freud followed Kant's complex epistemology, not the simpler empiricism of the British philosophers or the rationalism of the French; in this respect, he differentiated himself from his Viennese peers, the empiricist Ernst Mach and Ludwig Wittgenstein, the conceptual thinker. He was an aristocrat of the spirit, who preached that man must bow to *Ananke* (necessity), and he was skeptical about notions of fairness and egalitarianism. (It is scarcely possible to continue such a legacy in the America of the 1990s.)

When I visit psychoanalytic centers in Germany or Italy, I am often viewed as a link to that culture of Mittel-Europa under the Hapsburgs which gave birth to psychoanalysis. This is no longer familiar to present-day Western Europeans, while American colleagues tend to look upon the stigmata of such origins not in cultural terms but simply as peculiar attributes of my personality. (They also wonder why our discipline does not thrive in an America intent on disavowing its European roots!)

What does it mean to be Central European in outlook? How did the spirit of the region differ from Russia, the Balkans, or Western Europe? It has been an outlook oriented westward; the major intellectual journal in early twentieth century Budapest was called *Nyugat* (the West).[3] In his great wartime cycle of poems, *Swiat*, Milosz enjoins the children of Poland literally to train their eyes on Prague, Rome, and Paris. This prescription is undoubtedly the legacy of the region's millennial adherence to Catholicism. At the same time, this regional orientation was necessarily mediated through German culture—much of the area was long ruled from Vienna, and settlers from Germany were scattered all the way to the Volga. (My mother's maternal grandparents moved east from Alsace after the 1870 Franco-Prussian war.) The educational system was consequently modeled on German precedents and impelled its graduates to seek higher qualifications in German institutions—my grandfather Miksa in Vienna, my father in Prague, my uncle Gyula in Berlin. Every bourgeois family taught its children German as a second language; it took an eccentric like my mother to prefer that her son master English instead! But it was taken for granted that I would eventually learn German; that was self-evident. (*Das war selbstverständlich!*)

If all that makes Central Europeans cosmopolitan, they are bound, at the same time, to remain mired in a semifeudal past—simultaneously romantic revolutionaries and unembarrassed elitists. Where else could a writer like Vacláv Havel have spearheaded the overthrow of a tyranny? The concepts of duty and honor still possess a resonance in these antiquated societies that the jaded West only finds in the literature recalling the world before Waterloo, say in the theater of Racine or the novels of Jane Austen. In this code, on certain crucial matters one does not compromise; at the height of the Communist regime, when my mother was visiting relatives in Budapest, Éva Czecze's husband escorted her to her hotel and gave the bellboy an enormous tip. Mother, at her most unpleasant, said, "I thought this is a Communist country?" He replied, "But I am a Hungarian gentleman." My adherence to such conduct has often been taken for arrogance rather than as submission to an obligation. American psychoanalysts no longer believe that, to be therapeutically effective, we must be gentlemen—or gentlewomen (see in press, a).

Perhaps less characteristically for Mittel-Europa, I have truly repudiated chauvinism on the basis of national origins; my native language may have been Hungarian, but we were contented citizens of Czechoslovakia, and much of my family was committed to the international ideals of socialism. (Are there other analysts in America whose father shed his blood in such a cause—a glamorous but pathetic figure, reminiscent of Byron at Mesolongi?[4] It was 1919; he led a battalion of mutineers in defense of the short-lived Marxist regime against the Allied powers about to occupy Hungary. He also taught me to despise the slogans of his youth, like the martial song popular during the Balkan Wars, "Look out, look out, Serbian dogs; Bosnia will never be yours!")

The first time I visited the Hungarian Psychoanalytic Society, I met with their enthusiastic candidates, who were delighted to have an opportunity to hold a colloquium in Hungarian with a senior analyst from abroad. It gradually dawned on them, however, that I was not a true compatriot, and one of them finally asked me whether I missed Hungary. Naturally, I said no. Several of these young people burst into tears at my seeming indifference. (A Budapest taxi driver who discerned my situation was less sentimental about our motherland. He growled, "Anyone with brains left here a long time ago!") It is indeed ambiguous to live in a no-man's-land between two worlds.

That gray zone was nowhere narrower than at the 1993 Ferenczi conference. The Budapest adherents of Freud's "Paladin and Grand Vizier" are inevitably interested in proving to themselves, and to the outside world, that they have missed nothing essential through fifty years of isolation, that what Ferenczi's heir Imre Herrmann taught them, when he was practically the only source of analytic knowledge in Hungary, is sufficient to be au courant with contemporary psychoanalysis.[5] I can hardly conceal that I do not agree, that I consider the intervening lessons of American ego psychology to be indispensable for differentiating the circumstances in which Ferenczi was on the right track from those in which he was not. Those young Americans who also attended in considerable numbers want to make use of Ferenczi to make respectable their postmodern commitment to relativism, intersubjectivity, or the provision of a new, corrective object relationship. I have long insisted that such views are naïvely reductionist, and therefore magical (see 1981a [chap. 13], 1987c, 1988a [chap. 4], 1993j, 1994a, 1996i). Although the two groups scarcely understood each other, neither party missed the fact that I disapproved of both positions.

Perhaps the contemporary culture that best bridges the gap separating the ambiance of the old Hapsburg Empire from America is that of Germany. I certainly do not regret having exchanged the early nineteenth-century world of my childhood (and *a fortiori*, the nightmare world of the Communist Bloc) for the United States of the late twentieth century, but I am not at all sure that, if different possibilities had presented themselves, I might not have been better fitted for life in present-day Germany. At least I find I have much in common with many psychoanalysts from Germany, who seem to understand my values as a matter of course. I can easily imagine an alternative life of following my father's footsteps to the German university in Prague and seeking psychoanalytic training in Berlin, Munich, or Cologne. Or joining a thriving analytic community in that hypothetical Prague itself, where Jan Frank, a cousin of my mother's (later active in Topeka and New York) was one of the analytic pioneers.

When, after the Ferenczi conference, Mike Gunther and I reached Prague, I certainly felt nostalgia for the might-have-been. I did not have much success trying to intuit where and how my parents might have lived and worked in this "golden city," but despite the language barrier I felt more connected to the cradle of the Velvet Revolution than I do to Budapest, with its continuing flavor of latent fascism. Nor was I indifferent to the fact that my mother suffered a stillbirth in the Czech capital, or that in 1938 her youngest sister (who was a cardiologist in Prague) committed suicide there, after the West abandoned Czechoslovakia. Aunt Helen was chronically depressed—her end could have been precipitated by any number of stresses—but her reaction to the Munich Pact was an accurate diagnosis of the cataclysmic defeat of everything people of our sort stood for. In America, it sounds pretentious to note that, while she was injecting herself intravenously with morphine, Helen was listening to the Mozart *Requiem*. In Prague, in 1938, it was a statement of her beliefs. Exile has much in common with suicide; my father never recovered from it and never stopped dreaming that it might come to an end. (My mother, haunted by death since that of her father when she was 6, was indifferent to her surroundings, so that she seemed on the surface to have weathered emigration well. Wherever she was, she awaited catastrophe: the stillbirth, the early death of her mother, Helen's suicide; who would go next?) I decided, when I was 11, that I would embrace whatever new life was to come, and this is the first time I have looked back. I trust that, after fifty-nine years, I shall not turn into a pillar of salt.

I do not intend very often to focus the memoir of a life in psychoanalysis on my private affairs; I have included this account of a journey into the past only because I believe that specific childhood background (particularly its cultural context) accounts for much of my professional development. I was raised in a scholarly hothouse to be intellectually ambitious and fanatically diligent, like my paternal grandfather who came to Losoncz in the 1880s to teach at the local gymnasium. My father (and George, his beloved older brother) were bona fide revolutionaries who risked everything (and lost almost all) in the service of their dreams. (Of course, they were also mistaken in thinking that they were serving the cause of freedom, but their ideals were genuine.)

My life in psychoanalysis has followed the models provided by these previous generations. As my mother's only surviving child, I was indoctrinated to believe that only my own negligence and self-indulgence could stand in the way of fulfilling the duty of achieving a successful career using the intellect; work for me became a sacred task and the path to salvation, because its fruits guaranteed my mother's self-esteem and, consequently, her esteem for me. Nor was her side of the family devoid of shining examples, despite a prevalence of serious psychopathology. Not long ago, walking through an exhibit of André Kertész photographs at the Art Institute of Chicago, I noticed one from 1926, featuring a cello, that was commissioned by one of Mother's cousins while his string quartet was performing in Paris. Mother had a taste for puritanism, restrained in my father's lifetime by his categorical opposition to the opiate of the masses; as a widow she became active in the Presbyterian church. It is no coincidence that I generally make more effort than do others; I know of no one who has worked harder to master the subject matter of psychoanalysis than I have. If I have any talent out of the ordinary, it is the capacity to persevere in scholarly enterprises. Yet I also believe that nothing less can suffice in the endless effort to master the subject matter of our discipline, and that psychoanalysis must be subjected to permanent revolution[6] in order to remain viable.

All this has given many colleagues an impression that I consider myself superior to most. (But, contrary to my Calvinist mother, I really do *not* believe in predestination: yesterday's success guarantees nothing about future performance, and I am always in doubt about what I can achieve.) Because I have been intolerant of my failures and seldom feel really satisfied with my results, I have found others' view of me as a man filled with certitude difficult to understand. It is true that, like my mother (who took for granted whatever I could achieve), I tend to hold people to uncommonly high standards, and have thereby unintentionally offended many who are on easier terms with their conscience. Of course, I try not to show that I am just as hard on myself; I refuse to engage in public self-flagellation. Producing a hundred-odd pages of published material, year in and year out, for about three decades, has been my effort to atone for previous failures to live up to the highest expectations.

I must confess, however, that there is another side of the coin, although it did not surface until late in my life, when it led to my decision to retire as soon as it became financially feasible to do so. For this, I also had a wonderful precedent in the family: my great-uncle Oscar was still in his thirties when he modestly retired to Brussels. (The city had almost all the amenities of Paris, and it was a great deal more hospitable to foreigners.)

❖ CHAPTER 3 ❖

AN AGE OF GOLD

My oldest son, Paul, and his wife Ginta are currently candidates at the Washington Psychoanalytic Institute—a natural outgrowth of having been on the hospital staff at Chestnut Lodge. They know that if they want to develop a *psychoanalytic* practice, they will probably have to leave the Washington area—that most major metropolitan areas are saturated with psychoanalysts. They do not complain; they cannot even imagine a situation in which analytic patients could be plentiful. An older colleague recently told me that his latest analysand explained an interest in being analyzed as an addiction to lost causes. Such conversations with my contemporaries tend to end up in grief about the fate of the snows of yesteryear.[1]

I suppose that we did know, when we were candidates four decades ago, that we were beneficiaries of an analytic age of gold. I matriculated in 1956 with the largest cohort ever to enroll in Chicago; we were a class of sixteen, later joined by several refugees from Detroit, where, in the late 1950s, training was temporarily suspended. To make such commuting feasible, our courses were held on alternate weekends, from early Friday mornings to lunchtime on Saturdays. I found the Institute weekends exhilarating, especially after a number of like-minded people began to have ceremonious Friday luncheons at neighboring French restaurants. My cohort of candidates included several friends from my residency years, such as Leo Sadow and Mike Gunther, as well as other fellow residents from the three programs through which I had rotated. The occasional person who was new to the group soon joined in a spirit of genuine camaraderie.

Actually, the whole Institute was in pleasurable ferment, for a few months before our class matriculated a palace revolution had overthrown the regime of the founding director, Franz Alexander, who immediately left for Los Angeles, taking with him a number of his most loyal partisans, to bolster the Southern California Institute. Only the year before, a new five-year curriculum had been introduced—clearly a harbinger of the collapse of Alexander's dominance, a turn away from his emphasis on brief psychotherapy and psychosomatic medicine. There was high hope for the reformist regime that had taken over—Gerhart Piers as director, Joan Fleming as dean (a position that roughly corresponds to chairmanship of the Education Committee at other institutes); Thomas French provided continuity by remaining in charge of research. By today's gerontocratic standards, the entire leadership was young and vigorous, scarcely into their fifties. Therese Benedek, who was probably the oldest among them, had barely passed sixty. One still caught occasional glimpses of Edoardo Weiss, a last direct link to the Hapsburg era, but he was not one of our teachers; he seemed to be in exile in his South Side redoubt, where (according to reliable rumors) he was engaged in illicit private training activities.[2]

In retrospect, the heart of our didactic experience was a two-year course on psychoanalytic theory taught by Heinz Kohut. He was then 44 years old and a relatively recent addition to the faculty, but he had an absolute command of his material and led the discussion with efficiency and clarity. He was sufficiently aloof to create about himself a certain air of mystery. There was something about him different from other analysts from European backgrounds; despite his mastery of English, he retained the air of the Viennese intellectual to a remarkable degree. (Years later, at the Vienna Congress of the International Psychoanalytic, we took an evening stroll together through the Old Town. Heinz then told me that he never felt truly at home anywhere else.) In his class, he betrayed this lack of acculturation by insisting that everyone had to take notes while he lectured. I regarded this demand as absurd; I felt sufficiently depreciated by the lack of confidence in my ability to absorb instruction to parody Kohut's assignment by ostentatiously using a single sheet of paper, carried folded up in my pocket, to compress the lessons of thirty-six seminars: *multum in parvo*,[3] as Heinz might have put it. But he gave us a brilliant and faithful account of Freud's theoretical journey from 1892 to 1939. Among the seeming giants on the faculty, Kohut was clearly the greatest.

Kohut's intellectual brilliance was acknowledged by everyone. When, in 1957, the Institute celebrated its twenty-fifth anniversary, Heinz and Therese Benedek were chosen to give scientific papers to mark the occasion. Kohut presented his first major essay, "Introspection, Empathy, and Psychoanalysis," which laid the groundwork for the phenomenological bias of his subsequent work—an exclusive concern with subjectivity that I have been unwilling to accept, because it leaves out of account the heritage of the presymbolic era of infancy. Of course, in 1957 I was much too unsophisticated to grasp the radicalism of Heinz's viewpoint. The readers who refereed his paper (Kohut 1959) for the *Journal of the American Psychoanalytic Association* understood it well enough; many years later, Kohut told me that the journal published this work only because Max Gitelson insisted that it must not engage in ideological censorship.

Benedek taught only a brief course on psychological development in maturity, barely sufficient to give us a glimpse of her vast clinical experience and originality of mind. She was a tiny woman, stooped over and increasingly hard of hearing, and she exuded the aura of the Delphic oracle. I was fortunate enough to get her as my first supervisor—an experience decisive for my subsequent development as a clinician, for she taught me the centrality of affective vicissitudes in the transference. No doubt this was the legacy of her own analysis with Ferenczi just after the end of the First World War, but Therese never once mentioned his name to me. Shortly before she died (in her late eighties), I got up the nerve to ask her how it had been possible to complete an analysis with Ferenczi in just a few months. Therese smiled—it was clear that she was fond of me, and my impertinence merely amused her. She said that, before 1920, the insights of psychoanalysis were so startling and novel that their impact on an unprepared person was then much more powerful than it is now. . . . In sum, she was a *very* smart lady. It did not surprise me to learn that, when she was an adolescent in Budapest, her best friends had been the Polányi brothers, both destined to become world-famous scholars.

The tenor of my relationship with Therese might best be described in terms of an incident that occurred shortly after I arrived in Chicago to begin my internship. I attended a psychoanalytic conference at a fancy hotel with a fellow intern interested in psychiatry. The conference was capped by a festive reception at the Institute, a few blocks away, which we decided to crash. Far from being asked to leave, we were quickly approached by the very courtly Edwin Eisler, whom I had met during the course of my recent interviews in connection with my application to the Institute—as I have mentioned, at that time, it was possible to be selected at the same time one applied to the analytically oriented residency programs in Chicago.

Eisler invited us to join him at dinner at the elegant Ambassador Hotel; needless to say, we accepted. The other person in the company turned out to be Therese Benedek. When we got to the Ambassador, we were met by their respective spouses and two young ladies, daughters of each couple, whom we were asked to escort. A very nice occasion—incidentally, unthinkable in a contemporary context.

Like many candidates, I was most appreciative of our case conferences, for the skills of clinical practice cannot be learned from books. One is provided invaluable lessons by accounts of other analysts' clinical procedures. I suspect that as a candidate I gave most of our case conference leaders too much credit, for they seldom rose above transmitting, as a series of rules of thumb, the prevalent technical consensus of the era, that of ego psychology. Except for Gitelson, these instructors were only local luminaries, but most of them remained very popular with candidates, some for decades. They did a good-enough job of conveying the technical rules that were then part of the conventional wisdom; only Max was able to transcend that system to some degree. For instance, in Gitelson's termination seminar, Leo Sadow presented a case with a very atypical course. His supervisor held Leo responsible for the less-than-ideal outcome, but Max demonstrated that the analysis had, in actuality, addressed the patient's most important problems, so that criticism of the nonappearance of a transference neurosis was misguided. To his great credit, Max actually persuaded the progression committee to accept the analysis as satisfactorily terminated, contrary to the recommendation of the doctrinaire supervisor.

The Institute's commitment to implant psychoanalytic groups throughout the Midwest (over the years, it helped to spawn the institutes in Topeka, Detroit, St. Louis, Denver, and Cincinnati, and it is still trying in Minnesota and Wisconsin) has brought to Chicago not only commuting candidates but commuting faculty as well. In my time, the most distinguished among them was René Spitz, then finishing his career in Denver. He was already a renowned figure because of his demonstration of the devastating consequences of depriving infants of the opportunity to bond with one caretaker (Spitz 1945). As a medical student in New York I had still encountered babies at Bellevue Hospital who were dying of "hospitalism" as a result of inappropriate placement in impersonal settings, so that I was keenly aware of the revolution in child care Spitz had initiated. I was thrilled to be exposed to accounts of the latest work of this pioneer of infant observation, however infrequently Spitz spoke to us. Moreover, with his old-world courtesy and Hungarian accent, he was like an apparition from my childhood.

The most extensive presentation of original work within our curriculum was the full-year course offered by Thomas French on the integration of behavior.[4] French, like Spitz, was a gentleman of the old school, albeit American to the core. I cannot characterize him better than to relate an event that took place shortly after my graduation from the Institute. French was leading an effort to complete the long-term research on psychosomatic specificity initiated by Alexander.[5] In the face of some deadline, one member of the research team became unavailable, and (acting through George Pollock, the rising star in the group) they hired me to review a large number of protocols and make certain judgments about their contents as a test of interrater reliability. It was an assignment that captured my interest—I was, in addition, well aware of my selection as a vote of confidence in *my* reliability—and I completed the task well before the deadline. A few days later, I went to a meeting of the Chicago Psychoanalytic Society; Tom French caught sight of me as I entered the hall. His face lit up; he rushed down the aisle to greet me: "Dr. Gedo! Dr. Gedo! Isn't it wonderful? We disagreed on everything!"

Charming as this open-mindedness was in such a context, in his teaching, for me, it made French unendurable. Most of the time, we engaged in microscopic studies of bits of clinical material—a sentence or two excerpted from a longer transcript. After ninety minutes of backing and filling, French generally arrived at a reasonable understanding of probable meanings, but in most instances I was convinced on my first reading of the transcript that the data were best understood in that sense. His exercises in impeccable logic made me wildly impatient; I still do not understand why the candidates did not run riot in protest. After French's death, Heinz Kohut told me, with more than a touch of amusement, that Tom French was the prime example of an analyst who could not use empathy as an observational tool but was able more or less to compensate for this handicap through laborious intellectual operations. As usual, Kohut was more than half right, but in this case he was more tolerant than I am capable of being; French did not make use of empathic observation, but I thought he was also unable to perceive psychological gestalten through pattern matching. His career was a triumph of perseverance and ingenuity over certain cognitive handicaps. To characterize such problems, I later borrowed the neurological term *apraxia* (1988a [chaps. 11–14]). I could not understand why the Institute looked upon the process of his coping with such a deficit as a valuable teaching exercise. I was yet to learn that didactic work was seldom taken seriously as an essential component of a psychoanalytic education.

Overall, I found the curriculum to be an excellent stimulus for my own reading, and I made a serious effort to master everything of value in the entire literature of psychoanalysis. I read the major journals cover to cover as they appeared. During our first Christmas break at the Institute, it seemed natural to go over Otto Fenichel's (1946) synopsis of psychoanalysis—after all, it was on our list of supplementary readings for one of the courses. I was astonished gradually to discover that none of my fellow candidates found the time and energy to pursue such an agenda, and that nobody on the faculty noticed the difference—or cared! Most candidates worked crushingly long hours in their practice, whereas I had discovered relatively early that it made better economic sense to ask for higher fees from a smaller number of patients. We had a seller's market, and Mary and I were both accustomed to a standard of living considerably more modest than it has become customary to aspire to in psychoanalytic circles; when my parents arrived in America, they had an income of ten dollars a week, and my father-in-law started working in the West Virginia coal mines at the age of eleven.

Although it soon became apparent to me that, in academic terms, I was at least as well prepared as any other candidate and much better than most, I was much less confident about my clinical abilities. I had the fantasy that Benedek became my first supervisor because of our common origins in Hungary. In all probability, the assignment was made at random. I also do not really know how I came to be picked to be one of two candidates with whom Therese and Joan Fleming were planning to work as part of a study of psychoanalytic supervision. Benedek told me that she was recording our sessions for research purposes, but she withheld from me the true nature of her project. Ignorance was bliss. In the book Therese and Joan eventually published (Benedek and Fleming 1966), I was the candidate "G." (a disguise worthy of Edgar Allan Poe![6]); Benedek's account of our work is entirely fair.

Of course, such a scientific report could not include the transactions that were most meaningful for me. Take the very first and very last queries of our collaboration: Benedek started our enterprise by asking me, in her profound Hungarian accent, "Vell, are you going to confuse me viz your mozer?" This idea struck me as irresistibly comical, and I told her that there was no chance whatsoever of such an occurrence. I kept to myself my association that in several ways, including her obvious pleasure in my potential competence, Therese reminded me of my father. At the very end, she wondered what more she could tell me, and I asked her to give a general characterization of my work. She replied, thoughtfully, that my analytic attitude was rather unusual—it reminded her of a novelist's detached consideration of the characters he is trying to conceive. I suppose that she must have noticed that she was making me anxious, so she added, "It's all right—zere have been ozer good analysts like zat . . ." And she remained steadfast in her encouragement. When she heard, after my graduation, that I was seriously considering an overture by the St. Louis analytic group to get me to join them, she stopped me in the library to say that I should not leave because I had a better future awaiting me in Chicago. (The future turned out to be both very good and very difficult.)

The patient whose analysis Therese supervised was attractive and subtly seductive, a pious but promiscuous young woman who had already given away two illegitimate children. For her, Catholic morality precluded the use of contraception, but her inability to bear solitude rendered her unable to pass up sexual opportunities. Therese was enthusiastic about *our* opportunity: "Now I vill teach you all about vomen!," she promised. (According to my wife, even Benedek failed in that impossible task.) What she actually meant was that she would show me the role of shifting levels of estrogen and progesterone in the psychology of women—the conclusions of a superb piece of psychosomatic research Benedek had recently performed in collaboration with an endocrinologist (Benedek and Rubinstein, in Benedek 1973). In that aim, she succeeded admirably; these lessons consolidated the conviction that had grown in me as a result of my therapeutic attempts with hospitalized patients, that psychoanalysis is a branch of biological science.

Therese insisted that an analyst must actively promote analytic progress. If I was slow to convey our understanding of the material to the patient, she reproached me, "You vant zis pretty girl to stay viz you forever? Vatch ze countertransference!" With a naïveté only half assumed, I asked how to do that. Severely, Therese replied, "I told you! Vatch it!" But she also reassured me that our difficulties were inevitable concomitants of my analysand's character—she said that she had never encountered a patient as narcissistic as was mine. And she cautioned me to avoid being formulaic in my interpretations. When I thought it was necessary to inform the patient (who had learned to despise females at her mother's knee) about her penis envy, Therese laughingly told me that if I did that, I had to be prepared for the need of the young woman I would humiliate to castrate me in retaliation. (Some analysts were aware of intersubjectivity before the deluge!)

Benedek's clinical wisdom was profound; her supervisory recommendations almost always worked, so much so that the analysis made excellent progress, but I had the feeling that I did not know what I was doing right. Nor was I able to fit together these concrete events with my own analytic experience with Gitelson. I pleaded with Therese to correlate what she told me about my patient with some theory of technique, but she explicitly refused to do that; she implied that such a wish is an obsessive person's attempt to avoid the heat of the analytic kitchen. Perhaps she was right, but I still believe that my request was the first manifestation of my realization that with such an analysand the prevalent theories of technique made no sense—and this was the seed that sprouted my subsequent contributions to psychoanalysis. In retrospect, I also see that Therese was teaching me an analytic approach in disrepute at that time: the tradition initiated by Ferenczi.

As we were about to start the second year of courses, Therese indicated that she had some time previously recommended that I begin my next supervised analysis. She hinted that I was lacking in ambition because I had failed to seek this promotion sooner. I was quite gratified that even this seeress had failed to intuit that I was consciously curbing my haste to proceed, precisely because I knew that excessive ambition is my Achilles' heel.

My second patient was the fundamentalist minister I later presented to Gitelson's termination seminar. For supervision, I was assigned to Bernard Kamm, a German émigré, originally from Prague (like me!), who almost matched Benedek in seniority. At this point, I decided that the administration was thoughtfully trying to match me with supervisors who would have empathy for my un-American peculiarities—they were providing me with an approximation of a psychoanalytic apprenticeship in Berlin, circa 1930. Kamm made a reputation in that era as a therapist of psychotic patients and was one of the first European analysts imported by the Menninger Clinic. He certainly treated me in a highly individualized manner; when I expressed doubts about the analyzability of an obsessional religious fanatic, he replied that he would leave it to me whether to try it, although he thought that if I did so, I would find that the experience would be like a second analysis for me. There was a great deal to what he said; in any case, he could not have found a better way to ensure that I would feel honor-bound to proceed.

Thereafter, Kamm said very little in response to my accounts of the treatment. I was very much surprised to learn, a bit later, that he was generally regarded as an active and critical supervisor. Clearly, he had decided that what I most needed from him was to gain confidence in my own clinical skill and judgment. (He shared with me his surprise that, in America, whatever was not explicitly permitted was regarded as *verboten*, while back home it had been the other way around.) Much of the time, he greeted me by asking whether I would like to have some coffee, and he would serve it with some ceremony. In various subtle ways, he tried to wean me from my compulsive, chronological reports, based on notes scribbled during the analytic sessions. Kamm looked at my spiral notebook with contemptuous amusement. (He preferred to chat about the ways in which our patient might be compared to one or another character in the novels of Dostoyevski, a world in which he could see that I felt very much at home.) In this manner, he skillfully induced me to use our sessions to *think* about the analytic process.

Although I was still too resistant to external influence to change my procedure with the patient Kamm was supervising, I never afterward took notes in my consulting room. (For many years thereafter, I did dictate summaries of every session with every patient; as I gained confidence about grasping what was really important, I gradually reduced the frequency of such dictation to around once a month. During the Watergate scandals, when I heard that Nixon's operatives had searched the office of Daniel Ellsberg's analyst, in order to steal the patient's record, I discontinued this activity and destroyed my files. It was said that the gumshoes missed Ellsberg's chart because it had been misfiled under "L." Nonetheless, I remain convinced that an analyst should not put anything about patients on paper.)

After the unpleasant vicissitudes with my third supervisor, whose behavior was, as I saw it, worthy of Richard Nixon, for my last required case I was assigned to Joan Fleming. I initially thought that, in her capacity as the dean, she wanted to have a first-hand look at a candidate about whom his other supervisors wrote conflicting reports. When she began to record our sessions (characteristically, without a by-your-leave), it became evident that this was not her primary aim, and she soon revealed that she and Therese were collaborating on the supervision project. However, she always remained skeptical about my soundness. We had already had somewhat strained interactions at Michael Reese, where she had given a psychotherapy seminar I found both dogmatic and muddled. Fleming had started out as a teacher of physical education, and (as my prejudices led me to expect) she seemed basically anti-intellectual, while she perceived me as some kind of pseudo-intellectual impostor. She used her influence to push the Institute in the direction of providing technical training—as one of her favored pupils likes to put it, an "institution like a musical conservatory." (In my more critical moods, I would say, like a class in the martial arts.) Even the metaphor of an instrumentalist strikes me as inappropriate; psychoanalysis is not a technical performance but the practical application of an evolving scientific theory. Fleming always reminded me of the character in a German melodrama who has the line, "When I hear the word *culture*, I reach for my holster."

Forty years later, I realize that Joan's attitudes were not malignant and that her values were just as much a reflection of her cultural background as is the case with mine. Fleming was quintessentially the small-town career woman from the Midwest: devoted to pragmatism (she wanted to evaluate analytic candidates on the basis of a checklist of procedural therapeutic skills!), overly optimistic (she really thought that as a discipline psychoanalysis had reached maturity), contemptuous of a rationalist epistemology (and the obsessional characters who engage in studies of theoretical coherence), and committed to the American civic religion (of charity, cooperation, fairness, and so on). All of my encounters with such a person turned into a clash of Weltanschauungen.

From the first, I felt that Fleming misunderstood my patient and tried to push me to treat him in a conventional manner that was not appropriate for this highly unusual man. He was a professor of literature who believed himself to be the world's greatest unpublished poet; he was delinquent, bisexual, proud of having been cited by his real name in an academic novel as the most loathsome character the narrator had ever met! I did not know how to deal with such a Till Eulenspiegel, but I did not trust Fleming's certitude about the adequacy of standard technique with someone bent upon making a fool of anyone he encountered. I was also certain that she was wrong in condemning my tendency to communicate with this very sophisticated man by using a vocabulary laden with cultural allusions. (Fleming thought I was showing off; I was certain that because of my choice of language my patient felt *accepted*.)

By this time, I knew better than to argue with the czarina; for her part (as she was to reveal in *Psychoanalytic Supervision*), she was puzzled by my failure to acknowledge that her instruction had value. At one point, I did indicate that I had a complaint about her method as supervisor. She said she wanted to discuss the matter, and she turned off the recording machine. I was utterly shocked—she was refusing to document the most important transaction of the supervisory process she was purportedly observing. Her act filled me with disgust and contempt.

I do not know how well I succeeded in suppressing my indignation. Instead of talking about the present, I told her I wanted her to know about an incident from my childhood. This occurred when I was in first grade and received a homework assignment to complete certain exercises in a workbook. I was slightly confused about what I was supposed to do, and I asked my father to give me an explanation. He carefully inspected the workbook and began to do the assignment. I said nothing, and he did not stop until it was completed. I thanked him; he left the room; I tore the exercise book into shreds. Fleming said she understood. (So did another member of the faculty, who pointed out that Joan thought of supervision in terms of a gardening metaphor; this colleague averred that the process of learning had to be more active than that of being manured!)

Fleming never forgave me. As long as she remained in Chicago, she regarded me as a threat to the collegial atmosphere she believed she had established at the Institute. Of course, if collegiality means automatic deference to one's inadequate elders who claim to be betters, she was right. From my viewpoint, refusal to cover over what I perceived as her inadequacy was the most decisive change brought about through my analysis; as a child, I had disavowed the inadequacies of both of my parents through a smokescreen of idealization.[7]

I do not mean to imply that in her view of me Fleming was in any way distorting her usual criteria; she was merely prejudiced against anyone who disturbed her peaceful reign. I am sure that she was always sincerely trying to promote the welfare of the analytic community—the problem was that her conception of that welfare was highly questionable, but she could not even imagine that an alternative existed. But she was not engaged in a private vendetta; for example, she approved my request to take the final examination at the earliest time possible. Perhaps, in fact, it took some time for her mistrust of me to grow to the point where it caused her to take overt action against me; whatever my doubts, I retained some respect for the supposed analytic competence for which everyone gave her credit for some time after my graduation.

In those years, it was customary for candidates ready to take the written final examination to form private study groups to review the core of the analytic literature. I organized such an effort in conjunction with two friends from the University of Chicago residency group, Leo Sadow and Nate

Schlessinger. We expanded the study group by asking two people to join us whom I knew from Michael Reese (where I was still active as an attending psychiatrist) as well as from the Institute: the ever-popular Max Forman, and Mel Sabshin, still Grinker's right-hand man but shortly to become chairman of the psychiatry department at the University of Illinois and eventually medical director of the American Psychiatric Association.

It was an excellent and harmonious team. By distributing primary responsibility for blocks of subject matter among us, in about a year we were able to master broad areas of the literature of psychoanalysis. In fact, we enjoyed the collaboration so much that four of us decided to continue to meet beyond the examination. Only Forman declined to stay in the group, probably because he did not like the historical emphasis we planned to adopt. In any case, every member of the study group was to have a successful career—Sabshin in academic and administrative psychiatry, the others in psychoanalysis, both as training analysts and as contributors to the literature.

I took the Institute examination on the day of the Bay of Pigs invasion, and what I best remember about it is the ashen face of the Cuban exile who sat not far away, vainly trying to keep his attention focused within the room. I do recall, however, that I used every minute of the time available. This was a small victory over my own presumption (as Cervantes puts this about Don Quixote), because of a Russian roulette sort of game I had often played in medical school by leaving examinations as soon as anyone else did—and this time my poor colleague was compelled to leave early to get the latest news from Cuba. Perhaps this was the first occasion on which I spent much more time in thinking through what I should write than in actually writing—a method I have relied on with increasing emphasis with the passage of time, so that in recent years I have seldom needed to alter in any major way what I finally decided to put on paper.

It was Roy Grinker who first let me know that my examination paper had made a favorable impression on readers. He approached me in the hall near his Michael Reese office to congratulate me on having written the best exam—as he put it, my four essays were even better argued than those of Mel Sabshin's excellent paper. Thenceforth, he became even more helpful to me than he had been on the strength of my year as one of his residents; he recommended my first book, *Models of the Mind* (written in collaboration with Arnold Goldberg) to the University of Chicago Press; when it was accepted for publication, he agreed to write a very helpful foreword for it; afterward, because he felt *Models of the Mind* introduced systems theory into psychoanalysis, he invited Arnold and me to his club to meet the great theoretical biologist Ludwig von Bertalanffy. For me, that occasion had the significance of being knighted as a scientist.[8]

I received my certificate from the Institute in June 1961—the 189th Chicago graduate. I knew that, at age 33, I was one of the youngest in that series, and that such swift academic progress held the promise of creating an opportunity to make real intellectual contributions to psychoanalysis. I had begun to publish in 1959, with a paper on the difficulties of psychotherapy that appeared as the very first article in the first volume of the *Archives of General Psychiatry* of which Grinker was the founding editor.[9] (He soon began to give me opportunities to review books for him as well.) I had confidence in my writing talent; what I had never before allowed myself to acknowledge was the full extent of my scholarly ambitions.

Had I done so early enough, after my discharge from the Army I would not have gone to medical school, despite having sustained my morale in the service with the knowledge that a place was awaiting me there whenever I would be free to come. (I was drafted in April 1946, after being admitted to the New York University School of Medicine. This was a breach of the established policy to exempt medical students from the draft. I think the violation occurred because I lived on the margins of Harlem; overloaded with black volunteers, the services, which were still segregated, did not want draft boards to call up African Americans. I gave up my efforts to get the discharge to which I was entitled when NYU let me know that I could matriculate when I pleased. This decision led to a dazzling six-month stay in occupied Japan. Having satisfied my military obligations once and for all, I returned to New York in May 1947.) I lacked the initiative at the time to rethink the plan to attend medical school, although I knew I had little interest in what such an education had to offer. (My father wanted me to join him in Czechoslovakia to set up a modern health center—a utopian notion finally put to rest by the Stalinist takeover.)

At a less turbulent time, I suspect I might really have become a historian—in terms of language skills, I was ideally suited to focus on early modern Europe. In the decade preceding 1947, I had had more or less exposure to English, French, German, Spanish, Latin, Czech, and Hungarian. When one has to, one can master a new language fairly rapidly; my father and I began to study French in March 1939, when we learned that we could find shelter in Tangier, and that September I enrolled at the Lycée Regnault at my own grade level. (I have never again accomplished anything as difficult—and no academic challenge has ever seemed as daunting.)

The discovery of psychoanalysis as a respected branch of medicine permitted me to persevere with a medical education. Fortunately, from the viewpoint of emotional sanction for this new enterprise, my father was very much interested in psychological medicine and often referred patients to émigré psychoanalysts. Moreover, in college I had known a few people who had every intention to make a career of psychoanalysis. (Some of them actually did do that; more than one is a training analyst at the New York Psychoanalytic Institute, another is past president of the Academy of Psychoanalysis.) Until I was confronted with the actuality of medical school, however, the idea of indulging myself by devoting my life to a scholarly discipline simply because I enjoyed it made me feel too guilty to be taken seriously; I could take as many courses in history or literature as I pleased, but officially I had to declare biology as my major field of study. Four years later, at 19, I was still duty-bound, but I could compromise to the extent of settling on psychological medicine. When, fourteen years later still, I became a newly minted psychoanalyst, my original scholarly ambitions emerged once again. As a start, perhaps I could do some work on the intellectual history of psychoanalysis?

❖ CHAPTER 4 ❖

IS MORALITY SELF-EVIDENT?

Graduation from the psychoanalytic Institute closed a long chapter in my life, from the start of medical school, through internship and residency, to the early years of private practice and analytic apprenticeship. The change was a great liberation, for I decided not to fill the time I had devoted to unremunerative Institute activities with private patients—for the first time since before I left for army service, I had enough leisure to live as I preferred and sufficient income to enjoy it. Within a few years we moved to the gracious northern suburbs, and we began to travel. Mary returned to graduate school. Only my retirement, in my later sixties, has brought me a greater increment of freedom. Whereas finally leaving school at 33 was like a return to my expansive late adolescent whirl as a college student in wartime (almost like a three-year hypomanic episode), retirement reminds me of my earliest years in New York, from 13 to 15, when I had few human contacts beyond family, and I leisurely immersed myself in a world of books. And now I steep myself in memories as well.

Earlier than I can remember, it was already taken for granted that I would distinguish myself academically, and I did not seriously question these familial expectations. At University Heights, a small, all-male, New York University campus in the Bronx overlooking the Harlem River (sold in the 1970s to the City University of New York), which I attended as an undergraduate, most students were actually in the army—in classes separate from those for the ever-decreasing number of civilians. Until the end of hostilities in August 1945, the college atmosphere was feverish, in a spirit of commitment to the war effort. "They also serve who stay at home"—and try to gain admission to medical school.

In 1961, when I graduated from the Chicago Institute, I still felt some obligation to serve, for I had had three years of medical school and three of psychiatric residency at public expense—on the G.I. Bill and a Public Health Service Fellowship, respectively. In other words, I continued to obey my father's socialist ideals, all the more so because he had suddenly died some five years before. (I am still surprised by the fact that my coronary disease supervened only when I became ten years older than he was at his death.) Despite the fact that I no longer had a hospital practice (mostly because my schedule was gradually filled with referrals for outpatient work), I felt honor bound to continue giving my services to Michael Reese, where I was supervising residents in psychotherapy and consulting on one of the wards in internal medicine. I volunteered to take on a low-fee analytic patient through the institute clinic—an adventure about which I shall shortly have more to say. For some years, I made the long trek from the South Side (where we then lived) to Evanston to spend half a day each week at the Northwestern University student health service. I thought of this as a contribution to public health, because the entire campus was badly in need of instruction about mental health issues. (I can best characterize the atmosphere by recalling my first meeting with the dean of students, a lady in late middle age who seemed both amateurish and uppity. It was a social occasion, and I was with my wife, who was close to delivering our youngest child. Staring at Mary's abdomen, the dean declared, "Oh, Doctor, I am so glad to meet you both! Now I know that my girls are safe with you." One would have thought that appearances were to the contrary.) In summary, Central European socialists of the old school operated in a spirit of noblesse oblige,[1] and it took me half a lifetime to realize that in America this is seen as priggishness.

Beyond professional commitments, the spirit of activism at first led me to throw myself into community affairs in Hyde Park, the neighborhood around the University of Chicago where a serious attempt to create a racially integrated enclave was taking place. (As Mike Nichols and Elaine May described this, when they came back to their old haunts for a community fund-raiser, "Black and white together, we march shoulder to shoulder against the lower classes!") The intractability of America's urban problems and the naïve dogmatism of most people then involved in such community affairs gradually disabused me of the illusion that my activities could lead to some constructive end. The last straw was a well-attended PTA meeting, where I tried to argue that our children's education would be better served if we did not attack and deprecate their teachers, as a number of parents were doing. I said something to the effect that children will best learn from people they love. This statement elicited loud laughter from a large part of the assembly, and I realized that in the civic arena the voice of the intellect would not gain a hearing—whatever Freud promised in that regard.[2] I was ready to cultivate my garden in a more bucolic setting where my children would not be harassed on the playground.

I suppose I was also turned away from these fruitless struggles by the promise of opportunities for useful service in the professional sphere. Soon after our graduation from the Institute, George Pollock asked Mel Sabshin and me to assist him in teaching a course in research methodology for advanced candidates. In my last year as a student, I had just taken this excellent survey of scientific requirements in biological disciplines, and I was delighted to participate as a graduate, although George never clarified whether this was merely a private arrangement between us or an official faculty appointment. (Sabshin, recently appointed chairman of psychiatry at Illinois, also accepted the invitation, but, sensibly enough, he hardly ever showed up.) Although I was not expected to do very much as George's assistant, beyond setting up a recording machine before each session and storing the equipment when it was over, attending this course for two additional academic years did give me a useful foundation for my subsequent scientific efforts in psychoanalysis. In addition to a medical degree, Pollock has a Ph.D. in one of the basic biomedical disciplines, and in 1961 he already had a great deal of creditable scientific research experience. He selected readings that alerted me to the fact that, in order to advance knowledge, one must find data that constitute anomalies in terms of prevalent theory. All of my subsequent work has followed this principle.

George is in most ways a character larger than life. Not only did he have two advanced degrees, he also had a large brood of children, and he lived in two adjoining row houses that he and his wife had cobbled together. He has always been involved in multiple enterprises, confidently biting off more than anyone could thoroughly chew. I have always felt quite ambivalent toward him, because I thought he came on too strongly and had too much raw ambition; at the same time, I had to acknowledge that he was being both helpful and gracious to me. I still believe that, if he had devoted himself wholeheartedly to scientific issues in psychoanalysis, he could have made a truly major contribution to the field. But he could never resist the lure of empire building; by 1961 he had succeeded French as the Institute's director of research, although he was scarcely past his mid-thirties. The busier he made himself, the more impossible he found it to follow through with sufficient rigor on all his projects, and I gradually came to the conclusion that I had overestimated him as a person. Yet I suspect that his personal example helped me to overcome those aspects of my identification with my father's excessive altruism that stood in the way of pursuing my own professional self-interest.

Despite the complexities of our later relationship, I cannot but feel grateful to Pollock for giving me opportunities when I needed them—and not only as his teaching assistant. More than a year before my graduation from the Institute he sent me my very first private analytic case, and he responded to the report that the study group some of us had formed to prepare for the final examination intended to look into the intellectual history of the early years of psychoanalysis by offering to recognize it as an official function of the research division.

Mel Sabshin was (and remains) infinitely more sophisticated about academic politics than I, and he cautioned us that we would have to pay a price for everything we received. I learned that he was right when Pollock was both hurt and indignant because we did not make him a co-author of the group's first publication (1964b), although we had merely asked him to read the manuscript as a matter of courtesy. We decided to smooth over this contretemps by asking George to become a regular member of the study group. He participated constructively in the preparation of the group's next four papers (1966b, 1967c, 1968c, 1969), although he had difficulty in maintaining focus on our declared agenda; he probably spent more time and effort on tangential ideas stimulated by our discussions than on our joint enterprise. He also asked me to write a chapter with him on issues of research in psychotherapy (1967b). I did most of the work; George made all the arrangements, and he let me appear as senior author. I think we were both satisfied with this modus operandi, and it became the model for our later publishing ventures together, which invariably proceeded without difficulty (see 1976a, 1984a, 1985a).[3]

As a result of our contact in the study group, Sabshin soon approached me with an offer to join his department at the University of Illinois, on a part-time basis. He proposed that I spend one full day per week as an academic, teaching both medical students and residents in psychiatry and continuing to think and write about psychotherapeutic issues, as I had begun to do. (See 1959a, 1963a, 1964a, 1966a, 1967a, 1981a [chap. 2], and 1991a [chap. 8] for this sequence of papers.) The prospect of being paid, however modestly, to do work I had every intention of doing in any case was irresistible. Moreover, I had reason to hope that Mel would bring together a solid psychoanalytic cadre in the department, for as his residency director he had hired my friend Julian Miller, who had become a key pin in our professional circle. Sabshin made it clear to me that in the near future he would try to recruit the other members of our study group. We shared the fantasy that we could take part in the creation of a world-class institution for psychoanalytic medicine. John F. Kennedy was president; the American economy was booming—progressive enterprises had a bright future.

I joined the department at Illinois in the fall of 1962. To make this possible without shrinking my private practice, I resigned from the Northwestern Student Health Service and, with much greater reluctance, from the staff at Michael Reese as well. In fact, I only resolved my ambivalence about taking this step when my friend, the internist Ernest Mond, told me about attending a meeting of the committee formed to raise funds from the medical staff for a new hospital building. At this strategy session, the representative from psychiatry, an analyst-colleague of the older generation, named me as a potential obstacle to the success of the fund drive. According to this gentleman, the danger stemmed from my psychosexual predispositions (I forget what they were, but he spelled them out authoritatively)—at any rate, he guaranteed that he could forestall the problem by approaching me with these dynamics in mind. (Something in the nature of administering an enema, I believe.)

I decided that, despite my gratitude for Grinker's support, I did not belong in a setting where a colleague could feel free gratuitously to speak so disrespectfully about one. (I suppose this means that, as the standards of public conduct get looser and looser, I belong in fewer and fewer milieus. Fortunately, I am now free to enjoy solitude in my study. I look northeast across Lake Michigan; there is only blue water between my chair and Canada.) At least on this occasion, in contrast to some previous episodes of pique, I left not because I felt humiliated but because I regarded the procedures of the institution as shameful. However, I did not snub the organization in every respect: the forum of the monthly staff meetings of the psychiatry department remained available as a friendly arena where one could present works-in-preparation. I availed myself of the opportunity fairly frequently; that is where I became accustomed to facing a professional audience.

At the University of Illinois Department of Psychiatry, relatively little had changed since the year of my residency there, so that it was easy to fit in once again. I very much enjoyed working with a former teacher, Hugh Carmichael, a crusty old Scot from Canada who was in charge of medical student instruction. (When he retired, a few years later, Hugh initiated the program of continuing education for the American Psychiatric Association.) More important to me was the opportunity to become acquainted with George Moraitis, a faculty member newly arrived from Colorado, where he had his psychiatric training, to begin candidacy at the Chicago Institute. George is a member of a very distinguished Athenian family of artists and intellectuals; his attitudes about transplantation to America turned out to be very similar to mine.

In terms of teaching responsibilities, I was assigned to lecture on psychopathology to second-year medical students. I know now that what I presented was over their heads—it may even have been too complex for beginners in a psychoanalytic program. Although the course was therefore not a success, I was enormously pleased to find that I could speak spontaneously for a whole period about the various topics in the syllabus, and colleagues at my own level of experience found the lectures lucid and compelling. We all agreed that I might better be used to teach more knowledgeable students. I was gaining confidence as an expositor of psychoanalytic concepts.

Teaching psychiatric residents was, at that time, a gratifying experience, for Sabshin and Julian Miller recruited able people and infused them with enthusiasm for psychological medicine. A fair number among them went on to obtain psychoanalytic credentials, and a majority went through a personal analysis. In retrospect, our most distinguished student was Jim McDermott, who went on to Seattle to do child psychiatry and later became a congressman. Nowadays he is leader of the forces in the House of Representatives in the uphill struggle for a single-payer system of health care delivery. Now a generation older, on the television screen he looks as charming as ever.

Although Julian and I were never on campus at the same time, we had become rather close. On the Chicago analytic scene, he was probably the person best described as sophisticated—particularly sophisticated about cultural matters and public affairs. He was held in respect by all his peers because of his excellent judgment and seeming imperturbability. He had been a classmate of Leo Sadow's in medical school; he and I had been residents together at Michael Reese; he shared a private office with Nate Schlessinger. Julian also seems to have been Sabshin's closest friend; I presume this somehow came about because Mel's wife Edith had been Julian's laboratory partner in medical school. (The late Edith Sabshin was in my cohort at the Institute; Julian was in a later class because he had taken a two-year internship.) It was only natural that, as soon as he completed his work at the Institute, we asked Julian to join our study group.

The papers we produced in that group gave most of us our first experience in presenting to a psychoanalytic audience. The senior author of each paper—in practice, the person who prepared its first draft—would read it, for a start usually at the Wednesday afternoon research forum at the Institute. I made my first presentation of such a collaborative effort to the American Psychoanalytic Association (at the 1963 mid-winter meeting), as well as to the Chicago Psychoanalytic Society. The latter occasion also showed me Max Gitelson at his very best. He told me after the meeting how much he had liked the paper; he said he would have wished to take part in the discussion, but decided to refrain because he did not want to detract from my experience of having a solo triumph that evening. At any rate, when Julian Miller presented one of our works-in-progress for the first time at the Institute, he also scored a triumph. An hour after we left that meeting, as he was entering his home, he died of cardiac arrest. One may die of pure joy. Julian was 38 years of age.

Within our generation in the local analytic community, this was the first death. Most of us were thunderstruck. A colleague then in analysis with Therese Benedek reported that Therese expressed no surprise—she allegedly muttered, "He used up his emotional capital." I believe she meant that Julian was prone to burden himself with more responsibility, both in his home life and professionally, than any one person can carry with impunity.

When Julian died, most of us were concerned about his widow's ability to cope; only Leo Sadow, quite a *Menschenkenner*,[4] was shrewd enough to predict that she would quickly remarry. (Joan was neither conventionally attractive nor physically healthy; I could not imagine that she could manage this.) In a few months, she reappeared as the fiancée of a charming and erudite professor of Russian literature at the University of Chicago, Ralph Matlaw. I mention all this because some years later Joan was killed by a stray bullet that struck her outdoors during the intermission of a concert she was attending at Aspen, and Ralph asked me to give one of the eulogies at her funeral. Whatever I thought of Joan, I felt I could not refuse—I supposed someone from her past with Julian had to participate, and Ralph clearly wanted a performance his academic colleagues could respect. This idea almost paralyzed me—it was the only time in my life that I almost missed a deadline, and I had to stay up all night to manage. The academics seemed satisfied, probably because I ended the eulogy by quoting a poem none could identify. (By good fortune, no member of the Department of Classics happened to be present.)

I trust that I have conveyed the ambience of ambition, idealism, and uncertainty about career possibilities that characterized the first few years after my graduation from the Institute. Yet my decision to continue to participate in the Institute clinic by taking another low-fee analysand (without supervision), something most graduates in those years did as a matter of course, gave me a feedback signal that I was in favor with the powers-that-be. While I was reviewing the record of the first prospective analysand referred to me, I received a call from the clinic administrator that, on second thought, they wanted me to accept someone else. The second proposed analysand was a faculty wife from the University of Chicago, about ten years my senior, a friend of the director of the Institute, Gerhart Piers, of Heinz Kohut, and of numerous other senior psychoanalytic figures who lived around the university—albeit most of these people were undoubtedly attracted by her husband, an eminent scientist from an aristocratic European background. But the patient's very best friend was the wife of a training analyst, one of several who lived on her block in Hyde Park. I should have had the sense to decline such a challenge, but I was seduced by the thought that my teachers were entrusting me with one of their own.

Of course, they really were, and she knew it. She felt entitled to whatever she was provided and more, and she thought it was insulting on my part not to be in complete agreement with such a view. A generation before it became the fashion, she had perfected the art of accusing her associates of victimizing her. It did not take long before I joined her husband on her list of chief victimizers, and she spent a great deal of time in sharing these complaints with the wife of my senior colleague. One New Year's Eve, we were invited to a reception at the Piers home, where my analysand felt very much more *chez soi* than I. Maria Piers introduced me to my patient's husband, a distinguished figure about twenty-five years my senior, who was casually leaning against a doorpost. "Ah!" said he with a weary and condescending smile, "so you are the young man who is practicing on my wife."

I practiced and practiced, for something like five years, and made painful progress punctuated by crises that led the patient to denounce me, to ever more influential people, for various fictive abuses. The patient's intellectual paralysis was eventually overcome, and she was able to get a teaching job at a community college. In the context of the resultant change in her financial circumstances, I tried once more to address the issue of her sense of entitlement (in this particular instance, to a token fee), and she became so enraged that she dropped out of treatment. I notified the clinic about her decision and about my own not to take on further low-fee patients through the Institute. (If I was to write about psychoanalysis, I needed every spare moment for that enterprise.)

About three months later, the analysand returned to complete our work; she thought it would not take her long to reach a satisfactory termination. I was essentially in agreement, but I had no time available; I also clarified that I could only take her back as a private patient. We made arrangements to resume in the not too distant future, but shortly thereafter she called to announce that she had consulted her friend Gerhart Piers about the situation, and he had referred her to another analyst. The story is worth telling because Piers did not find it necessary to ask her permission to discuss the clinical situation with me. I was not surprised. I already knew that something was rotten in the state of Denmark.

I cannot resist recounting that, decades later, I met my former patient when I paid a condolence call on her best friend after the latter's husband died. She eyed me apprehensively across the room, and I joined her to talk over old times. She said she had done well, although she had had no further treatment, and she apologized for having been so very difficult and unreasonable with me. I told her that I did not feel that our shared travails were her fault or mine—I said that our mutual friends had put us into an impossible situation by making themselves witnesses of our transactions. She was very surprised to hear that I had felt under the gun.

I should make clear that my disillusionment with the Piers/Fleming regime was very gradual—the denouement of the foregoing analysis did not take place before 1967. In the earlier part of the decade, the Institute opened its doors to fresh blood in a number of ways, and many of us saw the leadership as progressive—a breath of fresh air after the twenty-three-year rule of the emperor Alexander. The very structure of the faculty was drastically changed: under the old regime, only an appointed "staff"—a praetorian guard of twenty—participated in governance; now the entire faculty began to play a part and decisions were to be made by an elected council. The Wednesday research meetings were opened to recent graduates active in various Institute programs, and many new faces were added to the teaching ranks.

Probably on the strength of a paper I prepared in the study group that dealt with the clinical evidence Freud cited in his early work, I was asked to redesign the course on Freud's case histories, offered in the first year of the curriculum. Although nothing was put in writing, I no longer doubted that I was on the faculty, and I acted as if it had been a matter of course that I would stop assisting Pollock in the research seminar. In addition to the five classical case histories, I decided to include in my syllabus not only Freud's cases from the 1890s but also the extensive secondary literature on all of his case reports. In the course, we tried to discern what specific aims were served by each case presentation, what changes in therapeutic technique were revealed where, how valid were Freud's clinical and theoretical conclusions, and what lessons for contemporary psychoanalysis were embedded in each case. I think I was loaded for bear, and the candidates appreciated the thoroughness of my preparation. There were persons of real substance in those classes; some, like Jerry Jacobson of Denver or Steve Post of St. Louis, later became directors of their institutes, when such organizations were established in their cities.

Around the same time, Gerhart Piers called to refer to me for analysis a psychologist who worked for a government agency that made grants to various institutions dealing with mental health, including the Institute for Psychoanalysis. As Piers put it, this man wanted to become a student of ours, the government would pay the Institute (which would then reimburse me), and I could look upon the referral as the first training analysis I was to perform—unofficially, of course. The implication was that we would cut through a variety of bureaucratic nonsense and gain a friend at court—and rules are made to be broken. I was afraid that in feeling uncomfortable about this I was, as usual, being moralistic—I had not yet heard the phrase "conflict of interest." If the august director of the Chicago Institute says that is the way of the world, is it not sheer narcissism to refuse to stoop to conquer?

As it turned out, the rules to be broken were more fundamental than I had imagined, although the patient did not make this clear for some time. I eventually grasped that he billed his agency for Institute "tuition," and our administration supplied him with documentation to support this claim, for the government would not fully cover the cost of the analysis as "treatment." I never did learn whether the patient's superiors were in on the plot, but when I indicated that I did not wish to join it, the patient felt utterly betrayed. We agonized over our dilemma for several months. Finally, we recognized that nothing good could come from such an arrangement, and the patient (with amazing enterprise) obtained an academic job in a distant locality, where he planned to resume analysis on a private basis. (A few years ago, I was invited to give a lecture at his university, and this man made a point of coming to greet me and to express his appreciation.) The point of the story is not that both of us ultimately managed to wash ourselves clean but that, by my standards and those of my family, the Institute was capable of corruption. I was as horrified as my mother used to be about Aunt Bertha's Budapest flirtations.

It did not help that Joan Fleming sent me the manuscript of *Psychoanalytic Supervision*, to get final permission to publish excerpts from the transcripts of the recorded material, and I found her comments unsatisfactory from several viewpoints. I wrote to her, granting my consent on condition that she include a statement, attributed to candidate "G.," setting forth my view of these disputed points. I received no reply. About a year later the book was published, and she sent me a copy signed by her and Therese. The condition I had stipulated for publication had been disregarded. Fleming's handwritten words of gratitude are inscribed, upside down, on the blank page preceding the back cover. Right or wrong, I took this parapraxis to mean that our transactions were topsy-turvy, that unconsciously she had to admit that she had mistaught me. From my perspective, this was corruption, compounded by tyranny.

It was all I could do not to denounce the sinners from the rooftops; this was another beneficial result of my analysis, for prior to that I would have preached against their abominations, like a Savonarola.[5] That is one of the things I mean when I say (as I often do) that I was raised to be unfit for human consumption. By the age of 35, I could more or less keep my moral anathemata to myself, although I no doubt betrayed my disapproval in countless nonverbal ways. It was not the best of dispositions for getting along in a self-satisfied community. But the comparison I have suggested to a papacy corrupted by worldly ambition did, in fact, apply to much of American psychoanalysis: it was scientifically complacent, and its leadership invested too much effort and energy in imperialist ventures to gain power within psychiatry, obtain subsidies from government agencies, and grasp other social advantages. A day of reckoning was drawing near.

❖ CHAPTER 5 ❖

AWAKENING

For about a year and a half before I completed my clinical responsibilities, I was working with only one patient—my very last analysand. I closed my practice to new referrals more than five years before the end, and I gradually decreased my clinical commitments as each of the eight persons who were then in analysis with me terminated our efforts. When I decided on this policy of (I hoped) dignified retreat, I did not realize that it would, toward the end, leave me with the patients with the most difficult problems. For several years, I had only tigers by the tail, and the last one may have been the fiercest tiger of them all. It turned out to be the lengthiest continuous analysis I ever conducted. Of course, it was very problematic from the first: an Institute faculty member referred this man to me, at a time when analytic cases no longer grew on trees, because he did not feel up to dealing with such an intimidating person. He made it clear that he thought I could not be intimidated.

When and where did I first hear such an assessment? (What a change for the excessively docile young man whom the Institute accepted in 1951!) It must have been a couple of years after I completed training, when Fleming asked me to present the patient whose treatment she had supervised in the termination seminar she took over from Max Gitelson when he died. I did not look forward to making public my dissatisfaction with her instruction, but I was determined no longer to keep silent about it. To my great relief, at the last minute she was unable to attend and arranged for Heinz Kohut to step in as a pinch hitter. I therefore felt no conflict about presenting my own view of the treatment of my psychopathic patient, one that emphasized that the crux of his difficulties was his vulnerability to narcissistic injuries.[1]

Although this class took place years before he published his novel views on narcissism, Kohut's discussion of the case was a revelation—not only because he was greatly interested in narcissistic characters, but also because he stressed that therapeutic success would depend on more than dealing with the patient's psychopathology. Kohut emphasized that my analysand was an artist, and that assisting him therefore depended on one's ability to promote his creativity. (During the treatment, when the patient actually changed from claiming to be the world's greatest unpublished poet to being a real, albeit modest, producer of respected poetry, Fleming blurted out that none of her analysands with artistic aspirations had ever become creative. Judging by my experience as her supervisee, she did not promote *anyone's* creativity.) At any rate, Heinz said that the sine qua non for helping such a person to be creative is not to be intimidated by his potential, and he added, "Obviously, Dr. Gedo was not afraid." It was the most original commentary I had until then heard about any psychoanalytic encounter. It was more radical in its implications than Kohut's subsequent "official" contribution to the field, the development of self psychology. It also happened to be very pleasing to someone who had only recently overcome his embarrassing timidity.

It was good no longer to be afraid of much! I have never forgotten what it means to be really afraid—as I was when forced to join a crowd of children in November 1938, to welcome the Hungarian reoccupation of Losoncz with chants of "Hitler! Hitler! Musso-lini!"—only a few days before my father was to be arrested for his anti-fascist commitments. At the age of 35, I was no longer afraid to proclaim that the premises of the psychotherapy then called "psychoanalytically oriented" did not make any sense. Through the mid-sixties, I worked on a series of papers on that topic, and I presented my ideas about what constitutes a set of rational therapeutic strategies at the Institute research meetings.

My objections to so-called psychoanalytic therapies involve the assumption of the majority of their practitioners that it is generally desirable to use a technique that comes as close as possible to the model technique of psychoanalysis, that is, one confined to interpretation. Exclusive optimism about the therapeutic power of quasi-analytic procedures in settings that fail to meet the criteria of an analytic situation (in terms of frequency of sessions, the use of free association, and so on) was probably even more prevalent a generation ago than it is now. In my experience, such therapeutic attempts generally ended in failure—in my own practice, probably because of my growing skepticism about these procedures. In recent years, I have concluded that an exclusively interpretive technique is largely ineffective even in psychoanalysis proper (see 1979a), because the difficulties of analysands are never confined to unresolved conflicts about mental contents. Clearly, this disjunction between the nature of the maladaptation and the measures intended to correct it is even more striking in cases that (in the era I am describing) were deemed not to be analyzable. Hence I joined that minority of therapists—prominently including Roy Grinker—who advocated looking for explicitly nonanalytic psychotherapeutic methods. I recall Heinz Kohut commenting, on the first occasion when I presented such ideas, that he liked my refusal to compromise, that is, to ape analytic techniques while working out of the framework required to create a psychoanalytic situation. I suspect that he liked courage (it was only much later that I discovered, to my chagrin, that this quality was not characteristic of his usual behavior. He was a prudent person—nobody could have become a dissident more reluctantly. In Hungary we would have said, "What can you expect of an Austrian?!") What was more important, he quickly recognized that I was willing really to struggle with conceptual issues and, unlike many others, he, in his turn, had no reason to be intimidated by intellectual competence.

Soon he began to refer patients to me for analysis. When he became celebrated for being able to deal with problems other analysts preferred to avoid, he was consulted by many people with the most severe difficulties. Hence, Heinz's referrals tended to be the most troublesome among my patients, but the first person to whom he happened to recommend me was among the least difficult analytic cases I have had to deal with. She was a young Stanford graduate, embroiled with neurotic parents. Her father was a long-term patient of Kohut's—Heinz told me as he made the referral, "Perhaps at least the daughter might be saved." In a relatively short time, she emancipated herself, married a brilliant Chinese scientist, and presumably lived happily ever after. (I recently saw her father's obituary, according to which the daughter and her spouse are still making progress in academia.) Heinz undoubtedly heard about my efficient work, and his confidence in me increased.

I later came to the conclusion that the decisive turning point in Kohut's dealings with me was the death of Max Gitelson, which coincided with

Heinz's election as president of the American Psychoanalytic Association. Heinz told me that Max had provided him with personal support, and his behavior toward me seemed like an effort to repay this by doing the same for one of Gitelson's analysands, largely by using the power of the office in which Max had preceded him. Whatever the reason, he gradually became my active supporter and, contrary to my personal inclinations, he made every effort to transform the relationship into one of social intimacy. To put the matter differently, I was reluctant to become friends with him, for however nice he tried to be, I never felt that his behavior was motivated by any personal regard for me. (In the vocabulary Kohut later devised, I felt I was one of his many selfobjects.) When he decided to become my patron, he was playing me the way one moves a rook in a chess game. More often than not, I was pleased by the position into which I got pushed, but I never felt gratitude, the way I always do when people show they care for me. I was keenly aware of a difference between what Heinz was doing with me and what is designated as "being used as a pawn": in this chess game, I was expected to play the part of a *rook*. Kohut saw me as reliable, powerful, and straight—*ein festes Burg*.[2]

Yet, for a number of years, I could not be certain that I perceived the situation correctly—after all, Heinz's behavior in many ways echoed the intrusiveness of my parents that I had had so much trouble in fending off. Later on, Kohut's own statements revealed that I had not misunderstood this emotional transaction. The clearest instance of such a revelation occurred at a meeting of an ad hoc committee of the American Psychoanalytic Association that Heinz chaired; he had me appointed as secretary of this body. In those prosperous days, such committees ate and drank lavishly, and at one dinner meeting, attended by only four or five people, Heinz had enough wine to loosen his tongue. Looking me straight in the eye, he intoned, "You know, except for Betty and Tom [his wife and only son], there is nobody in this world I care about." *In vino veritas*.[3] But I did not include this in my minutes. I am not certain whether Kohut's statement was literally true; it was, however, perfectly clear that it was meant for me alone. (I doubt that anyone else could have heard it.) I inferred that he was letting me know that he had no human regard for me, but that this exclusion from his caring might change if I would become *his*.

Although my feelings about Heinz's overtures were highly ambivalent, on the stage of everyday life I chose to disregard my doubts about the relationship because I thought Heinz was both a great man and the first person who discerned what I would be good for in psychoanalysis. When he approached me with the proposition that I take an assignment from the German psychoanalytic journal *Psyche,* for which he himself did not have the time (because of his commitments as president of the American Psychoanalytic), I was confident that he knew that absolutely nobody would do a more creditable job with such a back-breaking task: *Psyche* wanted an assessment of Ferenczi's manifold contributions to psychoanalysis (because the German edition of his writings had just been reissued). I labored over the assignment for over a year (see 1968b); Heinz was gratified about having exercised good judgment in pushing me into this slot.[4]

It was doubly satisfying to have one's strengths recognized by Kohut because he had become the unrivaled intellectual leader of Chicago psychoanalysis. At the Wednesday meetings, he invariably set the tone of the discussion, and what he said was always judicious, weighty, and relevant. He sometimes talked too long, not giving others as much opportunity to participate as they needed, but I always learned from what he had to say. Through the 1960s, he was a thoroughgoing adherent of Heinz Hartmann, and in Chicago nobody could hold his or her own with him, especially in theoretical matters. His public behavior was generally haughty, aloof, and mannered—but I had had cordial relations with much more objectionable characters, and in accepting his patronage I did not think I was evaluating him as a potential friend. He was very influential and was able to open doors for one: when he was president of the American Psychoanalytic Association, he appointed me to the Committee on Indexing, one of the few venues in the Association where active scientific collaboration was taking place. Having such a person in one's corner would have been very helpful even if I had been in universal favor at the Institute; because this was far from the case, I felt that I simply could not afford to pass up what Heinz had to offer.

Nor was I immune to the narcissistic seduction of being regarded as his intellectual equal by the most talented analytic theoretician I had encountered. Kohut's attitude seemed to promise that very soon I would be pitching in the World Series. My inability to resist these temptations is the most serious mistake I have thus far made in life. At the same time, it was a manifestation of a lack of confidence in the extent of my abilities—a defect in reality testing, if you will, that plagued me until I became a steady contributor to the psychoanalytic literature: I ought to have known that I could make my way without attaching myself to the coattails of anyone.

The situation was difficult not only because of my ambivalence; it was made worse by the fact that Mary did not like Kohut as a person either.

Heinz had impeccable manners that, as I was later to learn, he was able to put on or take off like an overcoat, and when he tried, he could be very charming. Yet he was not popular with women—according to Mary, he was hostile to them. She always felt depreciated in his presence, even late in our relationship with him, when he often quoted her scholarly work about Picasso (M. Gedo 1980) with enthusiastic approval.[5] Mary is almost always accurate in assessing people's attitudes, but I believe in this instance her view was too narrow: Heinz was contemptuous of almost everyone. He made a few exceptions—Hartmann, his friend the musicologist Sigmund Levarie, John Gedo—but almost no women were among these. Only his wife, Elizabeth (truly an admirable person—sensible, down-to-earth, generous, and intelligent), and perhaps Marianne Kris.[6] (He regarded Anna Freud as a perpetual child of a particularly amusing sort. He was fond of recounting that, when she was his houseguest while on a visit to the Institute, he caught her before breakfast one morning, raiding the sugar bowl for a goodie—just like her celebrated dream of early childhood about eating strawberries.)[7] Mary's reservations about much of Kohut's behavior also made our social contacts very difficult—on our part reluctant, reserved, formal. If Heinz noticed, he gave no sign of it; he relentlessly pressed forward to become one of my familiars.

The first time the Kohuts came to dinner, we thought, mistakenly, the proper atmosphere might develop in a party of European men married to American wives: we invited Ernest and Julia Mond (the internist I had met at Michael Reese) and Miodrag and Cathy Yokanovich. (Cathy is a pediatrician who had been Mary's college roommate in Urbana; she married Mio when, as an anti-Tito refugee, he became an intern at her hospital. He is a very glamorous figure from the high aristocracy of Montenegro; he had years of atrocious guerrilla warfare and forced labor behind him.) In this company, Heinz did not then stand out. Consequently, he was clearly out of sorts; he managed to put everyone down in turn, with sufficient subtlety to make it difficult to object. It is not the way to make oneself popular, least of all with us.[8]

Of course, most of my dealings with Heinz were professional, and we did a great deal of talking about analytic matters. On one occasion, I expressed amazement about how well most colleagues in Chicago thought of the research on parent loss in childhood, conducted by a study group led by Joan Fleming. To me, it seemed that making an actual external event the major independent variable in a piece of psychoanalytic research could yield no reliable result. As I saw it, the subjects in the study were not ill because they had suffered the death of a parent; rather, they had been unable to transcend parent loss because as children they were already ill. Heinz was in complete agreement with me—he was eager to see Fleming's thesis discredited because it was an avoidance of depth psychology. I asked him whether in our analytic community it was conceivable to say such things in a public forum about the work of a senior figure. He said that if I wrote a paper on the subject, it could certainly be presented at the Chicago Society, and he would be at the meeting to back me.

I was not particularly concerned about the consequences of offending Fleming because I knew that, in terms of career considerations, she had already decided to do everything in her power to stand in my way. Concerning my chances at the Institute, it did not help, either, that I joined Julian Miller, Leo Sadow, and one or two others in forming a small delegation to persuade Gerhart Piers not to purchase a building that we believed to be grossly unsuitable to house the Institute. It may convey the flavor of the interview to relate that, when I mentioned that the place did not have an adequate system of rest rooms, Gerhart replied, mockingly, that analysts are well known for their ability to regulate their bowels and bladders, so that they do not have to stand in line for a toilet. I did not bother to state that some of my patients did not possess this useful self-restraint or that I did not care to add such a training routine to the analytic regimen I offer them.

After this unpleasant interview, we received a lengthy letter from Piers, jocular in tone, promising to forgive our oedipal rebellion and giving us an ultimatum to sign on the dotted line within forty eight hours if we wished to be offered office space in the future home of the Institute.[9] (He knew very well that we had first to arrange the termination of existing leases, so that he was in effect making us unwelcome.) It is not irrelevant that one of our delegation did not show up for the meeting, later claiming that he had waited for the rest of us at the right time and place. This prudent colleague soon became a member of the Institute inner circle and went on to bigger and better positions in the administration. (The building we thought unsuitable was sold to the Archdiocese of Chicago—we learned that its owners had entered into negotiations with the Institute merely to inflate the purchase price.) At any rate, I was clearly unsuited to the political games one had to play for acceptance by the Piers regime.

I had amassed experience enough to be considered for training analyst status several years before this—even colleagues I considered mediocre who had graduated when I did had already been appointed or were actively being evaluated for the job. So I told myself, *"Tout est perdu, sauf l'honneur."*[10] As I have mentioned, in the antiquated society where I was raised, the question of honor was taken very seriously indeed. I was also beginning to suspect that persons lacking in honor (such as the powers-that-be at the Institute who disapproved of independent thinking) could not assist analysands to live honorably.

In retrospect, I suspect Fleming had already decided to blackball me because of the independence I had shown in withdrawing from the course I had been teaching at the Institute. Enthusiastic though I had been about preparing it, when I completed presenting the material for the second time, I felt that it no longer had much interest for me, and I looked for a way to tackle something new. I understood that it would not do simply to abandon ship, so I asked Arnold Goldberg, a recent graduate of outstanding intellect and enterprise, whether he would be interested in teaching the course with me. (Arnold had been a couple of years behind me as a resident at Illinois, disappeared into the service, cropped up as a resident at Michael Reese when I was a young attending physician, and went through the Institute four or five years after me. He was already the center of a coterie of young analysts, and he had asked me for advice about improving some papers he was preparing for publication. In my judgment, these efforts showed outstanding promise—one of the best predictions I have ever made.) When Goldberg indicated that he would be delighted to join the course, I managed somehow to get official approval for our plan—the relevant authorities were clearly cognizant of Arnold's merits.

The course Goldberg and I taught through the following year was the most successful I have ever participated in. Arnold is an outstanding teacher, lucid, witty, ever ready with relevant answers to good questions, skillful in fending off irrelevancies and in correcting misapprehensions without offending the students. Moreover, doubtless because he was aware that much was at stake for him, he took care to complement me in a way that set off my strengths in meticulous preparation, open-mindedness, and rationality. I knew that I would never be able to find a better collaborator. Toward the end of the academic year, I wrote Fleming (still the dean), that Arnold's excellence ensured the future of the course, so that I wanted to relinquish it, and I asked for another assignment—anything whatsoever—whenever one would be available. She replied that there was no opening for the moment, and I never heard from her again. It did not take me too long to discern that, at the Chicago Institute, I had become an internal exile. At least, unlike my father, I was not forced to emigrate.

Under the circumstances, I was ready to disregard potential torpedoes; I wrote a paper about the developmental antecedents that determine a child's ability to adapt to external events such as the loss of a parent. When I presented this to the society, Joan Fleming was my formal discussant, and she was, of course, hostile to my thesis. (I thought her arguments were confused and confusing, but she articulated them in her characteristically dogmatic manner.[11]) Heinz was not present, nor did he, a stickler for protocol, let me know that he would be unable to come. He had no way of knowing whether the presentation would be good or bad, for I had not shown him the paper in advance. It occurred to me that he was afraid to come, because he knew I would be forthright, and he actually did not wish to antagonize Fleming. Was it a case of "let you and her fight"? Perhaps he simply wanted to avoid something unexpected. (Although I was not certain at the time, my later experiences with Heinz convinced me that he had been afraid to attend.) Even if his broken promise had been an oversight, my confidence in Heinz's integrity was shaken; I became very wary of trusting his commitment, if that involved a risk, to safeguard the welfare of others. I can scarcely abide such a person.

My mistrust of Kohut was increased by a sequence of events that unfolded in 1969. Early that year, Heinz asked me whether I would be interested in collaborating with him in editing a volume of psychoanalytic polemics, the best arguments published over the years to rebut critics of psychoanalysis.[12] This topic was of no great interest to me, but at the age of 41 I still felt it was impossible to pass up an opportunity to co-edit a book with an immediate past president of the American Psychoanalytic Association, even if I had questions about his character, so I gave in to the temptation. Kohut asked me to do some library research and make suggestions for inclusion in the prospective volume.

I spent a fair bit of time on the project and sent Heinz an extensive memorandum about my findings. I did not get a reply, but he assured me that he would soon get around to drafting one. After a considerable interval, I ventured to ask whether he had yet thought about my memorandum. With unconcealed irritation, Heinz told me not to bother him about something for which he had no time. I was not particularly regretful that he had changed his mind, but I thought that his attitude was irrational and utterly unacceptable; he had been the one who pulled me into wasting *my* time. In contrast to Faust, however, I had to take my comeuppance, but I became determined not to allow Heinz to exploit me in the future.

I assume that the question of my status at the Institute must have come up for public discussion among the leadership, perhaps a bit after the 1967 society meeting where I clashed with Fleming. I made this inference because shortly thereafter Heinz took me aside to say, with a guilty air, that he felt the Institute was abusing me, and that he wanted in compensation to do something special for me. He proposed introducing me to Anna Freud, with the implication that this might open the way for me to become part of some covert inner circle consisting of those analysts who truly counted—mostly Central Europeans, of course. I have no objection whatever to elitism, but I could not grasp what I would gain from an acquaintance with Anna Freud, and I looked upon elites picked on the basis of national, even regional, origins with absolute horror. With amazing determination, Heinz insisted that a study trip to the Hampstead Clinic would do wonders for me, and he would arrange it. (When he got a bee in his bonnet, Kohut was impervious to outside influence. He could never be convinced that he could have made a trivial error, like the misidentification of a work of art, even in matters in which he had no expertise.)

At the British end, Heinz proceeded to put this plan into effect by writing Anna Freud in the following terms:

> Dear Miss Freud:
>
> My eyes are always on the next analytic generation who will have to continue our work, and I am trying to identify the all-too-few who show unusual gifts and who promise to become significant contributors to analysis in the future. You know what a difficult task this is and how easily and how often one does get misled. Once in a while however one thinks that one has recognized genuine talent in a young analyst and feels stimulated to do what one can to further his professional and scientific development. In Chicago there are unfortunately very few people who show such promise. One of them is I believe Dr. John Gedo, a comparatively young analyst (he became a member of the American Psychoanalytic Association just about five years ago) who, because of his uncompromising and original thinking, has become increasingly disengaged from the local structure around the Institute and has turned toward private research pursuits. In view of my high opinion of his scientific potential I have supported him to the best of my ability.[13]

Heinz might have been ruthless and self-centered, but how could I turn my back on a godfather who said this about me?

When the Hampstead journey was proposed, Mary was in graduate school, preparing for her Ph.D. qualifying examination, so that she could not take time to go with me to London for several months. Moreover, we had three children between the ages of 8 and 13, not to speak of some of my vulnerable patients, none of whom would profit from being left for very long. And Hampstead was inactive during school holidays. I protested that I could not possibly spend as much time in London as they required of visitors. Heinz was sure that he could get Anna Freud to make an exception for me, and when he actually gained her consent to let a protégé of his come for a mere six weeks, I was trapped—I felt I could not afford to refuse. Everybody was leaning over backward to accommodate me; I was not getting anything I desired, but I would have to be gracious or lose the only support I had in the Chicago analytic community.

It so happened that the 1969 Hampstead visit proved to be a decisive turning point in my professional life, although not in the way Heinz had implicitly promised. Those lures were, in any case, largely meant as payment for a service I was to render him, one he never spelled out in words but revealed in action as soon as I left for London. He kept calling Mary to find out what I said to her about my experience, either in letters or in phone calls. She told me this when I did call her (considerably later than Heinz, who was burning with impatience, imagined I would). This intimation that he had a hidden agenda so put me off that I waited several weeks before I even sent Kohut a postcard. His inquiries became ever more feverish; when I got home, it finally dawned on me that what he wanted to know was whether I had discovered Anna Freud's actual views about the radical papers on narcissism he had recently published (Kohut 1966, 1968). Mary had a different opinion, one that was too disturbing for me to accept. She thought that Heinz was so attached to me that he could not tolerate my keeping a distance between us. As she put it, "That man loves you."

After Kohut's death, the precise truth was articulated by his widow. I had turned my back on Heinz as a person (as well as on his psychoanalytic views) eight years before he died, but there had never been any unpleasantness between Betty and me. One evening, while I was waiting for Mary at the bottom of the great staircase at the Civic Opera House, Betty Kohut came down to greet me. I offered her straightforward condolences, and she began to cry. "Did you know how much you meant to him?" she inquired. I said I did. In a truly dignified manner that filled me with admiration, she concluded the story with her verdict. "It was not anyone's fault. You know, it could not be helped." Indeed. Although Heinz did not care for me in a manner I could accept, I was more important to him than anyone other than his wife and son. But in 1969 the drama was far from resolution.

What Hampstead did provide me was the longest period of real solitude in my life—an opportunity at the age of 42 to take stock of where I wished to invest my time and effort, and to what end. I was essentially alone because almost everyone at the clinic shared the delusion that it was the center of the psychoanalytic universe, so that visitors should be happy to be there even if they were offered nothing. (Moreover, the numerous Viennese on the staff tried to be more British than the English by staying aloof, so that scarcely anyone provided any personal contact. I did receive one dinner invitation, from Augusta Bonnard, an elderly, seductive widow with a magnificent Georgian house in St. John's Woods, complete with a Rachel Ruysch still-life over the mantelpiece.[14] She had been a friend of Max Gitelson's. She was the one who informed me about the amusing British customs copied by her non-English colleagues. She also understood that, in most ways, the psychoanalysis taught at Hampstead was that of the 1930s.)

I tried hard to be impressed with Anna Freud and Dorothy Burlingham. I must confess, however, that the only analyst I met whose ideas were of interest to me was a contemporary of mine from South Africa, Anne Hayman.[15] Unfortunately, she was then convalescing from a serious illness and did not feel well enough to spend time in exchanging views. I did attend some meetings of the British Society at their dazzling Robert Adam premises on New Cavendish Street.[16] On one occasion, I witnessed an unbelievably savage verbal duel between Masud Khan and Donald Meltzer there.[17] What I learned from this display was that the level of psychoanalytic discourse in Chicago was higher, as well as more polite.

At Hampstead, they were barely starting to turn their attention to the realms of pathology beyond neurosis—to problems of delinquency, addiction, and psychosis—with misguided confidence about the adequacy of Anna Freud's theoretical armamentarium to conquer these domains. The clinical experience of other analytic contributors was disregarded—for a guest it was not thinkable to mention the lessons of years of struggle treating hospitalized patients, such as my early experience at Michael Reese. One disgruntled staff member leaked the information that every word published by Hampstead personnel had to be approved by Anna Freud. People who had a spirit of independence tended to leave for greener pastures; respected figures, such as Joseph Sandler and Moses Laufer, had already established separate spheres of activity, and when they came to the clinic for specific purposes, their relations with "Miss Freud" seemed strained. A nasty scene took place when she brought me to one of Sandler's seminars without asking his permission. I found this overt rudeness doubly significant because he and I had cordial relations before this outburst, and these were later reestablished.

At the end of my third week in London, as the blessings of solitude were beginning to pall, I seized upon the fact that Mary needed a minor surgical procedure to announce that I had to go home. When she heard I was leaving, Anna Freud decided finally to grant me an interview, in her father's study. I suspect she understood that I did not find the visit constructive, and she felt some obligation to fulfill the promise she had made to Heinz. At any rate, she set aside a whole afternoon, and she arranged that Paula Fichtl, the famous family retainer from Vienna, first show me the Freud study and consulting room. She knew that I had done some writing about her father—not only the collaborative papers on the intellectual history of early psychoanalysis, but also something of my own (1968a), recently published, on Freud's self-analysis and the sequence of his scientific ideas. Anna Freud told me that she appreciated my evident effort to view the travails of a man of genius through affectionate empathy.

The tour of the Freud collection of antiquities was in the nature of a reward. I looked around with care, while Paula was giving her canned lecture ("And this is the piece the professor always kept on his desk . . ."). I was forcibly struck with what a magnificent milieu Freud provided for analysands—how he refused to hide his light under a bushel; on the contrary, he asserted that he was a great gentleman and a man of wide culture by surrounding his analysands with his wonderful library and fascinating artifacts. Of course, even the house itself is an early eighteenth-century treasure, and the most beautiful aspect it presents is the view of the garden from Freud's study. I wondered how American psychoanalysis has, by and large, let itself be squeezed into sterile spaces in ugly office buildings. Did I really have to remain content with that? Does it have anything to do with our progressive loss of prestige in America?

When Anna Freud joined me, we walked around once more, and I was really moved, despite my reservations about her *retardataire* role in psychoanalysis. I wanted to tell her how much I valued the experience she was providing me—"Have you any idea how much this is worth?" is what I said, indicating the entire suite with a sweeping gesture. And we both started to cry. She then told me that she would try to answer whatever questions I had about her father. We chatted for well over an hour; what was most memorable about the conversation was her reply when I wondered how Freud had managed to put forth such a prodigious amount of work—the sheer volume of writing he poured out while carrying a full clinical load. His daughter then talked about his energy and perseverance, his ability to make do with relatively little sleep. After a pause for reflection, she added, "Of course, my mother and I devoted our lives to making things possible for him."

The interview also had its amusing side, one that seemed to confirm Heinz's estimate of Anna Freud's childishness. While at Hampstead, I met her nephew, W. E. Freud, and I asked her whose son he was. She replied that he was the child of her sister Sophie—the one whose game of "*fort und da*" is described in "Beyond the Pleasure Principle" (Freud 1920).[18] I was confused, "Then how can his name be Freud?" I asked naïvely. With obvious sincerity, Miss Freud replied, "Oh, his name was Halberstadt, but the English could not pronounce that." In the British Navy, she would have been advised, "Tell that to the Marines!"[19]

In my stock-taking while in London, I had decided to renounce the goals that are generally considered the marks of success in psychoanalysis. If I was justified in thinking that I understood the actual problems faced by the field as a scientific and clinical enterprise better than the people I had met in London, it was foolish to be concerned about my role at the Chicago Institute, or the acquisition of administrative powers, about Viennese or Hungarian connections, or the personal feelings toward me of every Tom, Dick, or Harry. I needed a congenial environment and time to read, to think, and to write. When Mary had recovered from surgery, I told her about my interview with Anna Freud and asked her whether she would be willing to make it possible for me to try to do my best as a serious contributor to psychoanalysis. And she has more than done her part.

In retrospect, the seeming wild-goose chase I let myself in for was not as aimless as it appeared to be at the time. By 1969 my attention was focused on the disarray of psychoanalytic theory, and I needed to confirm the impression, gained on the narrow stage of Chicago psychoanalysis, that I was better suited to put it into some new order than anyone I had met. To engage in complex theoretical enterprises beyond my capacities would have been a wild-goose chase, indeed. The study trip to Hampstead, then at the height of its prestige, provided an opportunity to learn how my understanding of the unresolved problems of psychoanalysis compared with that of some of the best in the business. I returned home confident that, in these matters, I could hold my own with anyone.

❖ CHAPTER 6 ❖

COLLABORATION AND SOLITUDE

Not long ago, I received a laudatory review of the book that Mark Gehrie and I published in 1993. The reviewer is Boyd Burris (1994), an analyst I believed to be wedded to a traditional viewpoint—I remember how shocked he seemed when, about twenty years ago, he first heard me present some dissenting ideas at the Baltimore-Washington Psychoanalytic Society. In the interval, so many radical notions have arisen within psychoanalysis that my own have probably lost their shock value. It is also possible that the fundamental conservatism of my biological orientation to the phenomena of the mind has become apparent to an undogmatic traditionalist like Burris. I suspect that it also put me in a better light that, at several junctures in the book, we presented dialogues between Gehrie and myself; in the course of these, I generally took the more traditional positions, and Mark, whose analytic education at the Chicago Institute took place at the height of the local enthusiasm for Kohut's ideas, talked like a self psychologist.

Mark came to psychoanalysis from anthropology—he stood out among the candidates of his era for his scholarly bent, so rare among the medically trained. Shortly after his marriage, he happened to settle in the North Shore suburb where I was then living, and we began to run into each other with some frequency. He became very friendly with Mike Gunther, who also lived nearby—in other words, he was a natural recruit to the circles in which I moved professionally. About a dozen years ago, Mark and I agreed to organize an ongoing study group of some of his contemporaries who might want a more experienced person, like myself, to participate as an avuncular influence. We invited a number of well-regarded recent graduates of the Institute who had, at one time or another, consulted me privately or whom I had supervised during training. The participants turned out to have been well chosen—all of them are now on the Institute faculty, most have become training analysts, and several have significant publications to their credit. (In addition to Gedo and Gehrie [1993b], see Levin [1991] and several volumes of *The Annual of Psychoanalysis* edited by Jerome Winer.) As they got to know each other in this new context, they engaged ever more enthusiastically in candid clinical discussions about their most difficult cases.

I suppose that, in the course of this study group, we met close to a hundred times; having started without irreconcilable differences, we reached consensus on a broad spectrum of psychoanalytic issues. If, in our joint book, Mark and I articulated slightly different viewpoints, this was largely for didactic purposes. Naturally, as the participants' responses became ever more predictable, the meetings of the group lost some of their edge. With the passage of more than ten years, the time came to discontinue this activity—enterprises of this sort may have a limited useful half-life. At least, so I have found from my personal vantage point. I learned this lesson early in my career, when I took part in collaborative efforts (sometimes with just one other person) because I thought it would help me to produce publishable work. Of course, not every study group in which I participated even reached the state of being overripe, like the seminar Gehrie organized with me.

The one on scientific methodology, which had been so productive, was prematurely disrupted by the death of Julian Miller. I think we all felt that he would not have died when he did if our common effort had not made him dizzy with success, but the most profound response was that of Mel Sabshin, who seemed to lose interest not only in the agenda of our study group but in psychoanalytic matters in general. His relationship with Miller must have meant more to him than most of us realized—at least, when we no longer had the friendship with Julian in common, he and I drifted apart. Because I had mistakenly believed that a more personal bond existed between us, I felt disappointed and foolish to discover that, for Mel, I was now merely a member of the faculty who was expected to elevate the department's prestige. From then on, Sabshin seemed intent on promoting what he called social psychiatry, an ambition that remained fuzzy about data and methods. Of course, the study group could have gone on without him, but it had other troubles.

From my perspective, these took the form of a lack of equity in labor and rewards. We had agreed to take turns as senior author of succeeding publications, and that was fair enough. However, there was no way to determine who contributed how much to each paper, beyond drafting the actual text, and I thought that I was contributing more elbow-grease than anyone else. I began to suspect that I might work more efficiently if I did not have to persuade four of five collaborators to accept whatever ideas I would propose—that having to accommodate to the work methods of others may interfere with one's creativity. Of course, reaching consensus made it necessary to refine the statement of one's thoughts, so that the end product was very likely to be truly persuasive, and the process, conducted in a collegial atmosphere, also had its pleasures. However, it gradually dawned on me that some members of the group did not share my estimate of how much I was contributing, and I had a desire to demonstrate that I was underappreciated. When the paper Julian had drafted was accepted for publication, I decided to decline participation in another project. I doubted that my colleagues would do laborious research without me, and this prediction proved to be right.

I suppose I no longer had the time to listen to others if I wanted to think through my own scholarly agenda concerning the intellectual history of psychoanalysis. I was already working on the Ferenczi project for *Psyche*, and I was preoccupied with the question of how much Freud's self-analysis had contributed to the sequential articulation of his scientific ideas. I read whatever was then available in the public domain relevant to the Freud topic, but I was too busy to do further work on it. In 1967 I finally sensed that I was ready to write an essay on the subject, although I did not know what it would contain, except for the opening sentence; but then the next sentence came, and then the next. In thirty-six very stimulating hours, the essay was finished. It was a new beginning in my scientific life, and I found a fresh venue for it: I sent it to Harry Slochower, editor of *American Imago*, and he accepted it for publication. We established a very gratifying long-distance relationship—I never met Slochower in person. It was extremely encouraging for me that, on the basis of his high valuation of my previous work for *Imago*, Slochower asked me to take part in a succession of projects for his journal, and eventually put me on its editorial board. Until the mid-1970s, while he was in charge, I directed most of my interdisciplinary efforts to *Imago* (see 1968a, 1970b, 1978c, and 1981d).

I cannot easily explain why the way of producing the Freud essay gave me more pleasure than anything professional I had ever done before; I can only compare it to the experience of making love for the first time. The boost in self-esteem was even greater, for almost everyone can find a sexual partner, but I did not think that it has been common to write psychoanalytic papers essentially without conscious thinking. It was this intoxicating experience that turned me into a writer—the satisfaction I found in it has made the process of composition into the central activity of my vocational life. As I have mentioned, for more than three decades, I have produced well over 100 pages of printed material every year, mostly in this automatized manner. (It is not much, compared with Anthony Trollope's fifty-seven books, written in much the same way, mostly before he reported for his job in the post office every morning.) What this method has required of me has been to wait until I was certain that I had thoroughly mastered the relevant materials before attempting to write about any topic.

Needless to say, it took me some time to gain confidence in my ability steadily to produce publishable work through this reliance on unconscious processes. In the mid-1960s I still felt more secure in trying to succeed through sheer diligence and persistence—particularly useful in efforts such as those we made on the Committee on Indexing to which Kohut had appointed me. This enterprise reconfirmed the disadvantages of trying to work in a group of heterogeneous people. It was led in a very laissez-faire manner by its elderly chairman, Mark Kanzer, a respected figure in the New York analytic community. Kanzer never obliged anyone to carry out a specific piece of work but counted on our unfocused voluntary efforts. To that end, he encouraged members of the official committee to recruit assistants in their home cities. To make it easier to form a Chicago subgroup, I got George Pollock's agreement to organize an Institute research team on indexing—we even received a budget of five hundred dollars for expenses! Armed with this ready-made passport to Institute affiliation, I approached the most recent group of graduates who had prepared for the examination together: Arnold Goldberg, his intimate colleagues Michael Basch and Mark Berger, and my good friend George Klumpner.

Unlike the study group on scientific methodology, the indexing research group never did jell, partly because George was the only one among my recruits who found the work interesting. When Mark Kanzer was removed as chairman of the national committee in what to me looked like an underhanded political maneuver on the part of persons who coveted his position, I felt obliged to resign out of loyalty to this wonderful gentleman.

(Such are the rigid codes I was raised to live by. It was lucky for me that all this took place before Kanzer made a large donation to Yale University to support interdisciplinary efforts in psychoanalysis; if he had already done so at the time of the committee coup, I would have been obliged to avoid giving the appearance of currying favor with a potential source of grants. European codes of honor are often very inconvenient.) In the event, George Klumpner replaced me on the committee. (This succession could not have been more appropriate: George and Inger had agreed to be guardians of our children in case Mary and I both died prematurely.)

At any rate, it was George's idea to base psychoanalytic indexing on computerization; he eventually became chairman of the committee, and this activity has been the center of his psychoanalytic career. He kept me abreast of his highly successful leadership in this domain, and I helped him with one of his early publications about these matters (1976c). My role was more catalytic than collaborative—I merely handed the ball off to George at the right time; he then ran for a touchdown without further assistance.

In contrast to these frustrating experiences in trying to work in groups, I had a series of commissioned scholarly assignments that should have convinced me that I am better suited for working alone. (I have been slow to accept this verdict, probably because to do so condemns one to work in perpetual solitude.) After the happy outcome of the Ferenczi project, I was approached by the book review editor of *The Psychoanalytic Quarterly* to write a similar synoptic article on the work of David Rapaport. It seems that whoever had been supposed to review his *Collected Papers* (Gill 1967) for the *Quarterly* defaulted on the assignment. To make up for the omission, the editors felt that an article assessing the entirety of Rapaport's role in psychoanalysis would be appropriate. I was particularly pleased by this opportunity because I was familiar with only a part of Rapaport's work and what I did know about it made me think that, if I was ever to tackle theoretical issues successfully, mastering the rest was essential. Reading everything Rapaport published in the field was a laborious task, like that of covering Ferenczi's writings, although it was uncomplicated by any language barriers. (With the passage of two decades, my college German had become less than serviceable even for reading Ferenczi.) Jacob Arlow, then editor of the *Quarterly*, asked for some minor revisions but was otherwise quite pleased with the essay I submitted (1973c).[1] I have remained one of the reviewers in the stable of the *Quarterly* ever since, through the tenure of my medical school classmate Shelley Orgel as book review editor, as well as that of his successor, Martin Silverman.[2]

Shortly before I accepted the Rapaport assignment, Kohut brokered a second commission for me from *Psyche*. The journal was planning the publication of a recently discovered batch of the adolescent Sigmund Freud's letters to his friend Emil Fluss; the editors were interested in a commentary to be published in conjunction with the correspondence (Freud 1970). I thought that the nuances of language would be crucial for proper understanding of the letters, and I feared that, even armed with the best dictionaries, I could not do justice to this task. This was probably a rationalization, to cover over my reluctance to work alone. Through Heinz, I ascertained that *Psyche* would have no objection if I enlisted as a collaborator a colleague for whom German was the mother tongue. I had in mind Ernest Wolf, then a recent graduate of the Institute and somewhat at loose ends.

Ernest came to Chicago after a psychiatric residency in Cincinnati, where he had become acquainted with one of my old friends from college and medical school days; the latter urged him to contact me as someone who might help him to become acclimated to Chicago. We maintained a casual relationship for some time; then in 1960 Ernest and his wife decided to follow our example to buy one of a row of superb I. M. Pei townhouses in an urban renewal project in Hyde Park.[3] For the next four years, we lived two doors apart in identical dwellings and became much closer. Ernest started at the Institute considerably later than I, although he is several years my senior, and I had the impression that he was rather frustrated because nobody seemed to appreciate his potential. I too cannot claim that I had any idea, when I asked him to assist me with the Freud letters, about his abilities or the kind of career he would carve for himself. He did not behave in a manner that was overtly ambitious, although his young wife showed that she, by contrast, had great expectations.

I should have paid more attention to this phenomenon, for the seemingly smooth collaboration with Wolf was destined to come to an unhappy end. In a recently published interview (Hunter 1992), Ernest candidly describes just how ambitious and competitive he was at the time; to add to life's complications, he believed that I felt the same way.[4] I am afraid that, for an untroubled future, my actual attitude was even less favorable than he imagined. I felt irrationally sorry for Ernest and wanted to play Fairy Godmother to this imagined Cinderella. In my sixties, with colleagues fifteen to twenty years my junior, such a fantasy might be fulfilled; when I was barely forty, I should have known better, especially when dealing with someone older than myself. Ernest had an abortive attempt at analysis with

Max Gitelson on first coming to Chicago, and I believe that my ridiculous attempt to "help" him was in the nature of making restitution for having received the best that Max had to offer. (I had an older sibling who was stillborn. I rather think it was her loss for which I tried to compensate my mother through my subservience to her tyranny.)

Despite all this, the project on the Freud letters went very well. Ernest shared my commitment to promptness and diligence, and he turned out to have many original ideas. These were often too speculative for my taste, even visionary, in the tradition of German romanticism—not for nothing was Wolf raised in Germany—but he never seemed to push to include anything I could not endorse, and he was more than accommodating about my preferred notions. In other words, he behaved in the most sensible manner imaginable for a situation in which he knew himself to be on trial—not only with me but also with Kohut, inevitably the first reader of our manuscript. And he passed the test with flying colors.

In the next five years, we collaborated effectively on a number of historical and biographical papers (1970d, 1973b, 1975c, 1976b); we both took it for granted that these were primarily my projects, but Ernest's contributions were by no means confined to the exercise of his command of German. Nor did I openly object when he published a second version of one of our studies under his own name (Wolf 1971b), although I was utterly astonished and morally outraged about his failure to mention that I had collaborated on the research that led to his conclusions. By my standards, this failure to give credit to a close friend betrayed a flaw in Wolf's character, although there was no question of plagiarism on his part. I was rashly overconfident about my ability to tolerate such behavior in what should have been a nontherapeutic relationship; my lack of caution about the limits of my tolerance was to cost both Ernest and me dearly when our relationship later faced a greater challenge.

Of course, one reason for my inattention to such a danger signal was that these projects were relatively brief and could not compete for my interest with my decision to attempt to write a book on psychoanalytic theory. As I have already mentioned, I reached the conclusion that my concept of viewing all psychopathology primarily from a developmental viewpoint had to be expounded in a monograph because most people had difficulty in following the excessively condensed paper I had presented on this topic at the Chicago society. Although Kohut had absented himself from that presentation, he later agreed to read my manuscript, and he certainly did not miss its point. I found it both disturbing and illuminating that Heinz had no objection to my thesis but insisted that it would not be widely accepted unless I provided a credible metapsychological framework for it. (He had recently published his Presidential Address to the American Psychoanalytic [Kohut 1966]; this was a metapsychological exercise that subtly changed Hartmann's version of drive theory.) Kohut's trenchant advice helped me to realize that I had a monumental task ahead of me, although I suspected at the same time that he was being subtly deprecating about my paper because he thought that all good ideas should belong to him.

Some time in 1967 I talked to Mel Sabshin about my need for free time to prepare a book; I made it clear that I would only stay on at the medical school if he agreed to allow me to devote most of the time he paid for to scholarly work, off campus. To give Mel his due for excellent judgment, I need not have played hardball with him; he readily agreed to my request. As long as he remained at Illinois, I continued to be paid simply for listing my affiliation with the department on all my publications, and he soon promoted me to the highest rank available to a part-time person, that of clinical professor. Of course, the salary I received was negligible, but the fact that I was being paid to do work at home was a powerful moral force spurring me on to be productive. I should probably give even more weight, however, to the fact that I was persona non grata at the Institute: as Heinz was ever repeating, the greatest incentive for creativity is lack of appreciation. (Kohut even made the dubious claim that only the cult of Wagner, who was then regarded as the greatest living composer of opera, could have mobilized Verdi to transcend himself in composing *Falstaff*. I took this to be a manifestation of Heinz's German chauvinism.)

With the passage of time, more and more colleagues—even people who knew me well—began to suspect that, if the powers-that-be at the Institute found me unacceptable, there had to be some good reason for that unfavorable judgment. In this regard, only Kohut saw the situation clearly; he said, without equivocation, that my unforgivable sin was that, without regard for the consequences, I insisted on speaking the truth. It was a quality for which he had great respect. (Unfortunately, when he later found that this shoe could pinch him, too, he seemed to forget that I was committed to such a course of action.)

Of course, I retained the affection and respect of a number of analyst-friends, but some, such as Mike Gunther and George Klumpner, had not as yet been appointed to the faculty, and others, such as George Moraitis, were still candidates or had barely graduated. In other words, these "outsiders" were likely to identify with me because we were in the same boat. It was much harder for those whom the Institute had favored to acknowledge that its leadership was capricious and unjust. I have known a number of colleagues, mostly in other cities, who were subjected to such exclusion for a professional lifetime; they generally reacted with irritability and self-righteousness and were often labeled "paranoid" as a consequence. I was determined to avoid such a label by confining my reaction to the production of the best published work on whatever topic I tackled.

I suppose it was because I still needed affirmation of my theoretical conclusions that I felt I should enlist a collaborator to write the monograph; until I had a dozen years of exclusively psychoanalytic work behind me (that is, before the mid-1970s), whatever I wrote by myself dealt only with historical topics or the problems of psychotherapy. I think my policy was entirely sensible; public success as a scientific author depends in large measure on having a past reputation for solid, valuable contributions. The name of the game is to tackle problems of real interest that one is able to handle better than well. At any rate, in the late 1960s I asked Arnold Goldberg whether he would join me in writing a book on the topic I had selected. Arnold showed no hesitation before he accepted the offer.

We both took for granted that I would produce first drafts of most chapters, and that Arnold would go over these critically and amplify them as he saw fit; we then met to discuss how to reconcile our versions and further to refine our manuscript. The first draft was prepared relatively quickly and in an unusually cooperative spirit. Arnold's contributions were not merely those of a "first reader"—as his subsequent career shows, he has a lively interest in epistemology, about which I was somewhat unsophisticated at the time. (I have always found it extremely unpalatable to read philosophy and can only force myself to do so when I absolutely have to. I think the total lack of human referents in most philosophical texts makes me too anxious to function at my best.) Thus, Arnold contributed almost all of the metatheoretical content of our book; without his expertise, a book of some kind might have been written, but it would have been very different from the actual *Models of the Mind*. However, producing this monograph showed me that writing a book is well within my organizing capacities and that I am as competent as most to deal with analytic theory.

When I was in London, I mentioned to Anna Freud that a colleague and I were writing a monograph on organizing psychoanalytic theory on the basis of "lines of development," a concept she had used throughout a then recent book (A. Freud 1965). She expressed polite interest in reading our manuscript; on my return home we sent it to her. In due time, she let us know that she rather liked our scholarly approach, but she betrayed the fact that she had not grasped our intentions when she concluded that the hierarchy of models of the mind we proposed did not cover as much ground as her father's (she always said "my father," when she referred to Freud) tripartite model of 1923. Our principal thesis was directly contrary to her opinion: we showed that none of Freud's models was sufficiently inclusive, so that all of them have had to continue in use, each in different contingencies; we proposed a supraordinate, hierarchical schema that could accommodate all previous models proposed within psychoanalysis. Undeterred by this confusion of tongues, I asked Anna Freud whether she had any advice for us about how to get our book published. I received no reply. "Miss Freud" was not in the business of promoting sedition.

We did not expect *Models of the Mind* to have a popular success, so it never occurred to us to submit it to a commercial publisher. I no longer recall how we got the impractical idea to send it, instead, to be considered for the monograph series of the *Journal of the American Psychoanalytic Association*. (It had issued four volumes, by Hartmann, Jacobson, Schur, and Arlow and Brenner, and has never again published another.) John Frosch was then editor. He had been one of my favorite teachers in medical school; I believe twenty years later he still vaguely remembered me, but his affability did not help us: he was unable to get a definite verdict from his editorial board. This process dragged on for about a year and a half before we realized that, circa 1970, it was unthinkable to allow Gedo and Goldberg to appear in the monograph series sponsored by the American—even if the readers could not think of good reasons to reject our submission.

Arnold, who tends to be more impatient as well as more practical than I, finally took the bull by the horns. On the one hand, he asked Estelle Shane of Los Angeles, the wife of his old friend Morton Shane, to give our manuscript an editorial reading. Estelle, who has since become a psychoanalyst, had a graduate degree in English and proved to be a superb reader. On the basis of her advice, I was able to rewrite the book in its definitive form. On the other hand, Arnold asked Roy Grinker for his assistance—Grinker clearly looked upon Goldberg as one of the most promising of his "boys," as he called us. It was through this channel that we were recommended to the University of Chicago Press, which agreed to publish the book.

At the stage of actual production, Arnold proved less helpful as a collaborator: he let me do all the dirty work, such a proofreading, writing for permissions to use quotations, and preparing an index. Of course, I could have asked him to do his share, but I did not have confidence in his commitment to mundane tasks of that sort, and, once again, I shied away from confronting an issue that could fester. Obviously, we should have arranged for the index to be prepared by a professional, but I was still on the Committee on Indexing at the time, and I felt the responsibility of providing the most useful index possible. (Actually, the first index I prepared was so complete that the publisher insisted that I had to cut it by half. After I finished the second version, I felt I had discharged my responsibility to psychoanalytic indexing in perpetuity.) Arnold apparently felt some guilt about not taking part in these labors, for he made me a princely present when the book finally appeared. It was a magnificent leather sofa, an extravagance that did not fit into the Goldbergs' new domicile. We took it—I am looking at it as I write this—and I feel that I earned it, for I believe his participation in writing *Models of the Mind* established Arnold's scholarly reputation. Of course, it also solidified my own. The English version has sold almost 10,000 copies, and the book has been translated into Italian, Spanish, and Japanese.

The success of *Models of the Mind* can probably be accounted for by the fact that, by postulating that the disparate models then extant in the psychoanalytic literature (the reflex arc, object relations, tripartite, and topographic models) are applicable to different modes of mental organization (each derived from one of a sequence of developmental phases), we managed to preserve concepts that had seemed to be mutually exclusive. When arranged into a developmental hierarchy, this sequence of functional modes is clearly more inclusive than any of the previous models had been; in other words, the theory of mind toward which our monograph was pointed would not suffer from the gross reductionism which then characterized each of the competing theoretical viewpoints within the field.

Our ecumenical effort promised conceptual order without putting threatening emphasis on the revolution in the theory of technique it entailed. We did, however, spell out that the model technique of interpretation is specifically applicable in the mode of functioning best characterized by the tripartite model; when more archaic modes take over the regulation of behavior, other therapeutic modalities are more appropriate—pacification, restoration of self-cohesion (we called this unification), and optimal disillusionment were the modalities we described. I suspect that many readers failed at first to grasp that a radically new clinical theory for psychoanalysis had been proposed—at any rate, *Models of the Mind* received uniformly favorable reviews.

I have often heard it said, "Publish a book together—lose a friend." In 1973 I think both Goldberg and I felt that we had escaped this iron law. I knew that I would never again need the kind of assistance that I wished for while working on my first book, so that I was not likely to look for a coauthor in the foreseeable future. All in all, our experience left me with the conviction that collaboration should be reserved for the rare situations in which one could not accomplish the task alone, but that I could accommodate myself to some collaborators well enough to make it a feasible method of working for me. And I have persevered with such enterprises throughout my career—I have even had the nerve to publish a little book in collaboration with my wife (1992a). Only my cardiac bypass surgery put an end to the last two study groups in which I participated, the one I formed with Mark Gehrie and another, comprising faculty from the Institute younger than Mark's cohort.

❖ CHAPTER 7 ❖

THIS FAIR SUMMER OF YORK

I had mixed feelings about the invitation a few years ago to give a plenary address at the meetings of the American Psychoanalytic Association; it came years later than I thought it should, but on the platform at the Waldorf in New York, facing a packed ballroom, it meant vindication and acceptance. On the national scene, I have had all the respect anyone could expect, and it was my refusal to accommodate myself to organizational customs that caused the delay in getting to present a plenary. (It also did not help that, when my name first came up for consideration in the program committee, one of its members from Chicago—a functionary of the Institute whom I barely know personally—ended the discussion by saying, "That is unthinkable!" He was undeterred by the presence of several friends of mine on the committee. I still have no idea why this person thought that what actually came to pass was not to be thought of; I can only imagine that this was one example of what has become more and more frequent as I get older—I attract transference reactions like a candle does moths.)

I had not been shy about letting the program committee know that I thought I had earned an invitation for a plenary; I have participated in the scientific activities of the association in whatever capacity was proposed to me, including panel presentations, meet-the-author sessions, interdisciplinary colloquia, discussions of papers—I even introduced a plenary speaker, Robert Gardner. Finally, a recent program chairman, Chuck Rothstein, told me with a wry grin that I did not seem to understand how these things are done. "I have only one vote," he complained. But nobody gave me the magic password, and I was too proud to inquire.

Then, sometime in 1993, Leo Sadow sent me a copy of an elaborate letter he had written the program committee, spelling out in detail why my original scholarly work justified selection for a plenary. When I called to thank him, he said that Bob Gardner had put him up to this, that Bob was organizing a cabal on my behalf, and that the president-elect, Judy Schachter, was in on the plot. (Judy was at the New York University medical school in my time; we renewed our acquaintance when I led a site visit of the Pittsburgh Institute more than a dozen years ago, when we discovered that we saw eye to eye in organizational matters.) If you have the right key, it is not difficult to open the door—even sesame—without using magic.

Sitting on the platform at the Waldorf, waiting to be introduced, was an extraordinary experience of time warp. I could see Mary in the front row, flanked by our son Paul and his wife Ginta. Next to me sat John MacLeod of Cincinnati, whom I had asked to introduce me—Bob Gardner advised me against having a closer friend to do this, and he was absolutely right; I needed the endorsement of a widely respected figure who was not there because of personal sentiments. Yet John had been one of the fellow-candidates with whom I frequently had Friday lunch during our years at the Institute. Behind us, in a line of psychiatric residents who were being honored by the association, stood the stepson of a Chicago colleague whom I had known since he was a little boy. And the association was also honoring Melford Spiro, an eminent anthropologist whose application for psychoanalytic training I had refereed when I served on the relevant national committee. It was extraordinarily pleasurable that Spiro stopped to say hello on his way to the lectern—we became personally acquainted when I arranged to invite him to be one of the participants in the fiftieth anniversary celebration of the Chicago Psychoanalytic Society. When the lecture was over, Shelley Orgel came up to say a few affectionate words, and so did a colleague whom I have known since our days as undergraduates at NYU in the mid-1940s. That afternoon, walking through a Miró exhibition at the Museum of Modern Art, we encountered Arnold Modell, whose theoretical work I consider to be among the most significant in contemporary psychoanalysis; he made a point of joining us to give my lecture his stamp of approval. (Not long after, I persuaded the program committee to have him invited to give a plenary.[1]) And a little later, in the Waldorf lobby, Bob Wallerstein, a former president of the International Psychoanalytic, did the same thing. He said the presentation had been "lovely." The association is an extended family, *malgré tout*.

By the same token, the Chicago Institute is a nuclear family, but for at least a generation it has been dysfunctional. If in the late 1960s it labeled me a dangerous predator, like Kipling's Shere Khan, in the sunny period that followed it made me into something of a magical figure—a prodigal son for whom they would slay more than one fatted calf. My reputation on the national scene has depended on professional considerations; locally, it has been the subject of pure emotion. Around 1970, the winter of my Chicago discontent came to an abrupt end when Joan Fleming decided to move to Denver. It was like the happy ending of Hansel and Gretel—once the wicked witch was no more, I could look forward to psychoanalytic happiness ever after. I cannot say that it was a more astonishing change than the one I experienced in leaving Tangier, which, since the fall of France, had been under occupation by the Franco regime, to go to New York—but it came close to that. Suddenly, most of the Institute community thought well of me. No longer an out, I was very much in.

Inevitably, every summertime of high favor is to be succeeded by subsequent winters. But I was like the grasshopper of the Aesop fable, unmindful of changing seasons. The fattest calf the Institute immediately offered me was to be evaluated for training analyst status. At the time, there was a ritual to mark such an occasion: the person under consideration was invited to have a business dinner with the director, ostensibly to discuss whether an evaluation procedure would be of mutual interest. This custom constituted a travesty, of course: although in Chicago being a training analyst does not amount to much because they are as plentiful as blackberries, *not* being a training analyst is absolutely ruinous (if every Tom, Dick, or Harry is in, you must be pretty scummy to be out!). I cannot imagine that anyone has ever declined to be processed.

In 1970 the director was still Gerhart Piers, and our ritual meal at first appeared to be the stuff of high comedy. Piers pretended that he had had no role in allowing unnamed opponents to block my appointment. He wondered out loud whether my ethnic background had anything to do with the prejudices that had prevailed against me. Next he wanted to hear what kind of clinical work I was doing. I replied that I believed he was familiar with the quality of my psychoanalytic work, because one of my former patients was in a training analysis with him. (This was the person Pollock had referred to me ten years earlier, when the man was threatened with being dropped by his medical school. During my work with him, he successfully graduated and got the best psychiatric residency then available in this area. He then had to satisfy his military obligations; he was provisionally accepted by the Institute on his return to Chicago.) Piers then said that he had actually learned more about my work from a patient of his who was having an affair with the man he had referred to me. I became completely befuddled. I knew of no patient of mine who had had an affair with any patient of his. After a while I realized that he was talking about the functionary who had been in a position to make grants to the Institute. Obviously, after my unfavorable reception of the fraudulent scheme concerning fees as "Institute tuition," the poor fellow had been afraid to reveal this additional intrigue to me.

I tried to steer this uncomfortable conversation back to the other patient—at which point apparent comedy turned into overt pathos. Piers burst out with a stream of hatred for his analysand. I was too shocked to register his exact words, but the gist of the indiscretion was that he did not want to talk about such a low person. Fortunately, by that time the dinner had ended and we had reached his car. For a long time, I could not figure out the significance of this loss of control, but it became clear in due course that it was an early symptom of cerebral damage from the arteriosclerosis that was to end Gerhart's life.

The next step in the evaluation procedure was to have a series of six to ten monthly meetings with a senior training analyst, to present clinical material from the analysis of a patient with whom one had recently started work. I was asked to arrange such consultation with a widely admired and popular faculty member, one of the luminaries of the Alexander era. I had always liked this person, but, on the basis of his performance as a seminar leader when I was a candidate, I had my reservations about his high clinical reputation. At any rate, I was quite confident that I would have no difficulty in proving my competence to such a man: on the one hand, I thought he was fair and benign, and on the other, I knew that his expectations were modest. Consequently, I made no preparations for our initial meeting, and I told him about my most recent case in a spontaneous manner.

I could see, as I talked on for forty-five minutes, that the consultant was overly impressed by this performance. (It was routine in certain groups I frequented, but obviously not in his experience.) From my perspective at the time, because I had had a decade to practice analysis, I had to be able to talk about any current treatment in that manner—anything less would have driven me from the field in sheer humiliation. I learned gradually to keep such eccentric opinions to myself, but I still believe that psychoanalysis would have a higher reputation today if, at most, the better half of those who finish institute training had become fully qualified. (Levels of analytic competence are more than clear to members of every peer group.)

Although I had noticed the consultant's overreaction to our first session, I was not prepared for its extent. I discovered its magnitude when I returned a month later, only to find the lovely wife of a respected colleague in his waiting area. The dismay on his face when he emerged from his consulting room betrayed the fact that he had double-scheduled our appointments. I hastened to assure them both that I would be glad to come some other time, and we made the necessary arrangements.

Unfortunately, when I returned, the humiliated consultant was again unavailable; once more, he had mismanaged his appointment calendar. When he finally managed to meet with me again, his embarrassment was relieved because I told him, with genuine conviction, that I was completely at ease about what had transpired. I felt certain that it meant that he had already made the decision that I was well qualified, and there was no good reason to have further meetings. As if to confirm my off-the-cuff conjecture, at the end of this session he carefully entered our next appointment on his calendar for the wrong day. I was nasty enough to bring this error to his attention.

It certainly gave me pause that one of the most experienced and best regarded members of the faculty was intimidated enough by what I regarded as routine performance to have a need to avoid our meetings. If the standards of the Institute were as low as this phobic reaction suggested, the future of Chicago psychoanalysis was dark indeed. And how would those colleagues feel about me who did not even meet this consultant's minimum standards? (A few years later he told me that, in his view, about a third of the Institute's alumni had been granted a "compassionate pass." That led me to imagine that I would have flunked two-thirds of my colleagues! I am afraid it is really so!) When, in the spring of 1946, I was in basic training at Camp Polk, Louisiana, and I was the only college-educated person in my platoon, some hillbillies and rednecks had ganged up on me in a manner threatening enough to lead the master sergeant to move me to different quarters. If one cannot avoid being seen as a threat, perhaps the only defense is to overawe the lynch mob.

In due time we completed the initiation rites, and my appointment as training and supervising analyst was confirmed—according to Heinz Kohut, by a vote of three to two. It seems that criteria other than clinical competence weighed heavily with some members of this committee. (Could they have been prejudiced against natives of Nógrád County?) I had known that many on the faculty were so loyal to Joan Fleming that they would never forgive me for my poor opinion of her, but I was still surprised by the extent and passion of the opposition to me, even on the part of people with whom I had never had any personal dealings. I was puzzled by the source of this rancor, but I did not then worry about it, because it was driven underground by the positive attitude of the powers that be, especially after George Pollock became director.

Incidentally, some years later I attended a professional meeting in Aspen, and by sheer coincidence a Chicago colleague formerly in Fleming's entourage was vacationing there and invited us one evening when Fleming came over from Denver to see him. (This affability was once typical of the Chicago analytic community—whatever people felt, they smiled and smiled.) At any rate, Joan was by then old, frail, and nostalgic—she was obviously glad to see me. There are inconsistencies in people that continue to amaze me, however well psychoanalytic theories can explain them.

Of course, Fleming had always had her pathetic side. Before she had ever become the supervisor of my last case for the Institute, when I was writing my very first paper on psychotherapy, I asked her among others whether she might be willing to read an early draft—for the sake of old times at Michael Reese, so to speak. She was very gracious about this and one Sunday morning invited me to her apartment to give me her reactions. She lived in a new building in the most elegant area of the city, and I was therefore astonished by the lack of coherence of her furnishings. She offered me some coffee, and she did not possess matching cups and saucers to serve it in. As usual, I found her comments confusing, but in the published version of the paper I made fulsome acknowledgment for her assistance. Years later, she poignantly reproached me for not sending her a reprint—she experienced this as a hurtful rejection. Of course, my decision not to continue any personal contact with her was an expression of distaste, but it was dictated by a refusal to enter into a pretense of affection for her. From my viewpoint, it was a matter of being ethical. But Fleming wanted to be loved as a St. Joan of the Stockyards (to quote Berthold Brecht): a sad, lonely person.

The second plum to come my way shortly after Fleming's resignation was appointment to a committee to carry out the decision to establish a scientific publication as a function of the Chicago Institute. I do not know whose idea it was, but when I joined this enterprise its moving spirit was

George Pollock, and I have no doubt that it was he who wanted me to be on his team. I had little to do with the administrative side of the operation, but once it was decided to publish yearly, as a hardcover book (hence *The Annual of Psychoanalysis*), I was very active in soliciting manuscripts from the authors I most respected, in evaluating submissions and making editorial suggestions, commissioning local colleagues to carry out specific projects, and so on. Obviously, there is a lengthy time lag between initial planning and the appearance of the first volume of such a series; in our case, volume one was dated 1973.

I had been so active and enthusiastic about this project that George asked me to be volume editor for the 1974 *Annual*, and I did a lot of work on the 1975 volume as well. From the start, Ernest Wolf was also on the editorial board—certainly the first fruit of his previous collaboration with me. Deservedly, he was volume editor for 1975. Because the *Annual* did not become a commercial success, it gradually became more difficult to get contributions from prominent authors, who always want wide circulation for their work. We took justifiable pride, however, in the quality of the early volumes.[2] I was able to solicit a few of these submissions because I had become acquainted with the authors at professional meetings or committee work at the American Psychoanalytic.

In addition to internationally known luminaries, the *Annual* presented a number of Chicago authors, many of them in their publishing debuts. The late Mike Basch had important theoretical papers in each of the first three volumes. I recommended Mike Gunther as ideally suited to present some historical data about Freud's testimony at the famous Wagner-Jauregg trial—material put at our disposal by ex-Chicagoan Martin Grotjahn, who was not well enough at the time to complete the project. The first papers by followers of Kohut, those he teasingly called his "epigoni," such as Anna and Paul Ornstein, David Terman, and both Marian and Paul Tolpin, were included in these volumes. From the popular novelist Irving Stone, Pollock obtained some archival material about Freud's early medical activities at the Vienna General Hospital; these data were written up by Ernest Wolf.

I also had the opportunity to prepare a historical essay for the 1973 volume. Some years earlier, Kohut had put me in touch with K. R. Eissler, then head of the Freud Archives. Eissler wished to raise money to make it possible for a Romanian academic named Stanescu (who was in possession of a cache of letters from Freud to another adolescent companion, Eduard Silberstein[3]) to make a trip to Vienna. He was planning to come for the 1971 meetings of the International Psycho-Analytic Association in the

Austrian capital. I raised part of the necessary funds within the Chicago psychoanalytic community; in recognition of this small service, I was offered a chance to meet Stanescu in Vienna. Through correspondence, we made arrangements for a rendezvous at the Hofburg—it felt like I was taking part in a Balkan thriller. As I had suspected, Stanescu (who had permission to do "research" in Austria only because he was a professor of German literature) had smuggled the letters out of the country—they were, of course, considered to be Romanian national treasures, and their export was strictly illegal. He and I went for a walk in the Burggarten; he recounted his wish to emigrate as soon as his elderly mother died; in the meantime, he would leave the letters in Vienna—they would serve as his grub-stake in the West. He drew a manila envelope out of his battered briefcase and, higgledy-piggledy, took out of it a hundred thousand dollars' worth of Freud autographs. (I am talking in 1971 dollars!) He dropped a few on the grass, and we chased them down before they sailed off on the next puff of wind. After our chat, Stanescu gave me typescripts of a limited selection of the letters. I was relieved that the Securitate was not watching.[4]

When I studied the transcripts at home, they revealed that Freud and his friend had played a game in which they were supposedly a pair of Spanish-speaking dogs, Cipión and Berganza, members of an "Academia Castellana." There was a brief reference to such activities in the Jones biography, but their significance remained puzzling. I became very intrigued with the mystery and asked Mary, who was working on her dissertation at the time, to look up Cipión et al. in the Northwestern library. Wise in the ways of scholarly research, she stood on a chair and called out for someone working on Spanish literature. A courteous Castilian gentleman informed her that the dogs were characters from one of the tales in the *Novelas Ejemplares* of Cervantes. So I read these "jewels of truth," as one critic has called them, and they proved to be a key to the adolescent Freud's inner world. Of course, the Freud letters were mostly in German, so—once again—I asked Ernest Wolf to develop with me the paper I wanted to write about all this. This project (1973b) was as enjoyable as anything I have ever undertaken.[5]

For the 1975 *Annual*, Wolf and I provided a spinoff from what proved to be our last successful collaboration, destined for a book of Freudiana I was then editing. The primary aim of our study (1976b) was to identify Freud's predecessors in the introspective/humanist tradition that culminates with the sixteenth century essayist Michel de Montaigne. In pursuit of this research we read so much about Montaigne that we accumulated sufficient material for a psychobiographical paper on him. By this time, I had grown a bit uneasy concerning how Wolf might feel about the circumstance that he had invariably been the junior author of our joint papers, so I proposed that he draft the Montaigne study (1975c) and be listed as first author. My intuition about Ernest's resentment about playing second fiddle was on the mark (as he has recently confessed [Hunter 1994, pp. 174–175]), but my attempted remedy was unintelligent, for what mattered was not whose name was listed first. The problem was that whenever we worked together, I took the lead in determining the intellectual content of the product. I should not have prolonged such an asymmetrical working relationship; but instead of making different arrangements, I felt "generous" while I continued to "give" Wolf opportunities to show his worth—and even to borrow some of the credit I was earning. On my part, it was a self-indulgence and a grave error. It has been justly said, "Do someone a favor, and he will never forgive you."

The leading part I took in producing the first three volumes of the *Annual* was the happiest experience I had in the course of my affiliation with the Institute. The other compensation I received for my years as a local pariah was a new teaching assignment, and this did not turn out to be so fortunate. I was asked to join the late Charles Kligerman in leading a continuous case seminar for third-year candidates. Charlie, who was more than ten years my senior, seemed like an affable person, but he had taught the course for some time and could not accept me as an equal participant. I knew that he and Heinz had been friends since their days on the University of Chicago faculty in the 1940s, and I assumed that he agreed to have me assist him with the seminar because Heinz had pushed for this arrangement. At any rate, Kligerman was clearly unprepared for the active role I took in class. He got very angry when I disagreed with him (which occurred frequently), and he opposed my mentioning any of Kohut's then recent notions about narcissistic problems—with great heat. (In retrospect, this seems quite amusing, because after Heinz died, Charlie became a fervent supporter of self psychology.[6])

Charlie and I uneasily coexisted for a couple of years—he could hardly get rid of me simply because I was skeptical when he reached conclusions about clinical material that I considered to be arbitrary, and I felt stuck, especially once my evaluation for training analyst status started, because I knew he was on the committee that would vote on the matter. (In the event, he cast the deciding vote in my favor.) Before the tension escalated, Charlie asked me to be reporter on a panel on the methodology of analytic biography he was to chair at the American Psychoanalytic meetings; he told me that I was to present a paper, like all the other panelists. (Incidentally, these included Martin Bergmann, perhaps the most highly regarded lay analyst in New York, with whom I subsequently became close,[7] as well as the late Bernard Meyer, whose wonderful biography of Joseph Conrad [1967] I much admired and with whom I also kept in touch.) Needless to say, I accepted.

Some weeks before the panel was to take place, Charlie informed me about its agenda, which did not include a presentation by me. Fortunately, I realized that he had truly repressed his original offer, and I made no protest about this broken promise—the vote on my appointment was very near. It was Heinz who informed me that Charlie was one of the three who had voted for me. Thus, it was worth my while to swallow my indignation about what I interpreted as Kligerman's retaliation for my insubordination in the seminar. And the year after that, the wheel of fortune turned once more, and I was summoned to do a different teaching assignment.

At the same time, the dean called me to refer for training analysis the first candidate to whom the Institute gave my name. There followed another comical ritual: it was then a policy of the Institute to supervise the work of newly appointed training analysts through monthly consultations with one of their elders and betters. In my situation, this was particularly bizarre because for more than a year I had already been conducting a training analysis: in a fit of acting out, one of my patients (a young psychiatrist who started treatment with me during his residency) applied to the Institute, expecting to have to transfer to a training analyst if he were accepted. As it happened, his acceptance coincided with Fleming's departure, and the admissions committee recommended that he continue with me. Flexibility above all! To my relief, Fred Robbins (who had so generously taken over as supervisor in my Rip Slamming crisis) once again volunteered to serve as my consultant, and he treated the whole business with appropriate irony.

The fact that I was once again favored at court was reconfirmed when, shortly after these events, the dean made a second referral to me—that of a troubled candidate on leave of absence. In an institute with such a large surplus of training analysts as Chicago in the good old days, unofficial distinctions inevitably develop among them. There are those who have the title in name only, because the Institute never refers any candidates to them. There are others who might get one or two referrals in a lifetime, crumbs from the table of patronage, so to speak. Then there are the insiders who get the largest number of referrals and almost all the candidates who look like they might have an uncomplicated analytic course. (Needless to say, this group used to include the current director, the dean, and their kitchen cabinet.) I was soon to learn that I did not belong to any of the foregoing categories: I got more than my fair share of referrals, but these were invariably people with obviously difficult and potentially troublesome problems.[8]

The first candidate I was sent had started with someone else, had to interrupt treatment to go into military service, and on his return found that his analyst was mortally ill. (Just the situation for my debut as a training analyst!) The second referral was that of a woman divorced from a fellow-candidate; this man's sister was an influential psychoanalyst who supported her brother's wild accusations that my analysand was an unfit mother. From the first, a bitter child custody battle occupied the center of the analytic stage. Next, they sent me a young woman who had been totally unable to talk about her personal history during the admission interviews. After that, a Jesuit priest, seriously committed to his religion. And so on. I chose to look upon this pattern as a compliment to my clinical acumen, but I was also cognizant of the possibility that such idealization would be followed by disillusionment.

Yet one is tempted to gather one's rosebuds whenever summer comes, for it is always the shortest of seasons. A generation later, I can see that these were minor matters, for my organizational activities constituted a mere sideshow, more likely to distract me from my creative work if they went smoothly than during periods of friction that made me turn away from the Institute. I also realize now that it was absurd to expect my Chicago contemporaries to welcome my scientific contributions or to evaluate them on their merits; the majority of these colleagues literally could not even bear to read my works.

❖ CHAPTER 8 ❖

COSA NOSTRA

I recently sent my photograph to the Houston Psychoanalytic Institute, to be included in a rogues' gallery of the visiting lecturers they have invited over the years. The association with the Houston group has been one of the most fruitful collaborations of my professional life. I was last there in September 1993, for a lecture at the Baylor Medical School to honor the retirement of David Freedman. For the past generation, David has been one of the outstanding researchers at the frontiers of psychoanalysis and biological science.[1] I felt greatly honored by the fact that David wanted me in this capacity, all the more so because we had never had a social relationship. My personal contact in Houston has been Bob Gilliland, also on the faculty at Baylor and longtime director of the Psychoanalytic Institute. Bob had arranged most of my previous invitations to Houston—to Baylor, to the Institute, even for an interdisciplinary symposium at Rice University. Happily, in the process I established friendly relations with a number of people in the local analytic community.

As one might expect in Texas, there was an enormous, festive party to mark David's retirement, where I had a chance to chat with all my friends. Bob Gilliland is now in his late seventies, and gravely handicapped by the ultimate sequelae of a severe case of childhood poliomyelitis. He is as sharp as ever, and it is simply awful to witness such a man being betrayed by his failing muscles. Bob is one of the few colleagues I have met who has had significantly more clinical experience than I in doing psychoanalysis proper.

He is witty and modest, the salt of the earth, universally respected and cherished. A couple of years before the farewell for David, because Bob was already unable to travel, the CAPS group in which he and I first met held a reunion in Houston. (I feel embarrassed to admit that the acronym stands for Center for Advanced Psychoanalytic Study, a pretentious echo of the name of the celebrated scholarly institution in Princeton, New Jersey.) Although I had stopped attending the group's semiannual weekend meetings, I did go to the reunion to show my esteem for Bob. That turned out to be a happy occasion; our encounter two years later was more mournful than I can express.

It was in large part to avoid such occasions for mourning that I withdrew from CAPS. At the last meeting I attended, one of our charter members, Francis McLaughlin of Baltimore, announced that it would be *his* last, and a few weeks later he was dead. Previously, I had not had strong feelings for Francis, but his farewell to us was profoundly affecting, and I did not want to go through a series of such partings. When the group was organized, in the mid-1960s, I was its youngest member, just under 40. By the time I decided to withdraw, most original participants were past 70; today, many of the survivors are close to 80.

CAPS is a psychoanalytic organization, headquartered in Princeton, that assembles and administers ongoing study groups. CAPS is in Princeton for the excellent reason that, when the organization was founded, both the person who ran it, Sam Guttman, and the one who provided much of its initial financing, Muriel Gardiner, resided in the countryside around this pretty town. CAPS began in the early 1960s, apparently on the initiative of a small directorate that included Max Gitelson. For the first several years, one group of about fifteen participants was organized annually; each group consisted of promising analysts from all over the country, selected in a reasonably representative way in terms of numbers from each area. In practice, this meant that from Chicago someone was invited for every group; each group had several people from the New York area; smaller analytic communities were not necessarily represented in any particular group but would eventually be assigned a slot on a proportional basis.

I heard about this organization soon after its birth; I thought I might receive an invitation before long, because the first Chicagoans to take part were Gitelson and Kohut. Heinz's contemporaries, Sam Lipton and Charles Kligerman, were next to be invited—a sign of the organization's preference for people thought to be committed to a mainstream point of view. My expectations were fulfilled when I was invited to join group five. By that time Max had died, and I know that I owed the offer to Heinz's support; it could not have hurt, however, to have been one of Max's analysands.

I was elated about my selection, if somewhat mystified by the explanatory materials I received. We were supposed to get to the Nassau Inn, across the street from the Princeton campus, in time for a Friday afternoon session and to leave at lunchtime on Sunday. At our first meeting, the formal discussions were to be led by the celebrated Philadelphia analyst Robert Waelder.[2] Between sessions and at meals we were promised opportunities for relaxed private exchange. It sounded like great fun, but the point of the entire exercise remained obscure. It proved to be a not inexpensive hobby, although for some years CAPS covered part of our expenses, and I got an additional rebate because one of the first decisions of group five was to pool travel costs. (This impelled us to ride to and fro between Princeton and New York in the cars of local participants, thereby prolonging the camaraderie that soon developed in the group.)

I could leave Chicago at dawn on Friday, meet my driver in Manhattan by noon, and catch a plane back from Newark airport in time to be home for supper on Sunday. It made for exhilarating weekends of continuous talk. Participants from the West Coast found it utterly exhausting; after their initial enthusiasm, they tended to miss meetings and eventually to drop out. Nor was our particular group to everyone's taste, so that over the years there was some turnover in our membership—we even suffered some losses through the unexpected deaths of a couple of youthful participants.

In group five, the potential administrative vacuum was quickly filled by Ken Calder, a man of military bearing who had been chief resident in psychiatry at Bellevue Hospital when I took clerkships there in medical school. I did Ken an injustice in thinking of him on first impression as the very model of a modern major general, for he is the soul of kindness and generosity. He arranged for those of us arriving at La Guardia Airport on Friday morning to have lunch at his beautiful home on East 78th Street: Abby Calder (who in her late seventies is still an active professor of medicine at Columbia University) always prepared a fine meal for us; on each occasion she took the trouble to provide me with Hungarian strudel from Mrs. Herbst's Yorkville bakery.

Ken was not the only person in the group I had met in a previous incarnation; another member was Roy Whitman, now at Cincinnati, whom I had known during my year at the University of Chicago; a third was Alex Kaplan, who had served as my cicerone when I was being recruited to move to St. Louis. Both were graduates of the Chicago Institute, and we had many professional attachments in common. Fortunately, there were no disruptive elements in the group, and the collegial atmosphere quickly embraced everyone, even though the several participants from the New York Institute belonged to mutually hostile local factions. The only moments of serious tension were produced when, several years after the group jelled, an attempt was made to add the Cuban exile Humberto Nagera as a member. Humberto behaved as if his past experiences at the Hampstead Clinic and his closeness to Anna Freud made it both possible and necessary that he instruct the rest of us about Psychoanalytic Truth. Some of us were not reticent about showing our outrage, and Nagera chose not to return. By contrast, several latecomers joined the group without difficulty, notably Shelley Orgel, my classmate and a close friend in medical school. We had kept in touch over the years; whenever an opening in group five became available, I voted for inviting him and, when he became better known (largely through his work as book review editor of the *Psychoanalytic Quarterly*), in time a majority agreed with my recommendation.

Group five eventually became politically influential in the American Psychoanalytic Association; five members were elected president (Ken Calder, Francis McLaughlin, Ed Joseph, Becky Solomon, and Alex Kaplan), and Shelley became chairman of the Board of Professional Standards. Naturally, there was always a tendency to discuss the administrative problems of organized psychoanalysis, especially because several other members had leading administrative roles in their home institutes. Such derailments into side issues were almost always discouraged by those with a preference for dealing with clinical matters, among them, Bob Gilliland, myself, and Robert Gardner from Boston, whose clinical acumen is, in my experience, unmatched in contemporary psychoanalysis.

Very soon after the group was organized, I realized that I could get more out of private discussions with Bob Gardner than from the necessarily diffuse official sessions. We became more receptive to each other's ideas, as we gained confidence in each other's clinical judgment, than were the others to either his or mine. (Over the years, however, when Bob and I supported each other in the group, our voices gained more and more influence.) Privately, we consulted each other about the most difficult therapeutic problems, secure in the knowledge that neither would misattribute these dilemmas to mere personal deficiencies. As a result, we helped each other to perceive the shortcomings of existing theories of analytic technique.

It so happened that I greatly liked Bob as a person, and when she met him, so did Mary—her judgments about people are often exacting, but she always responds positively to persons of quality. Bob is urbane and witty, subtly ironic, and strikingly original. He is a great teacher and a legendary supervisor—at one time, he did close to thirty hours of supervision per week. Whether I talked to him about clinical problems, art, family life, or psychoanalytic politics, I always learned something unexpected. Apparently he also found what I had to say to be of interest, for we fell into the habit of spending many hours together, often walking around the Princeton campus or the university art museum. We have been very good friends for three decades—and not only at CAPS meetings. Bob's letters are works of art, which I have treasured and preserved, and his professional writings are as beautifully written as they are profound (see Gardner 1983, 1994, 1995).

In retrospect, I am puzzled about how I managed it, but I did avoid getting any political advantage out of being friendly with so many leaders of the American Psychoanalytic Association. But as a result of CAPS contacts, I was invited to participate in a great many scientific activities—in Houston through Gilliland, in Boston through Gardner, in Los Angeles through Joe Natterson of the Southern California Institute, in New Haven through Jay Katz (who also happens to teach at the Yale Law School). I also got an occasional analytic referral on the recommendation of colleagues in my group.

Although membership in CAPS was not the only reason for this, gradually more and more of my practice reached me through out-of-town referrals. I found such a state of affairs to be very advantageous, because I did not have to concern myself about damaging my ability to earn a living if I did not behave in ways pleasing to someone in Chicago. This lack of constraint emboldened me further to go my own way with regard to a psychoanalytic viewpoint—even to publish clinical reports more candid than most. I have written several papers about my analytic results, including detailed accounts of their limitations and outright failures (1979b, 1984a [chap. 2], 1991a [chap. 1]).

Regrettably, such candor has always been quite rare. When Janet Malcolm published her impressions of psychoanalysis in *The New Yorker*, I wrote her a fan letter; she graciously replied that she particularly appreciated my praise because, while she was preparing her articles, two analysts sent her my mid-career report on the results of my work. Ken Calder later confessed that he was one of the culprits. He also tried to interest his colleagues at the New York Institute in discussing some of my ideas, but he found no takers: the official line at the time was that nobody in Chicago practiced psychoanalysis.[3]

As I said, despite these marks of favor, none of my powerful friends in CAPS ever offered me a political plum. I do not know whether I would have accepted any such offer—positions of responsibility in psychoanalytic organizations are very time-consuming and, because they tend to involve some travel, entail considerable loss of income—but it would have been gratifying to be asked. Perhaps I gave the misleading impression that I was getting more than my legitimate share of gratification from writing and lecturing. I suspect, however, that the real reason for overlooking me was that I did not inspire confidence as a potential political figure in analytic organizations because I openly opposed the expansionist and monopolistic policies of the American Psychoanalytic Association. I have always believed that we had to improve our quality, rather than increase our numbers and that, in order to manage that, it would be necessary to recruit talented people from nonmedical disciplines.[4]

The only time I initiated a discussion of organizational matters at CAPS was during the difficult negotiations between the leadership of the American and the group of psychologists who were suing both the American and the International Psychoanalytic Association about the medical requirement for regular admission for training. (I had discussed the suit with a justice of the federal appellate court who long sat in the seat next to me at the Chicago Symphony. He made it clear to me that, if matters stood as I outlined them to him, the plaintiffs had an excellent case. I also had well-informed contacts among the psychologists and, on the basis of what I learned from that quarter, took their determination to fight maximally seriously.) I believe this discussion played a part in convincing some of the key figures in the American, notably Ed Joseph, then the president, to resume negotiating in a spirit of compromise. But one does not get much political credit for recommending the dissolution of an empire of any sort.

In the early years of the Princeton group, we often invited a senior colleague to lead our discussions—Waelder, who was present for our first meeting, came several times, and we also had weekends with Rudolph Loewenstein, Margaret Mahler, Hans Loewald, and (after he began to write about narcissism) Heinz Kohut—luminaries who have all since died. These contacts were most valuable in giving us a flavor of the psychoanalytic past, but they did not particularly raise the level of group discussions. Heinz alienated his audience by talking uninterruptedly through the entire weekend, unaware that those who were not infuriated had turned glassy-eyed. Mahler was imperious, arbitrary, vain, and unable to hear reasoned criticism of her ideas—after our encounter, I could not take her seriously as a theoretician. (Only her behavioral observations of the children at her nursery school have proved to have some value.) By contrast, Loewenstein was *menschlich*, humorous, self-confident, and very likable.

I felt closest to Loewald, who showed interest in me as a person and was willing to talk to me about his own past over a glass of scotch in the bar of the Nassau Inn. It is true that he and I had already formed such a relationship before this meeting in Princeton, when he chaired a panel at the American Psychoanalytic on which I was a presenter (see Meissner 1976). Although he was already quite ill, and his psychoanalytic views were extremely conservative, Waelder and I also got along very well. He was then writing a book on political psychology (Waelder 1967), and had apparently been bitterly attacked as a right-wing ideologue because of his skeptical views about revolutionary causes. He quickly grasped that I shared this pessimism about utopian programs—I think I have learned that much from my father's history. At any rate, shortly before he died, Waelder waved farewell to me as he was leaving Princeton, with the bittersweet exclamation, "So long, fellow-fascist." In the days of Herbert Marcuse, the New Left, and Reich's Greening of America, it was the ultimate accolade.

I often used the availability of these leaders of the previous generation to challenge the adequacy of the prevailing psychoanalytic theory of technique. At one of our early meetings, I proposed that we discuss what were the most valuable contributions to psychoanalysis since the death of Freud. In high good humor, Waelder replied, "Have there been any?" I was not prepared to answer that challenge off the cuff, but I decided to think through what should be said in response, and this was the germ of my first book, *Models of the Mind*. It was also the first indication I had that the psychoanalytic mainstream was not about to flow as quickly as I thought it was essential to do.

I got a further taste of the opposition I was bound to encounter if I challenged accepted technical assumptions on the occasion of our meeting with Loewenstein. I kicked off the weekend by asking what he thought about making an analytic intervention in the form of whistling a tune. He was scandalized and expressed strong disapproval. By the time this discussion took place, I knew that in this group one had to be ready to answer one's own questions, so I was prepared to persevere in espousing the usefulness of communicating with patients through nonverbal channels. I was not alone in providing clinical illustrations suggesting that words sometimes did not carry our intended meanings optimally. Loewenstein gracefully concluded the weekend with a suggested compromise: "Jewish jokes are kosher, but whistling is out!"[5]

With Mahler, we had two amazing experiences. She began the weekend by asking someone to present an analysis in which issues stemming from the separation-individuation phase (a prominent Mahlerian concept) had played an important role. I had concluded a treatment not many years before in which object loss around the age of 2 had been a crucial determinant of character formation, and I proceeded to give an account of it.[6] In my judgment, the clinical data did not bear out Mahler's developmental hypotheses; I do not know whether she realized this, because we never discussed the issues raised by the treatment. As I was finishing my account, Mahler asked whether after termination my divorced patient had remarried. She had not. Mahler wanted to know whether she was having affairs. I said that, in the very conservative circles in which this middle-aged mother of three adolescents moved, that is not how people behaved. (These were the good old days.) With great irritation, and without further comment about my patient, Mahler insisted that we should immediately go on to hear another case. For her, it counted for nothing that the analysis had helped the patient to overcome her chronic masochistic perversion, that she had resumed performing music in a community orchestra, and, for the first time ever, succeeded in supporting herself by catching on as a college instructor.

When Mahler's autobiographical confessions were published after her death (Stepansky 1988), it became clear that she had a very different value system with regard to sexuality than did my tradition-soaked analysand. It would seem that she conceived of psychoanalysis as an opportunity to inculcate those personal values in place of those of her analysands. I might add that, just a few months ago, my former patient (now aged 72) called me to check on a dubious recommendation by her physician. It was the first time I had heard from her in over twenty years. Among other good news, she reported that about a dozen years ago she remarried, happily. I thought she might enjoy hearing about Mahler's reaction to her life history, for she was well aware of the latter's reputation. She was greatly amused: "I have never slept with anyone other than my husbands," she proclaimed proudly. But this is more than an amusing anecdote, for Mahler's confusion of her own preferences with normative standards for human behavior has been all too common in psychoanalysis.

I was also amazed by the group discussion of Mahler's famous research project in the direct observation of toddlers, on the basis of which she had formulated her separation-individuation concept. Persistent questioning by several members of the group elicited the information that her entire sample (a handful of children altogether) had been obtained by advertising for volunteers in Greenwich Village and offering those willing to bring their child as often as the project required (and make themselves available as well) a free slot in an elite nursery school. When we asked what kind of people were likely to respond to such inducements, Mahler vehemently insisted that the Manhattan families interested in participating were representative of a normal population. To most of us who heard her account, her biased sampling called the relevance of her observations into question, so that her theoretical edifice sounded like a house of cards.

A few years after we began, when George Klein became a member, the overall tone of the group changed in the direction of more serious theoretical discussions. George was an academician, head of the Research Center for Mental Health at New York University and editor of the prestigious *Psychological Issues* monograph series. He was fully trained in psychoanalysis but did not have much clinical experience. In this, as well as in intellectual breadth, commitment to research, and logical rigor, he was the true heir of his original mentor, David Rapaport. George was to die prematurely but, in his lifetime, he was the leader of a cohesive group of Rapaport's students (roughly speaking, the *Psychological Issues* crowd). At CAPS, he was as interested in challenging accepted metapsychology as I was in questioning the theory of technique.

The most useful public discussion I participated in at Princeton was initiated by Klein: he insisted that the economic point of view of Freudian metapsychology was both redundant and misleading.[7] I attempted to defend existing theory by showing its explanatory value in a clinical event of the previous day: in response to my prospective absence on Friday, one of my analysands had reported on Thursday that she had a minor automobile accident that morning when, on her way to her session, she had started to drive too fast, without noticing that she was doing so. That I remember this detail of the discussion with clarity, almost thirty years after it took place, shows how significant an experience it was for me. Everyone present agreed that my analysand's haste could legitimately be seen as the result of increased stimulation—a quantitative or "economic" factor—but none of us was able to rebut George's objection that this formulation did not require that one postulate psychological energies, as Freud had done. Afterward it occurred to me that my patient's behavior could just as well be explained as the result of regression to a mode of psychological organization devoid of abstract thought. A revelation! Entirely new vistas in psychoanalytic theory were emerging.

At the next meeting of the group, I approached Klein to find out whether *Psychological Issues* would consider the theoretical monograph I hoped to write. George encouraged me to prepare an abstract of such a proposal; on the strength of what I then sent him, he promised to evaluate the book for publication in his series. When the first draft of *Models of the Mind* was done, late in 1968, I asked him whether he wanted to see it, and George said that he did. I am certain that we had miscommunicated, because instead of giving me the personal feedback I was looking for, he sent the manuscript to official readers who found it entirely unsatisfactory. (It was fairly raw, but these readers criticized it not for such remediable flaws—they were in radical disagreement with its methodology, which was entirely conceptual. They demanded empirical research.) George regretfully concluded that he would never be able to get the project approved by his editorial board. I felt he had mismanaged matters through inattention—there was something of the absentminded professor about him. But this contretemps did not impair our relationship, and I have continued to be grateful to George for opening my eyes to the need for radical theoretical revision in psychoanalysis.

On paper, transactions of this kind were precisely what CAPS was designed to promote, but the late Sam Guttman, majordomo of the whole enterprise, was not pleased by such revisionist activities. I am sure that he was not running CAPS without the approval of its board, but for those participants who knew nothing of what went on behind the scenes, Sam represented the whole organization. He was an ambitious man, independently wealthy—he lived in an early eighteenth-century country mansion with a pack of Great Danes and a succession of chatelaines. He shared offices in Philadelphia with Robert Waelder. I believe he saw his role as the defense of psychoanalysis against dilution, contamination, and error. His intentions may have been of the best, but, perhaps unavoidably, he handled CAPS as if it had been a secret society. For him (and many others, before and since) psychoanalysis was a *cosa nostra*.[8] He was capable, when he had a bit of drink in him, of teasingly pinching one's cheek and telling one, "You are a nice boy, John!" On several occasions, I considered punching him in the nose, but I decided every time that I would not allow myself to be provoked into any indiscretion. I suppose this shows that Sam's mockery had me properly pegged.

After George Klein's sudden premature death, our theoretical discussions petered out. George was temporarily replaced by Philip Holzman, another psychologist-analyst who is primarily an academician. (Phil and George had been together at the Menninger Clinic; before going on to Harvard, Holzman spent several years at the University of Chicago and was active at our institute, so I knew him well.) Contrary to expectations, Phil's interests had turned to biological research on schizophrenia, and he did not find our meetings worth his while. Although, by this time, I was deeply involved in psychoanalytic theorizing, without George's support I never felt free to raise my ideas with the group, most of whom did not bother to read my publications. This fact did not endear them to me, but I had no inclination to risk a real estrangement by making useless demands that they pay attention to my work.

In the mid-1970s, CAPS expanded its activities by organizing summer meetings in Aspen, mixing participants from various existing groups with people newly invited, more or less to find out whether they would make appropriate members for permanent groups to be formed later. I spent one fortnight at such a meeting, which I did not enjoy, despite the presence of Bob Gardner. Some of the participants were arrogant and contentious, and the discussion was maddeningly conventional. The only saving grace was the presence of René Major from Paris, whose hesitant attempts to introduce an unfamiliar point of view were, however, generally rudely overridden by unwarranted interruptions. René might challenge one of our shibboleths, like the general assumption that it is a sign of pathology to use potentially addictive drugs, and someone would behave as if his words had been *jamais entendus*,[9] by introducing an unrelated topic without a word of explanation.

René is a distinguished intellectual; he was then editor of *Cahiers Confrontation*, a serious cultural journal with a nonideological psychoanalytic orientation. He responded to the rough handling by uncouth barbarians with a tolerant but ironic smile. The fact that his feelings about the discussion group coincided with my own came to light in the last ten minutes of our last session, when he asked permission to relate one of his dreams of the night before. He spoke very slowly, although his English is excellent (René is a Montreal native). The dream was about the advent of one of those showers of falling stars for which the Colorado mountain skies are famous—he had hoped to see this phenomenon during his fortnight in Aspen. His dream made this wish come true: the stars were falling in a beautiful cascade, they fell and fell—and crushed the people around him. It seemed like the proper ending for my Aspen experience.

In subsequent years, I found the Princeton meetings less and less satisfactory as well. Some members of our rapidly aging group were beset with health problems, others tended increasingly to absent themselves. I began to skip an occasional weekend, and I made greater efforts to get together with Bob Gardner in other circumstances. The point of going to Princeton underwent a gradual change from fulfilling scientific/professional hopes to having a social occasion with old friends; still later, these holidays became less and less festive. Bob Gilliland could hardly travel any more; Ed Joseph had a series of heart attacks; Francis McLaughlin began to look moribund. I was now over 60 years old—there was no longer any reason to belong to a secret society. And so I wrote a letter of resignation; I hope it conveyed my conviction that for me as an individual CAPS had truly served the function its founders envisaged for it. Without input from Gardner and Klein (and to a lesser extent some of the others) and without the concrete evidence the group provided that my clinical and theoretical understanding of psychoanalysis would hold up in the most distinguished company, I could not have pursued the radical intellectual path I have followed.

Bob tells me that without my provocations group five has become tame. My old friends did me the honor of getting Leo Sadow to join them, as my Chicago replacement. When he and I were residents together, we never could make out which of us was being paged over the U. of C. public address system.

PART TWO

THE AGE OF DISCRETION

❖ CHAPTER 9 ❖

MACHINE POLITICS

A few years ago, a democratic revolution took place at the Chicago Institute for Psychoanalysis. George Pollock was forced out of the directorship when the faculty learned that a lawsuit was pending against him in which he was accused of improprieties in raising and distributing certain funds donated by one of his patients. George was convinced of his innocence and felt utterly betrayed by the faculty, every member of which was indebted to him for numerous professional favors. I suspect he was right to look upon the ostensible reason for the revolution as a poor rationalization. I certainly supported the revolution but not primarily because I was shocked by the charges against George. It was not clear whether these would prove to be valid; even if it were so, the exploitation of wealthy analysands is an inevitable concomitant of having a lay board of trustees, financially responsible for the Institute, most of whom were former analysands of members of the faculty. (Not that I approved of *that* system, for it inevitably compromises the scientific and therapeutic goals of a psychoanalytic institution, in favor of fund-raising and social climbing, but Pollock did not establish it—it has been in place since 1932!) I was most eager to be rid of the Institute's system of governance not because of such problems but because I hate tyranny, and I am convinced that, ultimately, it stifles all creativity. Autocrats must give priority to administrative activities; such bureaucratization and politicization of analytic life have been largely responsible for the current decay of American psychoanalysis.

When our tyrannicide was completed, a provisional regime was put in place while a constitutional assembly devised a new set of bylaws. Like other new republican governments, ours insisted on the responsibility of every citizen to contribute to the public good: allegedly, one would no longer have the privilege of refusing to serve when called to duty. The summons was to come from an elected committee on committees. When this body was in place, it asked faculty members to list their preferences for committee assignments. In due course, I was notified that I was to serve on the committee I had listed fourth (and last). Never would George Pollock have inflicted such an unwelcome task on anyone unless he wanted to chastise a rebellious vassal. Like artists and intellectuals in countries recently liberated from Soviet rule, I was not going to thrive under the succeeding democracy. Yet I still had one recourse: I arranged to go on indefinite leave of absence. (That compromise did not survive the election of Arnold Goldberg as the next director of the Institute.)

Although I could predict that I would thrive under a dictatorship headed by a friendly Pollock, when Piers resigned in 1972, I was strongly opposed to electing George to the directorship. Of course, I had no direct voice in the matter, because I was not on the council (a pro forma faculty senate). Nonetheless, I tried hard to persuade Kohut to block George's appointment. Heinz was puzzled by my passionate commitment to prevent George's succession, widely regarded as natural, although he did not dispute that we had reason for concern about the possibility that Pollock might show excessive hunger for power. Neither Kohut nor I shared George's undoubted interest in the Institute's extensive—and costly!—network of ancillary programs (which have always been operated at the expense of investing in the promotion of psychoanalytic activities as such). In talking with Kohut about this, I certainly made a tactless mistake by comparing the situation to the choice of the Soviet leadership in promoting Stalin to be party secretary—Heinz did not appreciate the implicit comparison of his role to those of Zinoviev or Kamenev.[1] He was very confident that he had sufficient prestige and faculty support to keep any director in line. (He could not then foresee that many colleagues would soon view him as a dissident and turn against him—just as the Stalinists had condemned their opposition—so that his political influence would practically vanish.)

Kohut did ask me who my candidate for director might be, and I told him that it was the only person who could win a contest with George—Heinz himself. Although he was clearly flattered, Heinz demurred on the ground that he needed every spare moment to continue his intellectual work. I argued that, with proper delegation of responsibilities, the directorship need not be all that time-consuming, but he did not have the stomach to put up a fight against George. I ended up pleading that he make a sacrifice for the sake of my generation of psychoanalytic scholars, but such moral pressure was unavailing with Heinz. George was chosen without opposition to succeed Gerhart Piers.

In terms of immediate effects, this change was quite beneficial for, by the time he resigned, Gerhart's progressive cerebral illness was increasingly interfering with his performance. The first public indication of his difficulties occurred at an Institute banquet where, ex officio, Piers made an after-dinner speech in which he compared himself to a bust made of chopped chicken liver. Many of us were embarrassed by what sounded like an inappropriate and failed attempt at humor; Mary, who had extensive experience in testing patients with chronic brain syndromes during her earlier career as a clinical psychologist, predicted that Gerhart would soon show overt symptoms of cerebral deterioration. (The strange behavior he had displayed when we met to discuss my evaluation for appointment as a training analyst now fell into place.)

Mary's prediction came true very quickly: within a few months, Piers wrote a furious letter to the president of the American Psychoanalytic Association, denouncing Heinz Kohut's conduct as chairman of the Committee on Scientific Activities, the final report of which had recently been published (Kohut 1970). Of course, I am not implying that being provoked by someone's conduct is a symptom of illness, but Gerhart's offensive letter was based on an untenable tissue of false assumptions. Needless to say, nothing came of this terrible episode: as secretary of the committee, I reported the actual facts to the president. When he equivocated in response, I insisted that he distribute my letter to all those who had seen Piers's charges, and his compliance put an end to this painful incident. I must confess that I acted particularly fearlessly about this matter because I wanted to show Kohut what I considered to be the proper standard of behavior in backing a "friend."

After I took arms against him in that imbroglio, I was naturally relieved that Piers abruptly resigned the directorship. The Pollock regime started auspiciously, with a real effort to make use of those talents available within the faculty that Piers had allowed to lie fallow. For me, the most immediate reward was an invitation to teach a course of my own, for fourth year candidates, to introduce Kohut's recent conceptual innovations into the curriculum. It was the current dean who discussed this proposal with me, and I told him that I would be pleased to do it, provided it were understood that I was free to absent myself for other professional activities (such as CAPS meetings and the increasing number of invitations to present to psychoanalytic organizations that had begun to come my way). The dean said that it was too late in the year officially to approve an additional instructor for the course, but he would see to it that this would be done in subsequent years. In the meantime, I should feel free to make informal arrangements for substitutes when I needed to absent myself.

I was quite pleased that, after a decade's hiatus, my teaching career at the Institute was finally back on track, and I tackled the subject matter of my new course with the same enthusiasm I had felt about devising the one on Freud's case histories. By coincidence, going over Kohut's writings through 1972 in preparation for the course permitted me to master that segment of his work in which his actual clinical discoveries were presented. To put this differently, I was able to teach the course about Heinz's past work without ambivalence, for that work had not yet abandoned my conception of psychoanalysis. The course was well received; the only untoward incident to occur was a nasty scene when, toward the end of the academic year, Heinz made a guest appearance in class.

As on the occasion when he was invited to my CAPS group, Kohut talked without pause from the beginning to the end of the seminar, unaware that many of his auditors were sinking into somnolence because of the passivity he was forcing upon them. I tried periodically to inject a little variety into the proceedings through some sort of interruption, without much success. On one of these occasions, Kohut was talking about people who try to restore their shattered integration by resorting to frantic sexual activities; he offered a clinical example that illustrated his point, but not convincingly. I interjected a clinical experience of my own that more clearly buttressed his thesis. Heinz looked at me with open annoyance, and sarcastically chanted, in imitation of a young child, "My patient is more potent than yours, hey?"

It was a fantastic misconstruction of my remark, and I was deeply offended by the implicit accusation that I had intervened out of infantile competitiveness or exhibitionism. I am, of course, perfectly capable of overt competitiveness, but I do not need to use any proxies to assert my potency. The rupture of our relationship was just over the horizon: Heinz showed that he could no longer keep in mind what kind of person I really am; rather, he began to confuse my motivations with his own. But more of that later.

After Kohut and I parted company, I was spared the embarrassment of teaching the course on his work. Shortly after the end of the academic year, Kligerman, who was chairman of the curriculum committee, called me to reconfirm arrangements for the fall. I repeated my request for the assignment of a co-teacher, and he promised to take this up with the committee. A few weeks later, while I was transacting some business about the *Annual* in the office of Pollock's executive secretary, Kligerman wandered in and informed me that the committee had turned down my request. Had he stopped there, I would simply have reminded him of the dean's previous promise, but before I had a chance to do so, Kligerman stated that the committee did not consider me to be a mature enough instructor to have such a privilege—he thought that in three or four years my wish might be granted.

Although I had no evidence for this, I was absolutely convinced that Kligerman had personally engineered this outcome: it was of a piece with his behavior concerning the panel on biography, not to speak of his unconcealed rancor about my activities in the course we had taught together. Unrestrained by any need to appease him any longer, I told him in a voice loud enough to be heard throughout the Institute's premises that he could shove his fuckin' course up his arse! I have seldom been so angry in my life. How could they do this to me, while, more than a decade earlier, they had already allowed Goldberg to be my co-teacher?

I think the intensity of my outburst was heightened by the fact that only the day before this scene, I had been appointed book review editor of the *Journal of the American Psychoanalytic*, a position that I thought required more "maturity" than does sharing a course with a colleague. The entire incident merely served to reconfirm that influential people on the faculty were determined to show me that I was no better than any of my peers. Yet in other analytic communities I was already being treated as one of the intellectual leaders to come.

It was typical of the Pollock regime that my refusal to be jerked around in this way had absolutely no consequences. (All that counted was how much political support one had.) They found other people to teach the course, and for a number of years I made myself physically scarce at the Institute. I was fully occupied with other responsibilities for which, however, I also had George Pollock to thank.

In the spring of 1973, George became president-elect of the American Psychoanalytic Association. One of the urgent items on the Association's agenda was to find replacements for John Frosch as editor of the *Journal* and Nathaniel Ross, his associate editor. The editorship went to Harold

Blum of New York, a man of my age well known to the previous leadership of the *Journal*. (Incidentally, Kohut declined to support me for the editorship on the ground that I was too young for the job. I thought he actually knew that age was not an obstacle to appointment; I felt that he was unwilling to help me to establish my own independent bailiwick.) George, ever eager to increase Chicago representation on national bodies, threw his support behind me to succeed Ross as book review editor.[2]

I doubt that Pollock's political influence would have sufficed to obtain this appointment for someone unknown to the *Journal* leadership, but I suspect it was decisive in nailing down the job for me. My qualifications were, in fact, well known to the relevant people because in recent years I had contributed two lengthy essays to the book review section, exhaustively covering the interdisciplinary literature on the visual arts, on the one hand, and on political and social affairs, on the other (see 1970a and 1972b). Neither of these pieces was commissioned; I had taken the initiative to propose them to Nat Ross, who encouraged me to proceed and was satisfied with what I then produced. Incidentally, each of these projects required months of scholarly research that I deeply enjoyed. I was particularly happy to immerse myself in the interdisciplinary literature on art and psychoanalysis because Mary was at the time engaged in writing a dissertation (M. Gedo 1972) on the autobiographical aspects of the work of Pablo Picasso; she was clearly on the way to a significant role at the frontier between depth psychology and the visual arts.[3]

My selection as assistant editor of the *Journal* (and subsequent election to its editorial board) shifted the center of my organizational activities from the local to the national scene. I did a prodigious amount of work for the *Journal*[4]; fortunately, Harold Blum instituted a policy that members of his editorial team (Selma Kramer for child analysis, Otto Kernberg for research, and myself) could not continue any affiliations with competing analytic publications. Hence, I had to resign from the *Annual*, as well as from the editorial board of *American Imago*, which Harry Slochower had asked me to join several years earlier. Pollock could not object to these consequences of an appointment he had helped to bring about, and I was satisfied to focus on my new job, because I thought that I had learned as much as possible from coediting a publication of limited influence.

At the same time, I was by no means interested in giving up fruitful collaboration with George. In place of working on the *Annual*, I proposed that he and I coedit a volume of papers on the history of psychoanalysis, all written by faculty members of the Chicago Institute. George was enthusiastic about the idea and, in short order, contacted Herbert Schlesinger (George Klein's successor as editor of the *Psychological Issues* series) about the possibility of publishing such a volume as one of their monographs. This time, there were no complications; the volume (1976a) was duly collected, accepted for publication, and produced by International Universities Press.

Needless to say, I was most interested in collecting in this volume my own past work on psychoanalytic history: the four papers on which I had collaborated in the workshop on scientific methodology, two published (in German) in *Psyche*, the collaborative paper with Wolf on Freud's adolescence, and my essay on Freud's self-analysis from the *Imago*.[5] Pollock was coauthor of three of the papers from the workshop, and he contributed three solo efforts. (When Schlesinger's readers objected to two of these on the ground that they diverged from the overall theme of the book, George was extremely gracious in agreeing to omit them.) Ernest Wolf was coauthor of two of my contributions; in addition, he agreed to include a fine paper (Wolf 1971a) on Freud's celebrated lecture on "The Aetiology of Hysteria" and a collaborative work, shared with Harry Trosman (Wolf and Trosman 1974), on one of Freud's *Doppelgänger*, Popper-Lynkeus. Trosman let us have two excellent published papers, on Freud's untenable views about the Shakespearean authorship controversy (Trosman 1965) and on his cryptomnesia concerning the origins of the technique of free association (Trosman 1969).

I wrote editorial introductions (and added a series of editorial footnotes) in order to knit these seemingly disparate materials into a coherent whole. In the process, I realized that the volume still needed both an introductory and a concluding chapter. George and I persuaded Kohut to provide the latter (Kohut 1976); I prepared the introduction in collaboration with Wolf (1976b). Our contribution was a review of the introspective tradition of humanism, with special reference to its greatest exemplar, Michel de Montaigne. As one might expect of a volume on intellectual history, its sales have been relatively modest, although the book received good reviews.

While this project lasted, Pollock and I would meet at intervals to discuss our progress, and we continued these occasional dinner meetings for several years thereafter. Although we never made it explicit, it was clearly understood that we could best get along if I did not concern myself with what was going on at the Institute. Early in his term, George offered to appoint me to one of the powerful educational committees. Had I accepted, it would have meant disrupting an analytic schedule that I strongly preferred to keep uniform every working day. By this time, I saw all my patients five times a week, and I remain convinced that an absolutely invariable schedule of appointments is a significant factor in getting good therapeutic results. Moreover, I was unwilling to substitute a Saturday schedule for the time devoted to committee work—I needed weekends for my scholarly activities. Consequently, I let George know that I was not interested in administrative assignments. Thenceforth, if he asked me to serve at all, it was on committees that never actually met—considerateness on his part that I still appreciate, despite our subsequent political differences.

Our smooth administrative arrangements became somewhat strained because George soon became embittered with the American Psychoanalytic Association. (The Board of Professional Standards had denied his request to grant the Chicago Institute an experimental exception to the usual training regulations—a move on George's part widely resented because many influential members thought it was inappropriate for a sitting president to propose a measure that favored his institute.) As he went into opposition to the association leadership (to me, it seemed that he fought them no matter what policies they advocated), George appeared to become more and more uneasy with my increasing involvement with the governance of the association. (Not only did I serve on the *Journal*, I was appointed to a succession of educational committees, to the permanent Committee on Scientific Activities that succeeded Kohut's ad hoc body, and to the board of the newly established Fund for Psychoanalytic Research.)

What particularly seemed to bother Pollock was that I did not owe any of these appointments to his influence, and I never consulted him about how to vote as a member of these bodies. George was continuously lobbying for greater Chicago representation on national committees, always complaining that Chicago was being slighted. By the early 1980s, he was seemingly so annoyed by my becoming independent of his patronage that, when an officer of the association reminded a Chicago lobbyist that I should be counted as one of the appointees from our institute, this satrap justifiably replied, "But John's *not* one of us!" The incident greatly amused Pollock's opponents and they made sure that the story got back to me.

When George originally became director, he suggested that the bylaws limit holders of the office to two relatively brief terms. I was scarcely surprised, however, that when the end of his second term was approaching, Pollock initiated a movement to amend the bylaws so that he would be able to serve indefinitely. I do not doubt that he heard that I was one of the people on the faculty who tried to persuade the council (which had to vote on this matter) to block this bid for extending his power. Pollock narrowly won the struggle to amend the bylaws; afterward, opposition became hopeless, for George controlled the nominations for election to the council and, when he felt it necessary, was able to organize campaigns to defeat anyone he wanted to chastise. For example, in 1978, when he felt that Kohut's followers were beginning to form an organized faction that might threaten his power, he engineered Kohut's defeat in the council election—without leaving any fingerprints, of course.[6]

After he eliminated the constitutional obstacles to his continued rule, Pollock's main political concern was the possibility that someone might organize a second institute in Chicago. He was particularly anxious about this after Bob Gardner's success, in the mid-1970s, in establishing a second approved institute in Boston, the Psychoanalytic Institute of New England (East), PINE for short. (I thought it was more than coincidence that opposition to Bob's initiative within the American Psychoanalytic was led by Joan Fleming. He defeated her at the Board of Professional Standards by delivering a thunderous, spontaneous speech on academic freedom. I looked upon PINE's opponents as an informal alliance of political bosses.) At one of our periodic dinners, George actually asked me whether I thought some faculty member (was it Goldberg? I am no longer certain) might try a similar move. The opportunity to twist the lion's tail was irresistible. Very soberly, I said, "George, you know there is only one person in Chicago who could possibly do that." "Who is that?"—in real alarm. "It is I"—portentously. "But *you* are loyal to the Chicago Institute?!"

No, I was not. Had anyone been willing to join me, I would have been delighted to form another institute—I even wrote an educational prospectus for one (1977b), a utopian vision that George actually published in the *Annual*. (I still believe that an analytic education would best be conducted on a tutorial system.) Few faculty members were as convinced as I that the existing Institute had deteriorated into a political machine. George Klumpner, who was maximally concerned because even the council was kept ignorant of the Institute's finances, tried to look into this and was defeated in the next council election. He was also removed from his committee assignments. At a dinner party at Klumpner's home, we elaborated a fantasy about forming a midwestern PINE, a Northern Illinois Psychoanalytic Institute, or NIPI (to be pronounced nippy)—but even our closest friends treated this as a joke. They owed George Pollock even more than I and had no stomach for nipping him.

Late in 1978 a colleague, about whom I was in possession of certain confidential information bearing on a defect of character, was about to be appointed as a training analyst. I had kept silent when this person was originally proposed, in the expectation that the evaluation process would have an unfavorable outcome. When this did not occur, I recounted the story to some friends at a CAPS meeting, to illustrate my objections to the machine politics of Institute patronage. Through these channels, the facts came to the attention of the national officers in charge of confirming training analyst appointments; they encouraged me to write to the relevant committee, spelling out the information in question. I did so and, as a courtesy, I sent Pollock a copy of the letter. George then asked me to confer with him and informed me that, if I did not withdraw these objections to the appointment, the person concerned would sue me for defamation of character, and sue the Institute and the association as well.

I pointed out that the person's resort to such a threat conformed precisely with the characterological attributes I had called to the attention of the committee. George agreed, but he pleaded that, to avoid trouble, the appointment should be made; he promised that the Institute would never refer a candidate to this "training analyst." So I shrugged my shoulders and stated the obvious, that the problem was not mine. In my opinion, organized psychoanalysis has been severely damaged by its refusal to apply appropriate quality controls at every level of promotion—but this is an issue for which I have never been prepared to wage a solitary war.

Later, I asked George how the appointee had learned that I had written the letter that had delayed the proceedings. He replied that he had shown this person my letter in order to explain the difficulty encountered by the proposed appointment. I objected that confidential information of that kind was not supposed to be shared with the person involved; George replied that the material would only have been confidential if I had reported it when the Institute asked for such information. I understood. (And how!) What I still cannot figure out is whether George had really shown my letter to the prospective appointee. After all, the entire story about a threatened lawsuit could have been a bluff.

Around the same time, George persuaded me to offer an elective course to advanced candidates; he knew that I was about to publish my first solo book, *Beyond Interpretation* (1979a), and he said he wanted a new cohort of students to have personal exposure to a faculty member who was doing original work. What convinced me to let down my guard against fresh harassment by opponents on the curriculum committee was George's assurance that the subject matter of the course would be left entirely to me. Yet I was not really appeased; by that time, I had become the person on the faculty most concerned in rethinking the theoretical problems of psychoanalysis, and I thought I should have been asked to teach the core of the theoretical curriculum rather than an elective. Still, I found it irresistible to tackle a fifth course at the Institute since my graduation. This time, I gave the course twice before the curriculum committee undercut me; Kligerman called in late spring to announce that Heinz Kohut was now ready to resume his elective course that, as Charley claimed I was supposed to know, was to alternate with mine, every other year. This time I did not lose my temper; I wrote George Pollock that I was unwilling to put up with the unpredictability of the curriculum committee and would not take part in the teaching program as long as Kligerman continued as chairman. (He only lost his fiefdom during the revolution, at which point I offered still another elective, one that led to a book [1993b] I coauthored with Mark Gehrie.)

During the 1981–82 academic year, both the Chicago Psychoanalytic Society and the Institute (which are organizationally entirely separate) were to reach the fiftieth anniversary of their foundation. Leo Sadow, who was president of the society in 1979–80, decided to appoint a committee to explore how these milestones might be celebrated and asked me to serve as its chairman. We quickly decided to attempt to organize a stellar scientific conference of national scope, and we realized that this would be most feasible if it were planned in cooperation with the Institute rather than in competition with whatever Pollock was planning to do to mark its anniversary. Leo was able to persuade George that such a collaborative program would be optimal, particularly after the society committee agreed to split the anticipated surplus with the Institute. We also promised to encourage the membership to donate the society's share of the profits to the Institute, as a commemorative gift.

We scheduled the conference for November 1981 and invited more than a dozen scientifically eminent participants from other cities. Almost everyone we wanted agreed to come, and we also imported the president of the American, Arnold Cooper, and the immediate past-president of the International, Edward Joseph. Needless to say, the out-of-towners were balanced by a wide representation of local speakers. I had hoped to have an imaginative cultural program in addition, but more sober heads prevailed; they argued that only clinical topics will induce registrants to pay a fee high enough to yield a profit. I had to content myself with a brief recital of Viennese lieder at the gala banquet by the soprano Claudine Carlson and a few sessions on interdisciplinary topics, involving mostly academics from Chicago.

Early during the planning process, I asked George Pollock whether he might wish to have the conference proceedings published, and he gladly accepted the idea. By this time, his publishing empire included several monograph series, so that his agreement amounted to an imprimatur. Although we did not get the author's permission to include every presentation at the conference, the ones made available to us amply filled two volumes (1984a and 1985a). We carried out this editorial task, largely through the liaison work of George's executive secretary, although other aspects of the conference had finally ended the residue of mutual trust between us. Characteristically, nobody ever questioned the decision not to share the editorial honors with anyone else.

Both Leo and I felt that the success of the conference depended on avoiding ideological polarization—in other words, it was essential not to discriminate either against self psychology or against its local opponents. In view of his stellar role at the meeting celebrating the institute's twenty-fifth anniversary, I thought that, a quarter of a century later, it was incumbent on us to offer Kohut the opportunity to present the plenary address. When the negotiation to gain Heinz's consent was successfully concluded, Pollock came forward with a demand for equal time. His power was then so absolute that I could not get the committee to oppose this inappropriate idea. It took very delicate diplomacy to keep Heinz on board without preserving a unique role for him at the conference.[7] As it happened, Kohut died a few weeks before the meeting, and his paper was read in his place by his son, Tom.

For his plenary slot, Pollock decided to present a filmed interview between him and Anna Freud, made close to the very end of her life. For some reason, he ordered an elaborate array of audiovisual equipment for this presentation; our treasurer told me that this cost almost as much as the conference made in profit. To my horror, the film was entirely pointless, as well as much longer than our schedule allowed; before Pollock got up to introduce it, he forced the subservient faculty member in charge of arrangements to announce that the session would be extended by half an hour and the rest of the program would have to start that much later. It was a gratuitous insult to all the other speakers and a lesson to the society about its actual subordination to those in power at the institute.

Largely through Leo Sadow's influence, I was elected president of the society for 1981–82, so that it fell to me to oversee the distribution of our half of the surplus earned by the conference. I appointed a committee, chaired by Mike Gunther, who was favorably disposed to our original plans, to make a recommendation to the membership, for the matter clearly had to be approved by their vote. I was not surprised to hear, from a number of sources, that Pollock suspected that I was trying to renege on our promise about the anniversary gift. On this matter, however, I insisted on proper constitutional procedure, and the society ultimately voted to earmark the funds for a project that has greatly benefited every member, the computerization of the institute library.

Pollock's vigilance about the preservation of his power knew no bounds. For example, at one time he circulated a questionnaire asking the faculty to suggest people who could be approached for donations or to serve the Institute in some other capacity. I named our friends Mary and David Green as excellent prospects for the board of trustees. Mary had had a fruitful analysis and has always been interested in working for the community; David is a highly successful industrialist and, at the time I put their names forward, he was the dollar-a-year right-hand man of the governor of Illinois—a fact I was careful to point out to Pollock. The Greens received a request for a donation—they probably contributed a token amount—but were not contacted about a board position as long as Pollock was in power. Soon thereafter, Mary was named a trustee. I inferred that George had not wanted a close friend of mine to have that much influence on the Institute's governance. My suspicion was strengthened a year or so after I sent in the Greens' names: George urgently called me to ask whether my friend was still working for the governor—there was some problem about the state subsidy for the Institute clinic! (To my malicious satisfaction, Illinois had by then changed governors.)

By the mid-1980s, the Pollock regime had become overripe. George installed one of his analysands as chairwoman of the board, and more and more of his energy was devoted to the politics of American psychiatry. (He eventually became president of the American Psychiatric Association.) On one occasion, a distinguished out-of-town art historian was invited to give a public lecture under Institute auspices. Because Mary was on friendly terms with this scholar, we were asked to a cocktail reception in his honor at the home of the board chairwoman, a magnificent, art-filled apartment on East Lake Shore Drive (the most exclusive address in Chicago). Aside from George Pollock, I was the only psychoanalyst present. Someone introduced me to a Mrs. Pritzker.[8] I stopped by a window that offered a magnificent vista of the lake and the "Gold Coast." George came up behind me, put his arm around my shoulders, and whispered, "John, *this* is psychoanalysis." Sodom and Gomorrah!

Shortly before the revolution that deposed him, Pollock was to reproach me for my ingratitude about all the favors he had done me. (He was right: one feels no gratitude to Tammany Hall.) What I found remarkable in his complaint is that he did not mention most of the significant actions on my behalf I have listed here but spoke instead about such things as the summer job one of my kids had in the library when he was a college student. "Oh," I said, "I didn't know that you had anything to do with that!" "Of course," said George, "everything of that sort has to cross my desk." With great satisfaction, I ended the discussion: "George, you have often done very kind things for me. But if I had known he had obtained a patronage job, I would not have permitted my son to take it." No, indeed. It was bad enough that I had failed to resist the temptation to accept George's patronage for myself. Or that of anyone else.[9]

❖ CHAPTER 10 ❖

ON THE NATIONAL SCENE

The day after I gave my plenary address to the American Psychoanalytic Association, Chuck Rothstein, then chairman of the program committee, collared me in one of the hallways of the Waldorf-Astoria and asked me to serve on the committee—as he put it, because the input of experienced contributors to the literature was greatly needed. The proposal seemed appealing, because, in preparation for retirement, I had severed almost all my ties to organized psychoanalysis, and serving on this committee seemed like an excellent way to avoid being forgotten as a contributor to the literature who is still living. I told Chuck that I was inclined to accept, although afterward the time and trouble of attending committee meetings kept nagging at me. The following May, instead of an invitation, I received a formal letter of thanks from the incoming president, Judith Schachter, about my acceptance of this appointment. Now I was trapped: when Judy was elected to the office, I had written to congratulate her and had promised to do anything she asked of me during her term as president. (I must confess that I had in mind something more glamorous than a seat on the program committee—perhaps chairing an ad hoc committee or acting as a private *consigliere*?)

Over the summer and fall, I was sent several prospective presentations to referee, and I was pleased by the weight accorded to my opinions by those who collated the referees' reports. The first meeting I was to attend was in December—as usual, at the Waldorf. Nobody told me what to expect, and I was greatly surprised by the proceedings. Over thirty people gathered around a table so large that it was difficult to hear what those at the other end were saying. I was horrified to discover that there were, in addition, a substantial number of absentees. I knew a fair number of the members from past visits to their home institutes or societies, as well as scientific or administrative activities with the national association. I was indeed one of a handful of senior figures on the committee: it seemed very appropriate that the others were Selma Kramer (with whom I had served on the *Journal*), Joe Lichtenberg (editor of *Psychoanalytic Inquiry*, who had published a major segment of my written work for more than a dozen years), and my old friend Shelley Orgel (who, as secretary and chairman of the Board of Professional Standards, had been instrumental in getting me appointed to the educational committees on which I served for over a decade).

As one might expect, the deliberations of an unwieldy group of thirty were excruciatingly inefficient and boring; I did my best to expedite matters by saying as little as possible. In fact, I intervened only to protest about the absence from the list of prospective plenary speakers of the active theoretician I most respect, Arnold Modell of Boston. To my amazement, there was no opposition to my emotional appeal. Chuck Rothstein crowed, sotto voce, that this incident showed that a single member can make a real difference. But I am now too old for this sort of thing; I had no real interest in any of the plans under consideration, and I felt much too weary to fight for ideas most people in the room might have found rather strange. The good news was that I had lunch with a young colleague I had once met socially, and she insisted on paying. O, brave new world!

I am no longer prepared to deal with a bureaucracy such as this committee. Moreover, the proceedings exemplified some of the errors in governance that have sapped the vitality of American psychoanalysis: the enormous expenditure of time and resources on unnecessary administrative activities, the politicization of essentially scientific decisions through the selection of the relevant committees on a geographic basis, the suppression of novel viewpoints because of their inevitable failure to gain majority support in democratic elections, and so on.

Once before, in the mid-1970s, when I was book review editor of the *Journal*, I had allowed my commitments at the American Psychoanalytic to grow unwieldy: I was serving on the Committee on Scientific Activities (CSA—the permanent successor of the ad hoc committee Kohut had initiated and for which I had been the secretary), on the board of the Fund for Psychoanalytic Research (as a delegate from the *Journal*), and I was finishing a second three-year term on CORST (the Committee on Research and Special Training, charged with reviewing the credentials of nonmedical candidates who wished to receive training in clinical psychoanalysis).

CORST is an organ of the Board of Professional Standards, the educational directorate of the association, and I rightly looked upon its work as the essential preparatory stage of a long-term campaign to eliminate the medical requirement for training within the association. The committee was discreetly packed with opponents of the medical requirement, many of them previously trained nonmedical analysts. They were eager to add to the committee psychiatrist-analysts they could rely on; I learned that they had requested my appointment on the recommendation of Chicago colleagues Phil Holzman and Merton Gill, whose terms antedated mine.

Morton Reiser, then head of the Department of Psychiatry at Yale, chaired CORST when I joined it; a few years later, he was succeeded by Herbert Schlesinger (then of Denver), George Klein's successor as editor of *Psychological Issues*. It was a small group, enlivened by Merton Gill's hypomanic humor and a firm consensus about the value of its activities as a contribution to the future of American psychoanalysis. Not only were the actual committee meetings highly enjoyable; I also took pleasure in reading the intellectual work the applicants had to submit (such as Spiro [1965] or Skura [1981]) to document that clinical experience in psychoanalysis would enhance their later contributions to their own discipline.

Although I have never believed that medicine is the only adequate preparation for a prospective psychoanalyst, I have also been opposed to the disastrous policy of expanding our numbers (heedless of the saturation of our markets) instead of attempting to upgrade our standards of qualification. Hence, I did not experience conflict about selecting only those applicants to CORST whose accomplishments in their original discipline gave evidence of outstanding talents. I was convinced that the medical requirement would in time be relinquished if the nonmedical candidates we trained turned out to be superior analysts and productive scholars. I therefore did not hesitate to vote against applicants with mediocre records or mental health professionals whose interests were merely clinical. (CORST applicants were expected to make academic contributions.) At the same time, I tried hard to open our doors wider to gifted persons with unusual backgrounds. This was work I thought it was worth my while to continue as long as the association's term limits permitted; hence, when I realized I was overcommitted, CORST was the only administrative activity from which I did not resign.

I had an additional reason to withdraw from a prominent role within the American Psychoanalytic: I was already stirring up more than enough hostility in Chicago through my scientific activities. (Some colleagues could not imagine that anyone as active as I then was could do all that work for reasons other than ambitions to obtain political power!) I was distressed by the fact that a letter objecting to the large number of reviews I was doing for the *Journal* came from one of my former teachers at the Chicago Institute whose good will I had never previously had reason to doubt. As I read it, this letter contained more than a trace of personal rancor; it then occurred to me for the first time that my serving on the *Journal* could arouse envy (even malice!), without much compensatory benefit. I can never get used to the fact that in psychoanalysis the rewards of merit do not include the support of one's competitors. (Contrast this with professional sports, for example!)

What I did regret giving up was the opportunity to meet regularly the other members of the editorial board—a very distinguished group in terms of leadership roles, for once including scientific contributions. While I served on the *Journal*, it included the contemporary theoreticians whose work I most admired, Hans Loewald, Arnold Modell, and Roy Schafer; half a dozen outstanding contributors on clinical topics, leaders of child analysis, and preeminent researchers. Our meetings provided ample opportunity for socializing and exchanging ideas in a collegial atmosphere. Of course, giving this up amounted mostly to relinquishing the narcissistic gratification of rubbing elbows with the crème de la crème.

There was much similarity among the people who served on the *Journal*, CORST, CSA, and the research fund: most of them were actually interested in promoting the intellectual agenda of psychoanalysis. However, CSA was a purely advisory body; this was the result of a compromise between the recommendations of the Kohut committee and the preference of most members not to involve the association in scientific enterprises. Lacking any power of decision, the deliberations of this debating society generally led nowhere. Robert Wallerstein, who was chairman, seemed to me to be resigned to the status quo—perhaps even satisfied with the fact that organized research had to take place in traditional academic settings, such as his own psychiatry department at the University of California–San Francisco. He showed no interest in proposals to push the association to establish some serious structures to make scientific work possible under its own aegis; I suspect he found such quixotic ideas more than a little ridiculous. I think he has lived to regret his complacency, because almost every medical school, including his own, has turned against psychoanalysis.

The entire effort to integrate psychoanalysis within medicine (particularly within its academic establishment) was hopeless as well as politically misguided, as recent events have shown. Not only did it cause the interdisciplinary wars with psychology and social work that prevented the development of a unified and rational training system; even worse, it diverted attention from the scientific evolution of psychoanalysis, in favor of imperialist efforts to gain influence in hospitals and medical schools through the pretense that psychoanalysts had a well-articulated and proven body of knowledge to peddle to their physician-colleagues. Hence the 1970 Kohut report failed to gain the unreserved support of the analysts who were in academic medicine, and the American Psychoanalytic was involved in research only in a token manner, through the recently established fund for research.

By channeling members' voluntary financial contributions to appropriate applicants, the fund did in a modest way encourage scientific activity. Initially, serving on its board meant that I could participate in setting up the procedures and criteria for making research awards. When the time came to serve as a referee for specific applications, however, I found that most of the submissions involved projects in academic psychology conducted at various universities. The methodological complexities of these (nonanalytic) studies did not interest me and transcended my expertise. All in all, it seemed appropriate to yield my place to someone better fitted to the task. At the same time, I was disappointed that our meager budget for research was awarded to projects in cognate disciplines; I had hoped that the fund might encourage conceptual research in psychoanalytic theory, for I saw the clarification of our muddled theories of mental function, development, psychopathology, and treatment technique as the most important task confronting us.

Why did I enjoy my service on CORST more than any of the other activities I had undertaken? Was it because of the unusual camaraderie within the committee? No gathering that included Merton Gill could ever be boring. (Alas, Merton has recently died. I spent much of the summer of 1996 in writing various essays [1996f, 1997b, in prep, b] to commemorate him.) After I completed the maximal term allowed, I was so convinced that the work of such an educational committee had real value that I simply accosted the then chairman of the board, to ask whether it was he who made committee appointments, and I requested another assignment. The chairman was taken aback, and I suspect that this impulsive move would not have succeeded if Shelley Orgel had not intervened to support me. As it turned out, for most of the six years of the assignment I next received, Shelley was chairman of the Committee on Institutes (COI) to which I was appointed.

COI is probably the most important committee of the Board of Professional Standards and its work is undoubtedly the most interesting. COI monitors the component institutes within the association by making site visits. Incidentally, COI was established on the recommendation of the team of Bertram Lewin and Helen Ross, who spent an entire sabbatical year in surveying psychoanalytic education in America (Lewin and Ross 1960). Early in 1957 they made a site visit to Chicago and sat in on one of my earliest sessions of supervision by Therese Benedek. I find it curiously moving that, recently, my son Paul recounted that COI visited the Washington Institute and sat in on one of his supervisory sessions. Moreover, the site-visit team was headed by my ex-supervisee, Lou Spitz (from Cincinnati), who shared with Paul some of the most inappropriate pronouncements I made during our work. I rather like the role of a "lion in winter."

When I was participating in COI, about four institutes were visited per year; this meant that each institute was surveyed at seven year intervals. As I joined, the modus operandi was rapidly changing from an adversarial one to an effort to offer assistance in a collaborative spirit. The composition of site-visit teams varied to some degree, depending on the size and administrative complexity of the institute in question. Before the actual visit, institutes were asked to submit extensive documentation about every aspect of their operations—financing, governance, auxiliary activities, housing, curriculum, record keeping, and the appointment of faculty. Where a child analysis program was offered, the site-visit team included a representative of the Committee on Child Analysis. The actual inspection usually took around five days and included sitting in on classes, on the supervision of candidates' clinical work, on committee meetings, then discussing the findings among the site visitors and with representatives of the institute. It was always a fascinating and exhilarating experience.

The penalty for having the privilege of serving on COI was the unremunerated commitment of substantial blocks of time: a whole working week for the site visit and several days each at the twice-yearly meetings of the association. On these occasions, the site-visit teams reported on their findings in order to get consensus about the formal report to be submitted to those who had been inspected. Committee members assigned to provide liaison with institutes between site visits kept tabs on fresh developments and reported these to the committee, and teams that had recently carried out site visits met with institute representatives to discuss the reports they had prepared. If one kept up this whirlwind of activity for two three-year terms, one had the opportunity thoroughly to learn about the state of psychoanalysis all over the country, to discover the varieties of pathology that can beset analytic organizations, and to gain a perspective detached from purely local considerations about the broader issues that determine the future of American psychoanalysis.

In retrospect, I must admit that the enormous effort poured into the site visits yielded relatively minor dividends in terms of their immediate impact on the operations of the institutes concerned. I believe nonetheless that this process of peer review does encourage, or even push, most institutes to make efforts to adhere to a few standards about which there is consensus in the association. It was also clear that colleagues who got appointments to COI tended to have more exacting expectations than those who do most of the work in local institutes. From my personal vantage point, many of the candidates I saw seemed unsuitable for the profession, many of the supervisors neither knew how to teach nor demonstrated an adequate grasp of the analytic process in their students' cases, many of the classes were pedestrian or worse, and most committees were ineffectual. In other words, as educational institutions, the institutes of the American Psychoanalytic Association are shamefully poor—comparable to community colleges rather than research universities. I could not see how we could continue to claim that our graduates are significantly better educated than those of training programs not affiliated with the association.

By the mid-1970s it had become clear that American psychoanalysis as a whole was producing a surplus of relatively poorly trained graduates, so that recruitment to the profession was becoming more difficult. Most institutes were responding to these developments by trying to become more "user friendly," that is, by keeping enrollment as high as possible (at the expense of competing institutes) instead of carrying out a program of downsizing by *raising* standards, thereby squeezing out the marginal candidates. In my judgment, this has turned out to be a drastic error—it has not really helped recruitment but continues to discourage the most talented prospects from participation in an increasingly mediocre and overcrowded enterprise.

In the past decade, conditions everywhere have begun to match the most severe problems I encountered circa 1980, yet analytic organizations continue their misdirected focus on training new practitioners. The pursuit of expansion and various forms of prestige still takes precedence over intellectual activity; competing orthodoxies still pronounce anathemata over each other. Today, I no longer believe that any of this is remediable, and in this dark age I am content to confine myself to setting down my views on paper, in the hope of some future analytic renaissance.

During my six years on COI, I participated in visiting both institutes in Philadelphia, the larger one in Boston, the institute affiliated with Columbia University, the one shared by the University of North Carolina and Duke (near Raleigh), and the Pittsburgh Institute. Each experience was unique; every institute was struggling with a different set of problems, every team of site visitors evolved a particular esprit de corps and met faculty representatives of widely differing personality types. Almost invariably, the assessment of a group's functional level in its professional and educational enterprises aroused strong passions. Every participant in COI while I was a member shared the conviction that these activities were vitally important.

The first site visit in which I took part was to the institute at Columbia University, a unit housed within the Department of Psychiatry at the medical school (with characteristic Ivy League snobbery, called "P and S"—the College of Physicians and Surgeons). This is located in Washington Heights, a neighborhood north of the Upper West Side in Manhattan, near the George Washington Bridge—the neighborhood where I had lived for several years after arriving in America, where I attended George Washington High School (in the same class with Henry Kissinger, Alan Greenspan, John Kemeny—the mathematician who became President of Dartmouth—and the former Israeli cabinet minister Moshe Arens). I had not seen that part of New York in decades, not since I was at P and S to take the specialty board examination in psychiatry, and I was stunned to discover that it had, at the end of the 1970s, turned into a somewhat rundown Hispanic barrio. A generation earlier, I had been the destitute newcomer to the city, too much an uncouth greenhorn to be accepted for elegant Columbia College or P and S. Needless to say, it meant a great deal to me to become an "inspector general" for such an institution.[1]

It did not take long, however, for my sympathies to swing to the side of our embattled Columbia colleagues. One of our first activities was an encounter with the chairman of the psychiatry department, a graduate of a well-reputed psychoanalytic institute whose experience as a candidate left him with a bottomless pool of hatred for psychoanalysis. He made it amply clear to us that he intended to derail the institute now under his jurisdiction from its analytic goals. (To the embarrassed relief of our Columbia colleagues, within a few months a fatal illness removed this nemesis from the scene.) Further to stimulate my protectiveness, some members of the site-visit team had prejudices about the Columbia Institute, based on the philosophy of its program under the regime of its late founder, Sándor Radó, a controversial and charismatic figure. From what I could observe, however, the Institute was leaning over backward to disavow Radó's outdated legacy; the most attractive feature of the place was its openness to a variety of psychoanalytic viewpoints. Excellent newcomers to the faculty, such as Jacob Arlow, Otto Kernberg, and Roy Schafer, had significantly strengthened a shaky program.

Those of the site visitors who had no wish to find fault with an institute eager to improve wanted to focus the committee report on the lack of statutory autonomy from interference with its functioning by university bodies or officials. The issue was especially timely because rather similar affiliations of institutes with universities had in recent years been ruptured in Cleveland and Pittsburgh. To our amazement, the Columbia faculty was unconcerned about this organizational issue; Otto Kernberg was the only member on its executive committee who shared the site visitors' concerns. (Otto was also the sole member of the executive who had experience in other settings and did not idealize Columbia University and its hallowed traditions.) In subsequent years, some of those who dismissed our worries probably lived to regret it, for the university did exercise its legal right to influence the selection of the institute's leadership, sometimes in favor of candidates the analytic faculty might not otherwise have chosen. This instance is the best possible demonstration of the seductive pull of academic medicine on allied analytic institutions.

An immediate problem even more difficult to handle was the incoherence of the site visit chairman's (oral and written) communications to the institute. Nor could the rest of the team cover over his unalterable contempt for the institute's alleged heterodoxy: he was one of the oligarchs who long wielded power in the association. The preliminary report he later distributed was full of unedited excerpts from the commentaries submitted by those who sat in on various exercises; not only did these name faculty members whose performance was being evaluated, they also identified the evaluator. (Some of my more critical comments earned me the lasting rancor of certain colleagues whom I was very sorry to have unintentionally offended.)

It scarcely caused surprise that the Columbia people indignantly rejected this disgraceful document or that the chairman proved incapable of rewriting it. By this time, Shelley Orgel had taken over COI; to help him out of this impasse, I volunteered to produce a report that would be acceptable to all concerned. Two and a half years after the site visit, this draft report was finally accepted, but the history of its production left too much resentment in its wake to make it possible for the institute to pay serious attention to its recommendations. I was then assigned to be the liaison person to the Columbia Institute, and I met with its new director, Ethel Person, on a number of occasions. Far from treating me as the ally who had protected her institution from injustice, Ethel seemed to regard me as a spy whom she needed to keep from learning what was happening in her boudoir. It did not help that I kept having the fantasy that she might bite me. Sharper than a serpent's tooth is the ingratitude of analytic politicians. And the Columbia politicians mirrored the prejudices of the site visit chairman.

My experience with this site visit brought home to me the destructive effects on psychoanalytic organizations of the misuse of membership for inappropriate personal ends, particularly in the narcissistic realm. The chairman of our team acted not like Gogol's farcical inspector general but like Dostoyevsky's grand inquisitor, and this arrogation to himself of the right to define analytic virtue whipped up storms of counteraggression. At the same time, all too many on the Columbia faculty used that affiliation as a mark of social cachet, as if *their* university connection had ipso facto made them superior to those teaching at "lesser" institutions. Much too much passion was poured into efforts to upstage rival analytic organizations in New York—even to court potential candidates by demonizing other institutions. These attitudes, in turn, provoked retaliation. I was to hear psychoanalysis as practiced at Columbia bad-mouthed on the ground that "those people" were contemptible because they tended to be sharp dressers! No wonder *The New Yorker* published pieces on psychoanalysis contemptuous of our attempts at social climbing.

The year after my exciting debut on COI, I was asked to chair the site visit to Pittsburgh, an institute recently forced by a hostile chairman of psychiatry to disaffiliate from the medical school that had formed its matrix. What was mere threat at Columbia had become an accomplished fact in Pittsburgh—but for the circumstance that, instead of buckling under to a hostile administration, the analysts had walked out. (Of course, they did not have to resist the seduction of Ivy League prestige.) Because

Pittsburgh is a city with only one serious psychiatric residency program, this disaffiliation essentially cut off the only source of potential psychiatric candidates. A trickle of CORST applicants kept the program going. Because the institute had focused almost exclusively on the training of prospective clinicians, the scarcity of applicants left it floundering without a mission; the energies of the faculty were irrationally concentrated on desperate remedies to regain some influence in the Department of Psychiatry.

To complicate the task of the site visit, James McLaughlin, the respected leader who had managed the foregoing exodus, had completed his term as director a little over a year before, and a period of dissension and administrative chaos supervened. The faculty was split about the wisdom of instituting efforts independently to reach out to the Pittsburgh community, without having the endorsement of the university. Thus, when we arrived on the scene, an untried leadership, representing a new generation on the faculty, had just taken over. Naturally enough, the prevalent atmosphere was gloomy. Most of the faculty thought that the area was oversupplied with analysts—some of the most enterprising younger people had recently moved to other cities. Relatively little analytic work was being performed, and by national criteria fees were unreasonably low, so that analysts had a strong disincentive to recommend analysis as the treatment of choice. (The ghost of Christmas future!) The whole analytic community seemed to be tilting in the direction of settling for practicing "dynamic psychiatry." Yet we found dissenters who had as much analytic work as they wanted. These exceptions blamed the pessimism and relative helplessness of their colleagues on excessive dependence on the former benefits of university affiliation.

In its desperate search for an institutional mission, Pittsburgh had volunteered to sponsor a group of faculty who had broken away from the Washington Psychoanalytic Institute in order to form a new institution on the model of PINE, to be known as the Washington Association for Psychoanalytic Education (WAPE). The American Psychoanalytic, perversely reluctant to encourage educational innovation, only agreed to allow WAPE to become a new training facility under the aegis of Pittsburgh; this meant that WAPE members had to qualify as Pittsburgh-appointed training analysts. In the manner we found to be characteristic for it, Pittsburgh took this delaying tactic with deadly seriousness and put the WAPE people, many of them very senior training analysts in Washington, through the procedures it normally used for its appointment of new training analysts.

Several WAPE "applicants" were initially deferred; some found the procedure too humiliating to carry through. Shortly before the site visit, the arrangement had completely broken down, and I received several written protests from WAPE members, one including the threat of a lawsuit. Much to my relief, our halfhearted request to review the records of these proceedings was refused by the Pittsburgh leadership on the preposterous ground that the participants had been guaranteed absolute confidentiality. As things turned out, without further ado WAPE simply disintegrated; probably as a result of this disaster, in the two decades since these events, no other attempt to form an institute on the PINE model has taken place.

Our site-visit team agreed that it was imperative for the Pittsburgh faculty to refocus on reaffirming a commitment to psychoanalysis proper and on raising the standards of analytic practice in the community; we wanted to discourage efforts simply to revitalize an analytic training program designed to turn out unneeded practitioners—or, even more uselessly, to engage in colonial ventures in Washington. Although this message was appreciated by one of the Pittsburgh factions (it certainly cemented my good relationship with Judy Schachter), it turned out that it was directly contrary to the aims of the new director; hence, it did not bear immediate fruit.

The contrast between Columbia and Pittsburgh could not have been more striking. Far from being puffed up, our Pittsburgh colleagues were deflated and paralyzed. Their position reminded me of that of the British ruling class after the loss of empire: they were unable to imagine how one could organize a new way of life. The Pittsburgh Institute had greatly overexpanded in the years when surplus graduates could be exported to underserved communities. Blinded by success, the leadership did not foresee that psychiatric residencies were about to abandon their psychoanalytic orientation. In this sense, the fate of Pittsburgh was a harbinger of the troubles that would a decade later overtake American psychoanalysis as a whole. I tried to shout this cautionary tale from the rooftops (see 1984c [chap. 12], 1990c, 1991a [chaps. 12 and 13]), but nobody would listen. What is left in the wake of these vicissitudes? A bloated bureaucracy, deprived of its reason for being.

In 1981 I was sent on the site visit to the Boston Psychoanalytic Society and Institute (BPSI), the first one since the split that had led to the formation of PINE, the rival, "elitist" organization created by my good friend Bob Gardner. Because Bob had kept me abreast of the dissension that produced the split, I was particularly interested in whether and how the truncated parent organization had managed to repair itself. As it turned out, the departure of a significant portion of the senior faculty had provided many worthy younger members with an opportunity to step forward to fill teaching and administrative roles suitable for them. Thus, contrary to the anxieties of those who had fought the establishment of PINE, the split had actually benefited both groups—exactly as Bob Gardner had predicted. But the site-visit report noted that many Boston candidates were only secondarily committed to their psychoanalytic progression or an eventual career in psychoanalysis. As I had understood it, the underlying cause of the PINE defections was unhappiness about the willingness of the parent institution to compromise its commitment to psychoanalysis proper. In this regard, conditions had not changed.

Although the BPSI was free of overt difficulties at the time of the site visit, the paroxysm it had gone through when some of its most respected faculty abandoned ship betrayed its institutional pathology, the secondary role it had accepted in its community vis-à-vis the powerful psychiatric establishment in its prestigious medical schools. These departments provided it with excellent applicants as long as analytic qualifications were regarded as desirable for careers in academic psychiatry, but too many of the candidates whose first commitment was nonanalytic remained marginal participants in psychoanalysis. In times of stringency, such as the present, these people tend to drift away from psychoanalysis; the analytic community as a whole thus begins to confuse psychoanalysis proper and various other models of therapy loosely based on analytic ideas.

The following year, I was sent on the visit to the Institute of the Philadelphia Association for Psychoanalysis, the more traditional, and arguably the more prestigious of the two institutes in that city. For the most part, the site visitors were a reasonably conservative group, yet we were in unanimous agreement about the extremism of the allegedly traditional viewpoint that was the only one represented at this institute; it seemed to most of us as if all of psychoanalysis were being reduced there to the dynamics of castration anxiety. Precisely because the internal workings of this institution were efficient and harmonious, there did not seem to be any remedy available for this unidimensionality.

As this site visit came to an end, I sadly concluded that, despite all my complaints, I was relatively well off in Chicago—there would have been no room for a person of my radical temperament within the Philadelphia Association. Here was the exact converse of the weakness we had found at BPSI: an institute of excessively strong and monolithic conviction—a veritable seminary, training missionaries to propagate a faith.

In 1983 I went on the visit to the North Carolina/Duke training program, a sizable group that had developed in relative isolation. Perhaps this state of affairs came about because its founders (originally from Chicago) were Franz Alexander partisans, alienated from the association, perhaps because many Southerners among the members had the attitude that they were the potential victims of Northern contempt and prejudice. Dealing with these issues made for a very interesting site visit. To my surprise, it actually served to mitigate the pathology of this institute, its self-imposed isolation and insularity.

A few weeks before I rotated off COI, in the spring of 1984, I took part in visiting the Philadelphia Psychoanalytic Institute, another organization that has been something of a stepchild within the American because of the reputation of its crosstown rival, the Philadelphia Association. Because I had no opportunity to participate in the follow-up conferences after this visit, I do not know about its impact.

When my service on COI came to an end, despite the disillusioning realities I had witnessed, I was still so enthusiastic about such work that I asked Shelley Orgel, just elected chairman of the board, to appoint me to another committee, one that was about to begin its work. The Committee on Non-Medical Clinical Training (CNMCT) was organized to monitor the acceptance of nonmedical mental health professionals by our institutes. The membership had by referendum decided to end the medical requirement for eligibility, probably in order to blunt the threat created by the lawsuit brought by a group of hitherto excluded psychologists. After the referendum, the suit was settled amicably. As part of this settlement, the association's subsequent actions vis-à-vis nonmedical applicants were to be subject to review by the federal courts. CNMCT had the task of ensuring that institutes dealt properly with such applications.

Shelley accommodated my request, although with some delay, so that I did not participate in the meetings that decided on a set of guidelines the institutes would have to follow as well as the committee's procedures. As applications to be processed started to arrive, the committee was expanded, and John MacLeod, director of the Cincinnati Institute, was appointed chairman. I joined with the hope of opening doors for applicants of quality; I had always been opposed to the exclusion of nonmedical mental health professionals, so much so that I was the only medical analyst invited to a conference (held at Clark University to commemorate the seventy-fifth anniversary of Freud's 1909 visit), organized by Division 39 of the American Psychological Association to discuss ways and means of setting up psychoanalytic training institutions for psychologists (see 1990c). I was happy to find that almost every member of CNMCT shared my outlook on the issue.

Almost from the start, a power struggle developed between CNMCT and certain institutes (notably Chicago!) about adherence to the guidelines for preparing applications. Far from putting prejudicial obstacles in the way of nonmedical applicants, these institutes were so eager to enroll students that they only went through the motions of assessing educational qualifications, analyzability, personal integrity, or therapeutic talent. When CNMCT deferred applications because of the deficiencies of an institute's procedures, it was accused of second-guessing the judgments of the local evaluators. (There was no guesswork in detecting whether or not serious evaluations had been done.)

A coalition of people opposed to the oversight functions of the Board of Professional Standards raised a hue and cry at board meetings and eventually succeeded in demonizing John MacLeod (the most conscientious of straight shooters!) and reducing the purview of CNMCT to rubber-stamping the applicants' paper credentials. John then resigned, and largely out of loyalty to him, I followed suit. (I also had no wish to be reduced to a rubber stamp.)

During this four-year struggle, I felt I was on the frontline of the engagement that would decide the future standards of psychoanalytic education, for it had become evident that in the future most applicants would come from nonmedical backgrounds, at least as long as a backlog of the formerly ineligible lasted. (These developments have made possible a decade's delay in confronting the actual crisis facing the profession by temporarily extending the usefulness of the bloated training organizations we have erected.) Heedless of the crucial issue of standards, the "states' rights" advocates who wanted to trim the powers of the board used CNMCT as the "elitist" scapegoat to achieve their aim. I know that Arnold Goldberg was one of the leaders of this coalition, and that he enlisted allies from several institutes with long-standing grievances about board policies or decisions, such as BPSI, Southern California, and Columbia.[2] (One tactful site visit will seldom repair the damage of past defeats over major issues!) At any rate, it was a battle worth waging, and reading the applications of more than a hundred would-be analysts provided a fascinating vista of the multitude of therapists of every stripe active in our major cities. A very small number of these even seemed to know what they were doing!

All in all, starting with the work on indexing, I had given the association over twenty years of committee service before I decided I had had enough. I had had the opportunity to make friends with outstanding colleagues of all ages, from those of an older generation, such as Grete Bibring, Mark Kanzer, and Hans Loewald, through contemporaries such as Otto Kernberg, Mort Reiser, and Bob Wallerstein, to younger people like Bob Pyles (recently elected as president of the American) and Bill Meissner (who is the only Jesuit in the association). It had cost a lot of time, sweat, even money, but it really had been worth my while. Never, before my experience on the program committee, had I felt that I was serving as window dressing: one vote out of thirty-eight! It was not a situation I could long endure.

❖ CHAPTER 11 ❖

ON AN OFF-SHORE ISLAND

Not too long ago, an interview with Ernest Wolf appeared in one of the psychoanalytic journals (Hunter 1992). The questioner encouraged Wolf to discuss the emergence of self psychology, including my brief participation in the Kohut circle. Wolf tried to keep his answers polite, but his ambivalence repeatedly seeped through in speculative statements about my putative motives for leaving the group or opposing its scientific positions. According to Ernest, I walked out because I was unwilling to take criticism; he claimed that I rejected Kohut's ideas in order to curry favor with the leaders of American psychoanalysis. For the first time in my life, I wrote a (mildly threatening) letter to the editor who published these misrepresentations[1]; the incident gave a strong impetus to my plan to write these memoirs and to spell out the full complexity of the personal issues that fueled the events Wolf wished to reduce to an incident of pique. I am afraid that, in some ways, my view of this painful story will cast my conduct in a less favorable light than did Wolf's.

Over twenty years ago, when I broke with Kohut, the hostility aroused by my actions was considerably more virulent than were Wolf's recent indiscretions. Some Kohut loyalists did not hesitate to spread the word that I had become psychotic; a psychiatric camp follower of self psychology actually tried to persuade one of my analysands to discontinue treatment with me because of this alleged condition. To be sure, for some years Kohut himself kept hoping for a reconciliation: on his sixty-second birthday, in

May 1975, he wrote to me, nostalgically recalling that I had given the speech explicating his accomplishments at the celebration of his sixtieth. At the same time, he sent us a photographic portrait of himself, affectionately dedicated to Mary and me.[2] In May 1975 he described how he thought about us in terms of "the unfissionable unity of observer and observed. Applied to my image of you, this means that you are my cherished friend . . ." (Cocks 1994, p. 323).

I responded with a polite letter, mentioning among other things that at the end of the year I was planning a Christmas trip to Morocco with my son Paul (who was scheduled to spend the fall semester studying in London). Kohut's inability to differentiate our personalities—the "unfissionable unity" between us he insisted on—was revealed in a letter he sent me that September:

> Your letter was a welcome gift. You are never out of my mind for very long. . . . [My work is] accompanied with a number of free associations concerning people who are important to me—and you have often appeared among them. . . . Your return to Morocco must be a great adventure for you. I can be empathic with you—and with your need to protect yourself by the presence of your son. I will never forget my first return to Vienna after the war—without the presence of Betty and Tom my playing with psychological fire might well have led into chaos. [Cocks 1994, pp. 324–325]

Kohut's vulnerability was truly pitiful.

(In 1975, hostilities on its southern border forced me to postpone a return to Morocco; later, when I did revisit Tangier, I reveled in staying at the splendid Hotel El Minzah—more fitting for film stars visiting Malcolm Forbes than for elderly psychoanalysts—and was surprised at how much smaller everything looked than it had to a child. It was a great pleasure to be able to identify some of the familiar vistas as the motifs of celebrated paintings by Delacroix and Matisse. Chaos? Psychological fire? *Au contraire*, as we used to say at the Lycée.)

When in 1977 Kohut published his second book, *The Restoration of the Self*, he sent us a copy, once again nostalgically dedicated to Mary and me. This gesture elicited the last communication I sent Heinz (see Cocks 1994, p. 348), a letter heavy with irony but couched in polite phrases of regret.[3] Between the lines, I was accusing him of stealing some of my ideas and then acting vengeful toward me. (In the volume of his correspondence recently published, the editor has included my letter as if it had been a tribute, although he notes that I claim it was ironic.)

I was less indirect in writing to Heinz that I was out of sympathy with most of his latest ideas, thereby inviting even more intense bitterness on his part. Shortly after this interchange, while I was away for a lengthy vacation, one of my former analysands had to face a family crisis and tried to get in touch with me to talk it over. When she was unable to reach me, she recalled that, some years before, I had expressed a positive opinion of Kohut, so she contacted him instead. He recommended that she discuss the problem in greater detail, but *not* with me (allegedly because I was unsuited for such mundane work), and he referred her to one of his disciples. I learned about all this from the couch, for (by sheer coincidence) one of my then current analysands was the therapist of the person whose difficulty caused the crisis for my former patient; the full story was related by one to the other in a professional context.

Early in 1979 Kohut underwent a coronary bypass operation. Afterward, I heard from two independent sources that, in a drug-induced delirium during his postsurgical recovery, he had been talking about me. (What he was alleged to have said so impressed hospital personnel that some could not resist spreading the story. One young physician recounted it to his therapist, who chose to share it with me. And so on.) I do not think it would be proper further to disseminate the specifics of statements made in a twilight state; one must even allow for potential distortions introduced into such reports through oral transmission. But there can be no doubt that Kohut was talking about our relationship during this crisis in his life. It was a remarkable and melancholy indication of his frustrated longings that I was on Kohut's mind at all, as he hovered on the brink of extinction, five years after I abandoned him.

While my relations with some self psychologists were deteriorating, other members of the group remained on friendly terms with me—most of all Mike Gunther, who understood precisely what my reasons for leaving Kohut had been. Because he and I have remained close, he was soon rejected by the most doctrinaire in the Kohut circle. This was the first instance of a pattern that became almost standard in later years: colleagues who became (or remained) my friends were strongly mistrusted by most self psychologists. By contrast, despite his role in Kohut's inner circle, to the end of his life Mike Basch never allowed my dealings with others to alter his relationship with me in any way.

Paul Tolpin also tried for a considerable period to transcend the state of my relations with more passionate Kohutians, including his wife, Marian. She never got past the group's sense of grievance against me, even though

I told Paul that the difficulty that led to my defection was entirely between Heinz and me and involved nobody else. Consequently, our old friendship with the Tolpins simply withered on the vine, albeit without untoward incidents. Perhaps it was most significant that Ernie Wolf tried for some time to maintain our friendship, although it was very difficult for him to swallow my increasingly explicit disagreements with Kohut. When I protested the statements he made about me in the 1992 interview, the person who recorded it tried to appease me by recounting that, as he was telling the story of our broken relationship, Ernest still could not help crying.

Perhaps the first indication that Wolf and I would be unable to overcome the effects of professional disagreements was a conversation we had, some time in 1975, about his increasing use of the term *the self*. Ernest acknowledged that he did not know what it means, because as of then Kohut had failed to define this term, so I asked him how he could justify basing an entire theoretical system upon such a vague idea. He looked at me with astonishment, perhaps even indignation. "Do you expect us to stop teaching on that account?" he cried. I said yes, I did. I was already planning a book of my own (the future *Beyond Interpretation*) that was to be centered on the concept of *self-organization*. My difficult struggle to explicate that process in precise terms made me feel indignant that people could pretend to promulgate theories when they knew that they could not make explicit what they were talking about.

A few months after that interchange, Ernest wrote to me on behalf of the Kohut group, asking me what I thought might be the most appropriate way for them to make some formal acknowledgment of my role in initiating and organizing their effort to produce a casebook (Goldberg 1978). This request was a piece of *politesse* with Heinz's fingerprints all over it, and I was determined to remain uncompromising in my disapproval of the use he was making of his followers, that of simply echoing his ideas. I replied, also by letter, insisting that I did not wish to be mentioned at all in connection with an enterprise so different from what I had in mind in organizing the study group. I added that I expected Ernest to grasp that I felt that, in seizing my project and deviating from its scientific aims, the group had kidnapped and murdered this "child of my hopes"; this was something I would not forgive.[4] I suppose a better way to view all this is that I could not forgive Wolf for being uncritically admiring of Heinz.

In the meantime, Ernest and I had been collaborating on a project to edit a volume of interdisciplinary essays for the Johns Hopkins University Press. Because ultimately nothing came of this, I can no longer reconstruct our full list of contributors or their exact topics. When the project collapsed, I salvaged a 135-page portion, about half of the original, by arranging with George Pollock to have it published, mostly as a special section in the 1978 *Annual*, under the title "Some Contributions of Psychoanalysis to a Science of Man." This included chapters on social science by Mark Gehrie and religion by William Meissner, and one by me on the Humanities (1978a,b); in addition, this volume of the *Annual* included a Joseph Lichtenberg essay on biography that I also brought to it from the Hopkins disaster.[5] Incidentally, I had to work hard to overcome the hesitations of Meissner, an active priest, to write about religion and psychoanalysis; subsequently, he has written more than one book in that interdisciplinary area (e.g., Meissner 1989). As for Joe Lichtenberg, he and Wolf had been medical school classmates, and I believe it is through Ernest that he became interested in Kohut's work. Conversely, it was through him that Wolf learned of the opportunity for the interdisciplinary project at Hopkins. In view of my subsequent estrangement from Wolf, Joe's ability over the years to remain friendly with both of us has been quite a feat.

By the time our editor at Hopkins sent us his readers' reports on the manuscript, my relationship with Wolf had become hollow. Ernest had already found his niche as a self-psychological elder statesman; people who did not know his history often assumed, on the basis of his chronological age, that he had much more analytic experience than in fact he had. As I then felt it, Wolf assumed a sententious air and a smug attitude that I had never seen in him before; partly because it proved that I had misperceived Ernest, I found this intensely irritating. He also began to talk a great deal about his interrupted analytic experience with Max Gitelson, whom he criticized mercilessly for an alleged lack of empathy (see Hunter 1994, pp. 159–164). The specifics Wolf cited seemed to me to have been appropriate analytic efforts to address ego-syntonic characterological attributes such as those I saw in Ernest's overt behavior around 1975; consequently, I felt that he was calumniating an excellent person who could not defend himself any more. In the 1976 *Annual*, Wolf published an article that I read as an effort to proscribe any analytic intervention that an analysand might dislike. I thought Ernest was propagating nonsense, and it became increasingly difficult to refrain from telling him so. Of course, my growing intolerance of Wolf's behavior was basically a response to his progressive unwillingness to take my psychoanalytic ideas seriously and to his total loyalty to Kohut. I had constructed a golem and it was no longer obeying me. I suppose it served me right.

The readers at the Hopkins Press were extremely critical of our manuscript; they felt that the quality of the various contributions was uneven and the tone of some chapters was self-congratulatory and lacking in self-critical rigor. I took this critique very much to heart; as I reread the book, I became convinced of the validity of the readers' judgment. Through Joe Lichtenberg, Wolf made discreet inquiries in Baltimore, and he reported that propsychoanalytic forces were no longer in charge at the Johns Hopkins Press. I thought that it was not worth our while to preach to the converted; books have to be persuasive for readers who do not have a bias in their favor. I thought out a plan designed to meet the criticisms of our first draft—a reorganization of the volume by leaving out the chapters to which those criticisms were most applicable, including two by Ernest Wolf. (It was an uncanny reprise of the need to eliminate two pieces by Pollock from the book of Freudiana.)

When I told Ernest how I thought we could salvage the book, he was adamant in his refusal to accept my plan—as I read his recollections of the incident (Hunter 1994, pp. 174–175) to him my proposal meant that I did not want him to be senior editor of the volume. This reading of my motives was manifestly absurd—my proposal would not have deprived Ernest of his agreed-upon seniority. Moreover, he himself acknowledges that through this struggle he was enacting some "narcissistic" wish. He had no concrete counterproposal to make about what we might do; it appeared to me that he was content instead to vilify the readers for "antipsychoanalytic bias." I was angered by his insistence on the inclusion of his contributions even if that would mean rejection of the entire volume, and I let Ernest know in no uncertain terms that I was sick of such egocentricity. (I listed several examples of similar behavior on his part in the past, such as his reusing our joint scholarly findings without crediting me.) For quite a while he listened with a hangdog expression; finally, he said he had had enough. The Hopkins project was kaput, and so was our friendship.

I finally realized that the time had come to meet the challenge of elaborating my ideas without collaborators. After fifteen years of full-time psychoanalytic practice, I finally felt that I had enough clinical experience to begin writing papers about various transference constellations and their psychoanalytic management. I began this new era in my career as an author with an essay (1975a) on the several possible meanings of the idealization of the analyst when this is encountered in practice; this was the first of my many efforts to integrate my clinical experience, traditional psychoanalytic hypotheses, and other analysts' novel observational findings (such as those of Kohut) in an ecumenical manner. When I organized the study group of Kohut's followers, I had the illusion that its work could go in this direction, in open-ended fashion.

My paper on idealization was surprisingly well received; it was included in a selection of recent contributions to the *Journal of the American Psychoanalytic Association* (Blum 1981), published in French translation under the aegis of Serge Lebovici, then president of the International Association. I followed that paper with one (1977a) on the management of what I dubbed "archaic transferences," the phenomena Kohut first named as manifestations of a "grandiose" (or "narcissistic") self; here I began explicitly to disagree with Heinz's developmental postulates. I also published clinical reports (1972a and 1979d) about the analytic treatment of two men who possessed genius; the vicissitudes of the fragile self-esteem of these individuals also cast doubt on the adequacy of Kohut's developmental schema.

I do not mean that I had any quarrel with Kohut's clinical observations (what he called [Kohut 1971] the "idealizing" and "mirror" transferences); I was objecting to his assumption that these transferences in adulthood reproduce childhood conditions that represent expectable (or normal) development. I was even more skeptical about the temporal order Kohut assigned to this putative sequence of infantile emotional positions—the arbitrary assumption that idealizing the caretakers presupposed some mastery of infantile grandiosity. Kohut never attempted to buttress these developmental propositions through the presentation of evidence of any kind.

Kohut's group published the casebook, *The Psychology of the Self*, in 1978, more or less contemporaneously with the appearance of an interesting volume on termination (Firestein 1978) that contained a comparable number of case reports about analyses performed by candidates at the New York Psychoanalytic Institute. This was the summer I attended a CAPS meeting in Aspen, and it was there that I read both works and conceived the idea of writing an essay comparing the results of the contrasting modes of doing analysis advocated in them. The paper I produced called out a plague on both houses for ignoring the import of each other's cogent findings and therefore being content with needlessly incomplete analyses. I submitted this to the *Journal of the American*, and it was duly accepted for publication. Harold Blum then proposed that, instead of publishing it as a regular article, my contribution be used as an essay in the book section. I no longer remember how this plan came to Goldberg's attention (perhaps I never did learn that); at any rate, he wrote Blum a strongly worded letter of protest, claiming that it would be unfair to let me review the casebook because of my quarrel with its authors. When Mike Gunther, who had read my paper, heard about his, he told Goldberg that the casebook was not likely to receive a review in the *Journal* more accepting of Kohut's contributions than was mine. Needless to say, neither Blum nor I cared much about how my paper was labeled, and it was published as a regular article (1980a). As I recall, Mike's prediction about the official review of the book did come true (see Moore 1981).

Thus, by the later 1970s, the self psychology movement looked upon me as one of its more dangerous opponents. At the same time, the more conservative analysts in Chicago knew full well that, in many ways, my views were quite radical—in this period, as usual, I frequently presented papers to the Chicago society, so that few colleagues remained uninformed about where I stood.[6] I remained at peace with the Pollock regime only by the expedient of staying out of institute affairs. All in all, my position in Chicago was rather isolated; because my office was in a lakefront building, I began to say that I was not part of the Chicago analytic community, because I practiced on an off-shore island.

Of course, this was hyperbole in more ways than one. There were a number of well-regarded analysts who did everything in their power to prevent the dissolution of the Chicago psychoanalytic community into hostile ideological factions, and some among them viewed the hierarchical model I had proposed as the conceptual tool that might best serve their ecumenical aims. The most direct effort to open channels of communication among serious scholars of varying views was initiated by Leo Sadow. He organized a new discussion group bringing together himself, Mike Gunther, George Klumpner, Nate Schlessinger, and me (a nonideological group of friends since our days at the U. of C.) with three nondogmatic self psychologists: Mike Basch, Paul Tolpin, and David Terman.

David was considerably younger than anyone else in the group; he had been in supervision with me when he was a resident at Michael Reese. Everyone had high regard for his intellect and talents. When I gave the course on Kohut's work at the Institute, it was David I asked to cover for me when I was absent. Ernest Wolf, David, and I had written a collaborative paper (1972c) in which adolescence is understood as a transformation of the self-organization; I persuaded George Pollock to accept this in lieu of requiring Terman to produce a graduation paper for the Institute, and later David certainly proved that our confidence in his capacity to make creative contributions was not misplaced. In the next several years, he presented several pioneering papers that carried a psychology of the self beyond where Kohut had then taken it, into the sphere of the oedipal situation. Unfortunately, David did not publish these until much later (Terman 1976, 1984/85; see also Robbins 1977). I thought he was immobilized by the fact that Kohut coldly repudiated David's ideas when he presented them at the Chicago Society. Of course, only a couple of years after that, Kohut endorsed rather similar concepts—without ever mentioning Terman's contributions.

The new discussion group functioned effectively for some time; in that private forum, at least, the participants reached a fair degree of consensus. (Yet, in public, few people had the courage to support any of my ideas.) In 1979, when my *Beyond Interpretation* appeared, the group went over it in great detail, and I believe this left some mark on the subsequent work of many participants. Shortly thereafter, however, Paul Tolpin discontinued his attendance; I have always thought that the tension between the positions he endorsed in our discussions and what he must have espoused in Marian's presence made him too uncomfortable. For more than fifteen years now, Paul and I have seldom encountered each other, but whenever we have had a brief chance to talk, I have expressed regret about our lost friendship, and Paul has made similar remarks, albeit never spontaneously.

David Terman's participation came to an end not long after Tolpin's. Although he became ever more committed to a radical brand of self psychology, I suspect he did not drop out because of any scientific disagreement but because his feelings about me turned more and more venomous. I have no doubt that the decisive turning point was my rupture with Wolf, because over the years David became increasingly attached to Ernie. Perhaps Terman also became uncomfortable because I kept urging him to publish the paper that Kohut had criticized. Moreover, I should not have allowed David to confide certain private matters to me; I compounded this error by responding, thereby increasing the chances of provoking a transference reaction. But these conjectures may be completely baseless—it is perhaps simply too difficult for me to admit that anyone could throw me over for the sake of Ernest Wolf.

The whole matter is a good illustration of what I resented about the way in which many local colleagues dealt with me. The situation came to a head in September 1980, when I presented a paper on "Transference, Fantasy, and Object Relations" (chap. 9 in 1981a) at the Chicago Society; Leo Sadow and David Terman were the formal discussants. Leo's remarks took my work very seriously and tried to place it appropriately within the intellectual history of psychoanalysis—I could not have asked for anything better.

David began his discussion with a string of personal compliments; he went on to say, at some length, that my paper missed the boat because it did not take up certain Kohutian concepts. Mike Basch intervened from the floor to point out that Terman had misunderstood the thrust of my argument; Mike explained that the ideas Terman missed in the paper had no bearing on its actual thesis. (My main point was that the analytic transference does not reflect the actual nature of early object relations but that of the childhood fantasies woven around them. Yet Terman had a point in calling attention to my disagreement with Kohut, albeit he was wrong about specific details: by 1980, most self psychologists dealt with transference phenomena as if they were homologues of early childhood transactions; my paper refuted that view.)

I was considerably stirred up by the lively discussion that followed, so much so that I felt I had reached the limit of my integrative capacity. I therefore asked the president to call a halt after the next intervention, because I could handle no more. He refused to honor my request because the audience was enjoying the controversy. I felt like an animal in a Roman arena, about to be sacrificed to the sadistic desires of the crowd. When it was time for me to respond to everything that had been said, I focused on underscoring the consensus among Basch, Sadow, and myself. Someone had commented on one of the clinical vignettes in my paper in a manner that called for an assessment of the actual personality of my patient's mother; I was casting about for an illuminating parallel for the patient's childhood experience. In my overstimulated state, in what amounted to a loss of intellectual control, I found myself saying that its ambience reminded me of my reaction to David Terman's discussion—that it was full of fatuous praise and irrelevance. After that, peaceful dealings between David and me were no longer possible.

I understand that, even years later, Terman complained about my cruelty in publicly humiliating him like that. He had a point; it would have been much better to let him have it in private, even though he had started this war. Leo later told me that David had shown him his discussion in advance of the meeting, and that he had advised David that its tone was unacceptably hostile. The fact that Terman did not send me an advance copy could only mean that he wanted his attack to achieve surprise, which it did.

Several years later, I reconfirmed that the cruel intention did emanate from David. Through the grapevine, I heard that he had presented something at a national meeting that elicited a hostile reception. Shortly thereafter, I was waiting for Mary in the crowded lobby at Orchestra Hall and found myself face to face with Terman. With malice aforethought, I asked him how his presentation had gone. David said it had gone well, but he was unhappy because he had let a hostile discussant get under his skin. In my avuncular manner of old, I said, "David, one should never be embarrassed, however one reacts to an attack. One should only be ashamed about giving hostile discussions!" Terman blushed crimson, and he offered to shake hands. But I hear from reliable informants that he hates me more than ever.

The desertion of two self psychologists almost entirely eliminated controversy within our discussion group. I stopped attending it after the anti-Pollock revolution, when I no longer felt any desire to preserve bridges to the local analytic world. It was quite disturbing to me that Mike Basch (who, in any public forum, was a loyal follower of Kohut) and Nate Schlessinger (who has shunned anything smacking of dissent from the mainstream) could, in private discussion, reach consensus with me, although I never moderated my radical views in the group. I suppose it is largely because to me this inconsistency increasingly appeared to constitute insincere political hedging on their part that I did not keep up a personal relationship with either man after I left the group. In my seventh decade, I felt that I could require people, if they wished to qualify as my friends, to make public their actual convictions.

In addition to the group organized by Leo, I was presented with another link to the local psychoanalytic world through my growing friendship with George Moraitis. George is a Greek émigré with whom my relationship truly blossomed when he graduated from the Institute. We are about the same age, and it was a bit difficult at first to manage our feelings about our different levels of psychoanalytic experience. As a candidate, George kept his own counsel; although he participated in the continuous case seminar I cotaught with Kligerman, I had no idea about how imaginative and clear-thinking he can be. The fact that he is a delightful, sweet, and generous person was, of course, evident from the first.

As soon as he qualified as an analyst, George organized two interdisciplinary seminars bringing together interested colleagues and local academicians. One of these focused on the social sciences, the other on the humanities, with special reference to literature. George asked me to take part in both, but I persevered only with the one on literature, largely because the other was so well attended that its sheer size diluted one's opportunity to participate. (Nonetheless, it was there I encountered Arnold Wilson, with whom I have recently coedited a book on the concept of hierarchies in psychoanalytic theory [1993c]. When we met, Wilson was a graduate student in human development at the U. of C. One of his professors, Bertram Cohler, was then a candidate at the institute and acted as George's coleader at the social science seminar. Arnold later moved to New York where he has had a successful academic career at the New School and Seton Hall University and psychoanalytic training at the Columbia Institute. Bert Cohler was later my son's dissertation advisor at the U. of C. [see P. Gedo 1988]. We have all kept up with each other.)

The humanities seminar was rather extraordinary because of the quality of many participants—so good that I arranged for Mary to attend, although she remained the only art historian in the group. George's academic coleader, Herman Sinaiko, was an expert on both Hellenic and Chinese philosophy. When the eminent Shakespearean scholar David Bevington also took part, the level of our discussions was at its highest. (This seminar furnished us with much of the talent pool for the interdisciplinary part of the program at the fiftieth anniversary celebration of the society.[7])

George Moraitis is the closest friend I have made in the last twenty years—both a like-minded colleague and a link to my European past. Organizationally, I may have retreated to an off-shore island (à la Chiang Kai-shek?!), but in George, Leo Sadow, Mike Gunther, and George Klumpner I had a phalanx of loyal friends who kept me within hailing distance of the rest of the Chicago analytic community. Ernest Wolf got it wrong when he claimed that I trimmed my scientific views to suit the preferences of those in control of American psychoanalysis, but I did have strong ties to people Pollock's minions called "John Gedo's Eastern friends"; as I have described, they helped me to participate in the affairs of the national organization. At the very least, those activities made me less likely to entangle myself in struggles against Pollock's rule; by making me better known in other localities, they brought me referrals, speaking engagements, and potential readers for my publications. Eventually, however, my dissenting scientific views made me persona non grata in the more conservative centers of psychoanalysis, whatever organizational role I undertook. It is a measure of the decay of the profession that most members no longer wish to hear views different from their own.

❖ CHAPTER 12 ❖

ON THE RIGHT TO A LIFE

When we were in Sydney last year, the Australian Psychoanalytical Society asked me to give a colloquium about my personal involvement with Heinz Kohut and the genesis of the self psychology movement. I made no explicit preparations for this event; I wished to respond spontaneously to the mood of the audience. It so happened that many Australian colleagues were concerned about the spread of a wild version of self psychology in the local mental health community, so that the majority at the meeting seemed to be rather hostile to Kohut. In this ambience, I found myself trying to do justice to my old teacher—as he would have said, by being as empathic as possible in describing his actions, and by correcting caricatural misrepresentations of his scientific views. For the first time in two decades, I was free of the sense of grievance that had made it so difficult for me to discuss the culmination of my relationship with Heinz—in some ways, the turning point of my professional life. I had only very recently written an account of our rupture for these memoirs that contained much too much spleen and not enough nostalgia. In Sydney, I felt I had found the right tone for recounting that lamentable history.

I was finally able to acknowledge that what had made an already difficult relationship unbearable for me was a change in Heinz's personality in reaction to the diagnosis of a potentially fatal illness. In 1971 he was found to be suffering from a chronic lymphoma. When I visited him at the time at the University of Chicago hospital, I perceived that Heinz was unable to remain calm in face of his mortality; his illness appeared to have enraged him. He emitted a stream of bitter accusations against a variety of culprits by whom he felt injured, principally the internist who, upon discovering his patient's rock-hard, enlarged spleen, simply told Heinz his conclusion that he had a serious malignancy. Kohut was fulminating against the physician's lack of empathy, although the latter's diagnosis had been confirmed by the specialists Heinz consulted at the university. The intensity of his grievance alarmed me, but not half so much as did his next communication. He proceeded to tell me that he thought his malignancy had been caused by his exposure, thirty years earlier, to putative radiation leaks from Enrico Fermi's experiments to achieve atomic fission, under the grandstands at the U. of C.'s Stagg Field. Beyond the lexical content of this fantasy, in Kohut's tone I heard a paranoid conviction of having been victimized; the thought that Heinz was becoming unraveled made me dizzy with anxiety.[1]

While I was trying to calm down, Kohut's mood changed, and he began to talk about our relationship and how much my visit to the hospital meant to him. In a voice trembling with emotion, he said, "I *knew* you would come!" I was horrified; Heinz was reading into my behavior an indication of personal attachment that was entirely fantastic, pure wish fulfillment. In "visiting the sick," I was merely carrying out the obligations of any civilized relationship. I did not know which would be worse, to let Heinz believe that he was right about my feelings or to outdo his internist in stating the bitter truth, without pity. I discovered soon enough that I had no choice in the matter. Without premeditation, I found myself saying, "Heinz, it is not like that at all. You know that, for a person like me, it is unthinkable not to pay a visit when anyone he knows is in the hospital." After that, neither of us knew what to say.

No, I had never loved him (to paraphrase King Philip's poignant lament in Verdi's *Don Carlo*), and I found his transference expectation that I reciprocate his attachment to me utterly unacceptable. The intensity of my need to rebuff Heinz was doubtless a function of my past difficulties in liberating myself from the suffocating embrace of my family, especially my mother. I was more or less aware that I was repeating the drama of my adolescence—the struggle for independence that had been delayed not only by the multiple dislocations of our emigration but also by my need to "make reparation" to vulnerable parents.[2] Yet I also knew that in keeping Kohut at arm's length, I was mastering "separation guilt"[3]—in Arnold Modell's lovely phrase, I was asserting my "right to a life." I believe that for me this was the emotional prerequisite of doing original scientific work without enlisting collaborators—if you will, to awaken to my own potentialities.

At the same time, there had always been many reasons for reservations about Heinz Kohut, even on purely social grounds. After he became ill, Heinz began to have great difficulty in behaving in a manner that could have elicited anyone's affection. To illustrate, only a few months after the terrible scene I have recounted, Kohut was visited by a young admirer from Germany, the journalist Tilmann Moser. For some reason, he decided to introduce Moser to some of his Chicago adherents in the context of a formal dinner party, at home. There were ten or twelve persons present, among them Constance and Arnold Goldberg, Mary and myself, and Kohut's son Tom, who at the time was a senior in college. Heinz, as usual, dominated the table talk, but Tom continually challenged him in an unpleasantly argumentative manner. To everyone's astonishment, Heinz never missed an opportunity to reply in kind, so that the whole evening constituted compulsory attendance at an oedipal duel. On the way down in the elevator, Moser reproachfully confronted Goldberg: "How can you put up with him?," he cried.[4] Arnold's reply was unforgettable. "Only because he is a living national treasure," he said.

Some years earlier, I might have agreed with Arnold; by the winter of 1971–72, I no longer believed that Heinz deserved indulgence because he would make further contributions of value to psychoanalysis. Although I still labored under the illusion that Kohut and I had a consensus about clinical matters, around 1970 I began to question the coherence of his theoretical position. I found it inexplicable that he insisted on trying to force his clinical findings into the metapsychological framework proposed by Hartmann. One of the principal conclusions Goldberg and I reached in preparing *Models of the Mind* was that Kohut's clinical discoveries transcended Hartmann's paradigm. Because he did not seem able to listen to such objections, I began to look upon Heinz as a superannuated leader of the previous generation, one about to be passed by because of the emergence of newer ideas. And since the discovery of his lymphoma and his increasingly egocentric behavior in response to illness, I also regarded him as a figure of pathos.

At the same time, I could not forget that he had supported me when nobody else would, and I do not believe in deserting a person in his time of troubles. Of course, the more openly demanding he became, the more I felt I had repaid my debt to him. In that regard, I had actually paid the largest installment several years previously. An early draft of *Models of the Mind* contained a conceptual proposal for a structural definition of *self*—the kernel of my subsequent theoretical work in psychoanalysis.[5] Heinz kindly agreed to comment on our manuscript; he responded to our work with a lengthy and detailed letter, generally encouraging and constructive in its thoughtful criticism.[6] He went on to ask that we eliminate the passage about the self concept, on the ground that this was his intellectual domain, although he had never defined what he meant by the word *self*.

Needless to say, I discussed the matter with Arnold, who agreed that Kohut's demand was outrageous.[7] Nonetheless, Goldberg felt that we had to comply with Heinz's demand; he reasoned that, even though the conceptualization in question was original with me, because Arnold had sat in on a recent course offered by Kohut where the latter's thoughts about a "psychology of the self" had been discussed, we could not deny the possibility that the idea originated with Heinz. (Obviously, it made no difference to Arnold whether he first heard this idea from me or from Kohut.) Although I felt that I was going to be robbed of the most important psychoanalytic innovation I was ever likely to make, I accepted the necessity for this sacrifice because of my sense of obligation for Kohut's past help. (Speak of "reparation.") Thereafter, I no longer felt that I owed Heinz much of a debt.

Actually, as it turned out, Kohut did not appropriate my idea, the purport of which he never did grasp—he merely laid claim to a label. In my judgment, by calling his contribution "the psychology of the self,"[8] Heinz was in fact *mis*labeling his own work, which is narrowly focused on those archaic object relations he came to call "self-selfobject" transactions: Kohut eventually called into question the very notion of the self-in-isolation. In contrast, the idea I have consistently espoused, for close to thirty years,[9] is that the focus of psychoanalytic theory should be the patterning of the basic structure of mind (that is, of the stable hierarchy of motivations that characterize each individual). This is the process I have labeled *self-organization*.

If Kohut's claim about ownership of the *self* concept sounds like the enactment of one of the narcissistic transferences he had described, such behavior merely confirmed a more valid claim he often made in my presence, that his clinical discoveries were the result of introspective efforts. (He was not above reminding one that, before him, only Freud could make such a statement.) Of course, he did try to compensate me for complying with his emotional requirements—with frequent analytic referrals, with praise that often verged on flattery, with introductions to Anna Freud or Marianne Kris, with indiscreet gossip about analytic luminaries and startling confidences about his childhood deprivations. (For some time, I had the fantasy that such confidences signified that Heinz wanted me to become his official biographer. I now think this was a defensive distortion on my part, a symptom of my reluctance to acknowledge that I had imprudently allowed an overtly needy person to develop an archaic transference toward me.[10])

Mary has been no more tolerant of misconduct than I—and with Heinz in particular, she did not have a debt to discharge. When Kohut's telephone call awakened her at 1:30 in the morning, she demanded to know the meaning of such an act of inconsideration. Heinz stammered that an electrical storm must have knocked out his clock; he thought it was "only" 11:30. Mary made it clear that she could not accept phone calls at that hour either. (It did not then occur to me that Heinz may have been intoxicated. Whenever I spent an evening with him, Heinz consumed prodigious quantities of wine, but he seemed well able to hold his liquor.) Mary's opinions of people weigh very heavily with me, and her coolness to Kohut buttressed my growing unwillingness to treat him as Arnold's "living national treasure."

From another point of view, Heinz actually began to seem psychologically impaired even before his illness was formally diagnosed. I noticed this when he attended my CAPS group, in the spring of 1970. A few weeks before this event, he asked me whether we could travel to and from Princeton together. I told him that I would be pleased to do so, but that on my way home I planned to go to the Metropolitan Museum of Art, to see a special exhibition of medieval French artifacts.[11] Heinz said that he would be very interested in such an exhibition, and we made the arrangements to go together. For some reason, Kohut was in a foul mood from the first; when, shortly after takeoff, I went to the washroom, he sarcastically asserted that air travel seemed to make me anxious. I knew better than to engage in any discussion about that, but it is not the sort of gratuitous insult I am likely to forgive. But much worse was to come; when we entered the exhibit at the Met, I made some enthusiastic comments about the ivories and enamels in the first display case—remarks that betrayed a modicum of knowledge about thirteenth-century France. About a minute later, Heinz insisted that we leave. I am sure that he really did not feel well, but I believe that an inability to tolerate that he knew less about the Gothic era than I did contributed to his malaise. And it never occurred to him that I might want to stay at the museum by myself. That was our nadir, but thenceforth it was not to be inconsistent with Kohut's general behavior.

In ordinary circumstances, Heinz started to make others feel at a disadvantage. When he discovered that neither Mary nor I knew enough German to follow him, he delighted in reciting long passages of German poetry in our presence. I once sent him a gift of Guy Sajer's *The Forgotten Soldier* (1971), an autobiographical account of the war experiences of an Alsatian volunteer in the German army. Heinz had often held forth on the necessity of empathizing with those whose positions are distasteful to us; I thought Sajer's account of his youthful illusions and their catastrophic consequences opened a rare avenue of insight into the mentality of Hitler's dupes. Kohut did not fail to give me his reactions to the present I had sent him; he rudely informed me that he thought the book was awful—he could not understand how I could have concluded that it was worth reading. It was a display of temper about my temerity in appreciating a work he did not like. It was incidents of this kind that convinced me that Heinz needed me to be his alter ego.

Even clearer evidence for this conclusion was provided when *Contemporary Psychology*, the journal of reviews published by the American Psychological Association, assigned Heinz's magnum opus, *The Analysis of the Self*, to a quirky reviewer who seriously misread the main thrust of the book (Apfelbaum 1972). His review was contemptuous and assaulted Kohut for allegedly eliminating consideration of the superego from clinical psychoanalysis. Heinz showed me this offensive piece and, when he heard what I thought about it, he began to emit an endless series of rhetorical questions seemingly addressed to Heaven, asking whether anything could be done about this misadventure. ("Who will rid me of this nettlesome reviewer?"[12]) Clearly, he was expecting me to intervene. I told him that I was confident that the journal would print a correction if I wrote one; our Chicago colleague, Phil Holzman, was on the editorial board and could serve as our go-between.

Heinz eagerly embraced my offer, and I wrote a letter to the editor critical of the inappropriate focus of the review as well as its censorious tone. Phil Holzman kindly transmitted this to the journal; to reassure Heinz, I sent him a copy. A few days later, Kohut returned my manuscript, covered with the corrections, additions, and deletions he insistently wanted me to make. I called him to say that it was too late to change the letter, because I had already sent it. I thought I was thereby making it clear that I did not wish to sign a letter composed by someone else. I do not know whether Heinz understood my meaning, but he simply went on to disprove my absurd contention that it was too late to make the suggested changes. A short phone call to Phil Holzman was obviously sufficient to arrange it all. I complied with what Heinz wanted, but I had reached the end of my tether.[13]

This anecdote illustrates how desperately Kohut needed to obtain the "self-selfobject relationship" he wanted from me. From my viewpoint, he wanted to rob me of my boundaries, and I was determined never to let that happen again. Contrast the story of the protested review with an incident that occurred four years earlier, in October 1969, when Kohut delivered the "Laudation" for Alexander Mitscherlich, that year's recipient of the Peace Prize at the Frankfurt Book Fair. This was a major cultural event, telecast throughout Europe, and Heinz was rightly very excited about the opportunity.[14] Before he left for Frankfurt, he sent me a copy of his speech, which he had written in German. I surmised that he would want to publish an English translation, and it occurred to me that to present him with one on his return would constitute a nice birthday gift. As usual when confronted with German texts, I turned to Ernie Wolf for help. He was very eager indeed to use this opportunity to make contact with Kohut and promptly produced a literal translation of the manuscript. I then rewrote the text with some care, producing what I thought was an English equivalent of Kohut's elegant but old-fashioned German.

When we sent this translation to Heinz, he was manifestly grateful. Incidentally, this transaction gave Wolf his entree into Kohut's circle.[15] Predictably, Kohut was not satisfied with our version, and he took the time to make his own translation of the speech. (In my judgment, his English version did not read well; its Teutonic awkwardness was characteristic of Heinz's prose.) There is no question that Kohut had every right to safeguard *his* boundaries in this manner—what was remarkable was not his preference for speaking in his own voice but his need to let me know, in a manner that once again verged on rudeness, that my effort was not good enough. I was unable to suppress my individuality sufficiently to qualify as his alter ego.

Yet, at this early date, I did not really take offense about this imbroglio. As I have mentioned, a few years later I asked Kohut to contribute a chapter to the volume of Freudiana Pollock and I were collecting. I wanted him to elaborate on a statement he had made at a public meeting about the significance of Freud's attachment to Wilhelm Fliess.[16] Although he was initially reluctant, Heinz yielded to combined pressure from George (Pollock had clout because he had arranged to pay Kohut a scientific subsidy out of Institute research funds) and entreaties from me. Our flexible editorial policy permitted him to produce a lengthy if rambling essay, one focus of which concerned what he called "the transference of creativity." His primary example was Freud, whose need for Fliess Heinz attributed to the stress of engaging in a great scientific breakthrough. He postulated that this supreme effort required the buttressing provided by a fantasy of merger with a messianic character such as Fliess (Kohut 1976).

In retrospect, I believe that Kohut's thesis was more applicable to his own creative efforts than to those of Freud, who was, in my judgment, seldom lacking in self-confidence. Tom Kohut told one biographer that both he and his mother thought that Kohut's celebrated case report, "The Two Analyses of Mr. Z" was autobiography—specifically, that while he was communicating his main discoveries he engaged in systematic self-analysis, presumably described in his paper as the second analysis of Mr. Z.[17] Beyond the congruence of historical details, I also find their interpretation convincing because it conforms to Kohut's thesis about the circumstances that produce a transference of creativity. To put this another way, I played the role in Heinz's mental life that he attributed to Fliess in that of Freud. The passages from his last letter to me that I have already quoted certainly fall into place as evidence for this conclusion.[18]

As an alter ego for Kohut, I was not expected to be messianic; I am confident that he relied on me not for certitude but its opposite: for good judgment in scientific matters—precisely as he relied on his wife for common sense in matters of everyday life. After I turned my back on him, Heinz (and some of his acolytes) kept saying that I had been his Jung,[19] but this fantasy utterly misinterpreted my actual role; in no way did I want to be accepted by Heinz in the filial position Jung had desired vis-à-vis Freud (see 1979c and 1981d). In fact, in terms of personality structure, I believe it was Heinz who had a great deal in common with the vulnerable Jung.

The clearest indication of what Kohut wanted from me occurred on the day Heinz Hartmann died. That event seemingly compelled Heinz to call me at 2:30 in the morning. With great urgency, he announced that Hartmann was dead. I said I was sorry to hear that, but that I did not understand the reason for the urgent telephone call. Kohut replied, half in exasperation, half in despair, "Heinz Hartmann is dead!" I am sure I was supposed to say that, from then on, Kohut would be the premier theoretician of psychoanalysis. In *my* exasperation about being pushed into such a transaction, the idea came to me in the nastiest form imaginable: "The Heinz is dead; long live the [new] Heinz!"[20] This time, I refused to indulge Kohut's need for affirmation.

After he participated in translating Kohut's Frankfurt address, Ernest Wolf became progressively more enthusiastic about Heinz's contributions, and he came up with the idea of organizing a celebration in Kohut's honor, to commemorate the latter's sixtieth birthday. Ernest at first tried to make this an official function of the Chicago Psychoanalytic Society, but that proposal aroused a storm of opposition, a consensus that no member should be so honored at the early age of sixty. Undaunted, Wolf managed to organize a festive conference, scheduled for June 1973, through an ad hoc committee that raised seed money from Kohut's supporters. Although I contributed a small share, by this time I was disaffected enough to avoid participation in these preparations. I was therefore highly embarrassed to be informed that before the address Heinz was scheduled to give at the Saturday evening banquet, he wanted me to present an extensive introduction that would frame his contributions within psychoanalytic history.

I had more difficulty in carrying out this assignment than I have ever had with any intellectual task. Emotionally, it was like having to give a funeral oration for Joan Matlaw after she was shot, with the added burden of having to attain a certain objectivity in evaluating Heinz's work. To refuse Heinz's request would have been tantamount to breaking with him, a step I was then still unwilling to take, because I had not given up hope that he would support the kinds of complexity in psychoanalytic theory and technique I was advocating in *Models of the Mind*. Yet I could not bring myself to speak positively about a man whose character I found increasingly distasteful. Was it possible to say nothing about Heinz as a person on an occasion organized to honor him?

For more than six months, I could not think of any way to bridge the gap between my actual feelings and the attitude appropriate to the task I had accepted. Finally, some weeks before the event, I wrote a detailed assessment of Kohut's psychoanalytic contributions, including consideration of several unpublished drafts he had shown me. Although his most recent work struck me as cloudy and unrealistic (full of expectations that his contribution would make psychoanalysis capable of effecting societal changes), I was content to describe these developments in his thinking as similar to the secular idealism of the plays of Euripides. And I ended the talk by wishing Heinz a productive old age by quoting Hölderlin's tragic verse (which the great poet wrote shortly before his permanent collapse into psychosis), "A *single* summer grant me, great powers/and a single autumn for fully ripened song" (see 1975b).[21]

I am not sure what Kohut's own understanding of my meaning was. Overtly, he implied that he was embarrassed by being compared to Euripides. This was a wishful distortion of what I had actually said: it was not his stature I had ranked with that of the great dramatist. Moreover, his protest does not prove that Heinz had missed that, in comparing him to Hölderlin, I had broadly hinted at his psychological vulnerability. Given the nature of the occasion, it is remarkable that nobody seemed to notice that my refusal to say anything about Heinz as a person was actually very rude. Of course, I was relieved. Yet one of the visitors from Germany did approach me at the reception the Kohuts held on Sunday to ask whether I knew that Hölderlin had lapsed into psychosis. I was content to let him believe that I was an American ignoramus. (In expiation of this prevarication, a few years later I made a pilgrimage to the poet's house in Tübingen.)

Shortly after this event, in the late fall of 1973, Kohut received an honorary degree from the University of Cincinnati. I believe it was once again Ernest Wolf who came up with the notion that it would be appropriate to attend this ceremony, and I thought we could not refuse to join a number of Chicagoans in doing so. One of these was Heinz's oldest friend in the city, a staff member at the university, whose manner strongly suggested that he was homosexual. Rightly or wrongly, I began to imagine that they had been lovers, and that it was a history of homosexuality that had stood in the way of Kohut starting psychoanalytic training soon after he settled in Chicago.[22] (The family's suggestion that Kohut himself was the homosexual "patient" he described in his case of "Mr. Z" is the first indication that my fantasy may well have been correct.) Heinz's hypotheses about the function of homosexuality as an adaptive solution for profound narcissistic difficulties would, if these conjectures were valid, indicate that he had lived in despair because his therapeutic analysis, "the first analysis of Mr. Z" (which ended with a temporary cessation of homosexual activities), had deprived him of a solution without dealing with his problems. A pitiful situation.

While we were in Cincinnati, Mary's irritation with Heinz finally boiled over, and she burst out with a sharp condemnation of Kohut in the presence of one of Heinz's analysands. (Of course, Mary did not know about their therapeutic connection, but I did.) I was quite chagrined about the inevitability of Kohut being confronted with our negative feelings about him by way of his patient's report, but thereafter in my own conduct I no longer bothered to hide the truth. At the Cincinnati convocation, Heinz delivered a paper about the promise of "empathic science" for the academic world (Kohut 1978). Afterward, as we were walking away from the hall, he asked me directly what I thought about his thesis. By this time, there was no point in veiling disapproval through irony, as I had tried to do in June. I showed my distaste for the grandiose religiosity of his address by saying, "Heinz, you should have saved such remarks for the Vatican." (One of the facts about himself Kohut had confided to me was how much he enjoyed giving an occasional sermon at the Unitarian church he attended.)

It is hardly surprising that within a year our relationship came to an end. The downhill course it had begun to take some years earlier became more precipitous, although Heinz tried desperately to ignore my growing skepticism about the direction his psychoanalytic views were taking as well as my increasing unwillingness to tolerate his need for me. In the summer of 1974 we both took long vacations that did not happen to overlap, so that we did not see each other for several months. When Heinz resumed work in late September, the Kohuts asked to go out to dinner with us. We had a pleasant enough evening; as we left the restaurant to retrieve our cars, Heinz took me aside and said, reproachfully, "John, it seems like forever since we have seen each other." The fervor of this avowal of longing was even worse than Kohut's misinterpretation of my visit to his hospital room, and I was even more pitiless in my response: "It is strange," I said, "how different people have a different sense of time. To me, it feels like we last saw each other the day before yesterday."

That was more than even Heinz was willing to bear. Within a month, he took revenge, after which I terminated our personal relationship.

❖ CHAPTER 13 ❖

ACROSS THE RUBICON

When Arnold Goldberg was elected director of the Chicago Institute, I was still on a leave of absence, and this status remained undisturbed for about half a year. Early in 1990 I received a toughly worded form letter from Arnold's office, declaring that I was delinquent in paying the considerable assessment the faculty had decided to impose on itself. I replied with a note, stating that I was not delinquent, because I had not been billed for the assessment—properly so, in my view, because I was on leave. Goldberg immediately answered this; he conceded that, due to an oversight, I had not been billed—according to him, improperly so, because those on leave had to pay anyway. (This bill of attainder was not directed at me but at George Pollock, the only other person on leave of absence. I understand that *he* paid up. Thenceforth, George actually greeted me when we encountered each other, although he allegedly gave no sign of recognition on meeting other colleagues. I wondered whether he thought I was on leave as a gesture of solidarity with him?)

As I have mentioned, I had arranged my leave because I was unwilling to do my share of committee work—but if I was not participating in Institute affairs, I did not think I should have to pay a poll tax. (I have donated a fair bit of money to cultural institutions, but I had stopped giving to the Institute midway through the Pollock regime, when it became evident that, in most respects, its aims and standards did not match mine.) I tried one additional gambit to maintain a loose connection with the program: I asked to receive emeritus status. Goldberg replied that, according to new regulations coming into force in a few weeks, emeritus status could only be granted at the age of 70. (He knew that I was then several years younger.) To invoke rules that were not yet applicable—and to turn a future deadline into a missed opportunity—struck me as a provocation, and I was determined not to permit Arnold to play cat-and-mouse games with me. Consequently, I wrote a letter of resignation, which I addressed to the new dean, Jorge Schneider.

Jorge is a pleasant, conscientious person. When I next encountered him, he told me that I could not resign because I still had one candidate in a training analysis, and it was against the rules for candidates *not* to be with a training analyst. He acknowledged that this was a local rule, and I told him that I was certain it could be waived. I also reminded him that, as far as I was concerned, this treatment was not a training analysis—the patient had come to me privately, and I had nothing to do with his later acceptance by the Institute. (In previous years, five of my private patients—four psychiatrists and one physicist—had become Chicago candidates. I do not think it is a coincidence, by the way, that the four clinicians all became members of the Institute faculty. I believe in helping analysands correctly to identify their assets and limitations.)

A few days after my resignation, I also ran into Goldberg, who now wanted to negotiate; he wondered what I really wanted—perhaps something could be arranged. I said I was content with the decision I had reached. As for the difficulty with the candidate, I reminded Arnold that the man was a psychologist, whose training came under the jurisdiction of the federal court (where the suit about the exclusively medical intake policies of the American Psychoanalytic had been settled). I thought the court would have little regard for internal workings of the Chicago Institute bureaucracy. This was the ultimate interchange of our long relationship. (It was mean and petty, but I deeply enjoyed it.) I suppose it is not surprising that Goldberg now calls me a very difficult person (Hunter 1994, p. 233).

Obviously, the passage of over fifteen years had failed to soften the mutual bitterness of our rupture at the time I walked away from the Kohut circle. It was quite an irony that when Kohut and I parted company, Arnold got the opportunity to take charge of publications for self psychology, for it was I who had convinced Kohut to overcome his apparent reservations about Goldberg. (In retrospect, I am ready to concede that Heinz turned out to be a better judge of character than I.) They had known each other for many years, for Kohut had been one of Arnold's analytic supervisors, but when I proposed that Goldberg be entrusted with summarizing Kohut's ideas at a workshop I was to chair at a 1968 meeting of the Chicago Psychoanalytic Society, Heinz initially showed ambivalence about Arnold as a person. (Goldberg has recently expressed the view that it was his performance of this assignment that seriously brought him to Kohut's attention [Hunter 1994, p. 233].)[1] Incidentally, Michael Basch also distinguished himself at the same workshop, and I was equally responsible for getting him on the program. Kohut said nothing about my recruitment of Mike, but he was clearly uncomfortable about it. This may have had something to do with the fact that he had been Mike's analyst.

Shortly after these events, around 1970, Kohut decided to invite a group of younger analysts to periodic meetings at his home, to hear readings of excerpts from the manuscript (Kohut 1971) that was to become *The Analysis of the Self*. He asked me whom I would recommend for such a group, and (as I recall) I named Basch, Goldberg, and Paul Tolpin. Heinz announced that he also planned to invite Anna and Paul Ornstein from Cincinnati, both of whom he had supervised when they were candidates in Chicago; otherwise, he accepted my recommendations.

I put forward Basch and Goldberg because, on the basis of our joint efforts on the indexing project, I was convinced that they were exceptionally able, energetic, and intellectually ambitious; Arnold and I had for several years been collaborating on *Models of the Mind*. Paul Tolpin had been in my cohort at the Institute; he was a particular devotee of Kohut, with whom he had long ago been in analysis. We and the Tolpins had been close for many years, and in the late 1960s we lived only a few blocks apart in one of the North Shore suburbs. I have always had the highest respect for Paul and thought he could become intellectually productive, although a mildly self-deprecating attitude stood in his way. (Marian Tolpin had taken a number of years off to have a family. She had only recently completed analytic training and was not at that time looked upon as a peer of the group Kohut invited to form his original circle.)

Although the meetings at Kohut's apartment were rather stiff affairs, they were undoubtedly very stimulating. Heinz profited from the difficulties of his audience in grasping his intended meanings to improve his presentation; he added the entire first chapter of *The Analysis of the Self* in response to questions posed by this group. He was very grateful for the positive feedback he received. For my part, I felt certain that his book would have a revolutionary impact, because it presented important clinical discoveries—notably, the description of a number of hitherto neglected archaic transference constellations. The excellence of this contribution temporarily overcame my reservations about Kohut as a person. To Heinz I predicted that the book would be a psychoanalytic best-seller. In response, Kohut professed great pessimism about its prospects, so I bet him a case of wine, of his choosing, if the book failed to sell ten thousand copies. About six months after *The Analysis of the Self* was published, he paid off the with a shipment of an outstanding wine. We always did get along best on the question of *bibenda*.[2]

I believe that the other participants in this first Kohut circle had not, on their own, attempted to analyze patients whose psychopathology stemmed from preoedipal difficulties by using methods that departed from those taught at the Institute. As Kohut well knew, I had conducted experiments in that area for more than a decade, especially so after I began my discussions with Bob Gardner. Earlier, my public disagreement with Joan Fleming's instruction in traditional methods contributed to my being blacklisted by her. And my reports on nonanalytic techniques in psychotherapy (especially 1964a, 1966a, and 1967a), which were precursors of my selective application of parallel interventions in specific analytic contingencies (whenever archaic modes of the organization of behavior prevail), had brought me to Heinz's attention in the first place. At the society workshop on Kohut's work—which he had attended—Heinz must have realized that I was able to grasp the value of his novel proposals in a way not accessible to colleagues who had never struggled to solve technical problems in an innovative way. Consequently, while the meetings about *The Analysis of the Self* lasted, Heinz clearly regarded me as the most significant recruit to his way of thinking, and he adopted a number of my suggestions—which I had the wit to make in private—about the subject matter of his book.[3]

Probably the most significant of these ideas was the distinction between disturbances in self-esteem, which constituted the exclusive focus of Kohut's clinical observations, and structural regressions that disarray the usual personality organization. Until we discussed this, Kohut merely described these dramatic events through metaphors, such as "fragmentation." (In the hierarchical model I was then elaborating, such a change constitutes one form of regression to a more archaic mode of behavior regulation. In my schema, self-esteem issues are predominant in mode III; the conditions Kohut called fragmentation involve a mode of functional organization I designate as "mode II.")

Of course, over twenty-five years ago, I did not realize that my initial enthusiasm for Kohut's work was based on a false consensus. What Heinz meant by "analysis of the self" had nothing in common with my conception of *self* as the basic structure of behavior regulation. Because Kohut's viewpoint was purely phenomenological,[4] he did not realize that the loss of cohesiveness which, misleadingly, he compared to the shattering of glass or ceramic was actually a return to an earlier and more primitive (symbiotic) mode of organization. In *The Analysis of the Self*, he adopted the terminology Goldberg and I put forward in early drafts of *Models of the Mind* and called what he thought of as the resultant fragments "nuclei of the self." However, Kohut never bothered to grasp my definition of this term. (Instead, he construed it in a phenomenological sense, as a *view* of oneself—a self-representation—as a disassembled collection of parts.)

Several years later, Kohut wanted to repudiate the conceptual confusion created by his odd assumption that infants initially saw themselves as disarticulated dolls; it took strong protests from both Goldberg and me to make him stop insisting that he had misunderstood nothing and that the error was ours. (I was highly offended by his all-but-explicit accusation that I was now misrepresenting what I had meant, simply to ward off a blow to my self-esteem. I concluded that, for his part, Heinz would not hesitate to suppress the truth in the service of covering up *his* errors.)

In retrospect, I think that the internal consistency and logical rigor of the hierarchical view of mental life I was then putting forward convinced Heinz that I possess good judgment in matters of psychoanalytic theory. Hence, he paid attention to my ongoing critique of his work in private discussions. (That commentary was, of course, based on the hierarchical model.) Perhaps the clarity of my critique contributed to evoking the "alter ego" transference that ultimately made the relationship insupportable for me. I believe that Kohut implicitly said as much when *Models of the Mind* was published and received serious attention, even beyond psychoanalysis. (It was considered for a National Book Award.) Goldberg and I were invited to appear on "Sunrise Semester," a local program on educational TV, to discuss the implications of our revision of analytic theory; we were asked to bring along a colleague competent to discuss our proposals. Naturally, we asked Heinz to play this role. In this very public setting, late in 1973, he fully endorsed the hierarchical view.[5]

Sadly, from the point of view of preserving a modus vivendi with Heinz, it never consciously occurred to me that my abilities could threaten him or that he might be tempted to muzzle me as a psychoanalytic theoretician. As our relationship soured, especially after his illness was detected, Kohut implicitly repudiated his endorsement of my work. In self psychology, there is no trace of a hierarchical viewpoint; Kohut postulates only two states of being, self-cohesion and fragmentation, and according to his published views, the former prevails throughout the life cycle whenever the glue of empathy is available—and the latter supervenes in its absence.[6] Such alternation between two states of being does not imply that one of those states is developmentally more (or less) mature than the other—the basic assumption of an epigenetic/hierarchical conception.

Kohut's flip-flop about the need for a hierarchical concept of mental functions convinced me that, to maintain a consistent theoretical position, he really needed the rational influence of a "selfobject," such as he had hoped I would be. As for Goldberg's later preference for Kohut's position, I still cannot decide whether he means it, in which case his acceptance of the hierarchical view as coauthor of *Models of the Mind* could not have been fully thought through, or whether he merely finds it expedient because it is popular.

After *The Analysis of the Self* (Kohut 1971) was published, I thought it would be useful to describe in detail the consequences of following an agnostic attitude to case material—this was the principal lesson, for me, of Kohut's demonstration that in automatically applying Freud's oedipal interpretations to all cases, we had misperceived the meaning of analytic observational data that were referable to more archaic phases of development. I thought that we were at the threshold of a new era of fresh clinical discoveries—as Cézanne put it about his historical position in painting, that we were the primitives of a new way to do psychoanalysis. It never occurred to me that Heinz could believe that his meager clinical reports were adequate as the basis of a comprehensive new clinical theory.

I was also unaware that Heinz was interested in putting together a casebook to illustrate his clinical procedures as a novel but finished schema of psychoanalytic technique.[7] Hence, I discussed my idea for a research project with those colleagues in Chicago who had shown the strongest interest in Kohut's work—Basch, Goldberg, Tolpin, and Wolf. All of them were very much in favor of forming a workshop to carry out this task and of asking Kohut to act as senior consultant for the project. It was also agreed that it would be desirable to have a larger number of participants. I proposed that we invite Mike Gunther as well as a woman colleague who was also from our social circle. My suggestions were accepted.

We then approached Kohut with our plans, and he not only approved but wished to be an active participant in preparing the casebook. I was taken aback; Heinz was invading a field of activity I had not envisaged sharing with him, but I was not in a position to demur, because the other participants were delighted with having him on board. I also thought there would be a problem because the person whose name I have withheld had started an analysis with Kohut, but Heinz assured me that their joint attendance at meetings would not create difficulties. In the 1970s Kohut began to allow himself to have social contacts with analysands, such as luncheons of a semiprofessional nature at his home. I was troubled by these departures from prudent practice (what nowadays we call "boundary violations"), but concerns about the way Heinz conducted himself as an analyst were less of a problem for me than the increasing difficulties in our personal relationship.

When, in the fall of 1973, the future casebook group assembled, Kohut once again brought along a number of former supervisees, including Anna and Paul Ornstein and a younger Chicago colleague. He also invited another former supervisee, who decided not to attend, but sent along a written record of the entire analysis. These notes were entrusted to Mike Gunther, who managed to construct from them a case report so convincing that nobody has ever detected that it was prepared by someone other than the analyst.

This group of about a dozen collaborators began to meet once a month on Saturday mornings, in a classroom at the Institute. At one of the early meetings, Kohut proposed that Goldberg take editorial charge of what the group produced. Heinz seemed fearful about my reaction to his arbitrary appropriation of a project I had initiated. I understood that I had so often rebuffed him that Heinz was beginning to take punitive action against me, but I failed fully to realize that this coup d'état might later make it difficult to ensure that my views would be represented in the publications of the group. In other words, I was still unaware of the fact that Heinz thought he had found the right way to do psychoanalysis, that my conviction that we had barely freed ourselves of the outworn procedures transmitted to us would be unwelcome to him, and that he would not tolerate any dissent from his views in a joint publication.

I had more than enough editorial work at the *Journal of the American*, on the book of Freudiana Pollock and I were trying to organize, and the Johns Hopkins project recently initiated by Wolf. Consequently, I accepted the plan to put Goldberg in charge of preparing the casebook. I made it explicit that my commitment to the project was exclusively scientific—I was not looking for publishing credits in the process. Regrettably, I was afraid further to disrupt an uneasy equilibrium, so that I neglected to discuss my concern that Kohut's unilateral decision violated one requirement of any working collaboration, that of prior consultation with all participants. I believe I could already sense that opening that can of worms would precipitate the inevitable break between us.

The group decided to discuss terminated analyses, to be presented by each participant in turn. It so happened, however, that (aside from the cases Kohut had supervised) I was the only member ready to describe suitable analyses. Ultimately, everyone was supposed to produce a written commentary about each case, to be distributed in advance of the discussion. Early in 1974, after the project started, I presented a difficult analysis, that of a middle-aged woman who suffered from a masochistic perversion. There was no controversy in the group about the conduct of this case, brought to a satisfactory termination after some six years of work (published as chap. 6 in 1979a). On the contrary, several participants, including Wolf and Basch, made laudatory comments about the treatment, as well as the organization of the case history; Kohut noted that the technique I described seemed spontaneous and effortless because it was informed by a consistent theoretical position.

That position required the exploration of every aspect of analytic material, without preconceptions about what would prove to be particularly important in pathogenesis—a program utterly different from the focus either on narcissistic transferences or oedipal ones Kohut was preparing to advocate. Heinz was apparently reluctant to argue the issue about a case with which he was not familiar, but he was much too perceptive to overlook that, if my conduct of this analysis was appropriate, the technical theory he was on the verge of adopting (see Kohut 1977) had to be discarded as overly reductionist. We were soon to learn, however, that Kohut was committed to the dichotomy of Guilty Man versus Tragic Man, simple alternatives that give the analyst a choice between two ready-made interpretive formulas. His position constituted the abandonment of agnosticism about the meaning of observational data, in favor of a priori assumptions about the issues crucial for maladaptation. I believe that, all but overwhelmed by his potentially fatal illness, Heinz was no longer prepared to acknowledge that any of his ideas could be improved upon.

Kohut's certitude about the validity of his hypotheses became overt at the next meeting of the group, when one of Heinz's former supervisees described an analysis that was terminated rather abruptly, a decision taken with Kohut's approval.[8] In the discussion, there were questions about this decision, and I vigorously espoused the viewpoint that the meaning of the analysand's sadistic propensities had been left unexplored.[9] When I next spoke to Kohut in private, he showed concern about my disagreement with the management of the case; he said that there had been no choice in the matter because he did not think the analyst would have been able to tolerate the patient's assaults if the treatment had continued. He left unclear why, under the circumstances, the case was suitable for presentation as a prototype of the appropriate conduct of the analysis of a "narcissistic disturbance" (as he then called these primitive difficulties). I could see that the issue was extremely significant for him, but I did not have the courage think through why this was so.

There followed the summer break to which Heinz and I had such different reactions. During this hiatus in our contacts, Kohut began work on his second book, *The Restoration of the Self* (1977). The opening chapter of that work takes up the controversy about the analysis concerning which I had disagreed with Heinz in the spring. In this discussion, Kohut no longer acknowledges that the decision to cut the treatment short had been a tactical compromise; on the contrary, he claims that it was a matter of principle—that, in the treatment of narcissistic disturbances, the appropriate time for termination is when some "compensatory structure" that makes better adaptation possible has emerged. In this instance of scientific flip-flop, I do not think that Heinz was being untruthful so that he could hide his shame from others; rather, I believe he was deluding himself.

In the fall, when the meetings of the casebook group were to resume, Heinz wanted to read this chapter to his circle of followers. He arranged to extend the first meeting of the group into the afternoon; in the morning, we were scheduled to discuss another one of my case presentations. (I later published this as chap. 4 in 1979a.) The analysis I described was unusually felicitous, and most members of the group thought it suitably instructive. Arnold Goldberg pointed out that my patient was a highly exceptional person, probably a genius, so that the unusually smooth course of the treatment might be attributable to his special talents. Arnold questioned the wisdom of using such a treatment as an illustration in a casebook. (What on earth was going on? I wondered.) The person then in analysis with Heinz interjected that the case report could not be used for a different reason; she declared, loudly, in a grating voice expressing absolute certitude, that the treatment did not qualify as an analysis because, before it started, I had allegedly instructed the prospective analysand about how to arrange to finance it. I was stunned by the virulence of this proclamation, and I did not have time to consider how best to respond.

What I found particularly odd about the situation was that Kohut was not present at the meeting. I was convinced that, if this person planned to object to the use of my case presentation, she must have mentioned this in her analysis, and this information had decided Heinz to avoid the meeting. Kohut had expressed no objection to my conduct of the other analysis I had presented to the group—a treatment that departed from traditional methods to a much greater extent than this second case. I concluded that his failure to show up when he knew I was going to be assaulted could only have been a deliberate act—an exact parallel to his avoidance of the society meeting where, as he well knew, Fleming was going to attack me. But could I be sure of what this meant? Perhaps Heinz merely had an aversion to quarrelsome situations?

Nor was the objector's attitude easy to understand. I had always regarded her as a brittle person, and she undoubtedly discerned that I had silent reservations about her, despite our ongoing social relationship. I particularly disliked her propensity to use ad hoc arguments, made up out of whole cloth, to override opposition—of course, this is precisely what I believed she was doing in objecting to my presentation. Yet she had never before expressed personal objections to me, so that her animus seemed startlingly out of character.

In my uncertainty, I chose to respond in the narrowest way possible: I tried to convince this critic that she had misconstrued an overly condensed report. I said I had not given the patient any instructions; I had asked certain relevant questions, well within the boundaries of accepted analytic technique. (I was trying to say that if she had known all the details, the transaction in question would not have seemed controversial.) A number of participants asked for further specifics and seemed satisfied with my answers. I was therefore thunderstruck when she resumed her discourse, in the sibylline manner she had used in the first place, as if my statements had been *non arrivés*.[10] As she intoned that the case did not qualify as an analysis, Mike Gunther (her closest friend in the group) tried to intervene by crying out, "Take it easy! take it easy!" But it was too late; I was flooded with outrage, which was evident in my contemptuous manner, my angry tone of voice, and my categorical contradiction of her claims. The hour was late, and Goldberg hastened to adjourn the meeting.

Over lunch, the group did not discuss this disruptive incident; rather, we talked about Kohut's wish to widen attendance for further readings from his new manuscript and the question of how to select those who might be added to the circle. I spoke with some passion for the desirability of holding an ordinary scientific forum, open to all analysts interested in participating. No doubt I was still wrought up by my encounter with a new Grand Inquisitor. (In retrospect, it is really comical that one of the future champions of self psychology could, in the fall of 1974, attack anyone for technical heterodoxy because of an intervention she looked upon as a departure from "classical" procedures!) I received no support whatsoever for my views about enlarging the group—those who spoke fully endorsed Kohut's preference for hand-picking recruits who would be sympathetic to his viewpoint. This symptom of clique formation added to my considerable discomfort.

The afternoon session with Kohut seemed uneventful—probably because I was still so overwrought that I could not attend too carefully. (It was only when *The Restoration of the Self* was published that I realized that the presentation had been an attempt to rebut the psychoanalytic views I had expressed at our last meeting in the spring.) As we were leaving, I told Heinz that I would meet him at the intermission of the Chicago Symphony concert for which we both had tickets that evening, and we agreed on a specific spot for doing so. On the way out, Arnold Goldberg reminded me that he had been opposed to the inclusion of the person who had attacked me in the casebook group; he meant that if I was now reaping the whirlwind, I fully deserved this fate. With absolute spontaneity, I told Arnold that he had been right, and now he must undo my error by getting rid of her. And I knew that I could never compromise on this demand, although I was slow consciously to grasp my reasons for this determination: if Kohut did not agree to my demand, his refusal would show that my assailant had acted on his behalf. I was beginning to realize that Heinz might wish to suppress my scientific views.

Before we left for the concert that evening, Goldberg called me, largely to find out whether I really meant what I had told him. It was pretty obvious that he had been in touch with Kohut, because he began to temporize, pointing out that it would be very difficult to do what I wanted, although he tried to assure me, unconvincingly, that his own wishes were congruent with mine. My conjecture about his having informed Heinz about my demand was confirmed when, at the concert, I hurried to the spot appointed for meeting and waited in vain for Kohut to show up. I have always despised such cowardice, and Heinz compounded the sin by calling a day or two later and opening the conversation with a reproach that, on Saturday night, I had failed to appear as arranged. I made sure that we had not misunderstood each other by asking where Heinz had waited for me, and he named the correct place. I was no longer surprised that Kohut would resort to deception, but I could not stomach the fact that he had not even bothered to make up a more effective cover story.

After this phone call, I was convinced that the critic had acted on Kohut's behalf. I did not concern myself about how explicitly he had made his wishes known to her; in the course of an analysis, both participants have multiple channels of communication at their disposal. I knew perfectly well that, if I understood the situation correctly, Kohut would not agree to bar his analysand from the casebook group for enacting his wish to punish me, but I had some hope that many of those who had witnessed her assaultiveness would support my position—as Goldberg claimed he was doing. Mike Gunther kept in frequent touch with me and affirmed that I had the right to demand that such behavior should not be tolerated in the group.

Several days went by without a decision; finally Goldberg called with a proposal that my opponent and I should attend meetings alternately—a senseless compromise I rejected out of hand. Goldberg fully understood the whole situation; I heard from Mike Gunther that Arnold stated that the objector was not the cause of the problem—that the difficulty was between Heinz and me. It was, indeed. Why, then, was Arnold proposing "remedies" that merely dealt with displacements? And if he knew that scientific disagreements were at the bottom of the problem, why did he fail to state where he stood on those issues?

The more I talked to Goldberg on the phone, the clearer it became that, in fact, he was stringing me along and had no inclination to make a stand. I felt he was betraying our friendship. I found it particularly painful and unempathic that he did not want to discuss the practicalities but injected into the proceedings more and more treacly "empathy" with my emotional situation. This was entirely out of character and sounded to me like a prescription for "managing" me, written by Heinz Kohut. I now realized that I had completely misunderstood the purport of Kohut's takeover of my casebook project: it was not to be a piece of scientific research but an instrument for doing Kohut's will and propagating his ideas. Heinz was not merely taking revenge on me for failing to meet his emotional needs—he was also provoking me to walk the plank because of our mutual realization that I was *not* in agreement with many of his clinical ideas, especially those about the theory of technique, and—what was worse from his perspective—I was probably right. The case my critic wanted to exclude from the book had been handled in a manner much more complex than those presented by Kohut's supervisees; hence it implicitly called Kohut's system into question. Some months after these events, one of *my* supervisees, Lou Spitz—later director of the Cincinnati Institute—presented a beautifully handled, terminated case to the group, and they rejected Lou's work out of hand. It did not belong either!

The more I thought about the situation, the more I felt outraged that Goldberg (and some others) would allow themselves to do Kohut's bidding for seeming political advantage. In midweek, I had a traumatic dream in which Kohut's analysand was attempting to kill me with a knife. As I awakened, I came to the realization that none of the participants would be willing to risk anything to defend me against such an assault, because it was sanctioned by Heinz; it was my ideas his agent was attempting to obliterate. I felt particularly bitter toward Goldberg, because I believed that he was genuinely convinced about the necessity of the hierarchical viewpoint that my case report illustrated. He also shared my estimate of Kohut's character, and (as I have already mentioned) continues to do so. Moreover, Arnold professed to condemn the critic's behavior.

Following my dream, I was flooded with the feeling that I could not continue to deal with a person who would not stand up for his beliefs, and I could not wait to let Arnold know about my decision. I was beside myself. It was 1:30 in the morning, but if Heinz could call at that hour, so would I; I phoned Arnold and read him the riot act. I told him that, unless I received satisfaction by midday, all was over between us. I then hung up before he could reply; that was our last communication for many years, except for a letter in which Arnold protested his innocence and called my behavior inexcusable. I was not inclined to excuse it, but I did apologize to Connie Goldberg for having disturbed her in the middle of the night.

Of course, my rupture with Arnold also meant that I was unwilling to have anything further to do with Heinz. I wrote the other members of the casebook group to let them know that I was withdrawing. Almost all wrote back, expressing regret. Ernest Wolf came to visit; he was literally in tears about my unwillingness to reconcile with Heinz. I understood that his idealization of Kohut was genuine, so that I was not angered by *his* loyalty to Heinz, although it was obvious to both of us that under the circumstances it would be difficult to maintain our friendship on its former basis. Finally, Kohut himself called to arrange a private discussion, face to face, and, as a last gesture, I joined him for dinner before a meeting of the Psychoanalytic Society.

Heinz wanted to know why I had reacted so strongly to the views of my critic. I tried to explain that I had found her impervious to rational discussion; I had attributed her hostility to some personal reaction beyond my ability to understand. I also expressed unwillingness to waste my time in arguments with people whose psychoanalytic knowledge and expertise did not match mine. Kohut stated that he would think over whether it would be feasible to share with me some kind of supervisory responsibility for the casebook—a tentative offer that stopped me from definitively closing the door on the possibility of salvaging our relationship. Of course, Kohut was not being serious; he went on to question my attitude toward his analysand. He said that I apparently had a low opinion of this person's potential; I acknowledged that I thought she was confused and overconfident about her intellect. I do not know whether Kohut's response amounted to a terrible indiscretion or a falsehood; essentially, he was asking me to overlook what had happened out of consideration for his analysand's difficulties. I said that I could not continue to expose myself to personal reactions that stemmed from transferences. (I often speak obliquely; I meant Heinz's more than his patient's.) "If you know it was a transference reaction, why do you object to it?" asked Kohut. The conversation ended when I replied that the person concerned was his patient, not mine. I did not bother to add that I was not his alter ego, whatever he wished in the matter, for I preferred to maintain a veneer of politeness in expectation of the unavoidable contacts we would likely have, willy-nilly, in our small psychoanalytic community.

Yet I knew that in taking such an uncompromising position, I would become anathema to Heinz and his followers. I had no interest in eliciting anyone's hatred, but it was much more important to me to preserve my freedom of thought. To remain in Kohut's circle it would have been necessary to submerge my own ideas in favor of Heinz's emerging comprehensive system. I am certain that such a self-betrayal would have stifled my creativity. To do him justice, Heinz did at one point realize that; he told me, as soon as the crisis occurred, that he understood it as my declaration of independence.

❖ CHAPTER 14 ❖

A SCHOOL OF ONE

When I completed the first draft of this memoir, I asked a dozen people, family and friends, in and out of psychoanalysis, to give me their reactions to the manuscript. I received the kind of feedback I wished for—none of my early readers was neutral. Members of my family were most critical; their objections were best summed up by my son Paul. Immersed in psychoanalysis and facing its bleak future, he looked at me reproachfully and asked, "What have *you* to be bitter about?" He was quite right—personally, I have profited from living in an era of milk and honey. (If I sound bitter, it is because the political leaders of American psychoanalysis have led it into ruin as I was watching, helplessly.)

In contrast, psychoanalyst-readers were most encouraging; from them, I received three letters that helped me to refocus this book in crucial ways. Mike Gunther's communication said certain things about me that I had not felt free to articulate about myself; I am not certain that I have been able to do it in the present version. Leo Sadow stressed that younger generations of analysts can scarcely believe in the reality of events he and I witnessed together. As an example, he cited his experiences with Heinz Kohut, one of his instructors at the University of Chicago medical school—transactions that led Leo to conclusions about Kohut's character similar to those I reached only after the awful misadventures I describe in this memoir.

Leo also urged me to say more than I did originally about the way my personal history influenced the kind of psychoanalyst I became. I have tried to be more explicit about this, although I find it difficult; if I go into detail about the manner of my upbringing, I shall mislead my readers about the personalities of my parents and the nature of my early relationships. My childhood took place long ago and far away, and it is impossible to translate its nuances into contemporary terms. For instance, what can readers make of the story that my father inculcated in me the code of honor of ancient Rome, as his fellow-Jacobin Jacques-Louis David tried to do for his compatriots through paintings such as his *Oath of the Horatii*?[1] Of course, he did not do this by swearing me to die for my country, as did the Roman patriarch with his sons as portrayed in David's painting. Rather, he endeavored to train me through ordinary transactions, for example in the course of playing ball with me.

Among his other glamorous qualities, my father had years of athletic glory to his credit; he had been the star striker of the local professional soccer team. By the time I was big enough to kick a soccer ball, he was too old for competitive play, but he eagerly tried to get me involved by engaging in one-on-one games with me. This might involve trading penalty shots within the enclosed space of our thirty-foot *porte cochère*.[2] I was not yet in school—perhaps 5 years old—and he shot the ball as hard as he could. After these cannonballs, what could a Joan Fleming send my way to make me flinch? (For some of us, the anxieties of the oedipal period take the concrete form of fantasies about decapitation.) Yet my father was a lovable, sentimental person. And in 1919, during the revolution, he had proved that he really believed that "It is sweet and worthy to die for one's fatherland."[3]

Enough of that. I find it easier to follow the course George Moraitis recommended. George pointed out that, although I spelled out the usual travails of a psychoanalytic career in America since the mid-century, I failed to particularize the vicissitudes of someone who tried to become a theoretical innovator in our era. If I did not say enough about that, it was not because I am shy about my ambitions; in 1981, when the *Chicago Tribune* sent someone to interview me about the festivities I was organizing to celebrate the fiftieth anniversary of Chicago psychoanalysis, I was candid enough to tell the reporter that I was embarked on a major intellectual effort in the field and hoped to become a rallying point for my colleagues, at least on the local scene. He actually printed this ambitious claim in the Sunday magazine (Cross 1982), to the disapproval of both the ego psychological and the self psychological factions at the Institute. (George Pollock was the angriest of them all because I told the *Tribune* that the Institute needed to adhere to higher standards.) By the time I published *Psychoanalysis and*

Its Discontents in 1984, I knew that my viewpoint had become so different from that of my peers that, in this era of clique formation, it was likely to be disregarded by the vast majority of analysts. Nor do I have the charismatic qualities of a Kohut, a Lacan, or a Melanie Klein, so that I knew I could not attract followers on the basis of personality, even if I had wanted to do so. In fact, I had a horror of following Kohut's example. Heinz himself had told me that he did not enjoy having seduced all sorts of people who did not really understand his work into joining a "school." Arnold Modell was to put this into the most appropriate terms, I no longer remember where. He wrote that, in contemporary psychoanalysis, every serious contributor has to become a "school of one."

In the dozen years since the publication of *Discontents*, nobody has disputed the therapeutic effectiveness of my technical recommendations (about which I have written periodic reports, such as chap. 10 in 1991a). At most, conservatives have steered clear of the issues I have raised (by calling my work "*not* psychoanalysis"), while many self psychologists have condemned me on personal grounds (in what amounts to a conspiracy of silence, hardly any of them has ever commented on my contributions[4]). Both groups have tended to do this behind my back, because I have acquired a reputation as a fierce public opponent. As I recall, the only person who has ever shown open disapproval of my ideas has been the Swiss psychoanalyst Olivier Flournoy, and he was exquisitely polite about it (*en français, à Genève*). Of course, Flournoy does not know one American analyst from another, and I suspect he disapproves of us all.

Not long ago, I wrote a sequential account (1993d) of my intellectual journey from the traditionalism in which I had been trained to the development of my school of one. Suffice it to repeat here that, well into the 1970s, I was convinced that I was a strict adherent of the fundamental principles of Freudian psychoanalysis, its biological underpinnings, its developmental viewpoint, and its insistence on clinical agnosticism. (By this I mean that I do not attribute a priori meanings to the analysand's associations but use inductive methods of inference to arrive at fresh and individual interpretations in collaboration with the analysand. Recently, this traditional prescription has been renamed "constructivism.") The foregoing principles inform the hierarchical model, which does not specify the nature or significance of the mental contents processed in the clinical situation. I began to acknowledge that I was embarked on a voyage into unexplored territory only when I was writing *Beyond Interpretation* (1979a), where the technical consequences of taking seriously the conclusions of our theories of development are finally confronted. In 1993, I completely revised *Beyond Interpretation* for its paperback edition, and I intend to highlight the main contributions of the book when I discuss its later version, in Chapter 15. Suffice it to say here that, in 1979, I wrote the book to demonstrate that the hierarchical model drawn up in *Models of the Mind* (somewhat modified, to eliminate anachronistic survivals of concepts tied to Freud's metapsychology of the 1890s) better serves to illuminate a broad range of clinical material observed in the psychoanalytic situation than do any of the other models extant. It follows from that demonstration that our theory of technique ought to be radically expanded in line with the variety of appropriate therapeutic interventions—beyond interpretation!—necessitated by the emergence of archaic modes of behavioral organization in the course of treatment, as the hierarchical model recommends.

It will be recalled that, in *Models of the Mind*, we had already concluded that the derivatives of every early developmental phase, when they present themselves in the course of analysis, require specific modalities of treatment; interpretation of the meanings of unconscious mental contents, formerly considered the cardinal tool of psychoanalysis is, in this view, merely the modality indicated in cases of unresolved conflicts among the three agencies of mind postulated by Freud—ego, id, and superego. Such conflicts occur only following considerable differentiation (in mode IV in my schema). I became a dissident by challenging in this manner the consensus that the model technique of psychoanalysis is one that uses interpretation alone.

I was launched on my solitary path in the mid-1970s, at a Los Angeles panel on metapsychology, chaired by Hans Loewald (Meissner 1976). This was the most significant of the public appearances that determined the future course of my scientific work. On that occasion, I was attacked by the ego psychologist David Beres, but I was able to hold my own. After the session, I was approached by Emmanuel ("Windy") Windholz and Jan Frank, classmates of my father's in Prague, and we had a tearful recognition scene. They reminisced about my father's sweetness of character, about his attendance at a delivery of Windy's sister. As soon as we parted, Loewald asked me to have lunch with him. We talked of many things (not shoes or ships or sealing wax), but Hans's purpose was to tell me that I must not let my ideas remain confined within a panel presentation for a few hundred who happened to come to this session—that these ideas deserved to be made into a book. I protested that the task was too great; it would take more than one book to spell it all out as he insisted it must be. His was the voice of conscience. I soon embarked on writing *Beyond Interpretation*; the seven additional volumes about these matters that followed have failed to complete the assignment I accepted from Hans that day.

A couple of years later, I participated in a panel entitled "Current Concepts of Object Relations Theory" (Spruiell 1978). On that occasion, there was an overflow crowd in one of the large hotel meeting rooms where such events are held, and I was hypnotized by the sight of Hans Loewald, arriving at the last minute, slowly making his way to the front of the hall and sitting down on the floor next to the podium, about eight feet away from me. No doubt he was there to learn what the panelists would say about his own proposals about object relations, but for me his near presence signified that the manner in which I would carry out my conceptual responsibilities to the psychoanalytic community was being overseen by Higher Powers.

Almost twenty years ago, the psychoanalytic consensus about technique was truly unanimous; as late as 1978, in the Kohutian casebook, Goldberg (1978, p. 9) asserted that interpretation constitutes the technique of self psychology. Even fifteen years ago, a traditionalist such as Dewald (1981) could, in an irritable mood, still claim that my *observations* themselves should be disregarded because they were not made in a standard analytic setting. He meant that noninterpretive interventions should be taboo. (Almost one hundred years before that, Charcot had cautioned Freud, *"La théorie, c'est bon, mais ça n'empêche pas d'exister."*[5]) Until the détente of the last few years, even the superior clinical results I was able to report failed to persuade the traditionalist majority that my work deserves attention; at the same time, most self psychologists perpetuated the boycott initiated against me when I broke with Heinz. Perhaps as a consequence of this (not so benign) neglect, neither my theoretical proposals nor my technical recommendations have ever been seriously challenged on their substance. (Indictments for heresy are another matter!)

I believe that my relative intellectual isolation (relieved only through personal contact with Bob Gardner and the Chicago study groups I attended) acted as a powerful spur for my writing. I was determined to publish my ideas, so that (if psychoanalysis survived at all) they would be available for consideration by a new generation. (He who laughs last is said to laugh best.) On the Chicago scene, I tried to gain a hearing through direct contact with the most promising of recent graduates; over the years, a number of these respected younger colleagues sought private consultation with me about difficult cases, and these opportunities allowed me to demonstrate my clinical approach to people willing to try it out. I still have a school of one, but by now a few people have studied there.

My rupture with Kohut was the most difficult contingency of my adult life; there was no turning back to some pre-Kohutian safe haven, and I felt my intellectual isolation keenly. I think I was able to continue to search for my own answers because I had been through such an experience before. In January 1939, after my father was released from political detention on condition that he emigrate, through Uncle Oscar in Brussels he obtained a permit to reside in Belgium. We wound up our affairs in Losoncz and started our journey by going to Budapest to take care of the remaining administrative details. Two days after we became homeless refugees, Belgium canceled our entry visas. For the next two months, we lived in the no-man's-land of a Budapest pension: there was no going back and no way to proceed. Tangier turned out to be the solution we found. Only those who have been through such ostracism know how bitter it can be to be betrayed by one's community.

I do not want to exaggerate; my isolation within psychoanalysis was never as profound as it was during our exile in Tangier, where, after the fall of France in 1940, my only friend, Pierre Forraz, was no longer allowed to associate with me—in a phase of national humiliation, the French turned their backs on foreigners. (Or they did worse; my teacher, Monsieur Duchez, slapped my face and called me a *sale voyou*—a dirty urchin—because to him I seemed disrespectful while he was discoursing on the greatness of *Maréchal* Pétain.)

Over the years, the analytic consensus has in fact moved in the direction I have pioneered. Perhaps the most convincing evidence for this claim is a recent issue *Psychoanalytic Inquiry* devoted to "The Clinical Use of Multiple Models," approximately half of which is devoted to my work.[6] The change in tone is already evident in the opening essay, an excellent synopsis of my clinical theories by Terry Rodgers (1994), a colleague whom I have not known in person. Rodgers notes that I have tried to articulate and explicate "a clinical theory for psychoanalysis that is comprehensive, coherent, and epistemologically sound," and he rightly states that basing the theory on a concept of self-organization that occupies a supraordinate position constitutes a new paradigm for psychoanalytic psychology.

Rodgers writes,

> The self-organization . . . is a psychobiological entity composed of a hierarchy of structured mental dispositions directed toward organismic needs and

> subjective goals as modified by a system of values. This patterned macrostructure evolves from the integration of preprogrammed biological needs and the subjective wishes that accompany the development of symbolic capacities—both in interaction with the external world. Once established it constitutes the basic core of . . . personality, a primary identity that is subject to later transformations only insofar as the individual acquires new systems of values. As the motivational fount for volitional behavior, it determines the individual's potentials for action and thus becomes the organizer of subsequent psychic life. [p. 238]

(I must confess with chagrin that Rodgers's summary of my proposed theory is the very best statement of my ideas to be found in print.)

I was most gratified by Rodgers's assertion that, in order truly to grasp my new paradigm, it is essential to become intimately acquainted with all of my writings. (I believe that, beyond other considerations, my work has thus far suffered relative neglect because it is not known in its totality to a sufficient number of informed readers.) Although not every commentator in this symposium was in sympathy with my viewpoint, it is notable that, in a refreshing change from the bad old days, none assumed that the burden of proof is on the person proposing a new idea. Estelle and Morton Shane (who are publicly committed to self psychology) described the conduct of an analysis from the perspective of my hierarchical model; they concluded their essay with the hope that it "conveys a sense of the clinical power of [that] conceptual formulation" (1994, p. 293). This was the first sign of acknowledgment by a self psychologist that, after my rupture with Heinz, I actually continued working. It was, of course, not at all unexpected that George Moraitis (1994) also endorsed my major contributions; the only critical voice was that of a younger traditionalist who attributed my favorable therapeutic results to my putative "talent" but condemned my theory of technique and called it "non-Freudian" (Druck 1994)—a feeble argument to make against a proposal that sets out to construct a new paradigm. (For my response see 1994a.)

Despite this objection, most of the 1994 contributors to the symposium on my work were startlingly receptive to it. At the same time, my overall position in psychoanalysis has shifted even further from the "classical" position that prevailed during my first three decades in the field. During the 1980s, I was widely regarded as a dissident, although many who thus dismissed me without studying my viewpoint mistakenly included me among Kohut's followers. The marginalization of my viewpoint was brought home to me when the eminent New York ego psychologist Charles Brenner and I participated in a panel (in Puerto Rico) where we happened to sit next to each other on the platform. At one point, as we were exchanging views in a friendly way, I laid my hand on his sleeve. Ever witty, Charlie grinned and asked, *"Là ci darem la mano?"*[7] He was calling me the evil seducer, Don Juan! I blurted out my disagreement, "The marriage of Figaro!" He thought I was displaying ignorance. "No, *Don Giovanni*," he said. "I know, I know," I replied, amid general laughter. Of course, among those who thought I had sold my soul to the devil, Charlie Brenner was both the nicest and the most cultivated.

In the early 1980s, a reputation for dissidence did not decrease one's opportunities to participate in scientific discussions at the American; on the contrary, in my case, this was the period when I was in greatest demand for its programs.[8] I felt, however, that I received these invitations not so much because I held views that deserved a hearing but because I could be counted on to put on an entertaining show. In terms of speaking engagements at local psychoanalytic societies, I tended no longer to be asked to the strongholds of ego psychology, even those where I had numerous friends. Under the circumstances, I became interested in the dynamics of dissidence within psychoanalysis,[9] and this topic became the central focus of my book, *Conceptual Issues in Psychoanalysis* (1986a). But that is a story that belongs among the sins of my old age.

I am confident that the theoretical future of psychoanalysis will be based on the hierarchical concept of mental functions, that is, on the integration of the simultaneous legacies of all previous developmental phases. The specifics of the hierarchical model I have proposed will undoubtedly be modified from time to time—just as I have modified them several times in the past twenty-five years (see especially 1979a, 1988a, and 1996b)—but I fully expect to get credit for the first explicit use of a hierarchical theory. I trust that this contribution has justified the great volume of my analytic writings; I hope that my cumulative bibliography (see Appendix) is not merely a sign of garrulousness.

When Goldberg and I originally constructed a hierarchy of modes of psychic organization, we based it on the correlation of several developmental lines then in standard use within psychoanalysis: object relations, narcissism, the sense of reality, typical situations of danger, and typical defenses. As our knowledge of psychological development has expanded (especially in the realms of cognition and communication), I have tried to adjust the hierarchical model by including among the lines of development it comprises these biologically determined functions. In the process, my view of psychic organization has come to lean more and more on such biological considerations; I finally realized that the hierarchical model should reflect (once the information available makes it possible, it must explicitly include) the progressive, hierarchical organization of cerebral functions.[10]

From this perspective, the therapeutic task of psychoanalysis is the expansion of psychological skills (that is, the maturation of cognitive abilities and the ability to communicate their results); in terms of psychopathology, this means that various hitherto missing procedural skills (conditions neurologists call "apraxic") must be acquired in treatment (see 1988a [chaps. 11–14]). We have recently learned that any such expansion of the adaptive repertory entails specific changes in neural organization; consequently, in my latest publications (1995c), I have equated Freud's concept of working through with the correction of apraxic deficits and changes in the central nervous system.

At the moment, such a biopsychological version of psychoanalysis is not in fashion. Contrary to all clinical evidence (not to speak of Freud's repeated insistence on the centrality of structural and economic factors for any change in mental functioning), most therapists—perhaps even the majority of analysts—labor under the illusion that the elucidation of mental contents suffices to produce adaptive change. If such disregard of the actual nature of psychopathology (that is, of the persistence of archaic forms of thinking and communications) were therapeutically feasible, some of our reductionist theories—for instance, those centered on object relations (such as those of Winnicott or Mahler) or Kohutian self psychology—would be sufficient. Conversely, such theories—popular precisely because they are simple enough to be easily mastered—do not address themselves to those transactions that actually matter therapeutically: the operations that result in working through.

One might even say that the scientific conception of psychoanalysis has been in retreat. This tendency began in France, where for more than a generation an alternative view has prevailed, that of a philosophically based Weltanschauung, only tenuously related to treatment for maladaptation. (The French generally equate adaptation with conformity.) In this country, I know of nobody who has gone that far, but a hermeneutic view of psychoanalysis (one confined to the search for "human meanings" in free associative material) is currently popular (see Gill 1994). The advocates of these notions are in a difficult position, because an emphasis on the indeterminacy of the meanings of texts (hence of free associations) is another fashionable intellectual import from France—and one extremely difficult to rebut. The "intersubjective" viewpoint about the nature of patients' communications is one of the ways in which the hermeneutics of psychoanalysis have been deconstructed and undermined. In other words, if we focus on mental contents alone, we shall forever remain mired in controversy about the putative virtues of one arbitrary interpretive schema against those of others equally arbitrary. (Klein? Kohut? Brenner? Mahler? Take your pick.)

In view of all this, a biological approach to psychoanalysis is the only option available that can address the crucial issues in a *scientific* context. Happily, an increasing number of respected contributors (for instance, Levin [1991], Lichtenberg [1989], and Modell [1992]) are espousing this view, so that my orientation on the fundamentals is not all that unusual anymore. In the last few years, I have focused much of my writing on metatheoretical matters, and these essays (1991f, 1994a, 1995c, 1995e, 1997b) have been well received by the establishment. Possibly the last book I shall write about clinical psychoanalysis (1996b) surveys the gamut of communicative channels used by analyst and analysand. These phenomena are, on the one hand, direct manifestations of human biology; on the other hand, adaptive improvement is contingent on prior change in the analysand's ability for intrapsychic and interpersonal communication. These matters are also best understood within a hierarchical framework. Hence, my farewell to clinical matters in *The Languages of Psychoanalysis* finally pulls together the various strands of my conceptual contributions.

Mine has been the most ambitious agenda a psychoanalytic author can undertake—which is not to claim that I have produced work of uniformly high quality. Yet I have thus far had no reason to repudiate any of the major hypotheses I have articulated in the past thirty years, and I continue to believe that I have chosen the most fruitful path. I react to the lack of widespread acceptance of my proposals with undiminished confidence in their value. If they fail to catch on, that fate will be the result of those unfortunate developments in the social matrix of American psychoanalysis that have largely turned its practitioners away from the search for scientific progress, in favor of seeking popular acceptance through some charismatic message.

I have only found it difficult to accept that, in the Chicago analytic community, some adherents of my intellectual opponents have occasionally treated me with disrespect. Of course, as a child, I was trained always to treat my elders as if they were my betters. And if that aspect of my upbringing has made me vulnerable to certain noxae, other early experiences prepared me for the lonely journey I have described. They may also explain the bitterness of which I am capable—a reaction that even my son finds inappropriate for the circumstances of my professional life.

❖ CHAPTER 15 ❖

THE HEART OF THE MATTER

Four or five years ago, I was replenishing my stock of unread paperbacks at Stuart Brent's bookstore and, as usual on such expeditions in pursuit of literary delights, I surveyed Brent's unrivaled stock of psychoanalytic titles to see whether my books were adequately represented. (Until he retired at the end of 1995, Brent was America's prime analytic bookseller, for about half a century. His premises were in the building where the Institute had been located when I was a candidate. Latterly, Stuart greeted me as a fellow-survivor from the good old days.) One of the numerous Brents of the second generation joined me and asked whether I was aware that *Beyond Interpretation* had sold out, and the publisher (International Universities Press) had no intention to reprint it. *Beyond Interpretation* had sold about four thousand copies—it was even translated into Italian—and it continues to enjoy modest but steady success over the years.

Adam Brent suggested that Northwestern University Press, which was then headed by one of his brothers, might be interested in reprinting the book—an idea I found intriguing because, when I finished the first draft of its manuscript some twenty years ago, I sent it to a third brother, David Brent, who had just become editor for psychoanalysis (and psychiatry) at the University of Chicago Press. David let me know, in some distress, that a reader whose judgment would have to remain final had found the book unpublishable. That is when I turned to the people I had come to know at International Universities Press.

Beyond Interpretation was an effort to spell out the technical consequences of consistently using the hierarchical model proposed in *Models of the Mind*. I was also eager to demonstrate that centering psychoanalytic psychology on a concept of self-organization did not necessarily mean acceptance of Kohut's recently developed theoretical schemata (a point also spelled out in 1987d); at the same time, I wished to put forward a theory free of the discredited energic assumptions of Freud's metapsychology of the 1890s (see also 1991f). I had become acquainted with the people running International Universities Press while working on the *Journal of the American Psychoanalytic Association* (until recently published by them). IUP also produced *Freud: The Fusion of Science and Humanism*, although on that project I had only dealt with them at second hand, through the personnel of the *Psychological Issues* monograph series. By the late 1970s, I was well enough known to the publishers and their editors to make it easy and natural to approach them—quite a change since my difficulties in getting *Models of the Mind* into print.

In the 1990s, although momentarily tempted by the potential symmetry of ending the book's journey *chez* Brent, as it had begun, I took it instead to a house I had frequently used since 1985, The Analytic Press. Its editor-in-chief, Paul Stepansky, has shepherded eight books of mine into print, and he seemed committed to making the core of my scientific contributions available for readers. Paul quickly agreed to my proposal to issue a substantially revised paperback edition of the book, and he explained how to obtain publication rights to the text; he suggested that computers could best retrieve the parts I wanted to reuse. I received the greatest compliment of my life from the operator who carried out this task; she wrote me a note to the effect that my case reports had caught her eye and, after reading them, she wished she could have had an analysis with me. After that, I did not even mind that I had been forced to hire her.

Once the book came back to me in the form of a computer printout, I rewrote it to reflect the changes in my psychoanalytic views between 1977 and 1992. The core of *Beyond Interpretation* is my account of three completed analyses and the comparison of the conceptualization of these clinical data in terms of traditional psychoanalytic theory (roughly, an up-to-date version of ego psychology, one giving appropriate weight to pregenital vectors) with the use of the most recently revised version of the hierarchical model first proposed in *Models of the Mind*. I did not change the case reports I had prepared fifteen to twenty years earlier—two of these were the analyses I had presented to the Kohut casebook group in 1974!—despite the fact that they did not represent my latest technical preferences, because fine points of technique are not centrally relevant to the aim of the book, that of testing the power of alternative *theoretical* schemata to illuminate psychoanalytic data. In other respects, I was amazed to find how drastically I had to rewrite the book (1993a) to keep abreast of the evolution of the theory I proposed in 1979.

When I sent my original manuscript to IUP, their reader cogently suggested that I focus the book more sharply, either on metapsychology or on the clinical theory of psychoanalysis. I decided to follow the second alternative, because in this manuscript I had made no original contribution to metapsychology. My specific contribution to the theoretical gestalt I wished to put together was in the clinical sphere; as I have already mentioned, acceptance of the hierarchical view of mental life entails the use of a set of differentiated technical modalities to deal with the pathological legacies of maldevelopment in each of the five phases of ontogenesis outlined in *Models of the Mind*. We entitled the work *Beyond Interpretation* (at George Klumpner's suggestion, I believe) because, in terms of a precise definition of the term, *interpretation* is only one of the modalities called for by this schema. If one accepts the necessity of using a variety of noninterpretive interventions in every psychoanalysis, it follows that one's procedures will be radically altered. Because these technical innovations improved my clinical results, I have over the years become bolder and bolder in departing from the traditional technique I had been taught. The cases I had summarized for *Beyond Interpretation* were handled in a relatively conservative manner, but I did not feel I had to demonstrate the subsequent development of my technical procedures in the revised edition, because I had spelled this out in a number of more recent publications (most extensively in 1981a [chap. 11 and Epilogue], 1988a [Epilogue], and 1991a [chap. 9]).

When the first edition of the book was published, Joe Lichtenberg had just taken over as editor of *Psychoanalytic Inquiry*, a new journal that planned to devote each number to a specific topic. Joe wanted to focus an occasional issue on a recent book he considered important, and he asked me whether I would be interested in such an evaluation of *Beyond Interpretation*. I was, of course, more than willing, and my book turned out to be the first one to receive such attention.[1] Lichtenberg invited half a dozen eminent colleagues to comment on the book at some length. He then sent me their papers, and I had the opportunity to write a response. These substantive commentaries were to be complemented by a brief biographical sketch to be authored by a person of my choosing. I asked Mike Gunther to prepare this for me, and he happily agreed, con amore (Gunther 1981).

Considering the radical nature of my book, the commentaries turned out to be surprisingly favorable. Merton Gill (1981) kept an open mind about my thesis, pending further clinical evidence about its applicability. Rangell (1981) did not see the *necessity* for theoretical revision, but he was not disturbed by the modifications of technique I introduced—as good a verdict as a radical proposal can get from a former president of the International Psychoanalytic! Appelbaum (1981) thought that my clinical innovations would prove to be particularly useful with hospitalized patients—she had intensive experience with such a patient population in Topeka. Meissner (1981), who confined his discussion to metatheoretical issues, endorsed the hierarchical approach to conceptualizing mental functions and looked forward to amplification of the theoretical schema I had presented.

On the other side, Dewald (1981) found fault with everything in my book that differed with the ego psychological party line; moreover, he cast doubt on the value of my clinical reports as psychoanalytic evidence because of my departures from what he regarded as correct technique. In contrast to this polemic, the critique of two prominent Kleinians (Segal and Britton 1981) was dispassionate. They noted that all the cases I described in the book were extremely "difficult," but they attributed what I regarded as reasoned technical innovations to the effects of unchecked countertransference.

The essay I wrote in response to these commentaries (1981b) is, in my judgment, the most closely reasoned and persuasive piece I have ever produced. I had so much pleasure in preparing it that I could not keep my elation out of the text, and I am still sorry that the copy editor insisted on deleting much of this evidence of high good humor. (There remain a few parenthetical exclamations calling on some epistemic referee to penalize my opponents for unsportsmanlike conduct, but my best sallies are gone.)

I found it noteworthy that none of the commentators acknowledged the excellent clinical results I reported, thereby denying their superiority to those obtained by traditional analytic means (such as the outcomes described in Firestein's recent book [1978]). To rebut arguments that noninterpretive interventions are not "analytic," I pointed out that in none of the illustrative cases did they interfere with subsequent elucidation of previously unconscious material; these analyses brought to light the gamut of significant mental contents generally encountered in the past. It was also in this essay that, for the first time, I called attention to the fact that certain psychological dispositions found through analysis are based on some kind of cognitive deficit—only by addressing that apraxia can its psychological consequences be eliminated. Moreover, I introduced the technical principle that analysts are most effective when they are able to find a private language they can share with their analysand.

In the realm of psychopathology, the hierarchical schema differs from previous conceptualizations in giving equal weight to vicissitudes in every phase of early development—in contrast, traditional theory attributed a predominant role in pathogenesis to the outcome of the oedipal crisis. Hence, in my version of psychoanalysis, it is necessary to pay equal attention to derivatives of every childhood phase of development—including, of course, the oedipal, which is frequently neglected by adherents of Kohut's system. The hierarchical view makes it possible to determine the relative importance for a given individual of various goals and of the legacies of various developmental phases; it is the stable configuration of these priorities that I have called "self-organization." Another way to define this term is that it refers to the sum of our clinical observations, considered from a structural point of view.

It is the task of a theory of self-organization to spell out what are the significant psychological dispositions that are thus structured in the course of development. In the 1981b essay I stated for the first time that the core of this organization is "the sum of those psychobiological patterns that become obligatory components of the compulsion to repeat" (p. 309). This is the conception that anchors my theoretical work within biology; it calls for an integration of psychoanalysis with neurophysiology (and neurochemistry). And in the clinical situation it dictates that analysts must expand their focus beyond the interpretable meanings of their patients' verbalizations to the repetitive, nonverbal, psychobiological patterns they can detect if they adopt the observational stance of a natural scientist. Patients tend to misattribute such preverbal problems to the vicissitudes of their object relationships; they have no awareness of the fact that their infantile patterns of relatedness have become obligatory because within them they received symbiotic assistance that compensated for various developmental deficits. (In other words, these archaic needs have never attained mental representation.) These obligatory behaviors, compulsively repeated in an active mode, form the core of what Freud called the Unconscious.

Beyond Interpretation was a true monograph; it presents one coherent thesis, and none of it had been previously published as a separate essay. (In retrospect, the chapter "The Status of Structural Theory" constituted a superfluous detour from the thrust of my argument. It *should* have been published separately, and in 1993 I omitted it from the revised edition.) It had taken me almost five years from the time I first began preparing the case illustrations to bring my first solo book to publication; during this interval, I had produced a number of papers, some published, others, presented hither and yon, that were only peripherally related to its thesis but were based on the theories outlined in the book (see 1975a, 1977a, 1979e, 1980a, 1980b). Moreover, some of my older publications (1964a, 1966a, 1967a) on psychotherapy now seemed to me to prefigure the technical modifications I had more recently espoused in a psychoanalytic context. I thought I had enough material more or less ready for republication in revised form to constitute a companion volume for *Beyond Interpretation*.

I sent the people at IUP some of these materials, to ask whether they would be interested in publishing such a volume, and they sent me an advance contract without further ado. (Since then, I have refused to write books "on speculation"—I have always made prior arrangements with a publisher.) Because the new volume (1981a) dealt with clinical topics, I entitled it *Advances in Clinical Psychoanalysis*. As many of the basic building blocks for this book already existed, I was able to bring it to completion much faster than my previous books; *Advances* appeared barely two years after *Beyond Interpretation*.

I was in frequent telephone contact with my editor throughout the project; he made many suggestions that promised to make the book clearer, more coherent, and more comprehensive. As our production deadline approached, we decided it would be desirable to add an entire chapter that would try to show that Kohut's then recent attempt to construct a nosology based on the putatively independent vicissitudes of specific lines of development (what he called Tragic Man and Guilty Man) was radically flawed, because it disregarded the epigenetic nature of psychological development. (Eventually, Kohut realized that he was on the wrong tack and, in his last book [1984], he dropped this faulty conceptualization. Thenceforth, instead of considering two alternatives, self psychology was further narrowed into a single formula.) I had to go to San Francisco for the spring meetings of the American Psychoanalytic and it was on that trip that I wrote chapter 7 of *Advances*, "Epigenesis, Developmental Lines, and Psychopathology." I completed it just before the plane landed on my return. An exhilarating experience!

In one sense, *Advances* was an effort on my part to forestall conservative objections to my proposals by publishing ample clinical material that shows adequate handling of the oedipal aspects of patients' pathology. Altogether, the book contains accounts of a dozen analyses; oedipal vicissitudes were clarified in all of them, but in none did they constitute the sole vector of maladaptation. These case reports show that each patient had difficulties referable to several developmental phases, in varying proportions, depending on the exact configuration of the personality. Based on the hierarchical model (and the multiple modalities of treatment it suggests), I endorsed the use of psychoanalysis in a very broad range of contingencies, and I urged a focus in treatment on patients' characterological attributes. I believe that the range of psychoanalysis is limited only by the emergence of regressions into helplessness, disorganization, or psychosis. (I illustrated these limitations via three cases in which analysis failed—one that necessitated hospitalization and two wherein I was unable to influence the analysands' covert delusional convictions.) From this viewpoint, the so-called borderline states cannot be seen as disease entities—they are heterogeneous syndromes that vulnerable personalities may develop in specific contingencies. Our analytic efforts fail not as a result of our patients' diagnostic status but because particular individuals turn out to be unable to assimilate new knowledge and skills through the clinical procedures we have applied.

When analyses are conducted in the "classical" manner, archaic issues are usually given short shrift (usually as mere regressive evasions of oedipal conflicts) and apparent improvements in adaptation are often contingent on the persistence of a silent and uninterpreted idealizing transference. Insofar as the disavowed problems are referable to the earliest phases of development, attention to the narcissistic issues stressed by Kohut will not suffice to deal with them, either; these patients do not possess some of the basic psychobiological skills essential to cope in adult life. Hence, Kohut's selfobject transferences are not central to archaic pathology—they are compensatory measures, learned in childhood, that patch over a developmental deficit. In other words, I completely disagree with Kohut's assumption that these transference manifestations echo expectable stages in early development.

Consequently, I make different recommendations from those of self psychology about the optimal therapeutic response to the emergence of grandiosity in the transference; I believe that the analyst must only make accurate statements about the analysand's actual merits, and that the problem can only be resolved if the reasons for having become fixated on these primitive attitudes are elucidated. I do agree, however, with Kohut's contention that transference idealization is not always defensive—nor is it always a reaction to prior disillusionment. It can represent the repetition of an early childhood state; typically the idealized other is a symbiotic object whose availability and perfection are taken for granted. Hence, a genuine idealization in the transference tends not to focus on the *person* of the analyst but on the latter's skills as a therapist.

Another area of disagreement I have with self psychology concerns empathy. Kohut was correct in identifying introspection and empathy as cardinal tools of psychoanalysis, but his view ignored that it is essential that analysts use additional cognitive operations: pattern-matching, and inferences about the analysand's motives based on our affective responses. In my judgment, empathy is most likely to lead to valid conclusions when we deal with human universals, particularly biological matters such as a person's affective state. Hence, in most instances it is best to enlist the analysand's cooperation to discern the meanings of verbal productions. Novel insights reached by such methods expand the psychological repertory of the analyst and create new templates for more accurate pattern-matching in the future.

In addition to the foregoing critique of self psychology (as it was at the end of Kohut's life), *Advances* contains a parallel critique of theories of object relations, especially of those that view internalized childhood relationships as determinants of later behavior. As patients' enactments within the psychoanalytic setting demonstrate, clinical focus on interpersonal relations is, in persons with alloplastic adaptive styles, of great practical importance. It is also important to understand the intrapsychic templates of these transactions (and of transference relations in general). The great pitfall of such attempts is the tendency to assume that adult behaviors constitute actual homologues of childhood transactions, for the child's capacity to elaborate fantasies forms a prism that deflects the effects of actual events in unpredictable ways. The earliest experiences are encoded in memory mostly in terms of their affective qualities, so that the object relations characteristic of the true self may be extremely difficult to discern. Hence, it is preferable to focus not on early object relations but on specifying the crucial *inner* experiences of early childhood. In this regard, it must be noted that certain transference developments referable to earliest childhood may be unprecedented in the adult experience of analysands, especially if unmet psychobiological needs lacking in mental representations are fortuitously (or planfully) fulfilled in the analysis.

From a metapsychological perspective, internalized object relations (that is, representations in the system of memories) cannot serve as an explanation of the source of all motivations. Hence, object relations theory has generally been used in conjunction with some form of drive theory. (Such was Kohut's position when he differentiated the problems of Tragic Man from those of Guilty Man.) Moreover, an exclusive reliance on object relations would clearly transform psychoanalysis into a psychology of nurture that illegitimately disregards biological considerations. Nor has any theorist specified how early object relations templates are supposedly turned into a source of motivation. Finally, it should be recalled that the quality of the infant's experiences is not determined by the activities of the caretakers alone.

The last section of *Advances* is devoted to various applications of the hierarchical model to analytic problems. First, I considered the paradoxical effects of interpretations (in particular, in the case of dreams) whenever they are offered in regressed states (that is, in modes I through III in the hierarchical schema). In those circumstances, analysands generally do not respond by grasping the meaning of the hitherto unconscious psychic contents; rather, they tend to take from the analyst's communication whatever can serve them to master the characteristic dilemma of the prevalent mode of behavioral organization: pacification (for mode I), integration of the self (in mode II), or the correction of illusions (in mode III). These paradoxical effects probably account for the fact that some analysts claim to have obtained good results in conditions beyond the neuroses through the use of a purely interpretive technique—they thought they were providing insight, but their analysands succeeded in getting something else from their therapeutic efforts.

A second major issue tackled in this section is that of the analyst's affectivity as it relates to management of the transference. The expression of affects may be essential as a primary avenue of communication with analysands unable to grasp the lexical meanings of ordinary speech—a circumstance that may either be chronic or may supervene acutely as a result of regression. Because emotion-laden interventions of this kind in no way interfere with the subsequent progress of analysis, there is no reason to avoid using the full resources of rhetoric (that is, varying the paraverbal aspects of speech) with the gamut of analytic patients. By extrapolation, it also makes sense to go beyond the music of speech and, wherever it may facilitate communication, to convey messages by means of music or gesture.

I also devoted a chapter to the problem of the choice of symptom, wherein I tried to demonstrate that the use of the hierarchical model is essential for its clarification. Every symptom is an attempted remedy for a threatened failure of integration within the prevalent mode of behavioral organization: for instance, neurotic symptoms resolve unconscious conflicts through attempts at compromise, resort to an addiction is a self-soothing (or self-stimulating) maneuver in the face of a failure of tension regulation, and so on. The specifics of the symptomatic behavior, however, go beyond the adaptive functions they subserve in this manner; they are codetermined by the particular historical circumstances within the phase of development when this given solution to the adaptive challenge supervened. In other words, the hierarchical model permits us to consider any piece of behavior simultaneously from a functional/adaptive and from a developmental point of view. (Because the model charts progress—or regression—along multiple axes, it can differentiate syndromes that represent mere regressions from others that constitute actual arrests in development. In such cases of arrest, functional development has never matured beyond the levels demonstrated during the period of observation.)

I trust that even these brief synopses of the development of my ideas in *Advances in Clinical Psychoanalysis* (and in my response to the discussants of my work in *Psychoanalytic Inquiry*) show that, only a couple of years after completing *Beyond Interpretation*, my scientific position had already left it behind in many respects—so much so, that my clinical procedures in the early 1980s were different enough from those in the cases described in the 1979 book to impel me to center another volume (1984c) on two lengthy accounts of analyses conducted in the new way I had developed. By the time I came to revise *Beyond Interpretation*, another decade had passed, and my psychoanalytic outlook had evolved even further.

My collaboration with Goldberg had been, for me, a maximally conservative stand—an effort to salvage as much of the Freudian paradigm of mental functioning as possible. Our book received a friendly welcome because readers could easily grasp this intention; we retained an extensive body of familiar constructs and jettisoned comparatively little of the baggage we were all used to carrying. Although *Models of the Mind* was influenced by previous critiques of Freud's metapsychology, the only overt concession it made to radical change was omission of the concept of psychic energy. By depriving Freud's theoretical system of an energic cathexis, we succeeded in reconciling (most of) the disparate segments of clinical theory at the expense of abandoning the principle of parsimony: these fragmentary concepts were based on a wide variety of disparate theoretical premises.

Except for matters of detail, I continue to stand behind the principles of the 1973 hierarchical model. By 1979, however, I was no longer satisfied with the theoretical compromise we accepted in *Models of the Mind*. Because neither a literal (biological) nor a metaphorical understanding of psychic energy is epistemically tenable (see Swanson 1977), a *scientific* version of psychoanalysis must repudiate any construct based on energic assumptions, as were most of the subsidiary concepts used by Freud (such as ego and id). I wished to articulate an elegant theory that would illuminate all of the observational data we obtain in the clinical setting of psychoanalysis—unlike both contemporary ego psychologists and self psychologists, who disregarded each other's cogent observations (see 1980a).

I prefer to define *metapsychology* as any psychoanalytic theory that is not derived from observational data by a process of induction. In my judgment, it is impossible to devise purely clinical theories, without reliance on deductive propositions that reflect our convictions about the biology of the human organism—that is, the latest conclusions of cognitive psychology and brain science.

In the 1993 revision of *Beyond Interpretation*, I asserted that the need to maintain the stability of self-organization is a supraordinate goal, at the summit of the hierarchy of personal aims. As Modell (1992) has also stated, without a stable self-organization (that is, internal order), the tendency to respond to stimuli in an ad hoc manner soon leads to chaos and intolerable anxiety. The goal of appetite satisfaction is also universal; it regulates behavior in the presymbolic mode of functioning through preprogrammed patterns of neural control. Early experiences of pleasure and unpleasure soon teach the infant to maintain physiological equilibria on the basis of anticipated affective reactions. Some of the sensorimotor patterns that subserve early appetite satisfaction may not gain mental representation—they remain out of the realm of subjectivity. It is to illuminate such repetitive behaviors that psychoanalysis must transcend the realm of symbolic meanings and build bridges to neurophysiology.

The hierarchical model presented in *Models of the Mind* actually constitutes a developmental record of progressive changes in self-organization. Mental life begins with a phase of uncoordinated, discrete goals that can be viewed as separate nuclei of function. Because at that stage experiences can only be recalled sequentially, one at a time, they cannot come into conflict with each other. From these sets of uncoordinated goals, the cohesive hierarchy of aims I call self-organization is gradually integrated—its stability means a relatively permanent set of structured potentials for action which are linked to characteristic affective consequences (both qualitatively and in terms of intensities). These affective parameters, established in the preverbal era, form the core of what human beings are compelled to repeat, at any cost, to maintain a sense of continuity. This developmental hypothesis implies that the compulsion to repeat is not, in itself, pathological; on the contrary, it is the principal guarantor of the stability of the personality.

Only after the achievement of self-cohesion (that is, psychobiological integration of the personality) does behavior begin to be regulated in accord with the principle of seeking "pleasure"—that is, satisfactions on the basis of purposeful choices. Any threat to self-cohesion must therefore be given priority (in any form of treatment) over the less crucial problem of conflicts about specific wishes. Intrapsychic conflicts can only become the central adaptive issue after self-regulation is achieved, usually as a consequence of the internalization of a set of moral standards. Prior to this development, self-cohesion is vulnerable to regression, particularly because of threats to self-esteem; these conditions place the burden of behavior regulation, in large measure, on caretaker-participants in the young child's milieu.

The foregoing developmental schema is grounded in biology, for it is built on the articulation of the interconnections among three lines of development (outside the realm of conflicts)—those of the maturation of the brain, of cognition, and of communicative skills. In the version of the hierarchical model presented in the revised *Beyond Interpretation*, these largely autonomous functions are correlated with those that tend to become involved in conflict: the child's object relations, the dangers typical for successive phases of development, and the typical defenses available to ward these off.

A theory focused on self-organization is preferable to the alternatives currently available (drive theories and object relations theories) because it can account for the entirety of the observational data of psychoanalysis, whereas the other theories do not do so and therefore have to be used in conjunction, despite their irreconcilable differences. (One good way to characterize these differences is to recall that drive theories represent a one-person psychology, and object relations theories are confined to dyadic transactions.) In addition, the repetition compulsion is unexplained by either theory, unless one accepts Freud's (1920) postulate of a death instinct (which has been generally rejected by psychoanalysts as heuristically useless and biologically incorrect). In other words, I believe the theory I have proposed is epistemically sound, clinically nonreductionistic, and internally consistent.

Anna and Mathias Gedo, Prague 1922

Mathias and John, Losoncz 1930

John, Tangier 1940

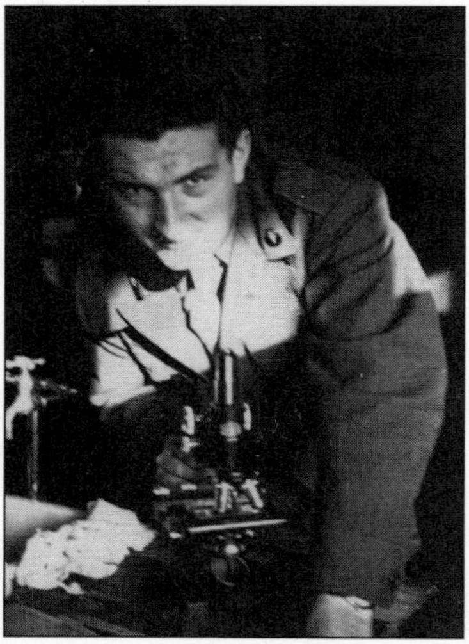

John, Osaka 1946

Mary and John, Chicago 1953

Front:
Andrew,
Paul, Nicholas
Rear: John
and Mary,
Chicago 1963

Mary, Paris 1966

Mary and Nick, Umbria 1971

Mary and John, Chicago 1987

Freud and friends, Chicago 1987

At the Chicago Institute 1995,
introducing Therese Benedek,
Heinz Kohut, Helen MacLean (top);
Thomas French, Helen Ross,
Franz Alexander (bottom);
Gerhart Piers (left); and
Joan Fleming (right)

Mary, John, and
poodle Cherubino, Chicago 1996

PART THREE

THE SINS OF OLD AGE

❖ CHAPTER 16 ❖

FESTIVALS

In October 1995 I gave an Edith Weigert Lecture at the Washington School of Psychiatry. What occasion could have been better? I had a new granddaughter just outside the Beltway, I love the city's museums, and I even got a chance to spend an afternoon with a colleague from Budapest, doing research at the Library of Congress in preparation for a book on Hungarian psychoanalysis. She interviewed me about the Hungarian diaspora in America and my own experience in the New World. It is simply gratifying to be asked to give named lectures, of course. Moreover, the invitation came through John Muller, formerly a candidate at the Chicago Institute, who has recently taken over as editor of the *Psychiatry and the Humanities* book series. Each volume of this interdisciplinary forum is organized around one or more public lectures by distinguished humanists, with commentaries by invited participants. My Weigert lecture is supposed to complete a volume on semiotics—John Muller's favorite subject, and one whose bearing on psychoanalysis I have from time to time also tried to consider (1984c [chaps. 8 and 9], 1988a [chap. 13], 1996b). I have no objection whatsoever to a token of esteem from a former student.

Yet I was decidedly surprised to get this invitation, for I once withdrew from a project with this organization in something of a huff. More than ten years ago, a former editor of *Psychiatry and the Humanities* asked me to write one of the commentaries about a position statement by the eminent neopragmatist philosopher Richard Rorty. I found Rorty's selective use of some of Freud's ideas objectionable, even to constitute a distortion, and I wrote a vigorous critique of his paper. A few months after I submitted this response, I received a communication from an editorial assistant that instructed me to review the copyediting of my manuscript and to return it within a week because the publishers had imposed a strict deadline; Rorty had taken too long to revise his lecture.

I was scandalized—Rorty had been dilatory, and now I was asked to approve printing my paper without seeing the final version of what I was commenting on! I called *Psychiatry and the Humanities* to protest—completely in vain. To add to my indignation, I got no further when I mentioned that I was, in fact, physically unable to work on the manuscript because I had just suffered a retinal tear and my vision was temporarily impaired by the resultant intraocular hemorrhage. (Under the circumstances, I thought even the Johns Hopkins Press would wait.) The functionary I was talking to used a tone of voice with me fit for a bureaucrat in a Kafka novel. I told her, in what I intended to be an echo of her tone, that I was withdrawing from their project. (I published a modified version of my essay as part of my next book [1986a, chap. 14].) The editor tried to call me, presumably to work out some compromise, but I refused to talk to him. (He was not directly responsible for the sadism of his functionary, but the decision to deprive the discussants of the opportunity to review the definitive version of Rorty's work was beneath contempt.) I suppose I was really prejudiced against this man, because I had heard that the last straw that had led to the defection of some in the WAPE group from the Washington Institute had been his appointment as a training analyst.

I was happy to find that this murky past history did not come back to haunt the October lecture or the festivities that surrounded the event. In terms of festive occasions, however, the Weigert lecture failed to match my experience the previous December, when I gave a Jerome Sashin Memorial Lecture under the joint sponsorship of PINE and BPSI. Jerry Sashin was a gifted colleague, affiliated with both institutions, who died young. Because of his personal qualities, the committee in charge of the event preferred a lecture dealing with creativity. They used an auditorium at Boston College, a gorgeous setting on a perfect autumn day. (Bill Meissner, who holds the only professorship of psychoanalysis in the United States at this Jesuit university, was able to make these ideal arrangements.) I chose to talk about the numerous personality traits indispensable to make creative achievements possible (1993i). The faculty member who introduced me spoke about Sashin's promise and accomplishments; he beautifully wove the theme of my presentation and the memory of the person in whose honor it was to be made into a seamless whole.

After the prepared lecture, Bob Gardner made a brief response, and for more than an hour I conducted a lively discussion with various members of the audience. I felt very much at home—I knew so many people there! How often did I indulge in fantasies of leaving Chicago to join Bob in Boston? How many times have I made the trek to New England, for how many different organizations? One of my papers on the rhetorical aspects of psychoanalysis (published as chapter 8 in 1984c) was prepared for a Tufts symposium that drew an astonishing audience of some twelve hundred. Ana-Maria Rizzuto, who was also a panelist on that occasion, was sitting in the front row at the Sashin Lecture. When the Boston Society celebrated its fiftieth anniversary, I was asked to discuss Arnold Modell's plenary address and to present an account of a terminated analysis (chap. 5 in 1984c). One of the commentators on that case report was also in the audience at Boston College.

I had once before lectured in that very hall—Bill Meissner had asked me to take part in an interdisciplinary series at the college, and I had discussed the meanings encoded in the Boston Museum's Gauguin masterpiece, *Where Do We Come From? What Are We? Where Are We Going?* (included in 1994b). Long ago, Bob Gardner invited me to give the first public lecture presented by PINE; that event took place at the Harvard Science Center. For that occasion, we had also selected a topic that might appeal to a broad audience, "Sigmund Freud and the Socratic Tradition."[1] The Boston Society once held a symposium about one of my books (1988a) with those outstanding experts on primitive personalities, Michael Robbins and Edward Shapiro (now director at Austen Riggs), as the principal discussants. There were three or four lesser occasions over the years, including some seminars for groups of candidates. Of course, I worked hard to cadge these invitations, to make it easier to get together with Bob.

Although I am not equally "among friends" in Washington, it has by no means been a terra incognita for me, especially after I became acquainted with Joe Lichtenberg. I think, prior to the Weigert lecture, it was Joe who secured almost all of my Washington engagements. The big exception was a joint invitation Mary and I received to take part in a conference at the National Gallery of Art about the psychoanalytic approach to the visual arts. This event was sponsored by the Center for Advanced Study in the Visual Arts (CASVA). CAPS is not the only organization to have copied the designation of the Institute for Advanced Study!

The CASVA symposium was a weekend of delights: a German art historian who had been analyzed gave an insightful public lecture on the eighteenth century Anglo-Swiss artist Heinrich Füssli (a.k.a. Fuseli) whose work is full of fetishistic imagery; we met the Gauguin biographer Wayne Andersen, arguably the most picaresque character of this prosaic age, fresh from designing mosques in Saudi Arabia; we were reintroduced to the celebrated Philip Rieff (whom I had met in Houston, when we participated in a conference on the unconscious at Rice University), once a serious Freud scholar, now turned into a figure of fantasy, dressed as an Edwardian gentleman.

Because Lichtenberg switched from one organization to the other, he managed to get me engagements for presentations and seminars at both the Baltimore-Washington Institute and the rival Washington Institute. A dynamo of activity, Joe has also been connected with the Washington School of Psychiatry, a Sullivanian training institution that is, despite its name, open to all mental health professionals. In 1989 he was the principal organizer of the fiftieth anniversary celebration of this influential academy. He brought together an array of speakers of various persuasions to address the topic that has divided Sullivanians from the rest of American psychoanalysis, the dilemma of encompassing both intrapsychic and interpersonal perspectives in our theories. He was able to attract many of us because he could ensure publication of the symposium as a number of *Psychoanalytic Inquiry*.[2]

In retrospect, that event was the most fruitful psychoanalytic colloquium I have ever attended. The interpersonal school was represented by Stephen Mitchell and Edgar Levenson (both from the Sullivanian organization in New York, the William Alanson White Institute), and the mainstream Freudian viewpoint by Sander Abend (then editor of the *Psychoanalytic Quarterly*). The infant researcher Daniel Stern and I presented concepts (incidentally, congruent with each other) that used a developmental perspective in attempting to resolve this long-time quarrel (see 1988b). Herb Schlesinger, Paulina Kernberg, and Ernest Wolf presented cases handled in accord with differing theoretical preconceptions, and the main discussants were Arnold Cooper and Bob Michels (from the Columbia Institute and Cornell Medical School), and Joe Lichtenberg. It was an open-minded scientific interchange among people with strong convictions that was nonetheless conducted in a spirit of rationality and civilized discourse. It rarely happens so.

The greatest possible contrast to such a felicitous outcome was my experience at the endowed lecture named after Sándor Radó that I gave about twenty years ago at the Columbia Institute. I suspect that they decided to invite me just before *Beyond Interpretation* was published; from their perspective, I was a scion of the analytic establishment but someone guaranteed not to put them down—say in the manner to be attempted by the chairman of the forthcoming 1979 site visit. By the time I actually appeared for them, they knew that they had compromised themselves by giving a platform to a radical. John Weber, who was then still director, was an upper-class New Yorker, and the institute was run along patrician lines. I was to wear a tuxedo; before the lecture, there was to be a ceremonial dinner at the Grolier Club; the great event was to be held at the New York Academy of Medicine. (It made me feel that the sarcastic mutterings about Columbia analysts and sartorial overkill had real substance!)

During my nine-year New York period, I had often passed the Academy's Fifth Avenue palazzo (for instance, en route to my first job as a 15-year-old delivery boy and doorman at the Longchamps Restaurant on Madison Avenue near 78th Street), but I had never entered its august premises. Nor have I owned a tuxedo since my internship at Presbyterian Hospital, which, alas! failed to introduce me into the social life of the Chicago elite; this may have been the third occasion in twenty-odd years for which I had to rent one. (When, at dinner, I groused about this to the reigning grande dame of the Columbia Institute, she assured me that it was desirable, because men looked so much better in evening dress. Henriette Klein was a lady of true delicacy!) The occasion reminded me of the single medical school reunion I have attended, in 1961 at the Plaza Hotel, where Mary was practically the only woman without a fur coat and some classmates arrived in enormous black cars that could only have been rented. Customs of that sort impel me to call the island of Manhattan a "ship of fools."

The night before I left home for New York to give the Radó Lecture, I had a memorable dream: I was the New York Yankee pitcher Ron Guidry, and I was at Yankee Stadium warming up for a start in the World Series. A number of reporters came to interview me; one of them asked, "Is it true that you have the best fastball in the business?" I paused before replying, "I don't know. We'll see. We'll see." I was flooded with intense satisfaction about having given this answer.[3] Because this dream showed how deeply I appreciated the opportunity the Columbia invitation had given me, as well as a modicum of modesty (newfound for the occasion), I decided to begin by sharing it with my audience. Some in the thin ranks in attendance did laugh—but the experience is etched in my memory because, on the way out, someone congratulated me for having invented such a marvelous fake dream to amuse the listeners. This confusion of tongues[4] turned out to be characteristic of the whole occasion.

The topic of my lecture was "The Problem of the Choice of Symptom" (chap. 12 in 1981a). As per custom, a synopsis (prepared by a recent Columbia graduate—Mahon [1980]) was to be published in an in-house organ, the *Bulletin* of the Association for Psychoanalytic Medicine. I knew nothing about the plan until I received a copy of this publication and was chagrined to find that, instead of a factual summary of my presentation, it contained a deprecating commentary that drastically misconstrued many of the points I had tried to make. For example, I had made an ironic reference to Sándor Radó's concept of "alimentary orgasm"—I hoped this attempted deconstruction of his pun would amuse the audience, because (by sheer coincidence) the case I used to illustrate a Radó Lecture happened to involve a real sexual perversion connected with eating. With condescending severity, the reporter of the *Bulletin* castigated me for concretizing Radó's abstract concept. *Mamma mia*! I wrote a private letter of complaint to the editor; he replied that he also thought the tone of the report was inappropriate, but he printed it as a matter of "academic freedom." He offered to publish a rebuttal. I thought his excuse was preposterous and the damage too trivial to dignify with a response. Yet this incident is fairly characteristic of the current tendency to politicize discourse in psychoanalysis.

I do not mean to suggest that only my opponents engage in polemics; however, I trust that, when I do so, I do not waste my ammunition on straw men. I have never hesitated to voice sharp disagreements in public: in the early 1980s, through the good offices of Helen Meyers, I took part in two symposia sponsored by the Columbia Institute (see 1986d and 1988c) where I was surrounded almost exclusively by colleagues from New York, decidedly out of sympathy with the views I was presenting. Such circumstances, I have found, loosen the tongue, enhance one's sense of humor, and unleash a bit of aggression—an excellent combination to spice up a reasoned position. I was able to defend my innovations against guardians of orthodoxy such as a grey eminence at the New York Psychoanalytic Institute about fifteen years my senior. My father taught me the Roman motto, "Si fractus illabatur orbis, impavidum ferient ruinae!"[5] Of course I had to have an analysis to be able to make use of the lesson.

I must say that when one is invited for some festive event, most groups treat one with greater consideration than I had received in New York, or at least with an appearance of greater tolerance for differences. For instance, some time in the late 1980s I gave a Franz Alexander Lecture for the Southern California Institute. (It was an opportunity I was particularly pleased about, both because of my personal encounters with Alexander a generation earlier and because I learned that the lecturer for this event is chosen by vote of the candidates.) This organization was able to fill a large lecture hall at the Mt. Sinai Hospital in Los Angeles, and my thesis (1987d) received a most friendly discussion despite its differences with the views prevalent at this institute. They also arranged a case seminar attended by about a hundred candidates and faculty, and some did not even take it amiss that I was highly critical of the presenter's clinical work.

Of course, such differences in ecology are not merely matters of geography. No place in America can actually compare with New York in terms of turning out a large crowd for a psychoanalytic meeting. Not long ago, the fiftieth anniversary meeting of the William Alanson White Institute had over a thousand registrants despite a hefty admission fee, and they did not boycott my presentation (1995f), as most of the members of the Columbia Institute had done at their open meeting years before. (It is not an organized plot I am describing, but the unanimity formerly attributed to a herd instinct.) When in 1985 I gave a Menaker lecture for the psychoanalytic program of the New York University Graduate School, they filled one of the largest auditoria at the university. (To be sure, my topic was a critique of self psychology [1989b], and that probably accounted for much of the attendance.) In other words, the issue is neither personal nor simply a matter of location or the size of the sponsoring group—it is that of fit between the speaker's reputed viewpoint and the perceived need for new input in that analytic community. From this perspective, organizations not affiliated with the American Psychoanalytic Association are more permeable to new ideas than those within the establishment. Nobody in Salt Lake City was shocked by my views when I gave a lecture at the University of Utah, nor in London, Ontario, when I presented there on several occasions. (There are psychoanalytic festivals in all sorts of unlikely places!) I do not know whether analysts at institutes of the American such as those in New Orleans, Atlanta, and various bastions of the Eastern establishment, are more rigidly trained than people from programs lacking the cachet of apostolic succession; perhaps the difference is merely a matter of having the nerve to snub presumed outsiders.

Of course, it helps if the speaker's way is prepared by word-of-mouth propaganda disseminated by friends. Boston has been a home-away-from home to me because of the publicity I have received from Bob Gardner. My trips to Houston were facilitated by the good words of Bob Gilliland.

For many years, I returned repeatedly to San Francisco because one of my medical school classmates kept recommending me to the faculty. In Cincinnati, I have had close relations with several colleagues, from John MacLeod to Lou Spitz; they have invited me on numerous occasions, culminating in a Maurice Levine Memorial Lecture, cosponsored by the Institute for Contemporary Art (chap. 5 in 1992a). As long as Maurice Tuchman was instrumental in preparing programs at meetings of the Academy of Psychoanalysis, he repeatedly arranged excellent opportunities for me to speak to large segments of its membership (1987e, 1988a [chap. 6], 1991f). (Tuchman and I have no social relationship, but it cannot be a coincidence that invitations to the academy have only come my way through him, and he is very friendly with Mike Gunther.) Yet friendship cannot help where the community will not accept one's viewpoint—one rarely gets asked to visit such groups and certainly never for their festivals.

At the same time, invitations are most gratifying when one is selected because of some specific expertise. This was the case with the Levine lecture, because the cosponsoring museum naturally desired a focus on a topic within the domain of the visual arts—a field that has attracted few psychoanalysts. The same was true many years earlier for a Sterba lecture at the Michigan Association for Psychoanalysis: Sterba lectures were always supposed to deal with a cultural topic. That meeting also took place in a beautiful museum setting, at the Cranbrook Academy of Art, and I chose to honor Richard Sterba (who was present for my talk) with a presentation on the character of Caravaggio (1983a, chap 9). Sterba had given a similar paper in Chicago about Michelangelo (Sterba and Sterba 1956)—one of the best efforts ever in psychobiography. I had no close contacts with anyone in the Michigan association, so that I was certain that I was asked to give the lecture on the basis of my published work on cultural topics. Now *that* is "The High Class Porno," as the flashing neon sign in Copenhagen used to advertise!

From a completely subjective viewpoint, any opportunity to teach in another community seemed like a festival to me, whether I met a group of graduate students in Knoxville, psychiatric residents in San Antonio, some study group of Manhattan colleagues, or classes at psychoanalytic institutes from Orange County to New Haven. Mary has almost never accompanied me on these trips, and they were never well remunerated, but five or six ventures of this kind, every year for some thirty years, have resulted in my getting to know the North American analytic world (not to speak of much of the country itself). These experiences also allowed me to compensate for the frustration of having remained a peripheral figure as an Institute faculty member in Chicago—they gave me feedback about my effectiveness as a teacher of a kind I never received among my neighbors.

Three decades on the lecture circuit have only whetted my appetite; I am still looking for invitations to Melbourne, Osaka, São Paulo, Geneva, Boston, or Washington. I love the feeling of being professionally valued by people who have a wide range of choices—something one does not get as a clinician, because most patients cannot afford to fire one simply because a Roy Schafer or an Otto Kernberg has more of a public reputation. My travels have also rubbed in the truth of the old saw about the impossibility of being a prophet in one's own country; I formerly experienced the contrast between the way I was received elsewhere and the tepid acceptance I long had in Chicago as very painful. It is true that I have had my turn as president of the Chicago Psychoanalytic Society, but this was no more a measure of the attitudes of the electorate than is attaining the presidency of a banana republic. A sitting president can hand-pick the next one to be chosen; I was put in office through the good will of Leo Sadow. (When it was my turn to choose, I offered the nomination to Mike Gunther. He declined for personal reasons at that time, so I passed the baton to Harry Trosman. Lest this sound like an old boys' network, it should be stated that it is not women who are discriminated against—the society has had a higher proportion of czarinas than of female members. The name of the game is to keep out political opponents. Only someone as generous as George Moraitis was capable of handing the office to Goldberg, with whom he had disagreed about almost everything.)

After Robert Waelder befriended me, when I was still young and full of idealism, he forewarned me of the fate that awaited me in Chicago; he told me that the raison d'être of the Philadelphia Association was to make sure that he would have no influence on Philadelphia psychoanalysis. Yet I have felt bitter about what I have experienced until recently as a form of ostracism in my own community—bitter enough to give as my presidential address to the society a sardonic piece I entitled, "The Artist in the Age of Mass Culture: Prophet in the Wilderness" (1983a, Epilogue). I do not know what my colleagues made of it; nobody mentioned that the talk was transparently autobiographical. Perhaps they could not imagine that I had the nerve to call myself an artist. At the same time, my detractors are fond of saying that my work has only borne fruit because "John knows how to write." (Although that implies that I do it artfully, it makes me enraged, as are the black athletes who sweat blood to acquire their skills and are then said to owe their success to inborn "athleticism.")

True, of late the Chicago atmosphere has utterly changed. I have been invited to participate in several events sponsored by the Institute. Last year, when I was walking to the lectern to discuss a presentation to the society, a few people actually applauded. The cream of the younger faculty, those who have been in my discussion groups, have risen into positions of responsibility, and they tell me that my ideas are creeping into the curriculum. The latest crop of fifth year candidates have asked me to give them an elective seminar, and the curriculum committee has managed to forget that I am no longer a member of the faculty. Not long ago, I presented something (1996c) at the Wednesday research meeting of the Institute, for the first time in at least a dozen years. How could I refuse when Hank Evans was the one to ask me? (Hank is a recent training analyst appointee, yet he stayed in private consultation with me until I closed up shop.) And how could I refuse Harvey Strauss, the current society president, who wanted me to kick off his scientific program? (see also 1996c). Harvey was the only candidate who ever asked me to be his advisor about writing a graduation paper. And he did extraordinary work with a close friend of mine whom I referred to him during her terminal illness—he followed her unto the grave.

Truth to tell, whatever I have felt, I have never refused to participate in the scientific functions of the society, although I have not volunteered to present for over twenty years. I have lost count of the actual number of presentations and formal discussions I have been asked to prepare—my files contain records of twenty-six appearances since October 1963. (We hold seven scientific sessions a year, let us say around two hundred in thirty-odd years.) By these calculations, the society has used me in one meeting out of eight; I felt exploited by this because I thought I was simultaneously surrounded by envy and malice.

My gorge actually started to rise in 1973, shortly after *Models of the Mind* was published. The following spring, the society was to hold a biennial weekend conference; Goldberg and I thought it would help to publicize our new book to have one session at the meeting devoted to it in some way. When we approached the program committee with this request, its chairman (allegedly a friend of mine) said that it would be best to postpone such an event to the conference to be held in 1976, so that the members could familiarize themselves with the book. (*Models* has an overwhelming 174 pages of text, including seventeen large diagrams.) That was the last time I volunteered for a Chicago presentation.

In a recently published oral history interview (Hunter 1994, p. 233), Arnold Goldberg (with admirable restraint) merely said that I am a very difficult person. The interviewer sent me a copy of her work; she was somewhat concerned about my reaction to this characterization. I replied that everything Goldberg said to her was scrupulously accurate. (I know how to be difficult. As a Chicago policeman told me when my car was stolen, while he was hitting everything within reach with his truncheon: "Police brutality?! There is no such thing as police brutality!! We only give them what they deserve!!")

So much spleen! And now, just when I can afford to give voice to it without restraint, everything has suddenly changed, so much so that it makes me feel depersonalized. A few months ago, I was notified that Fred Levin and Arnold Wilson have made plans to organize a Festschrift for my 70th birthday! Harvey Strauss has arranged to swing the society behind this plan by holding a festival in my honor, and the Institute has agreed to cosponsor it. I'll have to forgive them all, if I can. It was much simpler to feel like an internal exile.

❖ CHAPTER 17 ❖

THE ARTIST AND THE EMOTIONAL WORLD

About a year ago, I finally received the manuscript of Richard Spear's immense work-in-progress on Guido Reni.[1] Spear is now probably the preeminent American authority on Italian Baroque painting and a former editor of *Art Bulletin*, the most scholarly of art history journals. He had come to me almost ten years ago, out of the blue, to discuss the puzzling personality of the great Bolognese artist. We reviewed together the evidence in the early Reni biographies, which was indeed difficult to interpret—I suspect that Spear was most grateful for my statement that I was unable to reach any reliable conclusion about it. Years later, he sent me a reprint of a solid paper on Reni's psychology that he had delivered in Bologna, at festivities marking the quadricentenary of Guido's birth (Spear 1992), and we have since kept in touch. I promised to read the first draft of a book Richard is preparing on the influence of Reni's personality on his art—essentially as a consultant on matters psychological—and this chicken has now come home to roost.

I am sure that I came to Richard's attention as the author of *Portraits of the Artist*, for he has cited the book (1983a) on several occasions. Of course, when he was editing *Art Bulletin*, he also became familiar with Mary's *Picasso—Art as Autobiography* (1980), arguably the first book by an art historian to make a serious effort to correlate an artist's inner world with both his subject matter and changes in his style. Mary's introduction was generous in acknowledging my availability to her as an "in-house consultant," and Richard Spear may have wanted similar backing, for the methodology he planned to use was very close to hers—what she has dubbed "psychoiconography."

I have always been passionately involved in the interchange between psychoanalysis and the humanities, but Mary's decision in the mid-1960s to become a professional art historian naturally tipped my current interests in that arena in the direction of the visual arts. It was her immersion in graduate school that stimulated me to review the entire analytic literature on this topic for the *Journal of the American Psychoanalytic* book section (1970a). Before she began extensively to publish in her field, however, I more or less refrained from stepping on her turf, and my interdisciplinary work focused on literary figures; while I was collaborating with Ernest Wolf, we published biographical papers on Cervantes and Montaigne (1973b and 1975c); I wrote commentaries for *American Imago* on K. R. Eissler's book about *Hamlet* (1972d), a volume of Harry Slochower's literary essays (1970b), and biographical pieces on Nietzsche (1978c) and Jung (1981a). When the Freud-Jung correspondence was published, I wrote a lengthy essay about what it revealed about both men. I also continued to concentrate on questions of methodology; in the Panel Report on Biography (1972c) and in a paper about the meaning of "applied analysis" as a form of unsuccessful introspection (1970c).

The greatest impetus for putting together *Portraits of the Artist* was reading the correspondence of Vincent van Gogh (1959), newly acquired for Mary's library. I thought these letters were an unequaled source of data about a great artist's creativity—and a major literary accomplishment in their own right. In my 1970 review, I had severely criticized all of the considerable analytic literature about van Gogh, and I now wanted to propose something better. This resolution eventuated in two chapters[2] for *Portraits*, and these appeared to me to elaborate certain themes of my papers on Nietzsche and Jung, the idea of "the artist as prophet." I ultimately decided on a book of wider scope; I wanted to demonstrate that the motivations for creative activity were far more complex than any previous psychoanalytic theory had suggested. In fact, the great variety of these motives compels us to use a more complex model of the mind (such as the hierarchical schema) than those hitherto proposed by analysts. It then became evident that I had to start the volume by updating my 1970 review of the analytic literature on biography, creativity, and aesthetics. It also seemed desirable to include a clinical report I had published (actually, in two previous versions) on my analytic work with persons of "genius" (1972a and 1979d).

Thus, by the time I proposed the project to my editor, around two thirds of its eventual content already existed in some form. Most of what I added to the manuscript dealt with my clinical experience with creative persons—chapters on "the captivity of idleness" (a quotation from van Gogh!) and on the special challenges faced by women and homosexuals who engage in creative pursuits. In addition, I did embark on one venture into art history: I devoted most of a chapter, "The Paranoid Monster as Creative Genius" to the study of Caravaggio I had presented in an early version as a Sterba lecture.

I looked upon this volume as an integral part of the theoretical revision of psychoanalysis I was attempting, for the hierarchical view of mental life I had proposed postulates that creativity is characteristic of the conflict-free functioning ideally attained through mastery of the vicissitudes of the oedipal era (that is, phase IV in my schema). *Portraits* has had a good reception and has continued to sell over the years; at last count, some twenty-five hundred copies. The most favorable review was that of Aaron Esman (1986); this was particularly gratifying because Esman is one of a handful of analysts truly expert in these matters; Martin Silverman, in the *Quarterly* (1985), was almost equally generous. Even more important to me than the favorable psychoanalytic response was that of scholars in other disciplines, such as the respectful review (Collins 1990) published by the *Art Journal*. Best of all, the book brought me to the attention of an interdisciplinary group engaged in establishing "creativity research" as an independent scholarly discipline. Robert Albert, professor of psychology at Pitzer College, seemed to be the moving spirit behind this development, assisted by his former student Mark Runco, who was shortly to become editor of a newly established *Creativity Research Journal*.

To kick off their ambitious enterprise, Albert and Runco organized a ceativity conference in Claremont, California, and invited me to participate. The proceedings of this excellent symposium were published as a book, *Theories of Creativity* (Runco and Albert 1990); the chapter I contributed (1990a) was my first significant publication outside of the mental health literature. Mark Runco has asked me to send further papers to his journal and to other edited volumes—we have now maintained this fruitful collaboration for the better part of a decade (see 1990b, 1993j, 1996g). He also organized a monograph series under the aegis of the journal; Mary and I submitted a proposal to produce for this series a "methodological sampler" of the various ways in which biographical studies may be turned to good account in creativity research. Our proposal was accepted, and the end result was our only joint publication, *Perspectives on Creativity Research: The Biographical Method* (1992a).

Need I say that we had some misgivings about undertaking such a collaboration? We managed, however, to avoid squabbling about it, mostly because we decided that each of us would independently provide three sample studies. (Mary's contributions were an illustration of research focused on adaptation, through an examination of Goya's neurological illness and his use of art to master its emotional consequences; as an example of pathography, an account of René Magritte's decompensation into depression [and hypomania] and its effects on creativity; and to exemplify the use of interviews with a living artist, a study of the Chicago painter, Roger Brown. To avoid an exclusive focus on the visual arts, I chose to include an essay on Freud's personality that compared the differing viewpoints of several biographers; one on Mozart's adolescence, to illustrate focus on a specific developmental phase; and a paper on the pioneers of abstract painting I had presented as the Maurice Levine lecture in Cincinnati, to show how the correlation of the biographies of several persons may yield conclusions of wider applicability.) Thus, our actual joint work involved only three further chapters devoted to methodology. The project was somewhat frustrating because of endless delays at the production stage (and an elusive publisher who refused to answer phone calls or letters), but the actual book is handsomely done. We have even discussed trying to write another book together if we are ever simultaneously free of other obligations.

There is no doubt that the best entrée I have had to interdisciplinary endeavors has been Mary's editorship of *Psychoanalytic Perspectives on Art*. Through her, I met most of the art historians interested in using psychoanalytic methods or ideas, and her formation of a loose coalition of *PPA* contributors has led us both into a number of challenging activities. One of these was a series of annual conferences (also called *PPA*) Mary helped to organize at New York University, in partnership with Laurie Wilson, head of the NYU art therapy program. Laurie has expanded her scope from making art, through art therapy and a Ph.D. in art history, to clinical training in psychoanalysis by way of a CORST waiver.

For the *PPA* conferences, Mary was responsible for choosing good topics and for recruiting presenters; for instance, for a session on the psychology of Picasso, she was able to enlist the participation of her friend Françoise Gilot.[3] In time, Laurie found it too burdensome to organize these complex events, and we transferred this activity to the midwinter meetings of the

American Psychoanalytic, where we continued for some time to cochair an annual interdisciplinary colloquium on art. When the association once held its May meeting in Chicago, Mary arranged such a colloquium with Richard Brettell, then a curator at the Art Institute, who was organizing a major Gauguin exhibition. Brettell's data about the artist (and the outstanding show that followed) stimulated both of us to look into aspects of Gauguin's art and personality, and I presented portions of my conclusions at a number of scholarly events—among them one of the NYU conferences (1994b).

Mary has been an occasional lecturer at the Art Institute of Chicago for around twenty-five years; when she told her associates in museum education about our interest in Gauguin, they invited me to give a public lecture about the artist at the museum. This drew a large enough audience to induce the department subsequently to engage me to give a subscription series on creativity. And that went well enough to embolden me to think that, after I retired as a physician, I might aspire to call myself an "author and lecturer."

At one point Laurie Wilson was able to get a grant to establish a lectureship at NYU on psychoanalysis and the visual arts, and I persuaded her to name it the Ernst Kris Memorial Lecture, to honor the man who first built a bridge between these two disciplines.[4] The first lecturer she chose was the eminent, analytically sophisticated scholar Leo Steinberg. She also invited Kris's son and daughter, the Boston analysts Tony Kris and Anna Wolf, and asked Charles Brenner to give a brief talk about Ernst Kris as a person. I was to give a parallel résumé of his contributions in the interdisciplinary field. It was a very festive occasion, with an overflow crowd. The entire editorial board of *The Psychoanalytic Study of the Child* (the publication Kris had been most closely associated with) was in attendance. Brenner and I had been on a couple of Panels together at meetings of the American Psychoanalytic (see Abrams 1971, Rothstein 1983) and we have always been on the friendliest of personal terms, but this was the first occasion on which we truly agreed about anything—beyond civility.

Unfortunately, Laurie's grant to promote this enterprise was not renewed, so that she really had to scramble for funds to keep the Kris lectures going. When the series was about to expire, she asked me to give what she thought might be the last Kris lecture. The money for this final event came from the cultural branch of the Italian Embassy, and Laurie requested that I try to find a topic on Italian art. I decided to tackle the common denominators in the personalities of the pioneers of mannerism. By the time I delivered the Lecture, *PPA* had also fallen victim to financial constraints, so that there was no obvious venue for the publication of such an esoteric paper. Fortunately, just about then I heard from a group in Buenos Aires that was starting a Spanish-language equivalent of *PPA*, the *Revista Argentina de Arte y Psicoanálisis* (also known as *Eos*, after the Greek goddess of dawn). This journal is lavishly produced, as befits a venture financed by a foundation established by a bank! Not only have they published my mannerism paper (1994c—printed in both Spanish and English); they have also reprinted a paper on James Ensor (1990b) I did for the *Creativity Research Journal*, and they threaten to import me to Buenos Aires for some future project.

During the existence of *PPA*, I tried to be as helpful to Mary as possible by carrying out whatever assignment she deemed most necessary to produce a volume of high standards. For volume one, she asked me to write an extensive review article about Robert Liebert's (1983) recently published book on Michelangelo. Although Liebert's scholarship was as thorough as any psychoanalyst has achieved in interdisciplinary work (he had for years taught collaboratively with art historians at Columbia University, and the respected Michelangelo expert Howard Hibbard served as a consultant for the book), I disagreed with his understanding of the artist's inner world, which used object relations theory in a rather formulaic manner. I was embarrassed to write a negative review, because Liebert had been very gracious in throwing his support behind *PPA* instead of persevering with his parallel efforts to organize such an interdisciplinary publication.

Fortunately for the project, we did not know that Bob had a terminal illness, for that information would have stopped me altogether. As it was, I presented my view (1985d) of Michelangelo's psychology (and its significance for understanding much of his art) as an alternative dictated by my subjective responses to the artist's life and work. Liebert did not accept this *laissez penser*[5] position; he wrote an angry rebuttal (1985) that essentially rejected the implication that his view of Michelangelo's psychology was skewed by his own subjectivity. (How rapidly has the intellectual climate changed! A response such as that would today be unthinkable.) He may have been particularly sensitive on this score because, shortly before he received my piece, Leo Steinberg (1984) published a devastating critique of his thesis in *The New York Review of Books*, also based on the issue of the distorting effect of the biographer's subjective bias.

In volume two of *PPA*, I got involved in a dispute that was far more acrimonious. Mary arranged to publish an interdisciplinary dialogue about Paul Cézanne between the eminent Cézanne scholar Theodore Reff and myself. On a visit to Chicago, Reff came to see us, and the three of us agreed on a modus operandi: he would provide a bibliography, on the basis of which I would elaborate a psychological portrait of the artist (1987a); in turn, Reff would write a commentary on my essay. The first steps of this program went smoothly enough, but Reff was extremely dilatory in contributing his commentary. Mary was already prepared to proceed without his paper when, shortly before the publisher's final deadline, Reff (1987a) sent in a maximally hostile essay.

He did not directly address my portrait of Cézanne; the entire piece focused on the various sins he claimed I had committed as a historian, including my disregard of various additional references he now declared to be vital. (I still believe that I made very few historical errors in this paper, but even if I had been guilty as charged, none of these sins would have been relevant for an assessment of Cézanne's personality. Reff simply tried to discredit me as an author worthy of attention; he even stated that he saw no art historical value in articulating the kinds of insights a psychoanalyst could propose.)

Mary was naturally quite distressed by this intemperate outburst. She did not have such hostilities in mind in organizing an interdisciplinary forum! She would have rejected Reff's response if it would not have looked like a move to shield her own husband; she was particularly incensed by his failure to allow sufficient time for a well-thought-out rebuttal. Under the circumstances, I had to respond on the spur of the moment—or cancel the project in its entirety. With any other editor, I would not have hesitated for a second. I decided to use the opportunity to demonstrate the method of interdisciplinary collaboration developed by George Moraitis (1985)—to be sure, in his work, one of private consultation (such as my current contact with Richard Spear) rather than of public dialogue.

George began to experiment with such interdisciplinary work in the mid-1970s and asked me to participate in his project in a consultative capacity. His first collaborator was a young historian who was having difficulties in completing a dissertation on the life of Nietzsche; I believe they met in the workshop for social scientists where I became acquainted with Arnold Wilson. George devised the method of asking the specialist scholar to designate the list of materials to be studied together and then to discuss that scholar's work primarily in terms of transference/countertransference issues, in the manner developed in supervising the treatment efforts of analysts-in-training. (In later years, George collaborated in this way with historians of international reputation.) During the early phase of his experiment, George and I discussed each of his meetings with his collaborator; my main function was to provide consensual validation (that his assessment of the historian's subjective bias was in itself free of interference by George's own emotional biases). It was both great fun and an instructive experience—moreover, as a consequence I became so interested in Nietzsche that I went beyond the historian's reading list and ultimately wrote my own paper about the philosopher.

Of course, in writing about the distorting effects of Theodore Reff's identification with an artist he had studied intensively for decades on his assessment of my portrait of that person, I was turning the Moraitis method upside down by dispensing with privacy, tact, and consent. But, as the French say, "*A la guerre, comme à la guerre*!"[6] I produced what I regarded as an effective rebuttal (1987e) shortly before Mary's deadline. Unfortunately, in a fit of misguided courtesy, she sent Reff a copy, and (in an absolute rage) he insisted that he was entitled to the last word. He wrote a response (Reff 1987b) without delay; this was so poisonous that the publisher intervened to insist on toning it down, and Mary then courageously published it.

The story had an amusing coda: shortly after these transactions (and before *PPA II* was published), Reff was scheduled to present a paper on Cézanne at a *PPA* Conference at NYU, and Aaron Esman was to be his discussant. Aaron, who had not seen my Cézanne essay, put forward a view of the artist's psychology completely congruent with mine, and on this public occasion Reff meekly accepted his expert opinion. (In our exchange, he had called my claim of some expertise about psychological matters "authoritarian!") Mary happily obtained Esman's paper (1988) for *PPA III* and, in her editor's introduction (1988), noted the concurring opinions of two analytic scholars working independently about materials the significance of which had eluded historians.

Despite this contretemps, the *PPA* circle was largely harmonious; the attendance of several contributors at the Jerusalem Freud conference devoted to art and psychoanalysis was the apogee of its brief existence. Mary developed a particularly good relationship with Donald Kuspit, a superstar of contemporary art history and criticism, well informed about psychoanalysis through his analyst-spouse. A Manhattan resident, Donald was interested in formal education in the theoretical aspects of psychoanalysis, and I urged him to apply to the institute at the NYU Medical Center, the faculty of which includes an unusual number of people interested in interdisciplinary work. (Laurie Wilson was already one of their candidates.) I wrote a strong letter of recommendation for Donald—later I did the same when he was in line for a visiting professorship at Cornell—and he duly completed this program. (Donald is truly formidable; he has Ph.D. degrees in both art history and philosophy, one from this country, the other from Germany.)

In addition to Mary's complex professional ties to Kuspit, he and I have also done some interesting things together. On one occasion, we wrote the two essays (see 1987f) for the catalog of the exhibition "The Artist's Mother: Portraits and Homages" at the Hekscher Museum (on Long Island) and the National Portrait Gallery (in Washington). Another time, we were both panelists at a San Francisco meeting of the American Psychoanalytic; the topic was "Psychoanalysis and the Humanities: A Confusion of Tongues."[7] I expanded the brief position statement allowed by the panel format for a conference Donald organized on the same subject at Mountain Lake, Virginia (a beautiful, wild spot in the Appalachians). Both Mary and I were invited to this lively event, and Kuspit published our presentations (see 1988d) in the journal he edits, *Art Criticism*.

For the third and last volume of *PPA*, Mary received more material than she could accommodate, and the dilemma was resolved by leaving out articles both she and I had planned to publish in it. My submission was a paper I had prepared for a symposium on "The Art of the Insane" at the University of Chicago, organized in connection with an exhibition of selections from the celebrated Prinzhorn Collection at Heidelberg University. (Some years later, the Smart Museum at the U. of C. was the local venue for the touring exhibit of Freud's antiquities, and once again I took part [see 1992c] in the related symposium about "Freud as a Collector.") My paper on art produced during psychotic episodes languished for some years, until Mark Runco requested a contribution to the *Creativity Research Journal* about the adaptive uses of creative work. I then rewrote my case history of the art produced by James Ensor while he was undergoing a psychotic decompensation; in the published version (1990b), I focused on his work as a crucial component of his recovery.

The last project to come my way as a result of *PPA* activities was suggested by the San Francisco analyst Jerome Oremland. Like Bob Liebert, Jerry had for a long time invested himself in studying the work of Michelangelo, and he capped his efforts with a monograph on the iconographic significance of the Sistine Chapel frescoes. Over the years, Jerry and I established a good relationship—it was at one of the conferences he organized in the psychiatry department he heads at the Children's Hospital that I suffered a retinal tear; Jerry personally escorted me to ophthalmology and saw to my being well cared for. (Paulina and Otto Kernberg were also on the program, and I shall never forget their kindness about my difficulty.) Some years earlier, Mary and I had also worked with Oremland on a Picasso symposium cosponsored by the San Francisco Psychoanalytic Institute and Museum of Modern Art; Jerry was an excellent chairman riding herd on an unruly collection of art historians and psychoanalysts.[8] After he read my critique of Liebert's *Michelangelo*, Oremland asked me to write a similar commentary on his manuscript, to be included in the published volume. Alas, I no more agreed with his thesis than I had with Liebert's—in Jerry's case, not on psychoanalytic grounds but on those of historical plausibility. Jerry behaved entirely correctly about printing this less than favorable critique in his book (1989c), but I think he may have been hurt.

This whirlwind of activity in the interdisciplinary realm stimulated me to rethink the creativity question, and led me to plan a second book about it. I soon happened to have a chat with a New York colleague with cultural interests similar to my own; he mentioned that he was working on a book to be published in the new interdisciplinary monograph series sponsored by the Columbia University Press. I asked him to ascertain whether the editors, the analyst Arnold Cooper and the eminent literary scholar Steven Marcus, might be interested in a book on the creative personality.

He turned out to be a very efficient go-between, and I soon received a friendly letter from the editors asking me to submit a detailed proposal. I conferred with Jennifer Crewe, in charge of the humanities section, when she was in Chicago for a convention, and we agreed that the book should be aimed for a cultivated but nonspecialist public. There was no difficulty about the approval of the proposal I submitted, and I went to work with real enthusiasm. (By this time, I had begun to cut back my clinical responsibilities and had more leisure for scholarly work than ever before in my adult life. I began to feel an intellectual excitement similar to that of my intoxicating years as a college student at University Heights—the former NYU campus located in the Bronx—when I was fifteen!)

Despite my considerable experience of writing for publication, the challenge of communicating with nonspecialist readers was new to me, and it made the preparation of this book into the most troublesome venture of my life as an author. I submitted a first version of the manuscript about a year after I began work on it, and it clearly fell between two stools: one reader found fault with my inattention to certain scholarly requirements and conventions; another was put off by my clumsy efforts to hit a popular tone. For this person, it only sounded precious and patronizing. Jennifer

Crewe half expected me to give up, and I *was* severely discouraged. However, I asked our friend Sue Taylor (who was at the time a curator at the Milwaukee Art Museum) to give me a private reading, and she gave the project a good enough prognosis to revive my flagging spirits.

In the next eighteen months, I twice revised the manuscript, adding and subtracting material (even whole chapters), altering the sequence of presentation, beefing up documentation, eliminating foreign phrases (so Eurocentric!)—the whole obsessive panoply that renders rewriting so hateful. In the interval, I got feedback from still more readers until I was sick of it all and sent the last version I was prepared to produce to Jennifer Crewe. This time, I requested that she find a reader who had clinical experience, for I believe that those who found fault with the first version had missed the novelty of the psychoanalytic hypotheses I had proposed about the crucial role of personality structure, rather than conflict, in creativity.

It took a long time to find an appropriate person, but the wait was worthwhile: the book received an optimal reading, one that perceived its merits and made a number of concrete suggestions for improving the presentation. After a brief interval, the reader blew his cover of anonymity: Patrick Mahony, the Montreal literary scholar and psychoanalyst, called me on the phone to ascertain my reaction to his suggestions. I was delighted! Walking through the desert is not oppressive when the camel can smell an oasis. I was now happy to abandon my resolution and prepare a fourth draft (1996a) of *The Artist and the Emotional World*.

The principal thesis of this monograph is that success in creative endeavors depends (beyond the issue of specific talents) on a variety of personal attributes that vary in accord with the specific requirements and conditions of the particular domain of activity that is involved. Hence any single psychological characteristic may, in a given time and place (and within the prevalent social conditions), promote or hinder creative pursuits of different kinds. In broad terms, I attempted to describe those personality traits that are generally facilitating and those that are likely to inhibit creative efforts, and to outline developmental patterns throughout the life course that may lead to the structuralization of such patterns.

I differ from previous analytic commentators on creativity who have invariably explained the motivation for creative pursuits on the basis of their favored psychoanalytic theory of motivation in general—either a drive theory, an object relations theory, or one focused on the cohesion of the sense of self. In contrast, I assert that people always pursue creative goals because of the supreme satisfaction of exercising some unusual skill; other sources of motivation only play a subsidiary role in these activities. It follows from this conception that creative work is never a consequence of psychopathology; if anything, it tends to overcome various adaptive difficulties. (This is another way of saying that in the hierarchical model, creative activities pertain to a mode of function beyond conflict—what I have designated as mode V.)

❖ CHAPTER 18 ❖

BEYOND THE REALM OF MENTAL CONTENTS

In some ways, the reactions to *Beyond Interpretation* marked the apex of my acceptance by the analytic community. Donald Kaplan (1981) began his review, "John Gedo is one of the most interesting minds presently engaged at the conceptual frontiers of the practice and theory of psychoanalysis."[1] Even the *American Journal of Psychiatry* called it "an important book certain to stir extended psychoanalytic debate" (Swartz 1980). The reception of *Advances in Clinical Psychoanalysis* was considerably more ambivalent,[2] but those reviews only began to appear in 1984 and, by that time, I had published still another heretical volume (1984c), *Psychoanalysis and Its Discontents*. (This book also proved offensive to establishment types because it is concluded with a severe critique of the contemporary psychoanalytic scene, particularly in North America, similar in flavor to the splenetic aspects of this memoir.)

In the 1984 book, for the first time, I contrasted my viewpoint with the theory of technique espoused by all existing schools of psychoanalysis, the idea that the central therapeutic task is the elucidation of some set of unconscious fantasies. (Disagreements among schools invariably concern the question of which set of mental contents should be interpreted for maximal curative effect.) I differ from these assumptions by stressing that adaptive change is contingent on "filling in" prior deficits in mental functioning—the apraxias that render solutions by means of establishing symbiotic relationships necessary. In other words, I see the task of analysis as the promotion of further structuralization through learning[3]; the particulars of mental contents are not as significant as the manner in which they are being processed. (The hierarchical model shows five alternative possibilities for the processing of any bit of mental content. In mode I, only the biological resources of the organism are available; in mode II, sets of subjective experiences can be reactivated; mode III is attained when the person becomes capable of a holistic program of action; in mode IV, it is no longer necessary to use enactments—goals can be mediated through the channel of fantasies. In mode V, fantasies can be used creatively as blueprints for constructive activities.)

The task of identifying apraxias, of bringing them to the attention of analysands, and of assisting the latter to learn the procedural skills concerned devolves primarily on the analyst. (Success in this regard will enable patients to resolve their ubiquitous conflicts, so that my viewpoint actually does not *contradict* the widely accepted analytic emphasis on intrapsychic conflict; it merely shifts emphasis elsewhere.) At first, it may be necessary to enter into the analysand's life as an auxiliary who supplies the psychological skills unavailable to the latter. The need for such interventions can then be explained, and the patient stimulated to acquire the missing functions. If this occurs, symbiotic adaptation becomes superfluous and self-regulation supervenes. As I have already mentioned, *Discontents* contains two detailed reports of cases analyzed in accord with these recommendations.[4]

Another issue I first took up in this book is the potentiality of any psychoanalytic intervention—including the failure to intervene at all—to have simultaneous consequences at multiple levels of the hierarchy of organizational modes. For instance, the empathic understanding implicit in the provision of a valid interpretation often provides, beyond insight, both pacification through reassurance and prioritization among a confusing array of disparate goals. Accepted theories of technique have overlooked this kind of "multiple appeal" on the part of analytic interventions.

Although acceptance of the role of a symbiotic partner by the analyst need not jeopardize the stance of "neutrality" (with regard to the proper resolution of intrapsychic conflicts) that has been universally recommended in the literature, in *Discontents* I acknowledged that the problem is more complex whenever an apraxia involves the sphere of values. Many analytic failures are caused by the adherence of analysands with character problems to values directly contrary to those underlying the entire psychoanalytic enterprise, or even those of empirical science itself: analysands sometimes have commitments to dogmatism, reductionism, and irrationalism. In another group of difficulties, patients do not possess any authentic values at all; in such circumstances, the analyst's actions will inevitably serve as automatic "guidelines for the perplexed" about how to live properly. In other words, about certain fundamental matters (such as grave criminal offenses) there is no way to keep the analyst's values out of the therapeutic transaction. In those circumstances, I think it behooves us to make our attitudes explicit. Moreover, our analytic commitment to truthfulness, reliability, probity, and fairness to others—our shared professional values—should always be made entirely clear to analysands.

Such a focus on the issue of values in analytic treatment compels reconsideration of its current therapeutic limits, that is, examination of the role of delinquent enactments in causing analyses to fail. If the delinquent activities of an analysand do not overwhelm the analyst's anxiety tolerance, it is possible to promote an analytic process with patients who show such propensities, particularly if they have some internal conflict about their behavior. In these cases, the analyst cannot remain neutral; it is essential to support the patient's nondelinquent side. (Many delinquents form multiple symbiotic attachments; if one of their selfobjects takes the side of their delinquent propensities, the prognosis for analysis becomes extremely poor.) At the same time, it is well to keep in mind that delinquent behaviors sometimes serve as emergency defenses against threatened regression into states of confusion or helplessness, so that some patients correctly feel that they cannot afford to give them up. Often, therefore, chronic delinquency manifests itself in the course of analysis as a refusal to adhere to the basic rule of free association.

The last innovation introduced in *Discontents* was an attempt to think through the rhetorical dimensions of the analyst's communications. This thesis starts by acknowledging that the analytic dialogue cannot be completely understood on the basis of the lexical meaning of the words exchanged, for facial expressions, gestures, and the paraverbal aspects of speech greatly modify those meanings—not to mention the fact that human messages are not always intended to be taken literally. To maintain the holding environment required for therapeutic work, the analyst's messages must be encoded in one of the semiotic systems available to the analysand. The process of finding such a system can be called the establishment of a shared language. (Incidentally, this is facilitated by a schedule of sessions at the greatest frequency feasible.) Derailments in the use of the shared language are sensitive indicators of the emergence of a transference referable to early childhood, usually the era when consensual language was being acquired.

Often resistances stand in the way of achieving a shared language; such developments lead to fresh miscommunication that in turn makes it difficult to deal with these resistances. These complications often echo transactions that Mahlerians call the "rapprochement crisis," particularly the child's efforts to ward off external control—control the parents usually exercise by means of language. Yet we must keep in mind that verbal communication can also become enmeshed in conflict at later stages of development. As far as the analyst's rhetorical choices within the shared language are concerned, these are practically unlimited. The use of tropes (such as metaphors or metonymy) lends emotional power to our communications and builds bridges between the realms of the primary and secondary process. Yet patients suffering from communicative apraxias may only be able to grasp the affective component of our messages. (As I proposed in my 1981 book, this is often best encoded in the form of music.) In the process of such affective communications, analysts inevitably display some aspects of their subjectivity. Of course, even the specifics of the analyst's syntax and vocabulary will betray these covert attitudes, so that it is practically impossible to avoid provoking counterresponses to these subjective reactions (which are generally termed *countertransference*). Countertransference reactions may sometimes lead the analyst into making unfortunate rhetorical choices—even to abandon the shared language already achieved—although these interventions may seem academically correct. If analysands sense that the analyst cannot be trusted to adhere to a semiotic system they can understand, they will quickly despair about the joint effort.

I was somewhat surprised, when reviews of *Discontents* finally appeared,[5] that these contentions aroused little disagreement. Perhaps this meant that I was no longer seen as an ally of Kohut, more than a decade after breaking with him. Of course, a careful reading of the book reveals my explicit differences with self psychology, particularly in a chapter on the dynamics of dissidence within psychoanalysis. I trace these fissures in the discipline back to the a priori philosophical commitments of differing theorists to various assumptions about human nature. This is a subject with which I became increasingly preoccupied, so much so that it became the central focus of my next intellectual project and culminated in *Conceptual Issues in Psychoanalysis* (1986a).

The historical section of this book surveys three waves of dissent in psychoanalysis, each separated from the next by a generation—the dissident movements initiated in turn by Ferenczi, Klein, and Kohut. These analytic civil wars were succeeded on each occasion by ecumenical efforts grounded in epistemology. In every instance, both radical and conservative commitments seemed to be based on the personal subjectivity of charismatic faction leaders. Yet every wave of dissidence started with valid, new clinical observations (about ever more archaic aspects of mental life) which were made possible by gradual improvements in analytic technique. These clinical findings recurrently rendered obsolete the accepted theoretical schemata previously current. In the resulting confusion, various contributors would propose compelling hypotheses that, in their turn, proved to encompass too narrow a segment of the observational field. These proposals have always been stamped by the subjectivity of the theorist, and this circumstance foreordained their rejection by those analysts who did not share these a priori assumptions.[6]

Ferenczi's "deviation" stemmed from his discovery of an archaic syndrome that he conceptualized not in terms of putative libidinal vicissitudes but as a distortion of ego development, caused by early traumata. Unfortunately, he failed to realize that his clinical findings could not be properly encompassed by Freud's (1923) structural theory. Successful treatment of these patients necessitated technical modifications that transcended the kind of analysis of defenses introduced by ego psychology: Ferenczi insisted that, instead of simply overcoming resistances by interpreting their existence, we must discern their true functions. In this attempt, he experimented with noninterpretive measures of the kind Goldberg and I (1973a) were to call "pacification." In other words, Ferenczi's deviation was an effort to find solutions to unsolved problems that ego psychology had not succeeded in mastering. In retrospect, his dissent was an effective counterweight for Freud's exclusive emphasis on the neurosogenic conflicts of the oedipal period—as the ecumenicists of his generation predicted it would be.

Melanie Klein's dissidence stemmed from an assignment Ferenczi had given her—to extend analytic therapeutics to the treatment of (young) children. Her findings confirmed Ferenczi's conclusion that pathogenesis cannot be attributed to the oedipal period exclusively. The theories she formulated, starting in the mid-1930s, represent a doctrine of vitalism and innate fantasy systems (both contrary to empirical evidence)—yet she presented these in a confusing, pseudobiological guise. Despite the haziness of these conceptualizations, Klein's school has survived for over fifty years because, unlike the traditionalists (led by Anna Freud), she did not neglect the clinical problems that stem from developments in the preoedipal era. In particular, she gave proper emphasis to issues of primitive aggression.

The epistemological referee who transcended the Kleinian controversy was David Rapaport. He pointed out that the proliferation of object relations theories (that cannot be integrated with those centered on the drives) was a response to the inability of the structural theory to encompass the clinical evidence gleaned from patients with pregenital problems. He insisted that an adequate map of personality organization would have to include archaic functional modes integrated hierarchically with more mature ones—the prescription I have followed in developing the hierarchical model. Rapaport rejected all arbitrary developmental hypotheses (such as those of Klein); he rightly predicted that we have to learn about the development of cognition to be able to formulate hypotheses capable of empirical validation. In summary, he judged all existing psychoanalytic theories to be incomplete and inconsistent—and some to be untenable to boot.

At that juncture, Kohut made the important discovery that certain archaic transference constellations are focused on issues of self-esteem and self-cohesion. He also concluded that in these conditions (and, by extension, in all analytic treatment) therapeutic success is contingent on empathic performance by the analyst. In parallel, he began to see man's existential problems—the tragic difficulties of pursuing ideals and ambitions—as the central issues for the treatment. In other words, he relegated all previous analytic findings to a position of secondary import and elevated his own novel observations to one of primary significance. The central positions of most previous dissidents (Ferenczi, Klein, and even the interpersonalists) were retrospectively buttressed by Kohut's relegation of the empirical data at the core of Freudian psychoanalysis to the status of epiphenomena. But Kohut also attempted to supersede other dissident schools by proposing that a search for perfection is the primary motivating force in human nature. He therefore proposed a new value system for psychoanalysis, replacing Freud's parallel quests for knowledge and autonomy with the commitment to provide everyone with optimally empathic "selfobjects." A corollary of this position is that analysis cures by way of promoting the (automatic) internalization of certain qualities of such good objects.[7]

In summary, each of these three waves of dissidence reflected the accumulated dissatisfaction of a generation of analysts with contemporary psychoanalysis, both as treatment and as a science of mind. As long as the discipline retains vitality, we may expect analogous crises in every generation; the fact that such scientific ferment produces organizational strains proves our collective inability up until now to make rational choices among competing hypotheses. Theories tend to capture the allegiance of most practitioners without validation or even proof of their pragmatic utility.

Because fundamental disagreements among psychoanalysts have always arisen as a result of our actual ignorance about expectable psychological development in early childhood, a segment of the profession has turned to the direct observation of children in the hope of establishing valid criteria about this matter. The second section of *Conceptual Issues* examines some of the methodological problems encountered by these efforts—the difficulties of correlating the observable behaviors of young children with the psychological constructs that constitute our theories of mind. Margaret Mahler and her followers are among the most prominent of the analysts to have attempted such correlations, with equivocal results. The greatest pitfall of their work has been that of fitting their observations into the categories provided by existing psychoanalytic hypotheses and, at the same time, assuming that the possibility of such a fit constitutes an adequate test of those hypotheses. As a scientific procedure, this method is unacceptably circular. All Mahlerians, in fact, have continued to adhere to 100-year-old metapsychological assumptions and—despite their focus on object relations—to drive theory (in the version of Heinz Hartmann), and they have remained unconcerned about the incompatibility of these disparate theoretical commitments. In other words, I judge Mahlerian theories to be so confused conceptually that they cannot be taken seriously. Like the Kleinians, Mahlerians impute subjective motives to infants whose behavior is not yet regulated by the cerebral cortex—clearly, a biological impossibility.

Of course, other infant observers have not necessarily succumbed to the foregoing pitfalls.[8] Their cumulative data show that the developmental schemata of Klein, Mahler, and Hartmann seriously mistime the maturation of various cognitive capacities in normal infants. Above all, this evidence supports the assumption of the hierarchical model that behavior in the initial phase of development is regulated on a neurophysiological level. Hence, the action patterns that evolve during this phase are devoid of symbolic representation. This is one compelling reason to carry psychoanalytic theory into realms beyond subjectivity and the "meanings" of mental contents (the policy espoused by hermeneuticists). Finally, infant observation has demonstrated that much learning occurs while there is no interaction with the caretakers—contrary to most theories of object relations.

The therapeutic implications of these developmental conclusions are that the illumination of the analysand's presymbolic experience should constitute one aim of every analysis. These patterns may persist into adulthood in the form of defective self-regulation, bodily symptoms, cognitive difficulties such as alexithymia, and so on. Difficulties of this kind inevitably undermine self-esteem and predispose the individual to seek adaptation by means of symbiotic assistance—producing the syndromes formerly labeled "narcissistic." Theories that attribute the genesis of such syndromes simply to the vicissitudes of object relations confuse these compensatory adaptive efforts with the basic pathology they are designed to overcome. (This criticism is particularly applicable to the followers of Kohut, Mahler, and Winnicott.) Derivatives of the developmental phase transitional between the affectomotor organization of early infancy and the symbolic mode that normally supervenes at the end of the second year of life also persist into adult life; these matters are generally encoded in the form of mimetic enactments wherein words may not be the primary carriers of meaning. These behaviors, when they emerge in analysis, have to be dealt with in the manner Melanie Klein invented for translating the play activities of child-patients into a consensual verbal code.

The methodological section of *Conceptual Issues* ends with a chapter in which I attempted to show how an exclusively hermeneutic conception of psychoanalysis leaves certain vital matters out of account. Properly carried out, analytic hermeneutics are able to illuminate certain meanings of a literary text, for in written materials meanings that produce affective reactions are apprehended by means of the reader's *conceptual* capabilities. By contrast, in living transactions, notably in the psychoanalytic situation, affective communication takes place, in large measure, through paraverbal means—posture, gesture, facial expression, bodily events mediated through the autonomic nervous system, the music of the speaker's vocalization. A transcription of the verbal interchange cannot convey the entirety of the messages in question. I view the information the analyst needs to process as analogous to the performance of an opera: words are of some importance, but the heart of the matter is conveyed by the music. (I suspect that, in this regard, my position is the polar opposite of that of the school of Lacan.[9])

Efforts to ameliorate disorders of archaic origin might be called "developmental psychoanalysis." This therapeutic trend is an outgrowth of the successive dissident movements in psychoanalysis, for the defenders of orthodoxy have been reluctant to tackle the archaic depths of human subjectivity. In 1986 I expressed the hope that we were on the verge of reaching consensus about how such therapeutic ambitions might be fulfilled.[10]

❖ CHAPTER 19 ❖

THE LESSONS OF TRAVEL

In August 1996 I went to Brazil to take part in a Ferenczi Conference in São Paulo, a reprise of the 1993 meeting in Budapest. Everything about this experience was strange, from the modern luxury in a Third World atmosphere that has made psychoanalysis fashionable, through the timelessness of Brazilian life (I felt as if all clocks had stopped as soon as the plane entered South American air space), to the dominance of Kleinian concepts and terminology among our Brazilian colleagues. In this unfamiliar setting, I was not regarded as radically heterodox (as has long been the case at home)—if anything, the systematic quality of my work, its biological orientation, and the organized approach to archaic clinical phenomena (with which Kleinians feel at home) were seemingly much appreciated in Brazil. Yet I do not know whether they could grasp the real message of my presentation,[1] basically a plea to think through what parts of Ferenczi's legacy are actually serviceable today, instead of substituting him for the fallen heroes of yesteryear as the latest analytic prophet.

The clinical seminar I later conducted attracted a standing-room-only crowd, but various senior Brazilians interrupted it with long speeches, offering competing formulae that explained exactly what was what with the patient and what the analyst had to do about it, although the case presentation had not gone far enough even to hint at the nature of the analysand's inner world. It is true that, when I protested that the patient had not even begun to free associate and, from my perspective, we could not be certain of anything about her, many of the younger people in the audience burst into applause. But that partisan phenomenon was also utterly strange and only reinforced my conviction that psychoanalysis everywhere reflects the qualities of the society in which it has taken root. It is only when one becomes familiar with analytic communities in a variety of foreign countries, each very different from every other, that one can fully grasp that what in the United States we have regarded as the proper state of psychoanalysis is merely a variant (one possessing specific strengths and weaknesses) adapted to American conditions.

For the last fifteen years and more, I have had many opportunities to interact with analysts from abroad; I have seen them at international meetings as well as in their home communities. It has been quite an education in multiculturalism! This process only began with my fortuitous meeting with René Major in Aspen. Before that, on my 1969 expedition to Hampstead, and at the 1971 international congress I attended in Vienna, I learned little about the local analytic scene. I found such congresses too hurried and crowded to be worthwhile, and I did not go again until the international association met in New York. It was there I first became acquainted with French analysts, by signing up to participate in a francophone discussion group, in fear and trembling. The next opportunity came my way in Aspen, where Mary and I tried to be hospitable to René. He and I commiserated about the poor quality of our seminar group, and René made vague promises about organizing something better in Paris. I was really surprised when he later proved his ability to carry out this visionary idea.

I was to learn that René was quite a psychoanalytic entrepreneur. He ran an organization that published a beautifully produced, glossy psychoanalytic/cultural periodical, *Cahiers Confrontation*,[2] served as advisor to the prestigious Aubier publishing house, and regularly arranged conferences where diverse analytic viewpoints would be confronted. (He tried falsely to reassure me by claiming that in French *confrontation* does not have the hostile implications of its English cognate. Perhaps not, but our French colleagues turned out to be a combative lot!) In 1980 he organized a three-day *Rencontre Franco-Americain*, where representatives from each country would present papers for discussion. It was an irresistible invitation for early summer, just right to combine with one of those motor trips to the French provinces to which I am happily addicted.

Perhaps precisely because of his ecumenical stance, René was also a controversial figure within the Paris Psychoanalytic Society, despite having served as its president. Some years after the *Rencontre*, I ran into Janine

Chasseguet-Smirgel (possibly the most influential among French analysts in the international association) at a party in New York, and she assaulted me about having lent myself to the schemes of people who wished to destroy psychoanalysis in France. (I did not ask for clarification, because the scene smelled of the Inquisition. Nor did I take the assault lying down; I offered Janine a lift to the Waldorf, and when she snidely expressed "shock" about the bumpy potholes of Park Avenue, I said, knowing that she was bitterly opposed to the ruling socialists at home, "Ah, Madame, that is the price we have to pay for not having a socialist government." It was the best one-liner I have ever concocted.)

The *Rencontre* was held in a lavishly renovated academic center on the Rue Descartes, on the outskirts of the Sorbonne, complete with simultaneous translation (which, I was happy to find, I still did not need) and a lively audience of several hundred. Bob Gardner was the first speaker and, as usual on those rare occasions when he presents a paper in public, he scored a real triumph. (On the strength of this, René saw to it that Bob's [1983] book, *Self Inquiry*, got published in French by Aubier.[3] It is very telling about the anti-American bias of French psychoanalysis that the book did not sell.) I had chosen to present a clinical paper (1980b) illustrating the paradoxical results of (valid) interpretations of dreams if these are made when analysands function in modes that do not permit interpretive interventions. I should have known that I was heading for trouble when, in introducing me, René took great pains to summarize the thesis of *Models of the Mind*, in an attempt to bring the audience into the flow—*au courant*, as they say.

The formal discussant of my paper was François Roustang, a brilliant literary scholar and restless spirit, who successively abandoned the Catholic priesthood and Lacanian psychoanalysis. He construed the hierarchical model as a straitjacket and delivered a fiery revolutionary diatribe against all tyrannous theories. It dawned on me that the analytic civil wars in France had produced widespread revolt against the felt constraints of settled schemata, and that I would do better to demonstrate the complexities of mental organization through a concrete example than through theoretical generalizations. Hence, I responded to Roustang's blast by pointing out that he misconceived the consequences of using theory, as I would try to show by expanding the scope of one of the clinical illustrations. As I was doing so, more and more people interrupted with relevant questions, and an exhilarating discussion of the case took up the rest of the morning. At a reception that evening, I was told that such a candid report about clinical work had never been heard in Paris. (It may not be an everyday occurrence in Chicago, either, but by American standards there was nothing unique about it.)

At that, I fared better than some of the other American presenters: for example, Dale Boesky (then editor of the *Quarterly*), who gave a rather dry but competent paper on ego psychology, was altogether talking past the French. Aside from the invited speakers, there were only a handful of American francophiles present. I believe that only Warren Poland, an avid reader of French analytic publications, could follow what the French presenters were saying; the rest of us were just as bewildered by the natives as the French audience seemed to be by Boesky. (If they thought they understood Bob Gardner, it was likely that it was at the level of the poetry of his text.) A prominent Lacanian presented a case that sounded very much like one of psychotic decompensation, but she did not consider the nosological significance of the delusions the patient seemed to articulate. A dogmatic Kleinian talked about the effects of the death instinct in terms as concrete as if this force were a toxin. A deconstructionist lectured on the treachery of human communication. It was all highly clever and elegant, but there were no pretensions that these causeries aspired to the status of science. None of the French gave any thought to developmental considerations, and they showed no great interest in therapeutic outcomes either.

The experience in Paris convinced me that having a dialogue with most French colleagues was more trouble than I was willing to take. At the same time, the ones I encountered were intelligent, decent, hard-working, cultivated people. We saw how a variety of professionals live in Paris: from a patrician flat overlooking the Luxembourg Gardens, or a wonderfully renovated apartment in a piece of fourteenth-century real estate on the Ile St. Louis, through solid nineteenth-century bourgeois buildings, to an elegant private house a stone's throw from the Arc de Triomphe, and a depressing modern edifice in the squalid new quarter near Montparnasse. Analytic fees were low, so people worked long hours, but they had the satisfaction of being in a profession of high prestige. A Lacanian told me that psychoanalysis had conquered France because for the past generation French *literature* has been dormant. (In other words, psychoanalysis is regarded as *belles lettres*.[4]) I asked her whether the excellence of Marguerite Yourcenar did not disprove such a judgment.[5] She said, ruefully, that Yourcenar's books are, of course, popular, but not with intellectuals—only people like her own husband were enthusiastic about such work. The gentleman is vice president of a large oil company. The French are *different*. I suspect that psychoanalysis has a bright future in their country because of its millennial tradition of intellectual elitism.

René may also have concluded that Franco-American analytic dialogues are not presently fruitful, for (contrary to his original plans) he did not publish the proceedings of the *Rencontre* in *Confrontation*. He did ask me to send him an essay on psychoanalytic history instead; from the volume of Freudiana I showed him, he selected the paper Wolf and I had written on the adolescent exchange of letters with Silberstein (1973b).[6] The theme for that issue of *Confrontation* was that of correspondence. Incidentally, much of it dealt with the Freud-Ferenczi letters, with contributions by two of the Paris Hungarian contingent, Maria Török and Judith Dupont.[7] Hungarian analysts in Paris are, naturally, split into pro- and anti-Ferenczi camps.[8]

Despite the equivocal results of the *Rencontre*, René clearly wanted to keep in contact with some of the Americans he had invited; a few years later he proposed a week-long private colloquium featuring much the same cast, with but a few changes on each side. I was planning to vacation in Europe anyway (this was our year for Andalusia at Easter—the processions of Penitents re-creating the events of the Passion throughout Holy Week are unforgettable!), and a tax-deductible stopover in Paris seemed very attractive. Every morning, I walked through the heart of Paris from the Place Vendôme to the Rue Descartes; the group met until lunchtime, and then I met Mary for our customary explorations of the city. Bob Gardner and Warren Poland were there, and Peter Hildebrand of London, with whom René had in the interval organized a Franco-British *Rencontre*, also attended.

The absence of an audience failed to improve the possibilities of mutual comprehension between French and American analysts. Although the discussion was conducted in English alone, I found the proceedings just as dispiriting as they had been in Aspen, so much so that I decided to leave early. What became clear in the small-group setting is the fundamental anarchism of the French spirit. The young mistress of one of the senior French participants was driving us along the broad Boulevard St. Germain; when she spotted an illegal parking place on the opposite side, she made an abrupt U-turn and, heading into oncoming traffic, sped onto the sidewalk to take the spot. The same attitude characterized her conduct of a case she presented to the group. At one point, she said something about the analysand acting out by bringing payment in the form of a check. I could not believe my ears; I asked her how such a decision would constitute acting out. She replied that they had agreed that payment would be made in cash. I persisted, "*Chez nous*, such an agreement to collude in breaking the law would be regarded as a way of corrupting the patient." The young woman's mentor/lover/supervisor interrupted, "Ah! How I would love to live in a country where it is possible to obey the law!" Perhaps so; but I doubt that he would feel at home in one where such conduct is customary. Such attitudes probably interfere with the therapeutic effectiveness of those who hold them—but what a refreshing change they are from the conformity the Joan Flemings of this world have imposed on much of American psychoanalysis!

Despite my rude challenge to his friends and my early departure, René continued to maintain our relations for some time by sending me his newly published books. I found these increasingly difficult to read, despite my familiarity with the meaning of every word. I even checked my comprehension of the French as such by using a dictionary, but I remained puzzled about René's meaning. When I let him know about my difficulties, Major laughed. "You know," he said, "in Paris it is considered *un peu déclassé* to write in a manner that is easy to understand." I was able to follow a political essay he later sent me; in this, he assailed American imperialism for keeping Western Europe in thrall. I did send a response to this *confrontation*; I predicted that, within a few years, American isolationism would lead to our abandonment of European commitments. For some reason, this riposte put an end to our correspondence. Nowadays, it is the fashion in Paris to assail *les Américains* for their isolationist parochialism. *Sans blague*![9]

About a year after the second Paris *Rencontre*, Hildebrand had me invited to a conference at the Tavistock Clinic. I had other plans for that summer but indicated an interest in attending another time. They repeated the invitation for a week in July 1990—it was to be a colloquium on teaching psychotherapy, with participation allegedly limited to experienced or influential educators. It is a subject I was no longer interested in, but making an English country tour after the conference appealed to me, and I was curious about the Kleinian ambience at the Tavistock Clinic. (It was one of the rare occasions when I violated a resolution no longer to attend scientific meetings where I had no active role. As in the case of the Ferenczi conference in Budapest, the admission fee turned out to be a form of charity to an impoverished institution. Thatcherism has been no friendlier to analytic organizations than was Communism.)

Although a few visitors from abroad were featured on the London program, the conference was typically British in its condescension to the audience. (The atmosphere echoed the insularity I had experienced at Hampstead a dozen years earlier.) The therapy publicized by the Tavistock staff struck me as unrealistic in its ambitions and poorly thought through; it seemed to offer the standard Kleinian interpretive schema to all comers—even on a once-a-week basis. I made my usual noises of protest about using such magical formulae, like a shaman, but I knew it was really useless to object; I did it mostly to avoid sinking into bored passivity. I only found the experience worthwhile because I met so many interesting people—whether at the festive reception in the garden of the neighboring Freud house or at lunch in the deteriorating Tavistock building. One of these was an analyst from Stuttgart, with whom I discussed the possibility of a lecture tour in Germany.

Some of the English did, of course, deign to chat with visitors; they were always polite, if distant. I can best characterize them by recalling a lunchtime interchange with a young man who looked a bit like the actor Peter O'Toole. He turned out to be an analyst practicing in Oxford. I said that sounded wonderful, but I wondered what it was actually like. With obvious self-restraint yet a tinge of smugness, he conceded that it was lovely to see the tower of Christ Church from one's office window or to be riding one's horse in the fields of Oxfordshire, only fifteen minutes after leaving work. Then the dam burst. "Actually," he said, "I am a Cambridge man—but I decided to see how the other half lives." He was not even half-joking. (It was an incident worthy of one of Evelyn Waugh's novels.) When the conference was breaking up, Hildebrand assured me that if I ever wanted to do a bit of teaching in London, I would be welcome at Tavistock, provided I did not insist on being paid. I suspect that he thought he was offering me some kind of a plum.

The greatest contrast to the hollow arrogance I encountered in England was my trip to Budapest, earlier in 1990. As I have mentioned, this came about as a result of meeting two Hungarian colleagues in 1989 at the Freud Center in Jerusalem, on the occasion of the conference on art and psychoanalysis. When we next made a trip to Italy, I let my new contacts in Budapest know that from there we might go on to Hungary. They not only arranged a lecture at the psychoanalytic society but also a seminar with the Budapest candidates. Both experiences were stunning, but so was the entire visit. The first free elections in over seventy-five years were in progress on the very day we arrived, and I was amazed to discover that I could easily follow these events on Hungarian television, fifty years after last using my mother tongue.

My hosts translated the presentation I was to make at the society, and I stumbled through reading it in Hungarian—a challenge I found more difficult than it was to articulate the simple statements I could think up on my own. I brought along my cousin Gábor Antal, a retired journalist who had apparently written some articles favorable to the analytic group during their time of troubles under Communism, so that he was known to many of the senior members, and Gábor later edited the Hungarian text for publication.[10] It did not match my adolescent fantasies of returning to Budapest at the head of a conquering army, but it was very satisfying nonetheless. I realized that the reason visits to relatives had not been sufficient to lure me back to Hungary was that I first needed to feel that some significant entity in the country had acknowledged my potential value as a citizen.

The body that made proper acknowledgment was the group of candidates who gathered for my seminar in a turn-of-the-century apartment overlooking one of Budapest's major boulevards—bourgeois comfort gone to seed. These were the young people who cried when I made clear my lack of allegiance to Hungary. The presenter, Judit Mészáros, is a very capable Jewish psychologist; her patient was a bizarre and paranoid young man whose father had been a general in the Communist intelligence service. The patient had been raised with absolutely no information about his antecedents—even the family surname was clearly a pseudonym. One of his major preoccupations was a fervent belief in Jewish conspiracies to destroy the country. In view of these convictions, Judit was clever enough to focus her early efforts on inquiring about the significance of his choice of a Jewish analyst. (I thought I showed appreciation of her efforts, but when I met her in Washington, Judit told me I had been "very severe." I think this reveals the tenuous self-esteem of a group of analytic pioneers; what she took for disapproval was only pessimism!) Such are the travails of analysis in post-Communist Central Europe.

Of course, the Hungarian Psychoanalytic Society is not eager to be humiliated by colonialist advice. When I wrote to the president of the International Psychoanalytic to volunteer my services on the committee organized to promote analysis in the countries newly liberated from Soviet domination, nothing came of my offer; I suspect that my first visit to Budapest left the Hungarians with the impression that I thought they had a lot of catching up to do, and they did not welcome such avuncular assistance. Perhaps it was a mistake to send copies of all my books to Budapest.

The other country where I encountered the phenomenon of resistance to potential colonialism is Israel. I first went there in 1986, as a visiting professor sent by a group of American analysts (organized by Leonard

Comess of Los Angeles), ostensibly to beef up psychiatric education in Israel. Len and I had served together on the national committee on institutes; he is a warm, likable person who thought well of my published work and asked me, rather impulsively, whether I would like to have a subsidized trip to Israel. Well, of course! Why not? All expenses paid and a decent fee besides. I was told that Leonard's organization sent someone for three weeks twice a year, to academic institutions in Jerusalem, Tel Aviv, and Haifa, and sometimes to the Israel Psychoanalytic Society.

In actuality, the Israelis universally seemed to regard all this as unwelcome and patronizing; they were barely polite to quite rude to this visitor. I never heard from the psychoanalytic society or Tel Aviv University, and the psychiatry department at Haifa treated my appearance there as if they were doing me a favor by attending. (The chairman took us along while he went to Acre to testify at some trial, dumped us at the gate to the Old City, and told us to meet him there several hours later. The Crusader fortifications are fascinating and much of the medieval city is accessible to visitors through underground passageways. It is a beautiful spot, and Mary and I had a lovely morning there. But when our host picked us up, more than an hour late, he gave no apology or explanation.)

In Jerusalem, I was to teach at the Telbiya mental hospital, a state institution in the center of the city, just down a hill from the King David Hotel. In this nonacademic setting, my presence did not embarrass anyone; the place was run by a crusty Argentine-born psychiatrist who spoke no English but was entirely collegial. (He took us for a festive dinner in East Jerusalem, at a famous Arab restaurant repeatedly bombed because Israelis had invested in it. I believe the place has not survived.) He also encouraged me to offer a course of six lectures for any of the staff who cared to come, and I decided to present a truly psychoanalytic outline of psychopathology.

I have found that vacation trips often provide an excellent setting for thinking through my position on matters that do not require the immediate use of a library. I wrote such an essay (chap. 14 in 1986a) on a cruise up the Nile from Cairo to Aswan, mostly on deck under a brilliant January sun. Some years before, I had used a stay in a hotel on the outskirts of Dubrovnik, recently converted from a government guest house, as a similar haven of peace to write a long paper. (The place was destroyed during the Serbo-Croat war not long ago.) The seemingly interminable return flights from Europe have been intervals that I could sometimes use in the same way. My fortnight in Jerusalem allowed me to outline the monograph on psychopathology (1988a) that I eventually entitled *The Mind in Disorder*. I am sure the Israelis thought I was daft to insist on working; they wanted me to relax, enjoy my visit, and get to know the country.

We did see a great deal in three weeks—this was before the *intifada*, and it was still possible to go almost anywhere. Mary and I did get caught in a major riot in the Old City; fortunately we were walking around the surrounding walls, so it was easy to get to one of the gates and make our escape without being overwhelmed by tear gas. But Rami Aronzon, a young analyst on the Telbiya staff, kindly drove us into the occupied areas to see great isolated sites like the excavations at Qumran or Herod's awesome fortress in the Judean Hills. Rami is Norwegian-born and earned more than half of his annual income by working one month per year in his native land as a general practitioner above the Arctic Circle. In addition to his job at Telbiya, he spent one day a week providing psychiatric services for a kibbutz. (What have American analysts to complain about?)

The superintendent of Telbiya Hospital actually assigned a resident to be our chauffeur one day a week so that we could extend the radius of our excursions. A fierce young man born in Iraq, he had served as a paratrooper in the Israeli Army. We were not surprised that he had never before seen the Church of the Nativity in Bethlehem, but it was astonishing that he had never been to the Holocaust Memorial at Yad Vashem either, and that he expressed contempt for the victims for "allowing themselves" to be murdered. I think this lack of empathy is relevant for the understanding of the action-oriented ambiance within which Israeli analysts must function.

Fortunately for us, one of the members of the art history department at the Hebrew University had been in touch with Mary about publishing work in *Psychoanalytic Perspectives in Art*, and we notified this person about our prospective visit. Millie Heyd turned out to be a member of the Israeli elite; an uncle of hers was a former chief justice, her father an eminent scholar, and her husband a distinguished philosopher and a leader of Peace Now, the movement that advocated compromise with the PLO. Through her, we met a host of interesting people—even the psychoanalyst I most wanted to see, Pinchas Noy. Jerusalem is a place where such birds of a feather all know each other. Noy was entirely cordial, but he did not offer to arrange for me to meet other Israeli colleagues.

It was as a result of getting to know the art historians at the university that we got our second invitation to Jerusalem. Not only Millie, but several of her colleagues at the university proved to be interested in the psychoanalytic approach to art and in organizing a conference on that topic.

As it happened, shortly thereafter the Freud professorship at Jerusalem was for a year held by Sidney Blatt, a Yale psychologist/analyst whom I had known slightly earlier in his career, when he lived in Chicago. One of the responsibilities of the Freud professor is to head the periodic conferences held at the Freud Centre, and he was open to the art historians' wish to collaborate on an interdisciplinary effort. He was also more than willing to invite both Mary and me to participate.

The second trip to Israel was in most ways entirely different from the first. Because we had so recently visited the sites of greatest interest to us, we decided to stay in Jerusalem only for the duration of the conference. It was just as well; the *intifada* was at its height, and we were advised to stay out of Arab areas. However, this time we got the red-carpet treatment; invited participants were accommodated at Mishkenot Sha'ananim, a splendid government guest house built into the side of a hill overlooking the Hinnom Valley; from our windows, we had an unmatched view looking west to the Old City and, in the distance, the Mount of Olives. Intellectuals still count for something in Israel. This was underscored by a reception at the penthouse apartment of the financial backer of the meeting, the discerning Canadian art collector Ayala Zaks. From her terrace, one could survey the entire city—an unforgettable panorama as the setting sun burnishes in gold the uniform buttery stonework of the buildings. The modern art within was worthy of the best museums.

The conference itself, held at the fortress-like Mt. Scopus campus of the Hebrew University (surrounded by hostile East Jerusalem), was attended by a large and enthusiastic Israeli audience, with a scattering of European analysts. The first among these to make contact with me were two Hungarian ladies, Maria Csillag and Zsuzsa Varga. This is when they ascertained that I still understood my mother tongue and warmly invited me to visit the resurgent psychoanalytic group in Budapest. I indicated that, since we were exiled in 1939, I had never been back to Hungary, although my mother had several times visited family there. Undeterred, Zsuzsa promised to get in touch with me to discuss specific possibilities for such a professional homecoming.

Zsuzsa was then only starting her formal candidacy; she is a very sophisticated young woman, with serious intellectual ambitions—multilingual, an accomplished musician, widely read in the literature of Europe. Her mother, once a student of Piaget's, was a member of the Hungarian Psychoanalytic Society. Both her analyst and her academically distinguished father had died relatively recently, and Zsuzsa was explicit about appointing me as their distant successor—but the transferences are mutual, for she is the daughter I might have had if I had remained in Central Europe.

Even more remarkable than this encounter with a life-that-might-have-been was getting acquainted with Bettina Meissner, a colleague from Cologne who approached me carrying a bunch of my books that she asked me to autograph. She is the only upper-class European with whom I have ever become close—the daughter of an ambassador and the wife of an eminent academic—a person of extraordinary refinement. Needless to say, this friendship evolved more slowly than the one with my *Landsmännin*, for I am naturally more reserved with a woman somewhat closer to me in age. It was a new experience for me to make friends with a woman (rather than getting to know her because of prior friendship with her husband). When I saw the social setting in which Bettina moves at first hand, I got the impression that such a situation is not at all unusual for her.

In Jerusalem, however, we barely exchanged addresses; our correspondence actually started when I wrote her for an opinion about another German colleague who volunteered to present at our interdisciplinary workshop at the meetings of the American. At the time, I did not yet know that it is not only the French who are different. So are the Brazilians, the Israelis, the Hungarians, the English, the Germans. Oh, yes! The Italians, too.

❖ CHAPTER 20 ❖

THE HEIRS OF THE THIRD REICH

About a year ago, I received a reprint from a recent number of *Psyche*—a well-thought-out and well-researched article (Harsch 1994) on the effect on Freud of having had two primary caretakers. The author added a personal note to the effect that her essay was the elaboration of one sentence in my paper about the role of self-analysis in the evolution of Freud's scientific ideas (1968a). Wow! To add to my pleasure, she mentioned that the German candidates' newsletter/journal, *Psa-Info*, had published a translation of another paper of mine (1991b), one of the jeremiads about the ills of our profession I produce from time to time.[1] My correspondent added that she believes my pessimistic prophecies about psychoanalysis are applicable to the future of the profession in Germany as well. She may be right, but if so, such a catastrophe must be decades away, judging by my observations of the vibrant German analytic scene on my numerous professional visits.

One of the ways in which German psychoanalysis is unique is that, especially if they do not have to pay the transatlantic fares, our German colleagues are eager for input from experienced Americans—at least, they have been more than hospitable on the four lecture tours I have organized with the help of colleagues I had previously encountered. On the first occasion, Bettina arranged the tour for me, to include visits of several institutes of the *Deutsche Psychoanalytische Vereinigung* (DPV)—the organization affiliated with the international association. Bettina and I settled on a sequence of stops in Freiburg, Frankfurt, and Cologne. I tried to correlate this itinerary with a seminar for a group in Stuttgart, an institute of the *Deutsche Psychoanalytische Gesellschaft* (DPG), but this proved to be too difficult—a symptom of the continuing lack of cooperation between these rival organizations, almost fifty years after their split.

I flew to Strasbourg, an hour's drive from the extreme southwest corner of Germany where Freiburg is located. My lecture took place in a nineteenth-century mansion that houses the institute. I did not dare to read a presentation in German (I have several times come close to mastering this infernally difficult language, only to lose it again), but Bettina assured me that so many colleagues understand English that the lectures would be well attended. I was astonished to find, in this city of 150,000, an audience of almost fifty people. (I was informed that, for a regional population of a quarter million, Freiburg could boast of close to two hundred analysts, counting both DPV and DPG members.)

I presented a paper about the desirable form of psychoanalytic interventions, destined for a festschrift to honor Martin Bergmann on his eightieth birthday (1993k). Bettina had kindly prepared a German translation, which was available for those who might have difficulty following a lecture in English; judging by the lively discussion, the paper was understood. I wondered why Johannes Cremerius, whom I had met not long before, had not shown up, and I was informed that he had fallen out with the institute and was regarded as "impossible" in the analytic community. I was not really surprised; Cremerius had been an anti-Nazi resistor who ended up in a concentration camp; when I spoke to him, he was still fulminating against Germany and the Germans.

The following morning, one of the candidates—a very able young man who had some of his psychiatric training in England—presented an extremely difficult case to a seminar for about a dozen students. I was very favorably impressed with his clinical skill, as well as the general sophistication of the candidates, and they were obviously elated about the positive feedback they received from a senior visitor from abroad. (They seemed to fear disapproval simply because they are German.)

If possible, in the afternoon I wanted to cross over to Alsace to see once more the great Isenheim Altarpiece in Colmar. One of the candidates lived on the way, in the frontier village of Breisach, so she was asked to take me. Breisach turned out to be a community of around five thousand, now completely gentrified. The candidate's husband is the local obstetrician, and she also practices in the village. Psychoanalysis in a rural setting—such are the results of a responsible system of health care delivery! (At least three hundred analytic sessions are fully covered by the insurance system.) I was stunned, but my host could not grasp what I found so unusual about this, *Warum nicht*? Things are no different in Colmar; a town of sixty thousand, some three hundred fifty miles from Paris, has a resident analyst! Our continental colleagues have managed their affairs better than we have in America.

I was told that some of the older Freiburg faculty had started their analytic education immediately after the Second World War and had to make very unusual arrangements both for their training analysis and for supervision—so much so that some of the most experienced among them could not become full members of the international because of the irregularity of their credentials. One of these, a senior analyst of some reputation, invited me to meet her on Sunday morning for a tour of the cathedral.

There was a steady drizzle that day, so we shared an umbrella. While the cathedral was jammed with worshipers, we concentrated on seeing the exterior sculptural decoration; eventually, we inspected some of the capitals under the west porch, and she pointed to one portraying a particularly frolicsome and lighthearted human figure. "You see this? But appearances can deceive—look at it from the rear." On the reverse side, the same creature appeared to be a hideous devil. I knew this was not meant as a lesson in medieval iconography, so I kept silent. Then I heard, "You know, my father was a chemist who worked for the National Socialist regime. The Russians captured him in Vienna, and they gave him a hard time, but after a while they let him go. Then the Americans arrested him; and they treated him even worse." (Did he develop the poison gas used in the crematoria?) This was the first of a series of traumatic memories I was to hear from German colleagues; this tormented person's face was ravaged with grief and shame as she shared hers with me.

The Sigmund Freud Institute in Frankfurt is somehow sponsored by the state of Hesse, which has erected a modern four-story building in a fine residential area to house it. When I got there, the structure had just undergone a sprucing up—to give an idea of the ebullience of German psychoanalysis, the redecoration included an extensive piece of conceptual art, designed by the pricey American artist Sol Le Witt, that covered all the hallways and stairwells. (The analysts did have to pay for this out of their own pockets.) The bad news was that some kind of civil war was afoot within the institute, so that the atmosphere was tense and somewhat unreceptive to scientific distractions. About a year after my visit, two sources of this angst became manifest: the recently installed young director of the institute resigned under pressure, and a struggle among its editors over control of *Psyche* (produced in Frankfurt) broke into the open.

Despite signs of disorganization at the institute, the scientific sessions were well attended. Among those present was one of the editors of *Psyche* with whom I had dealt many years before, when I first had contact with the journal[2]; he had also answered me when I submitted a paper (1989b) to *Psyche* about a year previously. He now wanted to know whether I would let them publish my new paper as well, and I gladly handed him Bettina's translation.

In the power struggle that followed my contribution became the subject of a tug-of-war. More than three years later, it was finally published by the winning faction.[3] The civil war led to the appointment of a professional editor, who is not a psychoanalyst, to run the journal. In 1993 I met this person at the Budapest conference, and he expressed interest in continuing to publish my papers. He also suggested that, to make my recent contributions more easily understandable for the German analytic reader, it would be helpful first to publish an adequate synopsis of my body of theoretical work. After going through several drafts, we have reached consensus on such a position statement (also the epilogue in 1996b); Bettina once again volunteered to translate it for publication.

I was to conclude this first tour in Cologne at the end of the week; in the interval I wanted to visit Marburg. I had mentioned my plan for this excursion in a letter to Bettina, and she put me in touch with one of her good friends, who practices analysis in that university town. This person kindly showed me around Marburg, a small, charming community (one of the few in Germany undamaged by the war), and she invited me for dinner at her home. We were joined by another woman colleague, who happens to be a member of the rival DPG. Thus, because of a need for collegiality in a place with few analysts, political differences can be overcome. (My hostess belongs to the DPV institute at Giessen, another small university community about thirty minutes away by car.) Neither woman is from the Marburg area; I learned that in such a provincial setting this could be a handicap, particularly if one has a regional accent! They were ambivalent about their relatively isolated small-town existence; although to us it might seem easy to hop on a train to Frankfurt, these people have not as yet joined the commuter society.

The Cologne institute is located in an abandoned post office, behind the main railway station. Its facilities are unpretentious but adequate, and the lecture hall was filled, although, as Bettina later told me, a conservative faction of the membership was not in evidence. I was startled to see an Indian lady in the audience; afterward, she introduced herself and asked whether I would like to see a Max Ernst exhibition with her on Saturday afternoon. Nothing could have pleased me more.

Saturday morning we had a case seminar, with a junior faculty member as presenter. Once again, I heard an account of a difficult analysis, sensitively conducted, but without the benefit of a consistent clinical theory to guide it; those in attendance seemed grateful for the framework I tried to provide for them. Then Tapasi Gupta took charge of me, and we were off to the splendid new museum on the river front, just behind the immense cathedral. Her English is, of course, perfect (as one would expect of a well-educated high-caste Hindu), and she is fully conversant with twentieth-century art. Yet it seemed uncanny to be walking around an exhibition of German art with a lady in a sari, who had a scarlet dot on her forehead, chatting in English about surrealism and psychoanalysis. I finally burst out, "What are you doing in Cologne, Dr. Gupta?" She was amused. "Why? I am a German citizen!"

That evening, Bettina held a party to celebrate my visit. The Meissners collect Greek and Roman antiquities, and they also own several contemporary paintings of considerable merit. Bettina explained that these are by the late Georg Meistermann, whose widow was coming to the party—she is Edeltrud Meistermann-Seeger, the person who reestablished psychoanalysis in Cologne after 1945. She was then also widowed; her first husband had been a general. By contrast, Meistermann had been an overt anti-Nazi who barely survived the war through the unobtrusive protection of the Catholic church, for which he began to design stained glass windows. In this century, next to Chagall, Meistermann ended up as the most prolific artist in that medium, partly because his principal protector became the Cardinal-Archbishop of Cologne. Bettina's party was the elderly gentlewoman's first social engagement since Meistermann's death. She looked and acted the part of a person who had moved in the milieu of the most accomplished European intellectuals of the postwar era, and her analytic colleagues clearly revere her.

The person with whom I talked most extensively that evening was a man in his early fifties who impressed me as an intellectual of a type unknown in America. I first noted this when he handed Bettina a volume of French poetry—as a party gift. Of course, neither came to psychoanalysis from a background in the mental health professions: Bettina is a lawyer, her guest a sociologist. They are the kind of people Freud (1926) had in mind in advocating lay analysis. My new acquaintance told me something else about himself that I found illuminating about German society as well; he mentioned that his grandfather had been the sergeant-major of Kaiser Wilhelm's personal guard. Upward mobility of the kind demonstrated by this family is rare anywhere; until very recently, it was rarest of all in Europe.

We talked about the contrast between my attitude about analytic interventions—that one should not be afraid of making mistakes, for nothing could be more illuminating than grasping why some action of the analyst's was in error—and that of most German analysts, who seemed intent on always doing the right thing. When I said that I did have faith in a policy of *Sturm, Schwung, und durch!*,[4] my interlocutor could not integrate that I had spoken in German—I had to remind him that I was quoting Marshal Rommel's strategic doctrine of *Blitzkrieg*. He said, wistfully, "You may say that, but we must not even think it."

This repudiation of the German past is perhaps most evident among those who were young children during the war, most of whom had terrifying experiences of air raids, flight from advancing Allied armies, and deaths of family members—narratives I did not find it difficult to elicit when I inquired. Some members of an older generation proved to be less sensitive on the score of the Nazi past; a Cologne analyst in his seventies, who had been an artillery officer on the Russian front, agreed with me that his colleagues are excessively preoccupied with rules. He said, laughingly, that the war in Russia was lost because the German artillery always went "by the book" (one shell long, one shell short—observe, calculate—third shell on target). The Russians, by contrast, adjusted their gun-sights empirically (fire, observe, adjust), thereby saving one round out of three.

I returned to the Cologne institute about a year later; I was asked to discuss my disagreements with self psychology. This well-attended meeting was tipped in the direction of a passionate defense of self psychology (against what he perceived as my deprecation in an article [1989b] I published in *Psyche*[5]), by a single member of the audience, who spoke in a rapid German that had to be translated for my benefit. As he talked, it became apparent that he was unfamiliar with Kohut's ultimate positions (stated in his posthumous book of 1984)—finally, he mentioned that the views he was espousing were those of Michael Basch. I do not know whether the audience believed me when I replied that, in private, Mike had never taken exception to any of my analytic views, although in public he reiterated his allegiance to Kohut. This heckler was more or less appeased by my statement that his own positions were unobjectionable.

This lengthy interchange turned the remainder of the meeting to the history of the self psychology movement as I had witnessed it. Someone mentioned that Kohut's ideas initially swept German psychoanalysis by storm, only to be gradually abandoned by a great majority. She wondered whether this phenomenon might best be explained as collective expiation of guilt for the crimes of the Nazi regime. I assume she meant that an ex-refugee from Nazism received intellectual carte blanche, but I did not pursue this line of thought, because I did not feel fully prepared to discuss such an explosive issue in a public setting. *Ich bin auch ein Flüchtling*.[6]

Soon after my return from the first German lecture tour, I heard from my contact in Stuttgart, who wondered how soon I might be willing to return to Germany to make up for the missed opportunity at his institute. I had found the German experience so gratifying that I gave him carte blanche to set up a second tour for me; he had mentioned that he had good connections in Ulm and Munich. He obviously had great difficulty in organizing my itinerary, and I did not hear about the project for some time. In the interval, a colleague in Berlin contacted me with a scientific query, and through this person I made further inquiries about the possibility of presenting to one of the analytic groups there. It so happened that I eventually got positive replies from everywhere, and I felt honor bound to go through with both plans, although it proved to be impossible to schedule all the events for the same trip. We ultimately decided on separate trips to northern and southern Germany, a little over two months apart, in the winter and spring of 1992. Mary decided to accompany me on the earlier venture, the winter trip along the southerly route.

Shortly before we left for Germany, I sold the apartment in which I had been practicing and consolidated my remaining professional activities in a home office. This was a big step toward retirement, although it was to take me another two and a half years to wind up the analyses I still had in progress. I was considerably stirred up about shutting down an operation that had endured for more than thirty-six years; my introspective mood was heightened by the circumstance that the paper I planned to present on this tour (1993g) dealt with self-analysis and was largely focused on the issue of unexplored motivations for having chosen a therapeutic career. The leaden skies and widespread fogs that greeted us in Frankfurt reinforced the sense of existing in a dream-like state. For instance, when I thought I saw the director of the analytic institute at a performance of *Ariadne auf Naxos* at the Frankfurt Opera, I concluded that I misremembered what he looks like—only to learn more recently that he had indeed been present that evening.

The night before I was to read my paper in Stuttgart, I had a dream for which the opera clearly provided the day residue. In the dream, I had decided to discontinue an incestuous relationship with my mother, over her distressed objections. "I no longer care how you feel about it," I was declaring, "I have to do what is best for me." Like Theseus, I was abandoning the woman who had given me life.[7] It was clear to me that the dream was a reaction to guilt about refusing further to devote my life to the care of the afflicted; it also revealed that I had bribed myself to carry these burdens with the belief that, in the process, I had outdone my father as a man and a physician. I felt a sense of great relief to be done with it. Needless to say, I could not resist interpolating the dream and my understanding of it into my presentations to audiences of strangers, far from Chicago. I suppose that my freedom to do this also shows that, among German psychoanalysts, I almost felt at home. I must say, however, that they listened bug-eyed to this demonstration of self-inquiry in action. Needless to say, these personal indiscretions established greater intimacy with them than I usually have with audiences.

In Stuttgart, several psychoanalytic organizations share an old house, spared by the wartime bombardments. A few steps away there is a convenient *Weinstube* where, after the meeting, we downed a few glasses of Wurttemberger. This is where I got acquainted with János Harmatta, my future host in Budapest. The person who sat next to me was a beautiful, olive-skinned young analyst, the wife of one of the faculty members. Her English was limited, but we discovered that we could converse in French. She revealed that, as a child, she had lived in Paris; later she attended French schools in Germany. Her mother was German, her father an Algerian revolutionary of Berber extraction who disappeared when she was very small, presumably killed by the colonial authorities. An exotic flower on the banks of the Neckar River!

It so happened that, next morning, it was her husband who presented a case in my seminar. As usual, it was a thorny clinical problem; in this instance, a real impasse had supervened. I thought that the analysand behaved sadistically toward the analyst, so I tried to explore whether he could grasp that he had lent himself to the reenactment in the active mode of a childhood scenario in which the analysand had suffered passively. He was a bright and talented man; he understood instantly, and he commented that he often found himself trying to be more "giving" than was good for patients. That evening, we were to have dinner at the home of the medical director of a large inpatient facility, run by a consortium of insurance companies to care for persons who need psychotherapy as well as hospitalization. (The insurance system provided such treatment for six months, no questions asked—longer with peer review.) This "Klinik" is in a rural setting, just outside Stuttgart; the director lived on campus, in a nice, if modest, modern cottage. Among the half-dozen guests was that morning's presenter.

The conversation turned to the relations between the two psychoanalytic organizations in Germany, DPV and DPG. Everyone agreed that the split is senseless—if there ever were theoretical differences behind it, they no longer exist. Our host explained that DPG was a postwar reconstitution by analysts who had endured through the Hitler era of the society founded by Karl Abraham about eighty years before. Because these people had joined various professional bodies set up by the Nazis, the International Psychoanalytic Association would have no part of them; new analytic recruits, eager to be integrated into the anti-Nazi community, procured training by going abroad, and then founded the DPV. (These were the current hierarchs of psychoanalysis—Johannes Cremerius, Helmut Thomä, Edeltrud Meistermann-Seeger, and the late Alexander Mitscherlich.) I was also told that, although the two societies have roughly equal numbers, the DPV has more prestige. In fact, these colleagues were rather surprised that an American visitor would consent to teach at a DPG institute.

I turned to the husband of the Berber refugee and asked him why a man of his talent and promise had, under the circumstances, chosen to adhere to the DPG. After a considerable pause, he replied with great emotion, "My parents were profoundly implicated in the National Socialist regime, but I loved them, and I could not repudiate them totally by joining the DPV." One may be unable to repudiate beloved parents, but one can attempt to make reparation by taking care of refugees from North Africa or allowing unfortunate patients to be abusive. Out of my consulting room, I have never heard a comparable self-revelation. (By extrapolation, one could infer that many in the DPG expected Americans to boycott it as if this organization were still tainted by Nazism.)

I soon discovered that my DPG hosts were able to get me invited to the DPV institute in Ulm because one of them has a part-time research position at the university there, so that he knows the senior analysts, Helmut

Thomä and Horst Kächele, in their capacity as professors of psychiatry. A couple of days later, when we saw him on the grounds of the Ulm psychiatry department, I got the impression that he was being treated as a second-class citizen there. (In these days of threatened government cutbacks, even German psychoanalysts would do better to present a united front, but the DPV-DPG civil war does not seem ripe for resolution.) I was able to convince this person that we would like to reciprocate his hospitality, and, like the Meissners, he has since visited us in Chicago. We keep in touch.

When he was in America, my Stuttgart contact finally confessed that he had wanted to have me visit the DPG institute in Munich but had been bullied into sending me to the DPV instead! ("He belongs to us!" was apparently the clinching argument.) I did not ask who did the bullying. I wrote to the leading figure of the DPG in Munich, in the hope of clarifying that I had had nothing to do with this act of piracy, but my demarche bore no fruit—at least I never received a reply. In 1993 I met this colleague in Budapest and I reiterated my willingness to make reparation for the snub, but even this assertion of good faith was greeted with some skepticism.

In Ulm, Helmut Thomä proudly showed us around the impressive psychiatric/analytic empire he has built at the university. He is a man of prodigious energy: in his mid-seventies, scarcely a year after German reunification, he was already commuting to a number of psychiatry departments in the former East Germany to spread psychoanalytic influence. Although he has passed the reins of Ulm to Kächele, he continues actively to participate in the psychotherapy research that is one of the central goals of the department.[8] He has recently coauthored a massive textbook of psychoanalysis and was quite apologetic about having "forgotten" to discuss my work in it. (I prefer not to think about the dynamics of such a complex enactment; it is better in every way to exchange polite notes of mutual regard with such a man.[9])

Thomä is now the most senior of German analysts. At lunch, he recounted that he still feels shame about his prudent decision in 1939 to enlist in a program to train physicians for the *Wehrmacht*, as if exposing oneself to the hazards of combat were a point of honor, no matter what the cause in which one fights. He smiled ruefully about having been in medical school, in Berlin, precisely for the six years of the war, until 1945.

The analytic group in Ulm is relatively small, so that I presented my ideas on self-analysis in a seminar setting. Thomä's presence evidently inhibited the participation of most others in the discussion; wisely, he decided to stay away from the afternoon clinical seminar. The presenter was a candidate who is the wife of an American Air Force psychiatrist attached to a nearby military hospital. She was a very sensitive, intuitive therapist who was doing excellent work with a woman patient whose childhood had been one of continuous sadistic mistreatment at the hands of her father, formerly a member of the SS. The analysand's fantasies about the atrocities her father may have committed prior to 1945 formed an important part of the material. Everywhere in Germany, the psychoanalytic community struggles with the legacies of the Nazi era.

On arrival in Munich, we were whisked off to lunch by a pair of affable young analysts. Because we wanted to spend the afternoon at the Alte Pinakothek, they took us to a venerable Neapolitan restaurant close to the museum. When we were settled in one of the booths, they informed us, counterphobically, that the place is a real tourist attraction, for it was Hitler's favorite eatery when in the 1920s he lived in Munich.

That evening, the audience for my lecture was not confined to members of the smallish DPV group—for instance, my old friend Hans-Peter Kapfhämmer was very much in evidence. Ten years ago, I was surprised to receive a book on psychosomatic medicine by Hans-Peter (1985), who is on the faculty of the University of Munich. He wanted me to have his work because he had based his thesis on my hierarchical concepts. One thing led to another, and he asked me to give seminars in the psychiatry department and to his DPG analytic group—whenever I would be in the neighborhood. On previous visits, I had found Munich enchanting, so I decided to return at the earliest opportunity, which proved to be October 1987. The timing was poor; most people were still on vacation; as a professional venture, that trip was a bust. We consoled ourselves with a performance at the Munich Opera (yes, in Germany one can pick up tickets at the *Abendkasse* just before curtain time) and the city was as seductive as ever.

Before my lecture to the DPV institute, I was delighted to discover that its current director was a Count von Schlieffen, grandson of the celebrated strategist.[10] Unfortunately, his English was little better than my German. A case seminar the following day was almost anticlimactic, because, in a unique exception in my German experience, the presenter was rigid, incompetent, and intellectually limited. An American-born participant, who drove us back to our hotel, was convinced that he had used his influence in the university Department of Psychiatry, where he had an academic position, to get the privilege of presenting a case. The old traditions die hard.

The tour I undertook some ten weeks later grew out of a correspondence with a colleague in Berlin; she contacted several DPG institutes to suggest sharing my services. With Düsseldorf and Berlin, I arranged dates for late March 1992. When I mentioned this in a letter to Bettina Meissner, she suggested that I start the tour by returning to Cologne, where her colleagues were intrigued by my recently published article in *Psyche* about the merits and limits of Kohut's contributions. This is how the discussion I have already described, about the reception of self psychology in Germany, came about.

In Düsseldorf, the first stop was at the *Klinik für Psychosomatik und Psychotherapie* of the Heinrich-Heine-Universität. (Speak of expiation! Sixty years earlier, Heine's books were being burned.[11]) As I learned during the visit, German medical schools now have separate departments for biological psychiatry and what we formerly called dynamic psychiatry; they are turning out reasonably well-trained psychotherapists by the thousands. (This actually poses the greatest threat to psychoanalysis in Germany, for the health insurance system is bound to favor providers with therapeutic ambitions less radical than those advocated by analysts.) The Düsseldorf psychotherapy division is headed by a vigorous young analyst who rushed off to meet the state health minister, while I conducted a case seminar at the "Klinik." Both staff and trainees seemed competent and enthusiastic, but the twice-a-week therapy described to me was a case of biting off more than one could chew. (The patient was an Evangelical deaconess with a strong commitment to good works that seemed to patch over a cauldron of resentment about a brutal upbringing.) I had the impression that my preference for a more cautious approach actually gained a respectful hearing.

I was accommodated at a university guest house of spartan simplicity, just a few steps from a spiffy modern structure that houses the auditorium where my public lecture for the DPG group was to be given. The scale and quality of public facilities in contemporary Germany may best be conveyed by the fact that the walls of the extensive foyer in this hall are everywhere covered with a set of site-specific murals by the (very expensive!) American painter Roy Lichtenstein. In this setting, I presented the paper on self-analysis that had been such a good choice for other German audiences. Bettina, who on the spur of the moment drove over from Cologne to hear me, later told me that in this large auditorium, my English became hard for the audience to follow.

I had the better part of a week before I was supposed to get to Berlin, so I made a very enjoyable detour to Bremen and Hanover on my way. In the center of Bremen, I ran into a large contingent of police surrounding a small but exceedingly noisy crowd of skinheads who were chanting, "*Deutschland für die Deutschen: Ausländer 'raus!*"[12] This was the year of the most virulent attacks on so-called foreigners, and I wondered what Tapasi Gupta thought about that. The other side of the German coin was uppermost at a performance of *Il Trovatore* at the Hanover Opera; the costumes were vaguely suggestive of the Spanish Civil War, with Manrico's troops cast as anarchist Republicans and the forces of the evil Count di Luna presented as Phalangists wearing German helmets.[13]

I had seen much of central Berlin on previous visits, so I asked my hosts to take me out to Potsdam before the analytic meeting. The magnificent palace contains a glorious formal park; there, we came upon the spot where, some weeks before, the remains of Frederick the Great had been reburied. It is curiously moving to see the simple stone slab, with only the king's name on it, surrounded by seven smaller counterparts—the graves of the homosexual monarch's beloved greyhounds. This monument brought to mind that Heinrich von Kleist[14] committed suicide not far away—I asked my guide whether she knew where. She did, indeed, and she volunteered to take me there. The great dramatist chose to end his life on a beautiful lakeshore, surrounded by woods; a small commemorative stela now stands on the spot. Only the grave of Vincent van Gogh in Auvers has affected me in the same way. As we were leaving, however, my colleague reminded me that the lake is the Wannsee, and that the villa where the Final Solution was decreed stands within a stone's throw of the Kleist memorial.

In the course of the day, I also learned a great deal about psychoanalysis in Berlin. In 1992 the city boasted of five analytic institutes—of course, it also has three opera houses! The DPG had more than one, because there were more members and candidates than one organization could effectively accommodate. The most pressing problem for analysts in Berlin was the ever-present possibility of being squeezed out of their offices by the tide of commercial enterprises willing to acquire real estate at any cost. It is a world pulsing with change and optimism.

About a year later, Bettina informed me that the Cologne training committee wanted me to return for still another seminar. This invitation arrived just as Mary was having surgery. She had a wish to celebrate her recovery with another Jamesian sojourn in Italy—*Wo die Zitronen blühn*,[15] as Goethe put it. We decided that I would take care of business by myself, and we would then rendezvous in Milan and spend most of our vacation in Tuscany, which we first visited together some thirty years before.

I wrote Bettina that I could come in early spring but would like to use the opportunity to make presentations at more than one institute. As usual, she arranged everything; the Freiburg institute wanted me to come again, the people in Kassel were interested, and the whole tour could be compressed into the span of five days. It seemed to make sense to fly to Zurich and proceed north: Freiburg, Kassel, Cologne. I decided to present the paper I would read as my plenary address to the American Psychoanalytic in December, and Bettina once again undertook to prepare a German translation.

The amount of time I could spend in either Freiburg or Kassel was very limited, because of the crowded schedule, but in each place I was able to renew acquaintance with people I had met before, for the former director of the Frankfurt institute was now (back) in Kassel (whence he had gone to the big city.) He seemed like a different person—as if the weight of the world had been lifted from his shoulders. After the meeting, we had a leisurely meal and daydreamed together about organizing a great psychoanalytic conference on opera. As for my presentations, I noticed that my audiences had a harder time with this theoretical paper than with the others I had read in Germany. This impression was subsequently borne out by the reluctance of any of the German journals to publish it. The thesis is thought to be too abstract for German readers. Immanuel Kant must be turning over in his grave! In my judgment, the phobic reaction to theoretical matters stems from a reluctance to overthrow an analytic tradition with Jewish connotations.

I drove over to Cologne on a Friday morning and, at her instruction, met Bettina at noon in front of Stefan Lochner's *Adoration of the Magi* in the Cathedral.[16] (It must not be missed on a visit to Cologne!) She was very excited by the opening of a Lochner exhibition at the Wallraf-Richartz Museum, presenting all the known works of this rare and mysterious artist; that is where we spent much of the afternoon. Then we walked around the center city, looking at old churches and seeking out some of Meistermann's best stained-glass windows. (The entire church of the Holy Apostles, an eleventh century gem of the Rhenish style, is decorated with a cycle of Meistermann's design.) After dinner, we proceeded to the institute for the presentation.

On Saturday morning, there was a case seminar with candidates; this turned out to be the best teaching exercise I have participated in abroad, probably because on this third visit I felt thoroughly at ease with my hosts. When it was over, we were milling around the narrow street in this ancient quarter, reluctant to end an experience of unusual rapport. I finally asked that someone show me the best way to find the Autobahn to Frankfurt, and the candidate who had presented the case led me onto the route to the Frankfurt airport. A couple of hours later, I was on the plane to Milan.

My lecture tours in Germany have given me more satisfaction than my teaching efforts anywhere else, with the possible exception of Italy, largely because analysts in Germany are unique in being able to acknowledge that they can profit from what an experienced American colleague can offer them. This permeability to unfamiliar ideas may in large part account for the steady expansion of the influence of psychoanalysis in Germany. The profession tends to unravel whenever it reaches a sclerotic state that manifests itself as self-satisfaction about what we know.

❖ CHAPTER 21 ❖

HIGH WATER MARK

Last spring, on a trip to the Middle East, we stood on top of the mountain from which Moses caught a glimpse of the Promised Land he was destined never to reach. Across the Dead Sea, on a clear day, one can now discern the rooftops of Jerusalem; this year, I, too, was unable to visit the Holy Land because one cannot enter Syria (our main destination) after a visit to Israel. A decade earlier, when we were in Jerusalem, instead of taking the trouble to cross into Jordan, I had spent much of my stay outlining a purely psychoanalytic schema of psychopathology, eventually published (1988a) as *The Mind in Disorder*. I believe I chose the better part (to paraphrase Scripture), for the antiquities in Jordan have lost nothing in the interval, but (needless to say) I have lost a great deal!

The schema I then proposed is based on the assumption that the gamut of adaptive disturbances (that is, those in which neither tissue pathology nor a neurochemical abnormality is implicated) is explicable within the depth psychological framework of the hierarchical model as some resort to a mode (or modes) of behavior regulation of archaic origin. In such a schema, maladaptation is understood either as a result of apraxia or of the automatic repetition of old behavior patterns—or a combination of the two. The emergence of maladaptation or recovery from it generally constitutes a shift from one of the available modes of organization to another; there are, however, cases of arrested development in which the more mature modes of organization have never been attained. Alternatively, the self-organization may never have been fully integrated, so that certain nuclei of psychic function may become arrested in their development while other aspects of the personality seem to mature—as in cases that display a true self/false self dichotomy. The repetition of archaic patterns of behavior becomes manifest in treatment in the form of a sequence of transferences, including those stemming from the preverbal period. If these involve symbiotic modes of adaptation, that reliance on assistance inevitably leads to the persistence of apraxias, sometimes implicating the very capacity to learn. It should be noted that this schema of psychopathology is entirely unconcerned with the realm of mental contents; maladaptation is always a matter of the inadequate *processing* of information. (In this view, "mind" refers to the information processing functions of the central nervous system.)

Previous analytic conceptions of nosology have tried to subdivide maladaptive syndromes into distinct pathological entities (such as the transference neuroses, narcissistic disturbances, borderline conditions, and so on). In contrast, the hierarchical view entails the corollary that everyone has a complex repertory of alternative psychological patterns; this means that it is in principle possible (in the right circumstances) spontaneously to shift from one of the traditional syndromes to any of the others. In other words, each syndrome constitutes a (partially) *successful* adaptive effort, necessitated by a specific set of challenges, and it may be rendered irrelevant by a sufficient change in these adaptive requirements.

People tend to seek psychological assistance if their adaptive patterns turn out to be excessively costly or painful. Often, this dysphoria supervenes because some aspect of such an adaptive pattern becomes unacceptable, producing intrapsychic conflict. Sometimes the undesirable consequences of these patterned repetitions can be overcome if they are simply reversed (say from passive to active or vice versa) or inverted (for example, changing self-indulgence into self-restriction)—whether these changes occur through treatment or through fortunate life experiences. In the treatment of apraxias, however, it is almost always necessary to eliminate a learning disability that has stood in the way of acquiring the requisite psychological (procedural) skills—an accomplishment most likely to be achieved in an analytic context.

As a consequence, we must conclude that, in a fundamental sense, any maladaptation is "masochistic," because it involves the repetition of behaviors that produce avoidable pain or loss. Moreover, it usually takes some therapeutic work to bring patients to the realization that, to a large extent, we all bring about our unfavorable destiny—people generally try to explain their fate on some other basis, even that of a need for punishment. Very often, these masochistic patterns simply represent an identification with caretakers who behaved in analogous ways; in fact, a great variety of childhood ambitions and ideals can unconsciously produce repetitive behaviors that later seem masochistic.

The earlier the behavior pattern concerned was acquired, the more difficult it is to alter; this is particularly true whenever its genesis antedates the acquisition of consensual language, for behavior patterned that early may be built into the very core of the personality. Although many of these patterns are formed in the context of the infant's transactions with the caretakers, it should be kept in mind that they can also stem from the constraints of the child's physiology or the impingement of other environmental noxae. Of course, the earliest anlagen of the patterns later perceived as maladaptive are seldom detectable, so that they are often written off as constitutional givens. It was the endless consequences of matters of this kind that Freud (1920) named the repetition compulsion.

The most regressive mode of organization observable in adults is the traumatic state—not psychosis, as clinicians have wrongly assumed. With trauma, some alteration in consciousness usually occurs, and the ability to communicate on a symbolic level is lost, but these symptoms are usually quickly reversible. In contrast, psychotic disorganization involves the simultaneous loss of reality testing and of object relatedness; some defensive capacities are, however, preserved—mainly in the form of projection—as is some ability to communicate verbally. In psychotic regressions, the self-organization usually breaks down into uncoordinated motivational sets; in these circumstances, the reestablishment of a unified hierarchy of aims is the most pressing psychobiological need—one that has the power to override the pleasure principle. In such conditions, there is no intrapsychic conflict among the mutually contradictory goals of the various motivational sets; this lack of coordination produces a state of confusion.

In the course of childhood development, one (or more) motivational sets may remain split off from an otherwise coherent self-organization; the persistence of such a split is generally maintained through disavowal. Acute decompensation into psychosis constitutes the failure of defenses warding off such an unintegrated, archaic self-nucleus. And conversely: even in severe psychotic states, extensive areas of psychic function may remain unimpaired. In the analytic situation, the elimination of defenses against primitive mentation may, therefore, not infrequently produce "transference psychoses." In all such contingencies, therapeutic intervention must discern the *cause* of the disorganization, which often turns out to be tissue pathology or some biochemical imbalance that urgently needs to be corrected. If the regressive collapse has been precipitated by some acute stress, relief from that burden usually sets in motion a reversal of such a functional regression. It is, however, possible permanently to lose functional capacities (that is, to suffer *structural* decompensation) if some change in the somatic substrate remains uncorrected.

Whenever a child's entire psychic life (not merely a split-off segment) is arrested in its development, the more mature modes of behavior regulation remain unavailable in later life. The differential diagnosis between such an arrest and a functional regression may be difficult to make. Arrest will occur when the challenge of a maturational step defeats a child, either because of unfavorable external conditions or as a result of the accumulated handicaps of maldevelopment in earlier phases, or both. Problems usually designated as borderline most often occur in persons arrested at the start of the oedipal phase (phase III in the hierarchical schema) or earlier. In such cases, the patient's archaic core is generally in the open or barely screened by a pall of depersonalization or the impersonation of a better integrated individual that we call "as if" behavior. Sometimes such primitive personalities get by on the basis of forming a symbiotic relationship with a willing caretaker; lacking such assistance, they often require the provision of a supportive (hospital) milieu.

In certain contingencies, the usual organization of the personality may undergo regressive "fragmentation" (that is, a loss of cohesion), reverting to a mode of organization (mode II) characteristic of the childhood era of the self-in-formation. In persons with a symbiotic adaptation, such regressions follow an interruption of the symbiosis—in treatment, through the analyst's unavailability in this assigned role. Such a disruption of the usual self-organization amounts to an inability to continue the repetition of the fundamental behavioral patterns that constitute the core of the person's identity. The chances of suffering such a disruption are greatest in persons whose identity involves the obligatory repetition of relatively unusual and narrowly defined experiences, particularly if these require the participation of another person. (In many instances, however, self-cohesion can be restored by enacting the requisite patterns of behavior via reversal, inversion, or by following a template of the original form.) The polar opposite of traumatic states of overstimulation is stasis—the gradual extinction of a repetitive pattern because of a lack of external stimulation. These circumstances lead to subjective devitalization and inner emptiness but stop short of an actual rupture of self-cohesion.

Psychosomatic symptoms are often triggered by nonspecific stress—if some physiological subsystem happens to be vulnerable. (Attacks of mucous colitis, neurodermatitis, bronchial asthma, migraine, and epilepsy may be brought on in this way.) Other symptoms that involve somatic processes (including anxiety states and depression) reflect an inability to process certain quanta of stimulation through symbolic systems alone. In other words, these phenomena are the consequence of a type of apraxia; they constitute developmental deficits.

By contrast, in conversion reactions, the "language of the body" is utilized as an independent symbolic system that is however capable of being translated into a language of words. Still other somatic symptoms are expectable concomitants of states of conservation/withdrawal (mediated through parasympathetic activation) or their opposite (activation of the sympathetic system)—states of "fight or flight." These are the conditions Freud (1894) called the "actual neuroses." Threatened states of overstimulation are particularly likely to produce such anxiety states, without any correlation with symbolic contents.

Finally, certain somatic sensations constitute memories of infantile bodily experiences rather than contemporary alterations of function; in these cases, the memories have remained encoded in a perceptual-affective-action mode. In other words, they may be primarily sensory (as in hypochondriasis) or mostly motor (mimetic enactments). Conversely, if patients are unable to use bodily signals as guides for well adapted behavior, they are bound to develop syndromes of dysregulation such as bulimia/anorexia, constipation, chronic fatigue, and sexual dysfunctions without symbolic significance. The most serious among these apraxias is alexithymia, the inability to recognize and monitor affects.

From a biopsychological viewpoint, the boundary between psychic and somatic responses (in a person who has unimpaired symbolic capacities) is merely a matter of choice among the neural pathways available to process various stimuli. Obviously, such choices are made unconsciously, on the basis of patterned adaptive mechanisms, automatized during early phases of childhood development. Failure to encode matters in some symbolic form makes the unconscious unknowable, as Freud (1915) put it. (Psychoanalytic hermeneuticists, who would confine our subject matter to the realm of the symbolically encoded, inadvertently leave out of account these "unrememberable and unforgettable" issues [see Frank 1969].)

The mimetic enactments that are not under conscious control (such as tics or hysterical convulsions, torticollis or vomiting, coughing or affectless lachrymation, and so on) communicate meanings not through symbolic encoding, but by means of an affectomotor act. Such dramatic enactments may, however, to some extent make use of supplementary verbal communication. In any case, they constitute a *forme fruste* of reproducing memories inaccessible to awareness; in this sense, they should not be understood as *resistance* to recollection but as the only path available to that end—largely nonverbal communications, like pantomime, ballet, or the play activities of young children.

Doubtless most mimetic enactments are primarily intended to master emotional pain or, with lesser frequency, to achieve pleasure. In this sense, they have the same function as sexual perversions, autoerotic activities, most addictions, and other self-soothing behaviors. The only difference between these syndromes and dramatic enactments is that the specific *meaning* of the latter can be translated into words. Because many enactments repeat transactions from very early in life, in an adult context they may seem delinquent or at least irresponsible; at the same time, they sometimes reproduce those early behaviors that represented the child's compliance with social requirements. In still another group of cases, they stand neither for ego nor for id—for instance, they may represent the child's identification with an idealized object.

Beyond the illumination of specific symptoms, a psychoanalytic nosology must address the question of character pathology, which straddles the dividing line between the intrapsychic frame of reference and that of interpersonal relationships. (This bipolarity has permitted many analytic authors to obfuscate whether they are alluding to mental dispositions or to events on the stage of actuality.) In most instances, the mental dispositions we call character represent a compromise between patterned infantile transactions and the countervailing forces of self-restraint built into the personality in the course of later phases of development. Much of this psychic structure is established during the preoedipal era, often at the dawn of self-awareness. (One common instance of such an early deformation of character is the propensity to achieve adaptive equilibrium by entering a symbiosis.) When the archaic stamp of a person's character compels other people to participate (by gratifying *or* frustrating the subject) in a dyadic reenactment of the infantile past, the analyst is forced to use such interpersonal events (which constitute the archaic transference) to understand the genesis of these character traits. Through these transactions, the analysand implicitly demands from the analyst assistance with relevant problems in adaptation; although skilled clinicians have often provided such assistance, compliance with an infantile need has usually been looked upon as a countertranference-based therapeutic error. Yet it is only by making explicit what the patient needs to learn that this kind of dependence on external assistance can be overcome. Any refusal to enter into an apraxic analysand's life in this manner repeats the childhood caretakers' failure to provide the guidance such a person needed; a transaction of that kind usually leads to a transference crisis. Conversely, always giving assistance, without specifying what the analysand needs to learn to be able to function autonomously, merely perpetuates such character pathology.

In actuality, most psychoanalysts make a differential diagnosis on the basis of the sequence of transferences that unrolls as analysis proceeds. As this occurs, characterological predispositions tend to revert to the patterns of the original child/caretaker transactions, relived as interpersonal events in the analytic situation. The conflicts of an infantile neurosis (mode IV in the hierarchical schema) are reproduced in the form of a transference neurosis, and such a development is an all-but-universal occurrence in a properly conducted analysis. In most cases, however, these "neurotic" conflicts are embedded in character problems with a preoedipal genesis, and such preexisting handicaps prejudice the resolution of the oedipal crisis.

Some time ago, it was common to look upon the emergence of transferences of a preoedipal nature as a regressive defense; some even called these the defense transferences. More recently, it has been widely recognized that archaic transferences (those of mode III) are indicators of pathology distinct from the consequences of the Oedipus complex, and that careful attention to them usually yields great therapeutic benefits, especially if we succeed in specifying how these early difficulties influenced the resolution of the oedipal challenge. If the analyst refrains from tilting the process in any particular direction, both oedipal and preoedipal vicissitudes should come into play as transference. This is also what one would predict on the basis of the epigenetic view of development; preexisting conditions do not disappear when they are assimilated into the more complex ones of later phases. In other words, the potential for archaic transferences is not dissolved when a child enters the oedipal arena. In these terms, differential diagnosis is not concerned with syndromes or pathological entities but with the manner in which the legacies of earlier developmental phases have influenced the outcome of later ones.[1]

Whenever the presenting picture is that of a severe character disturbance, especially one that includes archaic features, analysts are thus confronted with syndromes produced by a combination of apraxic deficits and transferences that may stem from various phases of development. Very often, such analyses are slow and laborious, and success may depend on the cooperation of the analysand's social/familial support system. If the archaic transference emerges vis-à-vis the analyst, these patients are content to perpetuate the resulting symbiosis, because it protects them from the threat of further regression and disorganization. In favorable instances, the crucial transactions of early childhood are eventually repeated; in this context, the nature of the analysand's need for external assistance can be specified. (In the process, the transference sometimes reproduces features of a psychotic state in childhood.) It is essential to reconstruct the circumstances that originally led to the adaptive solution that left the patient with various deficits in psychological skills (such as disorders in thinking or communication). The particulars of the transference usually duplicate the manner in which caretakers helped the child to patch over some prior derailment of development. This, in turn, may have been produced by constitutional factors, parental failures, or both.

It is in intervals between the emergence of intense, archaic transference reactions that analysands are best able to learn new ways to deal with the challenges that defeated them as children—that is, in the context of a collaborative relationship that does *not* repeat the patterns established in childhood. In other words, it is the tendency for transference repetition that most often stands in the way of overcoming apraxic deficits. In this sense, most disorders of character handicap their victims in their ability to acquire knowledge or skills.[2]

Hence, the rational educational aim of psychoanalysis is instruction in procedural skills, particularly those of self-inquiry (see Gardner 1983). (In other words, the rationale of interpretive activity is not so much to convey a particular insight but, more importantly, to teach analysands to interpret their own associations and nonverbal behaviors and, in the process, to accept unpleasant realities.) To achieve these ends, it is often necessary to engage in novel patterns of cooperation with analysands—for instance, to adjust the analyst's modes of communication to the specific requirements of each patient. If the participants are thus able to establish a state of attunement, it even becomes possible to deal with issues that derive not from dyadic transactions but are best understood in terms of a one-person psychology. Noninterpretive interventions should be designed to instruct patients in a variety of cognitive and communicative skills hitherto missing in their repertory or to correct their faulty operations in these fundamental realms of activity. Such attention to the need of most patients to acquire new procedural skills fortunately does not interfere with the equally important task of elucidating their intrapsychic conflicts.

The Mind in Disorder received excellent reviews,[3] despite my failure to discuss every pathological syndrome or contingency. Nonetheless, I felt an obligation to fill these lacunae in my presentation, and I devoted a considerable portion of my next book, *The Biology of Clinical Encounters* (1991a) to further consideration of psychopathology, with particular attention to phobic avoidances, affective disorders, and obsessionality and magical thinking. To summarize briefly, I explain avoidances on the basis of a fear of being humiliated by a failure of self-regulation; I deem obsessionality to be a cognitive style that is crystallized at the very dawn of self-awareness, albeit the particular symptoms that characterize any one case may be acquired anywhere along the developmental axis and possess specific functional meanings. In my view, affective disorders are caused by apraxic defects in the modulation of emotional responses to the vicissitudes of life; these deficiencies are brought about by a combination of constitutional factors and early environmental noxae that alter biology. Perversions, addictions, and other primitive behaviors (such as gambling) may serve as desperate home remedies that cover over the vulnerability created by such a defect.

As the title of the 1991 book indicates, the main thrust of my argument was to show the advantages of a biopsychological conception of psychoanalysis and to demonstrate the need to correlate its findings with those of brain science. If we do this, the nature/nurture controversy dissolves into a meaningless differentiation of categories that in actuality continually exert great influence on each other: the nature of the organism is determined by nurture which, in turn, varies in accord with that nature. From this perspective, the crux of personality organization consists not of the contents of the various transferences evoked in the psychoanalytic setting (even if these turn out to be derivatives of phases of early development more primitive than the oedipal period) but of the underlying adaptive skills (especially those involved in processing information) that determine the predisposition to respond to certain contingencies with those transferential patterns. From this it follows that various transferences are evoked by the specific technical choices made by the analyst (generally on the basis of differing theories of analytic technique). The complex analytic technique suggested by the hierarchical model has the great advantage of making possible the sequential emergence of transferences referable to more than one phase of childhood development. Nonetheless, the analyst as a real person inevitably skews the material of every analysis—even by the rhetorical choices he or she employs. And the resultant indeterminacy of the analytic process renders the nature of the transference evoked unsuitable for diagnostic purposes; the shifting feedback mechanisms observed in analysis should never be mistaken for static intrapsychic conditions that characterize the analysand alone.[4]

The Biology of Clinical Encounters took up a number of other issues,[5] including the alarming decline of psychoanalysis as a profession in America. By the time I was completing this project, however, I was aware that *Beyond Interpretation* was out of print, and I was determined to produce a revised version of that monograph that would contain my recent theoretical innovations, so that I was content to eschew such topics in the 1991 book.[6]

❖ CHAPTER 22 ❖

RECESSIONAL

I am astonished to find myself, at the age of 69, retired from practice and teaching, engaged in completing a professional autobiography. Yet, without the stimulus of continued immersion in clinical work, I am less likely to have further things to say on matters of central concern to psychoanalysts. In any case, I have probably oversaturated the market. Most potential readers may assume that I say much the same thing over and over again (needless to say, I do not agree!). My work sells less well than one might expect on the basis of predominantly positive reviews. I fear that this may also be the fate of this manuscript; I do not even have one good sex scandal to relate!

Psychoanalysts lead prosaic private lives. A couple of years ago, I ran into Judy Schachter and her husband at a memorial service for Merton Gill. (It was a remarkable outpouring of affection from an overflow crowd of mourners.) We decided to sit together; Judy asked me how I liked retirement, and I told her that I was having fun recounting nasty stories in my memoirs. "Only nasty ones?" I then confessed that I had wanted to include the nice fact that Judy had been the most attractive woman in our entire medical school, but Mary thought this would not do as a characterization of the president of the American Psychoanalytic Association. Joe Schachter was delighted! He said that, to the contrary, I should certainly describe her in that way. So I promised—and this is the sexiest paragraph I have produced thus far. Oh, well! Horace advised writers to "fit audience find, though few . . ."[1]

Over the past decade, I have become more and more passionate about writing, and much less focused on any particular subject matter. I began to dream about retirement and (in emulation of Rossini's "sins of old age"[2]) writing a book about the operas of Mozart. The changes in the tax code brought about by the Reagan administration suddenly increased the net value of my retirement funds to the point where dreams of giving up the burdens of clinical work were no longer utterly unrealistic; early in 1988, I decided to stop accepting new patients. I expected to complete my ongoing clinical responsibilities by the time I reached 65; as things turned out, it took two years longer than that. I think I have paid sufficient homage to the gods of medicine; I served them for one year short of a half-century since I did my blood count on Hideki Tojo. As for psychoanalytic experience, I took my first patient just thirty-eight years before I said farewell to the last.[3]

To celebrate relief from work as duty, when I was asked to contribute a chapter to a book about the psychological significance of *Arbeit*, I wrote an essay (1996e) "In praise of leisure." (*Arbeit macht nicht frei!*[4]) I turned from writing on purely psychoanalytic topics to the creativity project with the Columbia University Press and to a variety of delicious nonprofessional enterprises. I have stepped up my consumption of *belles lettres*, always a priority for my leisure time, in proportion to my decreasing workload—I am gradually becoming nearly as well read as I have always wished to be. (It was also delightful that much of the preparation for *The Artist and the Emotional World* involved reading biographies, dozens of them, about amazing people such as Proust, Trollope, Turgenev, Nabokov, Lorca, or the Italian mannerist painters.) On a modest scale, I like engaging in philanthropic activities. Mary and I have arranged to donate to the Milwaukee Museum the works of art for which we no longer have room in our relatively tight quarters (it was our friend Sue Taylor who brokered this transaction), and we established a fund at the Art Institute of Chicago (in part with money generously contributed by others) for the purchase of paintings by contemporary Chicago artists. It has been tremendous fun to participate in choosing these works, especially because we are well acquainted with the painters who created them.

All this has been much more inspiring than watching the agonies of organized psychoanalysis. It costs me nothing (in either sense of the word) to remain a life member of the American Psychoanalytic or the Chicago society, but I have lost interest in their politics and obsessive concerns about governance. (When I still cared, nobody ever listened to my prophecies of doom or the draconian measures I advocated to save the sinking ship—see 1984b, 1984c [chap. 12], 1991b.) As I have mentioned, I do occasionally teach at the Chicago Institute, notably right after the overthrow of the Pollock regime, when its immediate successors offered me still another opportunity to conduct an elective clinical seminar for advanced candidates.

At that time, I enlisted Mark Gehrie as a collaborator, and for five consecutive trimesters we gave a course on the integration of theory and technique. I presented some of my clinical work to the candidates, and then we asked them to present cases to us; invariably, they selected those analyses that had run into major difficulties. The success of the first few seminars decided Mark to record the proceedings; these led to the transcripts we then used for our collaborative book, *Impasse and Innovation in Psychoanalysis* (1993b). In addition to one of my case presentations, the book contains three instances of analytic impasse described by other participants, supplemented by extensive commentaries by both Mark and me.

One of these stalemated analyses was presented by a graduate analyst who was afraid he had abandoned an analytic framework in various emergencies, such as his patient's intention to let herself succumb to an untreated malignancy. I tried to demonstrate that, contrary to his theory of technique, his effort to correct the analysand's faulty reality testing (which turned out to be in identification with a psychotic parent) was analytically indicated. Only recently, I received a copy of a letter the patient sent her analyst to report on the outstanding outcome of her treatment, since terminated. At the seminar, the majority of participants were skeptical about the possibility of bringing this analysis to termination, not to speak of a satisfactory outcome! (The analyst gave me periodic progress reports about their work, and I have no doubt that it was his freedom to intervene in a manner that could compensate for the patient's various apraxic deficits that produced this good result.)

My own case was also still in progress, and the analysand was almost as desperate as the suicidal woman treated by our young colleague. (This was the twelve-year-long analysis that turned out to be the very last one I conducted.) In addition to entering the patient's life as a symbiotic partner who compensated for his numerous apraxias, in this instance it was necessary to counteract the analysand's grandiosity that repeatedly led him into self-destructive behaviors. (For the most part, with this particular person, I chose to accomplish that through blunt confrontations that shocked many of the candidates, especially those who accepted the maximally soft tactics advocated by most self psychologists.) I have a recent follow-up on this analysis; three years after termination this person, previously unable both to maintain relationships and to work productively, was content in his recent marriage and a new vocation.

Needless to say, the stalemates presented by candidates (both very badly served by their supervisors) were not so easily resolved. In one instance, everyone concerned had colluded in creating the fiction that the analysis could be terminated, although the analyst was effectively paralyzed by her patient's rageful and uncontrolled behavior within the analytic situation. The candidate presented this case because, within a couple of years, her analysand returned with a complete relapse into her original difficulties. In this case, I focused on the analyst's failure to deal with the patient's uncontrolled hostility—worse, her tactic of blatantly denying its significance. (It is of interest that many participants remained convinced that the proper course would have been to be more empathic, that is, to legitimize the patient's rage. Such are the corrosive effects in Chicago of the elevation of self psychology into a belief system that does not need validation.)

I had hoped that Mark Gehrie would be willing to put this book together by himself because, as long as I was alone in claiming superior clinical results on the basis of my theoretical position, many readers naturally remained unconvinced. (I had the same hope concerning a contemporaneous project with Arnold Wilson, in which we were to garner outside support for the hierarchical view of mental functioning.) Unfortunately, Mark was so involved with other time-consuming activities that I lost patience and took the lead in planning and producing *Impasse and Innovation*. Moreover, his decision to play devil's advocate (on behalf of self psychology) hardly amounted to an endorsement of my viewpoints by my collaborator.

As I have already mentioned, my participation in institute activities ceased when Arnold Goldberg became director. The contentious events that led me to resign more or less coincided with the coup against John MacLeod's conduct of the committee to monitor the admission of nonmedical candidates and my subsequent withdrawal from that committee. In other words, I shrugged off any involvement with the national organization soon after casting myself adrift from the local one.

I have retained one important association in New York, with Arnold Wilson, the young analyst whom I assisted in editing *The Concept of Hierarchies in Psychoanalysis* (1993c). Arnold was a full-time academic at the New School for Social Research and a candidate at the Columbia institute when he informed me that he was engaged (with graduate students whom he was advising on their dissertations) in an elaborate program of research to make operational and attempt to validate the concepts embodied in the hierarchical model I had proposed. Over the years, he kept me informed about his promising findings, which have confirmed the internal consistency and predictive power of the model. We were naturally equally eager to publicize these results (see Wilson and Passik 1993). Herb Schlesinger, who was still editor of *Psychological Issues*, was then senior psychoanalyst in Arnold's department at the New School; when he was approached about the project, he suggested that I should associate my name with it, and of course I agreed. Beyond contributing a historical chapter (1993d) and rubber-stamping Arnold's meticulous work, I did little of the labor in putting the volume together. Perhaps contributors such as Bill Grossman, Joe Lichtenberg, Fred Levin, and Michael Robbins agreed to take part on the strength of their past association with me. Arnold recruited the psychologist Wilma Bucci (of Adelphi) and Edward Khantzian (of Cambridge Hospital); Stanley Grand and his collaborators (who have also done empirical research on a modification of the hierarchical schema[5]) were equally well known to both of us. As such things happen, our manuscript was completed during a period of turmoil at *Psychological Issues*, and Arnold swiftly transferred the volume to a publisher with whom we had both had previous dealings.

Perhaps the most pleasurable of my recent publishing ventures, however, have transpired in Italy, as an outgrowth of our friendship with a Florentine colleague, Emma Piccioli. We met early in 1987, when (on a lecture tour that included stops in Rome, Florence, Bologna, and Milan) I gave a talk to the small analytic group in her city. On that occasion, she rolled out a red carpet for us; we invited her to visit us in Chicago, and when she did, we became very fond of her. (Not for nothing is her nickname Joy—"Gioia.") Born and raised in the former Rhodesia, she speaks perfect English. In the last three years, we have exchanged further visits with her. In the meantime, she has become associate editor of the *Rivista di Psicoanalisi* (official journal of the Italian society), and this journal has, under her aegis, initiated publication of a series of books in English.

About a year ago, Gioia asked me to contribute a chapter (1996e) to their first volume, *Writing in Psychoanalysis*. Once again, the topic exactly suited my current preoccupations; I took the liberty of paraphrasing Rousseau by entitling my essay "Reveries of a Solitary Scribbler."[6] She liked this well enough to ask me to participate in her second collection as well, which is to be devoted to the analyst as a person. This also suited me perfectly (see in press a); if, as I believe, psychoanalysis is a matter of teaching procedural skills, our success in doing so largely depends on who we are.

Last summer, on her way home from the San Francisco meeting of the international, Gioia visited us again, and she and I recorded a lengthy dialogue about my work (1995g) for the *Rivista*. Because she has given my proposals serious thought, she was able to frame this interview so that it matches the Rodgers (1994) summary in *Psychoanalytic Inquiry* as an optimal synopsis of my ideas. It then occurred to me that *The Psychoanalytic Review*, where the offending interview with Wolf was published, owed me something; when I asked the editor to publish Gioia's interview in English, he readily agreed. It is gratifying to be able to collect such an IOU.

At this point, a substantial part of my work has appeared in Italian translation, including *Models of the Mind* and *Beyond Interpretation*.[7] The two papers I read to various audiences on the 1987 lecture tour were published in other Italian journals with a psychoanalytic orientation. Paolo Migone, a young colleague from Parma who made all the arrangements for me on this and two subsequent trips of this kind (in 1990 and 1993), has translated many of my papers and saw to their appearance, mostly in *Psicoterapia e Scienze Umane*.[8] This is the organ of the segment of Italian psychoanalysis that does not belong to the international association. Migone has on occasion asked me to contribute to this periodical short articles or discussions (1986b, 1993f) that have never been published in English (see also Migone 1985).

I have enjoyed my contacts with Italian psychoanalysis more than other professional activities because they have perpetuated my lifelong love affair with Italy. Since 1931, when my mother first took me south of the Alps, I have criss-crossed the Italian peninsula (and Sicily), from Turin to Trieste and from the Brenner pass to Bari and Agrigento. We accepted Gioia's invitation to spend a few weeks last fall in her country house outside Perugia; this glorious bucolic visit constituted my seventeenth Italian journey. Paolo Migone teases me with the inexact interpretation that my addiction to his homeland is in identification with Freud—in this respect, however, I have outdone the master, who was interested mostly in the classical past. I have immersed myself not only in Italian art, but in Italian music and literature as well; if this passion stems from an identification with an admired figure from the past, it is either with Goethe or with Montaigne, rather than with Freud.[9]

I have never formally studied Italian, but, over the years, the vicissitudes of these travels have increased my comprehension sufficiently to enable me to read all but the most difficult texts and not to need translation for most of the comments made in bilingual seminars. (Speaking is something else again.) I have a good enough feel for the sound of the Italian language to have emboldened me to read Paolo's translations of my papers on my lecture tours. This effort was highly appreciated by most audiences, especially those at universities. (One Marxist heckler in Florence yelled that my accent sounded just like "*il Papa polacco*,"[10] but I was able to shut him up by promptly replying, "Il Papa? No! Arturo Toscanini!" The politically savvy students laughed; they knew I meant not so much my white hair and bald pate as my antifascist past.) I should add that the moment of highest pleasure in my entire life was when in a seminar in Trieste I caught a mistranslation of what I had just said in English. This felt to me as if I had just learned to fly.

Another factor that makes it extraordinarily pleasant to deal with Italian psychoanalysts is that, almost without exception, the sophisticated colleagues I have met come from well-established, cultivated families; they do not have to rely exclusively on their current earnings to maintain a high standard of living. It is not irrelevant that, for the past fifty years, the grande dame of Italian psychoanalysis has been the Princess of Lampedusa, widow of the author of *The Leopard*. To illustrate from my personal experience: in Bologna, I became acquainted with Fabiano Bassi, who once took us on a walking tour of the historic city center. Like most Italians, Fabiano gave evidence of intense local patriotism; he wanted to show us treasures usually inaccessible to tourists, like the celebrated inner court of the fifteenth century Palazzo Bevilacqua, where he knew the custodian. As we were admiring this gem of the Renaissance, I asked Fabiano whether there are any Bevilacquas left in Bologna. "Oh yes," he replied, "they live on the second floor, there. The Duchess is a very nice girl." A light went on inside my head. The main street in Bologna is the Via Ugo Bassi.

Fabiano was embarrassed when I asked him how he knew "the Duchess." He muttered that, when the province did a survey of child care in the city, he had been assigned to interview her. Because of his discomfort, I curbed my curiosity, and then he felt compelled to tell me something about his actual social position. We had just left the palazzo when he volunteered, "This is my tailor, here"—pointing to an establishment of unusual elegance. I ventured, "Do you live around here?" Fabiano became vague: "Not far—just around the corner." (This is a quarter urbanized by the Etruscans!) Then he told me that his family has occupied the same apartment for more than two hundred fifty years. There is no civilization to rival Italy's. Happily, the International Psychoanalytic organized a conference on representation of mother–child relations in the visual arts for spring 1997, which took place in the Palazzo Vecchio in Florence. Mary and I were invited to give a joint paper; we discussed the psychological significance of Claude Monet's lily pond at Giverny, for neither of us had the leisure to do justice to a Renaissance topic in the time available for preparation. It turned out to be quite a climax to our love affair with Italy!

While my Italian journeys and other overseas adventures have been very gratifying, until I was asked to give the plenary to the American, my professional life at home had been more routine. Before the plenary, the program committee did ask me to participate in meet-the-author sessions concerning books by Lawrence Friedman (1988) and Joe Lichtenberg (1989)[11] as well as panels on psychoanalysis and psychotherapy, and on the contributions of Sándor Ferenczi.[12] Although this level of activity should perhaps have satisfied me, these exercises left me cold. I suppose this reaction was analogous to the progress of one's experience in drinking wine; almost anything will do at first; later one has to start being selective; late in one's seventh decade, one has to disburse many more bucks for the same bang. Nothing can equal the thrill of the first panel I participated in, in San Francisco, with Wallerstein, Brenner, Modell, and Sam Abrams (see Abrams 1971). I was then still anxious about being attacked for my radical notions; fortunately Brenner and Modell got into a rancorous dispute, and I escaped unscathed.

For some years I was disappointed by the negligible impact of my ideas on American psychoanalysis, despite favorable reviews of my books. At first I told myself that my work had an intellectual agenda that appeals to relatively few people. This was especially true of the volume of Freudiana published by *Psychological Issues* (1976b) and *Conceptual Issues in Psychoanalysis* (1986a), which was focused on the history of ideas.[13]

By the early 1990s I was ready to acknowledge defeat in my thirty-year effort to have an immediate impact on American psychoanalysis. Organizationally, mine was a lone voice in the wilderness—for example, even after the Pollock debacle, I was almost alone in Chicago to suggest that relying on a lay board of trustees was a poor idea. (Mostly appointed by Pollock, the trustees had stubbornly opposed the faculty's determination to oust him. The faculty responded by arranging to have several of its members appointed as trustees. On the whole, the analytic community is narcissistically gratified by opportunities to rub elbows with socially prominent, wealthy people.) Nationally, the MacLeod committee's losing struggle to maintain a modest minimum standard underscored my disagreement with majority views. My position was widely (and sincerely) regarded as arrogant and elitist. Of course, I see the current disrepute of our profession as a direct result of having abandoned any hope of being a therapeutic elite. The only advertising for psychoanalysis that could possibly be effective is the actual accomplishment of superior therapeutic results. These are obtained only by the very best among us.

Under the circumstances, I also lost hope that my exceedingly complex theoretical schemata could at present gain a serious hearing; repeatedly, I saw at first hand that many of those who read my work simply could not grasp the meaning of what I had written. (Those who did understand my writings have assured me that the problem was not any lack of clarity in my text.) My proposals require analysts to think through the significance of every bit of human behavior in terms of the specific context in which it takes place; most analysts prefer to classify behaviors in terms of some simple schema. (In practice, even the simplest, such as Kohut's ultimate classification of selfobject transferences, is further reduced by most users into a choice among two or three patterns.)

If I have not given up altogether, it is because my experiences in Europe suggest that psychoanalysis may be reborn even after it has been seemingly annihilated, as it was by both the Nazis and the Communists. I have begun to look upon my study as a present-day monastic scriptorium—Lake Michigan can easily stand in for the Irish Sea. I continue to write about the crucial unresolved issues in psychoanalysis, and I think my recent work is the most sophisticated I have produced.

PART FOUR

THE OTHER SIDE OF THE COIN

❖ CHAPTER 23 ❖

BEFORE CHICAGO

In 1995 Mary and I were invited to Australia to participate in the annual Freud conference that takes place in Melbourne. We ended an exciting fortnight in that delightful country in Sydney, where I was to address the Australian Psychoanalytic Society. When we showed an interest in visiting some of the outlying areas of this widespread metropolis, one of the local analysts kindly volunteered to have his Hungarian mother-in-law show us around in her car. We had a very enjoyable day of sightseeing around the magnificent harbor; as she was about to drop us off at our hotel, my compatriot exclaimed that she should have introduced us to her artist friend, Judith Kaszab. What serendipity! I have known Judith Kaszab since 1950; she was married to one of my father's best friends. When I stammered out this information, I was told that, contrary to my assumptions, Judith's husband John was still alive. (By my calculations, he had to be 97!) I had barely enough time to get ready for the analytic meeting, and we were scheduled to depart early the next morning, so I sent him a message of apologies and love, as well as chagrin about having missed our chance for a reunion.

Ten minutes later, the phone rang in our room, and I heard a familiar voice from my childhood, for the first time since we said farewell to each other in Salzburg, forty-five years before. In Losoncz, John Kämpfner visited us at least once a year; trained as a chemical engineer, he was before the war superintendent of the Slovakian estates of the counts Schönborn (of Vienna), properties where the principal activities were the brewing of beer and the production of slivovitz (plum brandy). Every Christmas, my father received a sample of the best from the count's cellars. After the war, my father grasped the nature of the Communist regime in Hungary when he asked John to give his personal regards to one of his roommates of the early Prague years, who had reemerged in 1945 as a high official in the Hungarian police. Kämpfner was told that General Nógrády had never heard of Mátyás Gedö. In a country where the police chief is in terror, even my father did not wish to live. Darkly, he muttered, "Stalin is a pig!"

In Sydney, John and I reminisced about the good old days, and about our own 1950 encounter, just after the Kämpfners escaped from Hungary, as soon as John realized that the Communist regime would not continue to employ him to run the country's biggest brewery. He had just married Judith, a much younger woman, and they awaited an Australian visa at Bad Ischl, on one of the mountain lakes near Salzburg. Judith was an artist who was to become a celebrated portraitist (her clients have included Queen Elizabeth and Winston Churchill), and she made an oil sketch of me as a souvenir of our stay at Ischl. (Alas, it was ultimately ruined by a flood in the basement of one of my suburban houses.) I was surprised that she remembered those days as clearly as I did. Of course, with John, we talked about prehistory, the years of his bachelorhood when I was a child.

In 1950 I was 22; it was the summer of my last vacation in medical school. With my classmate Bob Drye (who was to follow me to Chicago to obtain analytic training), I arranged to go on a grand tour via a student charter—eight weeks in Europe on a budget under eight hundred dollars. (I did run short near the end; I had to wire my father that, if he ever wanted to see me again, he had to send me a loan of fifty bucks.) The Korean War started a few days after we flew off to Luxembourg; our charter airline was compelled to ferry troops to the Far East, so that our return flight was delayed. They put us up in an old château near Diekirch, and we were recompensed with a garden party at the embassy in Luxembourg. Our ambassador was the famed "Hostess with the Mostest," Perle Mesta—she provided each of us with one glass of Coca Cola!

It had been a wonderful trip, crammed with eye-opening experience; it addicted me to European travel. (To be sure, I could not manage to go back again for over a dozen years—the lean years of internship and residency, succeeded by the infancy of our children—but in the last three decades, I have returned at least once a year.) From the viewpoint of my intellectual development, the 1950 grand tour made me determined to immerse myself in the Western tradition—in art, architecture, history, literature, music.

Of course, this might have happened without going on this pilgrimage from London to Naples, through Paris, Toledo, and Vienna—but the trip followed three years of hateful toil in medical school. My enthusiasm about everything I encountered acted as a revelation that I was not meant to follow in my father's footsteps, after all. I should have known this in the first place (in undergraduate school, I took numerous courses in history, and before starting medical training—while I was in the Army—I had unrealistic fantasies of earning a master's degree in the subject during breaks of the school calendar), but I was unable to imagine that I could choose a life different from that of my admired father.

The fact that it took three years of forcing myself to deal with subjects I found uninteresting to come to my senses was partly caused by my father's wish to return to Czechoslovakia to found a modern health facility that would serve the underprivileged. He abandoned the idea after the 1948 Communist takeover, when a young relative whose education in Prague he was subsidizing started to write letters that assailed him as an "American imperialist." (The Czech Stalinists were no different from those in Hungary.) Until then, my need to differentiate myself from Dad was focused on making the decision to stay in America, whatever my parents planned to do. In a European family, such independence did not then come easily, and it was made doubly difficult for me because I did not have the financial resources to live away from home while I attended college and medical school, both at New York University. My parents flatly refused to subsidize any such venture, nor could they have afforded it very easily. Beyond enrolling me in high school when I was 13, they did not know enough about life in America even to advise me about my education.

As a wartime undergraduate, without a single pause for breath from September 1943 to May 1946, it made sense to me to pursue a premedical program; few people wanted to end up as infantrymen after they got drafted. (Of course, by the time I reached 18, at the end of 1945, the fighting was over, but it remained preferable to be assigned to the medical corps.) I had a slot waiting for me at the NYU medical school while I was in the Army; when I was unexpectedly discharged during the 1947 demobilization, I scarcely had an opportunity to reconsider what I had best do before it was time to matriculate at Bellevue (everyone called the school by the name of the historic municipal hospital next to which it is still located). So, for the next four years, I commuted from the Upper West Side to First Avenue and 28th Street.

It strikes me as very fitting that I arrived to start medical school in the fall of 1947, after serving in Japan, and that the definitive end of my clinical career (termination of the ultimate treatment I conducted) was followed by my second visit to that country. I was hoping that the experience would be emotionally resonant—if not as gripping as a return to Hungary, at least as nostalgic as my visit to Tangier, some four decades after living in that North African outpost. I was astonished to discover that going back to the very places I had seen before—Osaka, Kyoto, Nara, Tokyo—failed to evoke anything of my past. Perhaps contemporary Japan has been constructed to bury the shame of defeat. The only history to which a temporary visit can now connect is the one that came to an end when Commodore Perry opened Japan to westerners.

I was especially gratified to attend a scientific conference in Osaka because I had been stationed there as a soldier. After leaving there, I worked at the hospital that served the Sugamo Prison in Tokyo, where the persons on trial for war crimes were incarcerated. At the age of 19, I was enormously impressed by their code of conduct, which impelled them to ignore their captors by observing total silence. That is where I had my encounter with Prime Minister Tojo, about which I had concocted the myth for my children.

Needless to say, just fifty years ago, when I was a rather immature adolescent in an Oriental wonderland, the confusion of tongues between me and the Japanese I met was enormous. When they found out I was European, some of the civilian employees in the biological laboratories, mostly medical students or young biologists, became interested in me. (Perhaps it helped that Hungary had fought on the side of the Axis?) They were particularly delighted to discover that we could practice French conversation together. I suspect that my experience of being invited to an upper-class private house in the Japan of 1946–47 was highly unusual for members of the army of occupation. (Ironically, nothing of that kind recurred in 1994, however many Japanese colleagues I encountered!) Of course, I tried to reciprocate with small gifts of items from the Army stores, especially food, which was in very short supply for the civilian population.

I kept up a correspondence with my Japanese friends for about a year after my return. Their letters became more and more disturbing because they gradually revealed a grave misunderstanding of my position in America. Instead of seeing me as the penniless immigrant I then was (and a medical school freshman to boot, than which there is none more abused!), all these people assumed that I was a person of wealth and influence—like their own families at home. They began to ask me for various kinds of help I was utterly unable to provide; to my eternal shame, instead of telling them so, I simply failed to answer.

This first experience in Japan climaxed my adolescence, such as it was, in view of having lived it on four continents, in a whirl of disparate civilizations. I have always thought the Japanese interlude was crucial in the consolidation of my identity as a person beyond national loyalties: I was so impressed by the dignity, optimism, and diligence of the Japanese I encountered that my sympathies were entirely on their side. (I was shocked by the racism, arrogance, and exploitativeness of many of my fellow soldiers.) In the Army hospitals, much of the actual work was performed by Japanese, and these educated people did not fail to notice how I felt.

Obviously, there is no way to resurrect such an ambience today. The Japanese professionals I met on my return may still harbor some awe of their American counterparts, but it is unthinkable for them to *show* in any way that they feel at a disadvantage. I refused to curry favor with them by bragging about the fact that my daughter-in-law Terry Ozaki is of Japanese extraction—as I like to put it, I am prepared for the twenty-first century, because I have three quasi-Japanese grandchildren!

My original experience of Japan crystallized my interest in the arts and taught me that, even on a modest budget, one could build a respectable collection of artifacts. Unfortunately, the pay of a private first class during the occupation barely sufficed to keep one in beer and to pay fares to and from the Red Cross Club—to make any acquisitions, one had to trade on the black market. People willing to steal a few vials of penicillin could obtain museum-quality works, and there were ways of getting these shipped home. Almost everyone traded in cigarettes, not quite as valuable as scarce medicines, but in great demand everywhere. I was rightly convinced that all this black-marketeering was a way of robbing a deprived community, and I righteously refused to participate. (My mother would have been proud of me, if I had had the generosity to let her know!)

A few weeks before I was scheduled to be sent back to the States, the Red Cross Club held an exhibition of *ukiyo-e* (woodblock) prints—editions made just before World War II of classic eighteenth- and early nineteenth-century works. It was my first exposure to such art, and it swept away my moralistic scruples. One carton of Lucky Strikes (a couple of bucks for a GI) paid for some three dozen fine prints—in terms of today's commercial values, worth over five thousand dollars. I cherished them for many years; they eventually made a fine present for my daughter-in-law. In five decades of collecting, I have never again made such a lucky strike. As my grandfather would have said, *Vae victis!*[1]

I was prepared to appreciate a strange civilization such as that of Japan by the encounter with the colonial ambience of Tangier, just seven years earlier. In 1940, when I was in the *quatrième* class at the lycée, my teacher of history was a gentleman past 70 who told me about having been born at Suez during the construction of the canal. He gave me a slim book he had written on the history of Tangier, based in part on archaeological digs he had conducted when he explored the basement of its largest department store. He was also in charge of the French lending library, where he got me hooked on historical novels. He was the embodiment of France's *mission civilisatrice*; if I am somewhat civilized (he would have said, *"un homme moyen cultivé,"*[2]), I owe it to him and some of his successors among my high school and college instructors in New York. I came honestly by my lifelong enthusiasm for myth and history.

I must confess that, having lived in an extravagantly romantic colonial setting, I have remained a bit of a colonialist. It is scandalous that an American professional should be unable to afford to buy his wife a decent gift if she cannot accompany him to Japan—not even after the rebate of the 30 percent sales tax the natives have to pay. I should have traded in penicillin while the trading was good!

I suppose it was fortunate for me that in 1947 the NYU College of Medicine had just instituted a very progressive curriculum, with ample provision for electives and a minimum of rote learning—even so, I was barely able to endure the drudgery of medical training—memorizing mountains of facts I knew I would never use. Our flight from Losoncz to Tangier and on to New York took place in tandem with my uncle George and his family; his son Tom, almost three years my senior, was like a sibling to me. (He was even more hostile than older brothers generally are, for his father clearly thought that I was abler than poor Tom.) When this cousin returned from the Army, he was in considerable psychological difficulty, and my father referred him for assistance to a psychoanalyst—someone of Hungarian origin, of course.

I suppose it was this coincidence (and my malicious pleasure about the fall of my nemesis) that stimulated me to begin reading Freud. I was excited and fascinated by this material; my pleasure was not spoiled by the guilt I experienced when I turned to history or literature instead of "studying." To ascertain whether I wished to pursue a career in psychoanalytic psychiatry, I took as many electives in the subject as the curriculum allowed;

altogether, while still in school, I spent almost a full academic year working in various psychiatric settings.

In retrospect, I now realize that what really occupied me from 1947 to 1951 was the completion of my delayed adolescence. When I started college in 1943, I was just 15 and still bewildered by the complexity of American life. The year I spent in the Army—basic training in Louisiana, the dreamlike six-week voyage to Yokohama through the Panama Canal, a half a year in Japan—helped to restart my emotional development, and my time in medical school was in most ways the equivalent of the college years of contemporary youngsters. Another way to say this is that I insisted on having a good time, however mind-numbing medical studies turned out to be. I was fortunate to make friends with a rather sophisticated young woman who worked in the fashion industry, and we explored the resources of New York City together—restaurants, the theater, music, and museums.

At times, all this experimentation made me somewhat giddy: I adopted the principle that it was necessary to spend the evenings before major examinations "on the town"—I might go to a performance at the old Metropolitan Opera House on 39th Street, where one could buy a standing-room ticket at the last minute, or attend an NYU basketball game at Madison Square Garden. What I lost by refusing to cram was probably regained in the form of added self-confidence, but I could not make the same claim for the compulsion that gained a hold on me to walk out of examinations, whether I was finished or not, as soon as any other student got up to leave.

After the pivotal European trip, I decided to devote my last year of medical study to two major artistic enterprises: writing a class chronicle for the senior yearbook and collaborating on the production of a musical satire about medical education, to be performed just before graduation. The class play tradition generally provided an outlet for the students' accumulated resentments, and it gave me a rare opportunity to indulge my suppressed rebelliousness. (At the same age, my father fought in an actual revolution!) The story for the yearbook was my first actual publication; it is a first-person account of the subjective experience of a medical student who is ostensibly unaware of his own absurdities. Even today, I am rather proud of it; the great trouble I took to produce this piece of ephemera was the harbinger of a future that became more and more dedicated to writing.

In the Army, during basic training, I had made friends with a fellow New Yorker, Fritz Heimann. Fritz was of German origin and reached America shortly before I did. By coincidence, he was to finish at the University of Chicago Law School when I would graduate as a physician. I had the fantasy that we might start our parallel professional lives together; this and the need to put distance between me and my parents' increasingly constricted way of life, decided me to focus my search for an internship on Chicago.

I must confess, however, that I also longed to be accepted for an internship at Bellevue Hospital, where NYU students received their clinical training, and I abandoned this idea only as a result of a debacle during my clerkship in obstetrics. (To discern its meaning for me, I must remind readers that in Europe my father had been a well-trained obstetrician and that my early years were filled with listening to his accounts of difficult deliveries performed in primitive rural conditions.) One night, we admitted a woman in labor, transferred from the acute psychiatric service. She was flagrantly psychotic, utterly uncooperative with hospital personnel, and she was also alleged to have severe rheumatic heart disease. The chief resident immediately assigned her care to me because of my declared interest in psychiatry; the patient would have to be handled with some skill, to soothe her so that her struggles during parturition would not precipitate a cardiac catastrophe. Everyone regarded this as a dire emergency.

We put the patient in a private labor room, and I attempted to establish some kind of contact with her. She continued to babble senselessly, but she permitted me to begin the requisite physical examination. Occasionally, some comprehensible phrases emerged from her stream of verbiage, such as "The baby is coming." I was most concerned about her undetermined cardiac status, and I was using a stethoscope to check this when the chief resident came in to monitor the situation. He uncovered the patient's abdomen, and—to his utter delight!—found a healthy infant under the bedclothes. Everyone congratulated me on my miraculous management of the delivery. To add insult to injury, when all participants were cleaned up, the head nurse placed the newborn in the patient's arms, adding the routine Bellevue formula, "Mother, here is your baby." Acidly, with impeccable logic and a suspicious glare, the patient replied, "That is not *my* baby. Everyone knows that, to have a baby, you have to go to a delivery room and put your feet in stirrups." Such are the rewards of producing miracles. I felt so ridiculous that I lost my taste for Bellevue Hospital. The scales tilted toward the decision to leave New York. (It never occurred to me that, from the viewpoint of clinical psychiatry, my intervention in the case had been successful enough.)

At Thanksgiving, 1950, I made a scouting expedition to Chicago, and set up headquarters in Fritz's Hyde Park apartment. I had arranged to have interviews at various teaching hospitals; at the old Presbyterian Hospital (now part of Rush Medical School) the interviewer, Howard Sinclair Armstrong (oil and cork!), socialite head of the Department of Medicine and a friend of psychoanalysis, immediately offered me a place (provided, contrary to regulations, I would also commit myself). I was dazzled by Armstrong's wealth and glamor and very impressed because he was the first person in America to pronounce my name in the Hungarian manner, sounding the umlaut, "ö," that I never bother to write any more. I was very happy to accept the offer and to stop obsessing about the future. I took the train back to New York in the middle of the season's first blizzard, with just enough change in my pocket to take the subway home from Pennsylvania Station. (I felt like Otello, in act one of the opera, returning to port after he vanquishes the Turks.)

I arrived for the internship with one medium-sized suitcase, a pair of white loafers for work, a tuxedo (just in case Howard Armstrong decided to be sociable!), and something like forty dollars to my name. I drove with a friend; we arrived in downtown Chicago as the sun rose over Lake Michigan. An auspicious beginning! I spent my money on an FM radio and a reproduction of Lautrec's *Au Moulin Rouge* from the Art Institute, and I was ready for a new life, on my own for the first time.

Unfortunately, Fritz Heimann left Chicago just as I arrived: he went to work for the Atomic Energy Commission (whence he moved to General Electric's atomic products division), so that we never have managed to live in the same city, and my hopes of finding a ready-made social matrix in Chicago came to nothing. I was dating a very decent nurse at the hospital who eventually found me a bit too bourgeois to suit her. *C'est la vie*. But these circumstances scarcely threw cold water on my exhilaration about having become an adult. I was determined to live on my own earnings. (We had no salary, but the hospital paid interns a premium if we wished to sell our blood, and well-to-do patients would tip us from time to time; I received a generous honorarium from the widow of a prominent corporate executive, probably because she had exclaimed at my clumsiness as I was vainly trying to revive her husband.) I received lessons in frugality from fellow house officers who came from places like China and Lebanon.

Within a few weeks, it was time to apply for psychiatric residencies, and, largely because I was delighted with Chicago, a city possessing all the amenities of a major metropolis without being as difficult to manage as New York, I wanted to obtain a position here. When this soon proved to be feasible, I felt on top of the world; just a year after I realized that I was out of place in medicine, I knew that I could enter a psychoanalytic community I regarded as an avant-garde of humanism. What a year it had been! How drastically I had reformulated my future!

Forty-six years have passed since: Judith Kaszab is a distinguished Australian painter, Bob Drye has retired to Arizona, Fritz is the most senior figure in the legal department at GE, Kämpfner has outlived his entire generation, and I have returned to writing subjective chronicles, in the first person. Next year should come even closer to fulfilling the deferred ambitions of my adolescence: I have just been invited to serve as visiting professor "of psychoanalytic thought" at the University of Chicago. Happily, the appointment is not in the medical school, but in the Division of the Humanities. Franz Alexander had the same position when he arrived in America in 1931, and Bruno Bettelheim played a similar role while he directed the university's Orthogenic School, but neither man was free of clinical responsibilities or the training of professionals. My cup runneth over.

❖ CHAPTER 24 ❖

ENVOI

I have recently heard from Sidney R., an elderly but vigorous financier who was formerly one of my patients. He called in high good humor to let me know that he had pulled off a great coup—one of his patented deals of Byzantine complexity—that would simultaneously promote a number of excellent causes and only cost him two million tax-deductible dollars! He wanted me to share his gratification because one of the difficulties that had brought him to seek assistance was an obligatory miserliness. (In our work together, I often called him Fafner the Dragon, because all he could do with his gold was to sit on it, like Wagner's pitiful and obtuse giant.[1]) Now, in the closing portion of his own Ring, Sidney has found new avenues for creativity that match his youthful ideals—he has turned into the most imaginative of philanthropists. And he has had the generosity to keep me informed of our joint success.

This call confronted me with the paradox that in these reminiscences I have avoided saying anything about the core of my professional life, clinical work with more than sixty analytic patients. However burdensome I have found it to take responsibility for the care of others, my writings bear testimony to my fascinated immersion in the intricacies of psychoanalytic technique. Moreover, I have greatly appreciated the opportunity to become intimately acquainted with a variety of individuals the like of whom I could never meet in the course of ordinary social or working relationships. I suppose one reason for shying away from this subject is that I have published a greater volume of detailed case reports than any other psychoanalyst, ever. (And I may not be done yet; I have just uncovered, in the back of a storage closet, the transcript of my supervision with Benedek—returned to me after her death by her niece, Eva Sandberg, who was registrar at the Institute and has long assisted me in preparing my manuscripts. Therese was better than I remembered! I think that I, too, may have been better than I have hitherto dared to believe. What a wonderful book one could make of this! How about *What Have We Learned in the Past Forty Years*?)

Of course, case reports necessarily focus on the maladaptive behaviors analysis should overcome, but what is truly worth remembering about analysands generally lies beyond the realm of pathology. There, precisely, is the rub; one can hardly describe those matters without committing some breach of confidentiality. How could I discuss the young woman who, many years ago, wrote a roman-à-clef about her analysis with "Doctor Green" (a man who sometimes had a spot on his tie), without committing some indiscretion? That novel has been widely regarded as the best fictionalized account of an analytic experience—it is still in print as a paperback, decades after publication. Have I already pointed a finger at the author, now very well known as a serious woman of letters? (Once, at a literature and psychoanalysis conference at one of the California universities, some of her critical admirers recognized her, although I did not reveal much more about her than I do here.) Yet working with this person has brought me the greatest reward of any analysis I have performed: the dedication of a book of verse, "To John Gedo, a Master Builder," and characterization in *The New York Times Book Review* as a "wise and gentle guru." (Mary questioned the characterization, but she did recommend that I advertise, "*The Times* says, he is," etc.)

Persons of similar distinction and interest I would like to describe but may not, such as the anonymous architect who designed the underground silos for the American ICBM arsenal or a mathematical genius about whom full-page stories have appeared in the press, were not simply remarkable for professional accomplishments and as ideal analysands—they were rare and admirable human beings. I have also seen more than an expectable number of fascinating religious believers, starting with the fundamentalist minister I treated as a candidate, through an official of the Baha'i faith (my suburban house was within walking distance of its U. S. headquarters in Wilmette), to the Jesuit psychiatrist who was referred to me for a training analysis. To turn from the sublime to the pathetic, I have also treated my share of picaresque delinquents—about some of them, I could recount sexual scandals worthy of TV drama. Alas, it cannot be done.

About former patients, I have to content myself with one unusual anecdote. This concerned a young woman who, in explicit identification with what she observed about me in looking around my office-apartment, began seriously to collect art. The difference between us was that her resources in this endeavor exceeded mine literally a hundredfold; thus, to console herself for a (temporary) interruption of the analysis, she casually purchased an old master painting fit for a great museum. She was convinced that the analysis had saved her life (and I rather think that she was right on that score). However much I charged her (and it was always enough to cause consternation in the analytic community), she was burdened with a sense of not having reciprocated sufficiently for my efforts—she often wanted to *give* me something, beyond the fee. I always dealt with this fantasy by trying to discover its transference significance[2] and by reminding her that it would be unethical on my part to take anything beyond the fee we agreed upon. I finally tired of this recurrent refrain and told her that, if she still felt she owed me something after termination, she could make a gift in my honor to the Art Institute—a common enough arrangement on the Chicago medical scene.

What turned out to be uncommon was that *this* grateful patient donated a hundred times the amount I had imagined she might give—the veteran curator who received the money told me that he almost fell out of his chair when he looked at her check. She designated the funds for the purchase of a suitable drawing that would be to my taste. I made the choice in consultation with the famed connoisseur, Harold Joachim, who elevated the quality of the Chicago drawing collection to rank among the best. We settled on a 1913 charcoal portrait of Alma Mahler by Oskar Kokoschka—a work widely recognized as the artist's best on paper. It was prominently featured in the Kokoschka exhibition at the Guggenheim Museum some years ago; we saw the show when we were in New York for one of the December meetings. Many analysts were at the Guggenheim that day—when he saw the label with my name on it, I thought one of them might fall over the railings into the bowels of Wright's snail shell.[3] Such are the fantasies of eternal exiles. (Consult *The Inferno*.[4])

What else have I given short shrift in surveying my professional life? Not much that would interest anyone—perhaps only some of my private disappointments, like the deaths of certain dear friends, such as Brahm Baittle.

We met at the U. of C. in 1952; when I went into private practice, he was one of those with whom I shared a suite. Brahm was a sweet teddy bear of a man; his pace in life was never faster than adagio. He married late and adopted a baby at 47. In 1967 the Baittles came with us on a leisurely tour of Burgundy—they were the only couple we have known who could agree to the kind of antiquarian itinerary we always follow as travelers. Brahm was seriously involved with music—he once had dreams of being a composer—and he was my guide into the world of the preclassical repertory. At the age of 50, after a horrifying struggle, he died of a sarcoma.

Ernest Mond, who had until then been my internist, told me that henceforth he could not take care of people who were his friends. About Brahm, he said, "He even chose the hour of his death so that he would cause no trouble for anyone." (It is a memory I kept uppermost in my mind during my illness and surgery three years ago. That and the need to preserve one's dignity.) I gave one of the eulogies at Brahm's funeral, and this one came from the heart, without inhibition. Over the years, I have often dreamt in sorrow that Brahm has been avoiding me, for reasons I could not discern. In this way, he has come to symbolize everything about psychoanalysis about which I have reason to feel nostalgia.

Needless to say, I have also had therapeutic disappointments, about which I have invariably reported in some detail (1981a [chap. 3] and 1984c [chap. 7]).[5] I am infuriated by failure; one reason for my relative success as a therapist is that I stubbornly refuse to admit defeat. I am capable of great obstinacy. My patients have generally discerned that I fought on their behalf, above and beyond the call of duty; consequently, I have parted on good terms with all but two or three analysands. (I do not count among these a handful of people who decided during an exploratory period that they did not want to work with me. Almost invariably, these were individuals who for some reason struck me as psychopathic or a little bizarre, and they no doubt sensed my unease in their presence.) I tend to believe that those who failed to experience my analytic attitude as helpful and benign were paranoid, that analysands who did not eventually see that their anger at me was a transference reaction were demonizing me. In two instances I know about, former patients have loudly disagreed. It is par for the course, but I prefer to beat par. Moreover, I have a letter I wrote to my mother on my eighth birthday (she had the decency to preserve it until she died), in which I apologized for all the trouble I had caused her and promised to do better. I probably have not done better, but I long ago stopped apologizing for my existence.

I have had disappointments of another kind, when my best efforts did not suffice to obtain something I wanted. Much of the time this happened because I disregarded certain political necessities; if I wanted a voice in running the Chicago Institute (and I did), I should have supported George Pollock; if I wanted my books to be analytic best-sellers (as who would not?), I should have swallowed my distrust of IUP; if I do not want to provoke the anathemata of Kohut's followers (and I have no interest in eliciting anyone's hatred), I should not reveal such disillusioning stories about their hero—as I should slowly have marginalized myself in Heinz's circle, without provoking a rupture. But, as cousin Eva's husband told my mother, "I am a Hungarian gentleman." (He did not mean it literally, either.) Hungarians do not stage their revolutions only when there is a good chance of success, but *honoris causa*.[6]

Occasionally, I have sustained reverses for which I cannot blame myself; this was the case in my negotiations with the Freud archives. I became acquainted with K. R. Eissler through his "friend" Kohut. (I put it this way because I gradually gained the impression that they hated each other.) After I wrote reviews of some of Eissler's interdisciplinary work (see esp. 1972b),[7] we began at intervals to correspond; he even asked me to write an endorsement of his book on the Freud-Tausk relationship, *Talent and Genius* (1972). As I have mentioned, he also enlisted me to raise funds in Chicago for some small projects of the archives. Then, in the mid-1970s, after my rupture with Kohut, Eissler proposed that I take a greater role in the affairs of the archives, starting with raising a hundred thousand dollars for the purchase of the Freud-Silberstein correspondence. He asked me to come to see him in person—as he put it, to determine whether I had the "presence" to induce old ladies to donate money.

One evening when we were in New York, Mary and I called on the Eisslers and we were graciously received. I knew Ruth Eissler had been Kohut's (second) analyst, and I wondered what her attitude would be about my repudiation of Heinz. I did not have long to wait—they both made it entirely clear that they did not disapprove of my decision. We chatted about the possibility of my editing the correspondence after it was purchased; Eissler expressed confidence that I could bring my competence in German up to the necessary standard. (I thought so myself; I had less confidence in my talent for charming wealthy old ladies.) The soirée ended very pleasantly, and Eissler promised to keep me informed about the next steps to be taken. Silence followed. About three months later, I was about to leave for some weeks of European travel, and I sent Eissler a note to let him know that he would not be able to reach me in that interval. He responded by thanking me for my considerate letter. I understood, of course, that he had decided to drop me, and, in fact, I never heard from him again.

Needless to say, when it turned out that I had been aced out by the notorious Jeffrey Masson, I felt a fair bit of satisfaction about the manner in which my successful rival skewered the archives, and even more about the delicious exposé about the whole matter by Janet Malcolm (1984). And it has gone on and on, with news reports about Masson's suit against Malcolm, trials and appeals—a veritable orgy of schadenfreude. Moreover, if I had succeeded Eissler at the archives, I would never have focused my efforts on theoretical innovation. It is not that I have *chosen* the better part—it has been thrust upon me, to juxtapose two celebrated statements on the subject.[8]

What I have not mastered still is some difficulty about asserting my true worth. It is not merely that it is unseemly to toot one's own horn or that *un dottore di mia sorte* (to echo Rossini once again)[9] cannot dream of voting for himself in an election. I have no conflict about adhering to these values of my upbringing. Beyond such niceties, any tinge in myself of my mother's characteristic smugness fills me with the dismay I felt when I realized that her pretensions were empty. I think it may interest people that in high school I sat next to Alan Greenspan, but I put it in parentheses, as an afterthought, because it may sound like name dropping. Can I mention that I once received a *Good Housekeeping* seal of approval—or is that just a piece of showing off?[10] I never know, and I probably err in both directions.

At the same time, a professional memoir such as this only shows certain facets of one's personality and, of necessity, these are the most polished. If they were not, who would publish such a book? And who would undertake to write hundreds of pages about a life of failure? Yet a description of my forty-four years as Mary's husband would in fact make a better story, and it would certainly avoid the suspicion that I am boasting. When my father met Mary, he declared, "My son, you have chosen cleverly!" *Vissi d'arte, vissi d'amore . . .*[11] (Mary and I got married six weeks after we met; many years later, Leo Sadow confessed that a betting pool was established among our acquaintances not about *whether*, but *when* we would get divorced.) I feel no spleen about the parts of my life that constitute the nonprofessional side of the coin.

Some of the friendships I formed entirely outside the mental health/medicine nexus have been as meaningful—and more interesting—than the ones I have had the opportunity to describe. (Fritz Heimann, whom I met in the Army, when we were both 18, is full of fascinating stories about service on international bodies or presidential commissions—a man of decency, intelligence, humor, and common sense. Robert Darvas, a 1956 refugee from Budapest, has designed astonishing structures all over the world—he, too, is the salt of the earth. Claudio Aspesi, who twenty years ago lived with us as an exchange student, and whom we have seen frequently in Chicago, Rome, Milan, and other European cities, is now a partner in the Chicago office of one of the great consulting firms; he is also one of the most cultivated and urbane persons of his generation.)

When I tell people that my career in psychoanalysis has been like a marriage of convenience that has lost its advantages, they are generally incredulous, because I fully committed myself to make the best of the bargain. Yet I have had other passions, and some of these have meant more to me. I would certainly rather read Iris Murdoch or Marguerite Yourcenar than Melanie Klein, I prefer Kafka to Kohut, Mann over Freud. (I have not even named the authors I truly love, because I want to compare like to like.) I prefer writing about the history of culture to writing about the history of psychoanalysis. I would never exchange listening to live music or looking at serious art for a chance to do treatment. Commissioning the design of a unique house—a modernist version of a small Roman country villa—and filling it with art was the most satisfying creative accomplishment I have participated in. Sophisticated friends tell me that this is idle talk—that a person must work to maintain self-esteem. Of course, I had to work in order to earn a living, but it is perfectly feasible to do that through scholarship in any of the endeavors I have listed here as passions, and in a number of others I love almost as well. Perhaps, after all, I have been inclined to be splenetic because until very recently I did not give myself the opportunity to pursue my true passions.

Some colleagues have actually been angry because I have dared to retire—not because they cannot afford to do so, but because they view me as a deserter. (I tend to add insult to injury by reminding them that, when a ship is sinking, one cannot be called a rat for abandoning it.) I could claim, if I chose, that writing one's memoirs is valuable work, but it has been pure joy, and I prefer *not* to view it as labor—it is no more work than reading *Vanity Fair*, *Sentimental Education*, or *The History of the Peloponnesian War*, visiting the churches of Rome, Cologne, and Burgundy, or the studios of our artist friends in Chicago. Or following public affairs, the opera, and the Chicago Bears.

NOTES

Chapter 1

1. Petrarch, Sonnet 133: *"L'oliva è secca . . ."*

2. To put it more precisely, the poisonous wrangling over a divorce settlement is portrayed in *Humboldt's Gift*; the vast apartment in a luxury building that an elderly U. of C. professor abandons to his beautiful but callow young wife is described in *More Die of Heartbreak*.

3. I have described some of this self-analytic work in greater detail in J. Gedo (1993g). (Henceforth, references to my publications, listed in the Appendix, will be cited by dates alone, without my name.)

4. In 1975, as he was starting to fail, Grinker wrote a brief memoir about Chicago psychoanalysis, highlighting the period from the mid-1930s to the mid-1950s. Publication was deferred until everyone named in this passionate diatribe had died (see Grinker 1995). Compared with Grinker's essay, this book is filled with mildness and clemency; he was especially caustic in his characterization of Gitelson.

5. The specific issues implicated in such attitudes were brilliantly highlighted by Modell (1965).

6. See Gitelson (1973). My brief (unsigned) review appeared in the *Journal of the American Psychoanalytic Association* 22:700–701; prior to 1974, the majority of books reviewed there received such brief, anonymous "Notices."

7. In 1973 we began to publish evaluative Book Notices and soon realized that it was unfair to leave these unsigned. As soon as we changed policy, it became apparent that most notices were prepared by me, and we received a number of protests about this practice. To my regret, after producing about fifty notices, I

had to stop this challenging activity. Because thenceforth the job was purely administrative, when my term was up I decided not to seek reappointment as book review editor.

8. See Malcolm (1981).

9. In tribute to Max, one former student published a collection of Gitelson's most illuminating statements while that person attended his seminar. See Kramer (1967).

10. For details, see 1993g.

Chapter 2

1. *Borovička* is distilled from the juniper berry, like gin.

2. Abbazia (now called Opatija) is a Croatian resort town on the Adriatic. Until 1918, it was within the Hapsburg empire; because it is the seaside location closest to Hungary, it continued to attract a bourgeois clientele from the Danube basin through the years between the wars. From 1919 to 1945, the town was part of Italy. The *corso* is the street in an Italian city where the bourgeois take a ceremonial stroll before dinner.

3. Ferenczi formed part of the intellectual circle that published this avant-garde journal. They met in a famous café called the New York, still decorated with witty caricatures of these early twentieth-century luminaries, including Ferenczi. Although they kept the splendid art nouveau interior intact, the Communists forced the establishment to give up its pro-Western name; in 1990, when I visited, it had just been renamed the New York.

4. Lord Byron assisted the Greeks in their War of Independence against the Turks and died at the siege of Mesolongi, often transliterated as "Missolonghi."

5. Herrmann, born in the nineteenth century, was old enough soon after the Communist regime took over to be officially "retired." The authorities were not particularly interested in the professional activities of pensioners, so that Herrmann was able inconspicuously to conduct analyses in his home, albeit at some risk. In addition to this heroic resistance to tyranny, Herrmann made significant contributions to the Budapest school of psychoanalysis, extending the emphasis of Ferenczi on the significance of the preoedipal phases of development.

6. "Permanent revolution" was Leon Trotsky's recommendation for the socialist commonwealth.

Chapter 3

1. I echo the title of Rezzori's memoir because it would have been most appropriate for my own. The line comes from the refrain of a celebrated Villon poem: *Où sont les neiges d'antan?*

2. These rumors were later amply confirmed; some of Weiss's students began to practice psychoanalysis. Recently, they formed the nucleus of an analytic training program under the aegis of Division 39 of the American Psychological Association.

3. Latin for "much in a small compass."

4. This was also the title of a multivolume work French (1952/1953/1958) published over the years.

5. Alexander and his collaborators were testing the hypothesis that each of seven distinct psychosomatic diseases is (partially) caused by specific psychological predispositions. The outcome of the research was equivocal. More recently, the specificity hypothesis has received little credence. In the Alexander study, psychological data were used to postdict which of the seven diseases was present; the problem was that it was practically impossible to eliminate from the protocols nonpsychological clues about the diagnosis. My task was to survey the protocols for such cues. See Alexander (1951) and Alexander, French, and Pollock (1968).

6. In Poe's tale, "The Purloined Letter," a document is concealed by being left in plain view.

7. Some years later, I wrote a paper on this topic (1975a) and proposed to call such a reaction formation against disillusionment "pseudoidealization." In *Psychoanalytic Supervision*, Fleming characterized my responses to her as signs of narcissistic vulnerability.

8. Ludwig von Bertalanffy was then at the end of his great career as a theoretical biologist and one of the pioneers of systems theory. Although he was officially Viennese, his origins were aristocratic and Hungarian; for me, these facts underscored the fantasy of being knighted. See von Bertalanffy (1968).

9. The fact that my first publication (1959a) was the lead article in the first issue of Grinker's *Archives* may have been a coincidence, but I chose to interpret it as a vote of confidence and a signal honor.

Chapter 4

1. Noblesse oblige implies that the higher one aspires, the better one's conduct must be.

2. In 1927, Freud optimistically predicted that, "after a countless succession of rebuffs," the voice of the intellect will be heard.

3. In addition, Pollock and I played important parts in editing (with other members of the Institute faculty) the first three volumes of *The Annual of Psychoanalysis* (1973, 1974, 1975).

4. Literally, a "knower of men"—a judge of character.

5. Girolamo Savonarola (1452–98), Dominican monk who attacked the moral laxity of the church hierarchy with such passion that the authorities he condemned ultimately had him burned at the stake, thereby proving his charges.

Chapter 5

1. Prior to 1966, I had no idea that Kohut was preoccupied with problems of narcissism; I did not encounter his first paper on the subject until it appeared in print that year.

2. Martin Luther called God *"ein festes Burg"*—a mighty fortress.

3. Latin for "in wine [there is] truth."

4. For Kohut's satisfaction about this transaction, see his letter of October 26, 1966, in Cocks (1994, pp. 152–153). For Kohut's general assessment of my potentials around this time, consult his correspondence, on file in the archive at the Institute for Psychoanalysis, Chicago. Most relevant is the letter in which he describes me to K. R. Eissler.

5. Kohut had early access to the research results that led up to this book; these were first reported in a dissertation (Northwestern University, 1972) on "Picasso's self-image." Kohut was fascinated with the finding that cubist faceting of the human figure reflected Picasso's subjective states of disintegration.

6. Marianne Kris, an eminent analyst in New York, one of the editors of *The Psychoanalytic Study of the Child*, was the widow of Ernst Kris, one of the leaders of ego psychology. She was the daughter of Freud's best friend, the pediatrician Oscar Rie, and a lifelong intimate of Anna Freud, and (in her own right) she was universally respected.

7. Reported in Freud (1900, p. 130).

8. The tension at this party culminated in the only incident in our decades of keeping dogs in which one of them bit someone.

9. I have retained this treasure in my files.

10. "Everything is lost, except honor." These were the words of the French King, Francis I, in a letter to his mother announcing that he had been captured by the Spanish at the disastrous battle of Pavia.

11. Because many found this paper to be difficult to follow, I never published it as such, although it contained the germ of many of my later ideas, particularly that of the systematic application of a developmental viewpoint to psychoanalytic observations. A summary of the meeting at the Chicago Society was, however, published (Siegel [reporter] 1968).

12. For Kohut's letter of January 28, 1969 to the publisher of International Universities Press, in which he proposed to edit such a volume with my collaboration, see Cocks (1994, pp. 224–225).

13. For Kohut's letter of July 12, 1968 to Anna Freud, proposing this invitation, see Cocks (1994, pp. 206–207).

14. St. John's Woods is a fashionable district of London, just west of Regent's Park. Ruysch was a Dutch artist of the early eighteenth century and the outstanding proponent of the "flower piece."

15. Hayman (1969) had just published a theoretical paper of fundamental importance that challenged Freud's structural theory.

16. New Cavendish Street, just south of Regent's Park, is in the most elegant part of Central London. The institute is located close to the intersection with Harley Street. Robert Adam was the outstanding British architect of the second half of the eighteenth century. The institute building is a national landmark.

17. The late Masud Khan, reputed to be a Pakistani prince, was at the time one of the intellectual heirs of D. W. Winnicott. Donald Meltzer, of American origin, is a vigorous spokesman for Melanie Klein.

18. When his mother died, the little boy repetitively made a toy disappear and reappear, with the comments, "gone" and "there."

19. The expression originated in the British Navy, where landlubbers (such as the Marines) were plied with absurd tales about seamanship and foreign parts.

Chapter 6

1. A revised version of this essay is included in 1986a (chapter 5); a German translation appeared in 1976 as "David Rapaports Beitrag zur Psychoanalyse," *Psyche* (30:306–326).

2. Among the score of books I have reviewed for the *Quarterly*, the following were probably the most significant: G. Klein (1976), M. Gill and P. Holzman, eds. (1976), (for my review, see 1977d), V. Rosen (1977), P. Gay (1984), H. Searles (1986), H. Rosenfeld (1987), F. Pine (1990), V. Tähkä (1993).

3. Ming Pei is the celebrated Chinese-American architect, probably best known for the glass pyramid he built for the Louvre and the East Wing of the National Gallery in Washington. His Chicago townhouses prefigure his design for the latter.

4. This material was reprinted in Hunter (1994); for subsequent references to this interview, I shall cite the 1994 version, pp. 143–182.

5. I retain this (typewritten) letter of August 20, 1969 in my files.

Chapter 7

1. Modell gave his plenary in December 1995; it will be published in the *Journal of the American Psychoanalytic Association* in 1997.

2. In 1973 we published work by Hartmann, Waelder, Loewald, Benedek, Kohut, Kanzer, Modell, Searles, Kernberg, Masud Khan, Roy Schafer, and Pinchas Noy, to mention only the best known contributors. In volume two, we had papers by Heinz Lichtenstein, Bill Meissner, Leo Stone, Melitta Sperling, Henry Krystal, and Bob Stoller—again to list only those already well known. In 1975 we were finally ready

with the translation of a superb metascientific essay by Helmut Thomä and Horst Kächele (we had solicited this for volume one); we also had contributions from Augusta Bonnard, Paula Heimann, Krystal, Ping Pao, Paul Parin, and Kohut.

3. These were eventually published in book form; see Boehlich (1990).

4. The Securitate was the Romanian secret police under the Communist regime.

5. The conclusions we reached in this paper are included in the volume edited by Boehlich, without a reference to our work, as if they were self-evident.

6. For Kligerman's reservations about Kohut's work during the latter's lifetime, see Kohut's letter of Oct. 6, 1980 (one year before his death) in Cocks (1994, p. 413).

7. For a *Festschrift* to honor Martin on his 80th birthday, I contributed an essay (earlier published in German) on the rhetoric of interpretation. See 1993k.

8. For Heinz Kohut's congruent opinion, see Cocks (1994, p. 90).

Chapter 8

1. Freedman has observed the development of individuals born with a variety of handicaps—the congenitally blind or deaf, the famous child raised in a sterile bubble because of a deficient immune system, and so on. From these observations, he has derived careful conclusions (for a sample, see Freedman 1984).

2. Waelder came to psychoanalysis from physics and acquired a well-deserved reputation as a rigorous scientific thinker. His most lasting contribution was enunciation of the principle of multiple function—the idea that every piece of behavior simultaneously satisfies the disparate requirements of the several agencies of the mind. See Waelder (1930).

3. The incident is documented in Douglas Kirsner's chapter on the New York Psychoanalytic Institute, in a book still in preparation, a version of which he kindly shared with me.

4. In 1987, in the newsletter of the Massachusetts chapter of Division 39 of the American Psychological Association, I articulated what I believe to be a rational program for American psychoanalysis: "[We] need to avoid the temptations besetting every organization to compromise on quality in order to gain adherents. In clinical work, there is no substitute for sheer talent . . . its absence cannot be repaired by good training or the attainment of mental health. The psychoanalytic community can thrive without growing, but not without improving."

5. Over the years, I have laid more and more emphasis on questions of communication in the clinical situation, culminating in a recent book on this subject (1996b).

6. See 1979a (chapter 6) for a full account of this treatment.

7. For his theoretical views, see Klein (1976).

8. I am using the Italian phrase in its literal sense, "our thing," as the Mafia must originally have done. Clearly, there is nothing unlawful about secret societies as such.

9. Literally, "never heard." The French phrase is used in neurology to designate a kind of cognitive lapse.

Chapter 9

1. Soviet politicians who allied themselves with Stalin during the power struggle that followed the death of Lenin. Zinoviev and Kamenev were later purged by the dictator.

2. According to Geoffrey Cocks, editor of Kohut's correspondence (Cocks 1994, p. 28), Kohut did support my appointment as assistant editor by writing to the relevant committee.

3. See M. Gedo (1980, 1985/1987/1988, 1993).

4. In addition to onerous administrative duties, such as finding reviewers (without secretarial assistance from the association), and the steady preparation of book notices, I participated in the regular work of the editorial board. At that time, this involved biannual meetings and service as a referee for about twenty papers every year. I found it remarkable that of about a hundred submissions I read, the judgments of all readers were identical in over ninety. It only happened once that a paper I recommended for publication was turned down by the other referees.

5. Listed as 1964b, 1967c, 1968c, 1969, 1970d, 1968b, 1973b, and 1968a, respectively.

6. For Kohut's response to these events, see his letter of June 1978 in Cocks (1994, pp. 368–371). He wrote, "My removal from the Council came about as the result of a carefully organized campaign among the Faculty" (p. 369). I can testify that his impression was correct because, as a voter, I was contacted by that campaign.

7. His contribution at the conference was Kohut (1985).

8. The Pritzker family is reputed to be the wealthiest in the Chicago metropolitan area.

9. Douglas Kirsner of Deakin University (Australia) is preparing a book on the social and political history of American psychoanalysis. This work will be focused on the evolution of four large institutes, Chicago among them. As part of his research, he has tried to interview as many participants in the events he wishes to describe as he can get to cooperate. After we talked on three occasions, Kirsner and I realized that our assessments of Chicago analytic history (as developments determined by the institute's bylaws for governance) are practically identical.

Chapter 10

1. I am *not* implying, however, that, like the hero of Gogol's play, the COI site visit teams played a game of imposture.

2. The BPSI leadership resented the board's handling of the PINE split; Southern California and Columbia were the domains of those former mavericks, Alexander and Radó, and many of their graduates favored the Academy of Psychoanalysis—hence, these organizations were for a long time viewed with suspicion by those in power within the American. In my judgment, Goldberg joined with these disaffected institutes because the leadership of the American has not looked with favor on self psychology. In my opinion, the Chicago Institute has always received more respect from site visitors than it deserved.

Chapter 11

1. Published in *Psychoanalytic Review* 80:309 (1993).

2. I have donated this object to the library of the Chicago Institute for Psychoanalysis. To my chagrin, it has never been on display.

3. I wrote in part, "Many of your proposals go in the direction I have espoused for many years, as you know. . . . It is, of course, very gratifying to have been judged to be correct by a person of your caliber." Further, "I shall always remain grateful to you for setting me free through your work, not to speak at this moment of all the other kindnesses you once showed me" (Cocks 1994, p. 348). I meant, of course, that he was no longer doing so.

4. Letter of January 15, 1976 (copy in my files).

5. *The Annual of Psychoanalysis*, Vol. 6 (1978). "Some Contributions of Psychoanalysis to a Science of Man" (pp. 67–164); "Psychoanalysis and Biography" (pp. 397–427).

6. Between October 1975 and September 1980, I presented six papers of my own and discussed one by the eminent Mahlerian Calvin Settlage.

7. See 1984a, Part III ("Creativity and the Life Course"), with contributions by David Bevington and Mary Gedo. Part II ("Interdisciplinary Problems") used people from the social science workshop—George Moraitis, the sociologist Donald Levine, the anthropologists Mark Gehrie and Waud Kracke, and the historian Mark Schwehn.

Chapter 12

1. In retrospect, I believe I made too much of Kohut's immediate reaction to his illness, in part because I did not then know the salient fact that his father's early death had been caused by leukemia. See Cocks (1994, p. 7).

2. The concept of *making reparation* was put forward by Melanie Klein. In her terms, it refers to efforts to make up through good works for one's fantasied destructiveness. The phrase also conveys the notion that the person involved is "repaired" through these actions.

3. *Separation guilt*, a term introduced by Arnold Modell, arises when a person believes that the rupture of a symbiosis will greatly damage the abandoned partner. See Modell (1965).

4. Moser eventually communicated his disgust to Kohut directly, judging by the latter's response (in a letter of October 23, 1973) to their meeting in Switzerland in the summer of 1973. See Cocks (1994, pp. 291–292).

5. A structural definition means one focused on relatively permanent consensually observable *mental dispositions*. Kohut always dealt with *self* from an exclusively phenomenological (i.e., subjective) perspective.

6. Kohut's letter of January 20, 1969 is available at the Archives of the Chicago Institute for Psychoanalysis.

7. In his interview with Virginia Hunter (in Hunter 1994, p. 234), Goldberg's assessment of Heinz Kohut's character is entirely congruent with mine; he describes Kohut's lack of concern with giving credit to other contributors for their previous work.

8. The label was first adumbrated when he entitled his 1971 book *The Analysis of the Self*, but it did not become explicit until the Kohut group named the casebook *The Psychology of the Self*, some time prior to its 1978 publication.

9. In *Models of the Mind*, I wrote, "It is insufficient to conceptualize [memories of one's past transactions] as mental contents alone; they are more than the passively recorded percepts of the activities of one's own person in the past. By virtue of their continuing dynamic effects, they must be understood, in addition, as an actuality in the real world—the organized personality as a whole" (pp. 63–64). The book appeared in 1973, but its first draft was finished before my trip to Hampstead in 1969, so that this passage should be dated ca. 1968–69. In May 1972 Kohut was a formal discussant of a presentation on the self concept at the Chicago Psychoanalytic Society, and he sent me a copy of his remarks, which I have preserved in my files. He stated, "I prefer to define the self as an abstraction derived from psychoanalytic experience, i.e., I see it as a content of the mind. . . . There are selves in the ego, the id, and the superego. . . . However, there is . . . one which is experienced as the basic one . . . the nuclear self."

10. I first used the term *archaic transference* in 1977, to designate transferences of earlier origin than those replicating the Oedipus complex. I had in mind the "archaic" sculpture dug up from under the fifth century B.C. Parthenon.

11. The Year 1200: A Centennial Exhibition.

12. The murder of Thomas à Becket was provoked by Henry II's "rhetorical" question, "Who will rid me of this nettlesome priest?"

13. See letter to the editor, *Contemporary Psychology*, 18:571 (1973). See also my rebuttal of a reply from the reviewer, in *Contemporary Psychology* 18:685 (1973).

14. See Kohut's letter of September 9, 1969 to Anna Freud (in Cocks 1994, p. 240).

15. This is also Wolf's opinion—see Hunter (1994, p. 171).

16. Kohut said this in a 1966 discussion at the Chicago Psychoanalytic Society of Max Schur's "Some Additional Day Residues of the Specimen Dream of Psychoanalysis" (1966).

17. See Cocks (1994, p. 4). It is possible, of course, that an analysand (Mr. Z) did exist whose inner life happened to resemble Kohut's, but such an alternative would not change the inferences drawn by Kohut's wife and son.

18. "My work always involves the deeper layers of my personality, the hours over [*The Restoration of the Self*] are always accompanied with a number of free associations concerning people who are important to me—and you have often appeared among them" (Cocks 1994, pp. 324–325). In this passage, Kohut claims that his book is produced via self-analysis and that (in 1975) I am one of the objects that such introspection was focused on. This is precisely what he meant by a "transference of creativity."

19. This insinuation tried to portray me as disturbed and emotionally unable to accept psychoanalytic truths. Such a characterization was also grossly inaccurate when it was applied to Jung by political/scientific opponents.

20. Conventional formula to mark the decease of an English king.

21. The published version of my remarks is abridged. The editor of Kohut's correspondence, Geoffrey Cocks, uncritically accepted Kohut's misinterpretation of my Euripides reference (see 1994, pp. 28, 292)—despite the fact that he himself avers that Kohut adopted the "liberal tradition" of the anthropology of Euripides (1994, p. 24). Hölderlin's poem is entitled "An die Parzen"—to the Fates. The poet compares creativity to living "like the gods, and more is not needed," that is, one should be ready to accept death: "sated . . . my heart may more willingly die." To my taste, Kohut's continual preoccupation with mortality was not attractive.

22. Kohut reported the deferral of his acceptance by the institute in a letter of September 2, 1946 to his former analyst in Vienna, August Aichhorn. See Cocks (1994, p. 52).

Chapter 13

1. Unpublished letters in the Kohut Archive at the Chicago Institute confirm Goldberg's conjecture.

2. Latin for "[things] to be drunk."

3. For Kohut's opinion about my professional status at that time, see his letters of March 10, 1967 (p. 172), and July 12, 1968 (pp. 206–207), where he "introduced" me to Anna Freud, in Cocks (1994). For additional information on this issue, see the editor's introduction (Cocks 1994, p. 28).

4. We owe this insight about Kohut's viewpoint to Arnold Modell (1992, pp. 2–3).

5. Kohut had already endorsed the hierarchical view in 1970, in a discussion at the Chicago Psychoanalytic Society (summarized in 1970e).

6. For his ultimate views, see Kohut (1984). For a full critique of Kohut's work, see my 1986a (chapters 7 and 8) and 1989b.

7. Kohut's wish to produce a casebook is reported by E. Wolf in Hunter (1994, p. 173).

8. In the casebook (Goldberg 1978) this case history is labeled "Mr. M."—it is presented as chapter 3.

9. In advance of the meeting, I was assigned the task of writing a commentary on the account of the treatment from the viewpoint of "working through." I retain a copy in my files; in part, it follows:

> In this protocol, I want additional data about termination—the interrelated issues of sadism and being the one who keeps the parents (the mother, the analyst) happy. The concern about becoming addicted to analysis raises the possibility that the rapid and therapeutically gratifying termination is an enactment of the need to be a good patient and avoids the working through of that aspect of the negative transference that is expressed in [Mr. M.'s] sadistic fantasies (in relation to the analyst, echoed in the dream of the Jewish ball—probably a reference to [matters he had noticed about her] which had stimulated him so markedly in the intial interview). I would feel more secure on this score if there were some sign that he could accept the analyst's pleasure in her own success.

10. [Something] has not occurred.

Chapter 14

1. David's canvas of 1784 shows Horatius swearing his three sons to fight for Rome, unto death. When I was at the lycée in Tangier, I memorized long passages from Corneille's drama, *Horace*—at the age of 12, I had encountered nothing as stirring as, "Rome, l'unique objet de mes ressentiments . . ." The Jacobins were the most radical among the revolutionaries of 1789–95.

2. An enclosed carriage-way leading from the street into an inner courtyard.

3. Roman motto. In 1919 the revolutionary regime in Hungary attempted to prevent the dismemberment of the country by the victorious Allied powers. Ironically, when the revolution collapsed, it was that partition that allowed my father to escape to Czechoslovakia.

4. The only exceptions (if they can be classified as committed self psychologists) are Estelle and Morton Shane. They contributed an intelligent appreciation of my conceptual work to the 1994 symposium on "The Clinical Use of Multiple Models" (Shane and Shane 1994). Much to my amusement, in view of the imme-

diate precipitant of my rupture with the casebook group, in this essay they report on a case analyzed by Estelle that started with an interview between the analyst and the patient's father in which he was persuaded to finance the analysis. *Bravissimi*!

5. "Theory is good, but it does not prevent [anything] from existing." (See Freud 1892–94, p. 139.)

6. *Psychoanalytic Inquiry*, Volume 14, Number 2, pp. 235–312.

7. Don Giovanni's aria, addressed to Zerlina (the peasant girl he wants to seduce)—"There we shall give [each other] our hand[s]." For the panel, see Rothstein (1983).

8. See Lytton (1984) for the report of a panel where I presented 1983b, and Weich (1986) for the panel where I read an early version of 1984a.

9. See 1984b, an essay I first read as an "After Dinner Speech" at the banquet at the fiftieth anniversary celebration of Chicago psychoanalysis. Unfortunately, for publication, I felt obliged to cut the jokes.

10. For this expansion of the theory, see 1991e, 1991f, 1993d, 1995c, 1995e, 1996c, and 1997b.

Chapter 15

1. In *Psychoanalytic Inquiry*, volume 1, number 2 (1981).

Chapter 16

1. I also presented that material as the first public lecture of the Friends of the San Francisco Psychoanalytic Society, and it was published in the journal of that organization—see 1977c.

2. This was volume 8, number 4 (1988).

3. On one hand, this satisfaction marked the dream as a sign of mastery over the temptation to see the occasion as proof of being one of the elect; on the other, the speech in the dream quoted a characteristic phrase of Bob Gardner's—now a (nonbaseball) Yankee, but originally from New York.

4. "Confusion of tongues between adults and the child" is the title of a seminal paper by Ferenczi (1933).

5. "If the globe were broken up, I would be borne on its ruins, unafraid."

Chapter 17

1. Guido Reni (1575–1642), Bolognese painter, in his own time esteemed as one of the greatest masters in the history of art.

2. Chapter 7, "On van Gogh, Picasso, and the Dynamics of Creativity," and chapter 8, "Creativity and Psychopathology: van Gogh and Gauguin as Prototypes."

3. Gilot once lived with Picasso, and they had two children together. She has written extensively about this experience.

4. Kris was originally an art historian (and a curator at the Kunsthistorisches Museum in Vienna). His book *Psychoanalytic Explorations in Art* (1952) established interdisciplinary work on a solid footing.

5. "Let [everyone] think [as they will]," as in laissez-faire.

6. "In a war, [wage] war."

7. Available on cassette #129 from the American Psychoanalytic.

8. For the proceedings, see *Dialogue*, Volume 5, Number 1 (Fall, 1981).

Chapter 18

1. For other reviews of *Beyond Interpretation*, see McLaughlin (1983), Katz (1981), and Michels (1982).

2. The principal reviews of *Advances in Clinical Psychoanalysis* were those of Jaffe (1984), D. Goldberg (1985), Silverman and Silverman (1983), and Gill (1983).

3. I first presented this idea at a meet-the-author session devoted to both *Beyond Interpretation* and *Advances* at a meeting of the American Psychoanalytic Association in Philadelphia early in the 1980s.

4. In addition, the book has a chapter in which I summarize my results in fifty consecutive cases treated in psychoanalysis. Termination via mutual agreement was achieved in forty-two (that is, 84 percent)—a rate considerably higher than those reported for more traditional analyses by Erle (1979) and Erle and Goldberg (1984).

5. See Wallerstein (1986), Mehlman (1987), and Modell (1988).

6. William Grossman independently reached similar conclusions in his superb studies of two other dissidents, Wilhelm Reich (Grossman 1976) and Karen Horney (Grossman 1984).

7. Although I was less than explicit about it, the thrust of my argument in *Conceptual Issues* was that my own role in psychoanalysis is that of the "epistemological referee" who has inherited Rapaport's mantle. This implication so offended one reviewer that he wrote a highly deprecating response, largely on the basis of the *tone* of my book, which was (admittedly) that of being "above the battle" (see Friedman 1988).

8. These studies were competently reviewed and summarized in Lichtenberg (1983).

9. In the epilogue of *Conceptual Issues*, I made several other points about the epistemic gap between Lacan and all other psychoanalysts. These philosophical differences are so wide that I find it is beyond my abilities to compare Lacan's propositions with those of other psychoanalytic schools.

10. These premature hopes were perpetuated by the reviews of Gabbard (1988), Elrod (1988), and Skolnikoff (1989).

Chapter 19

1. A slightly different version of this presentation constitutes chapter 11 in 1996b.
2. Literally, "the confrontation notebooks."
3. As *Enquête sur Soi* (Paris: Aubier, 1985).
4. "Letters" in the sense of "arts and letters."
5. Marguerite Yourcenar, Belgian-born novelist who lived in America for half a lifetime, was the first woman elected to the *Académie Française*. Her best work was published after World War II.
6. It is typical of the French that they included an editorial note to the effect that the paper overlooks the work of a French literary scholar who had something significant to say about the Cervantes novella Freud had emulated. That work was published after 1973 and, as far as I was able to grasp, was not relevant to our thesis.
7. Dupont was editor of the French version of Ferenczi's *Clinical Diary* (her edition appeared in English in 1990). She is one of those now working to publish the Freud-Ferenczi correspondence.
8. The opponents of Ferenczi are led by Béla Grünberger, who reached France in the 1930s. See Grünberger (1980).
9. *Sans blague* means "no joke." *Un peu déclassé*: a bit lower class.
10. In Hungarian, 1986f appeared in the journal *Pszichológia*. I was correctly listed as "Gedö János," but my middle initial was left as "E." I had hoped that my cousin Gábor, who acted as my agent for this transaction, would get it right: "Emeric" is my arbitrary rendering of Imre. At age 13, I condensed the German equivalent, "Emmerich," and the medieval French name, "Aimery."

Chapter 20

1. Gedo, J. (1992). Das belagerte Troja: Ein Zehn-Jahres Bericht. *Psa-Info* 39:99–111.
2. In connection with the commentary on Ferenczi (1968b), on Freud's adolescent correspondence (1970d), my review of the analytic literature on art (1970a), and the article on Rapaport (1973c).
3. Gedo, J. (1993). Zur Form psychoanalytischer Interventionen. *Psyche* 47:130–47.
4. Attack, impetus, breakthrough!

5. Gedo, J. (1991). Selbstpsychologie—eine post-kohutianische Betrachtung. *Psyche* 45:1–16.

6. I, also, am a refugee.

7. *Ariadne auf Naxos* contains a play-within-the-play about Ariadne's abandonment by Theseus, the Athenian youth whose life she had saved when he was sent to Crete to be sacrificed.

8. Thomä and his team have joined forces with an American consortium that includes such prominent psychotherapy process research figures as Wilma Bucci and Hartvig Dahl, as well as George Klumpner, and others.

9. In a letter of October 7, 1980 (in my files), Thomä wrote me, "I read with great interest and agreement your recent monograph 'Beyond Interpretation' as well as your paper on a comparison between the Firestone Report [sic] and the case book of the Kohut group."

10. The Schlieffen Plan was the strategic doctrine the German general staff devised for the 1914 attack on France (by way of Belgium).

11. Heinrich Heine, the early nineteenth-century German-Jewish poet, was a native of Düsseldorf.

12. "Germany for the Germans! Foreigners, out!" (Contemporary extremist rallying cry).

13. Although Verdi's opera casts Manrico in the role of hero, the actual political point of the narrative is that he and the count are brothers and their war is senseless. To equate this with the civil war of the 1930s utterly subverts Verdi's drama of sibling rivalry.

14. The work of Heinrich von Kleist, the outstanding German dramatist/short story writer of the Napoleonic era, formed the principal subject matter of chapter 13 in 1986a.

15. In Goethe's *Wilhelm Meister*, the foundling Mignon asks everyone she meets whether they know a land "where the lemons bloom"—her only memory of her birthplace, Italy. Like many of Henry James's American heroines, Mary has always felt rejuvenated by Italian journeys.

16. Lochner was a fifteenth century Cologne painter of great accomplishment; very few of his works survive.

Chapter 21

1. Careful attention to archaic phenomena reveals that analysands will often repeat patterns of behavior even more primitive than those of mode III; these "crises" may be characterized by disorganization, states of apparent helplessness, and grandiose fantasies. The coexistence of mutually contradictory attitudes, without subjective discomfort about this dissonance, is pathognomonic of orga-

nization in mode II. When such behaviors recur as transferences, they do not constitute emergencies in the present; they are merely mimetic reenactments of the past.

2. Two chapters of *The Mind in Disorder* are devoted to a review of apraxias commonly encountered in psychoanalyses: in chapter 13, I discuss disorders of communication (including language, affects, and vegetative signs), and in chapter 14 disorders of thought (particularly obsessions and magical thinking). A further chapter (15) considers the manner in which the spectrum of sexual behaviors is explained in the foregoing schema of psychopathology.

3. See Carlson (1990), Rodgers (1990), Shane and Shane (1993), and Wayne (1991).

4. Chapter 9 of the 1991 book is devoted to further discussion of epistemic problems, namely, the question of how modifications of standard analytic technique influence the observations that follow as psychoanalytic evidence.

5. Chapter 11 is my ultimate assessment of Heinz Kohut's contributions to psychoanalysis and of self psychology (as he left it at his death) as a theoretical system.

6. For reviews of *The Biology of Clinical Encounters*, see Meissner (1992), Zabarenko (1993), and Orr-Andrewes (1995).

Chapter 22

1. In "The fine art of criticism," *The Satires and Epistles of Horace*, trans. S. P. Bovie (Chicago: University of Chicago Press, 1959).

2. Voice and piano works by Rossini, produced after he retired at the age of 39 from composing for the stage.

3. To be precise, I performed analytic work from early in 1957 until September 1994. In that interval, I worked with sixty-two analytic patients; of these analyses, fifty were terminated by mutual consent, six were interrupted, and six had to be changed into nonanalytic treatments.

4. The Nazis had signs at the gates of concentration camps that proclaimed that work makes one free. I deny this.

5. Grand et al. (1993). See also Grand et al. (1988).

6. Rousseau's work is entitled "Rêveries d'un promeneur solitaire"—a solitary stroller.

7. *Modelli della Mente* (Rome: Astrolabio, 1975) and *Al delà dell'Interpretazione* (Rome: Astrolabio, 1981).

8. "L'Arte Della Psicoanalisi come una Tecnologia dell'Instruzione," 21:25–39 (1987); "Una Epistemologia del Transfert," 24:7–20 (1990); "La Teoria Psicoanalitica e il Rasorio di Occam," 28:19–32 (1994). See also "La Nosologia e gli Scopi

Terapeutici della Psicoanalisi," *Prospettive Psicoanalitiche nel Lavoro Instituzionale* 5:195–214 (1987), and "La Elaborazione come Metafora e come Modalità Terapeutica," *Il Ruolo Terapeutico* 67:4–11 (1994).

9. Montaigne's *Travel Journal* about a journey to Lucca (where he "took the waters" to combat his kidney stones) was the first literary treatment of the theme; Goethe's *Italienische Reise* was probably the most influential. Freud was undoubtedly acquainted with Goethe's book, at least by reputation.

10. The present, "Polish" pope, John Paul II.

11. Available on cassettes #140 (Friedman) and #164 (Lichtenberg) from the American Psychoanalytic Association.

12. The former is available as cassette #142 from the American. For my presentation at the Ferenczi panel, see in press, b.

13. *Conceptual Issues* had one unexpected outcome: a major article appeared in *Psyche* about my differences with Kohut's views (Elrod 1988). I received a copy of this early in 1989, and (as I have recounted) this sign of interest in my work in the German analytic world led me to contact *Psyche*, after a lapse of more than a decade, to ask whether they would like to receive submissions directly from me; this *démarche* eventuated in my subsequent fruitful contacts with the German analytic community.

Chapter 23

1. *Vae victis*—woe to the vanquished. (A Roman general's terse comment about the fate awaiting defeated Barbarians.)

2. *Mission civilisatrice*—civilizing mission. This was the French version of the British justification for colonialism, "the white man's burden." *Un homme moyen cultivé*—a man of average cultivation.

Chapter 24

1. In Wagner's *Ring*, Fafner is one of the giants hired by Wotan to construct Valhalla; his fee is the Rhinegold. To guard this, Fafner magically turns into a dragon.

2. That is, how this proposed enactment would have repeated some childhood transaction with a significant figure.

3. See Guggenheim Museum (1986), *Oskar Kokoschka* 1886–1980 (New York: The Solomon R. Guggenheim Foundation), Cat. Number 125. The spiral ramp of the museum overlooks its atrium from a height of several stories.

4. Dante was in exile while writing *The Divine Comedy*.

5. For an overall summary of my analytic results, see 1991a (chapter 10).

6. By reason of honor. (This is the phrase universities use to designate honorary degrees.)

7. My review of the literature on art, 1970a, dealt with several of Eissler's works.

8. "Some are born great, some achieve greatness, and some have greatness thrust upon them" (Shakespeare, *Twelfth Night*, Act II, Scene 5); the Gospel of John 12:2–8.

9. In *The Barber of Seville*, Bartolo sings, "A doctor of my sort . . ."

10. "The 327 Best Mental Health Experts." *Good Housekeeping*, February 1994; see p. 77.

11. Tosca's aria, in Act II of the Puccini opera, "I lived [a life] of art; I lived [a life] of love . . ."

APPENDIX

Chronological List of John Gedo's Psychoanalytic Publications

The following list is arranged in the order of first publication; however, the bibliographic information is given for the first appearance in English. Works that have also appeared in translation include the relevant information in parentheses—first the language, in abbreviated form—French: F; German: G; Hungarian: H; Italian: I; Japanese: J; Spanish: S—then the year of publication.

1959a: Some difficulties of psychotherapeutic practice. *Archives of General Psychiatry* 1:3–6.

1963a: A note on non-payment of psychiatric fees. *International Journal of Psycho-Analysis* 44:368–371.

1964a: Concepts for a classification of the psychotherapies. *International Journal of Psycho-Analysis* 45:530–539.

1964b: (with Sabshin, M., Sadow, L., and Schlessinger, N.), "Studies on hysteria": a methodological evaluation. *Journal of the American Psychoanalytic Association* 12:735–751.

1965: Unmarried motherhood: a paradigmatic single case study. *International Journal of Psycho-Analysis* 46:352–357.

1966a: The psychotherapy of developmental arrest. *British Journal of Medical Psychology* 39:25–33.

1966b: (Schlessinger, N., Pollock, G., Sabshin, M., Sadow, L., and Gedo, J.), Psychoanalytic contributions to psychotherapy research. In: L. Gottshalk and A. Auerbach, eds., *Methods of Research in Psychotherapy*. New York: Appleton-Century-Crofts, pp. 334–360.

1967a: On critical periods for corrective experience in the therapy of arrested development. *British Journal of Medical Psychology* 40:79–83.

1967b: (with G. Pollock), The question of research in psychoanalytic technique. In: B. Wolman, ed., *Psychoanalytic Technique*. New York: Basic Books, pp. 560–581.

1967c: (Schlessinger, N., Gedo, J., Miller, J., Pollock, G., Sabshin, M., and Sadow, L.), The scientific style of Breuer and Freud in the origins of psychoanalysis. *Journal of the American Psychoanalytic Association* 15:404–422.

1968a: Freud's self-analysis and his scientific ideas. *American Imago* 25:99–118.

1968b: The wise baby reconsidered. In: J. Gedo and G. Pollock, eds., *Freud: The Fusion of Science and Humanism*. *Psychological Issues*, monograph 34/35. New York: International Universities Press, 1976, pp. 357–378. (G, 1968).

1968c: (Sadow, L., Gedo, J., Miller, J., Pollock, G., Sabshin, M., and Schlessinger, N.), The process of hypothesis change in three early psychoanalytic concepts. *Journal of the American Psychoanalytic Association* 17:608–623.

1969: (Miller, J., Sabshin, M., Gedo, J., Pollock, G., Sadow, L. and Schlessinger, N.), Some aspects of Charcot's influence on Freud. *Journal of the American Psychoanalytic Association* 17:608–623.

1970a: Thoughts on art in the age of Freud: a review. *Journal of the American Psychoanalytic Association* 18:219–245. (G, 1973).

1970b: Mythopoesis and psychoanalysis. *American Imago* 27:329–337.

1970c: The psychoanalyst and the literary hero: an interpretation. *Comprehensive Psychiatry* 11:174–181.

1970d: (with E. Wolf), The "Ich" letters. In: J. Gedo and G. Pollock, eds., *Freud: The Fusion of Science and Humanism*. *Psychological Issues*, monograph 34/35. New York: International Universities Press, 1976, pp. 71–86. (G, 1970).

1970e: (with A. Goldberg), Models of the mind in psychoanalysis. *Bulletin of the Philadelphia Association of Psychoanalysis* 20:74–79.

1972a: On the psychology of genius. *International Journal of Psycho-Analysis* 53:199–203.

1972b: The dream of reason produces monsters. *Journal of the American Psychoanalytic Association* 20:197–223.

1972c: Panel report: the methodology of psychoanalytic biography. *Journal of the American Psychoanalytic Association* 20:638–649.

1972d: Caviare to the general. *American Imago* 29:293–317.

1972e: (E. Wolf, J. Gedo, and D. Terman), On the adolescent process as a transformation of the self. *Journal of Youth and Adolescence* 1:257–272.

1973a: (with A. Goldberg), *Models of the Mind*. Chicago: University of Chicago Press. (I, 1975; paper, 1976; S, 1980; J, 1982).

1973b: (with E. Wolf), Freud's *Novelas Ejemplares*. *The Annual of Psychoanalysis* 1:299–317. New York: Quadrangle. (F, 1984).

1973c: Kant's way: The psychoanalytic contribution of David Rapaport. *Psychoanalytic Quarterly* 42:409–434. (G. 1975).

1974a: Review of *Sigmund Freud and Lou Andreas-Salomé Letters*. *Journal of the American Psychoanalytic Association* 22:211–218.

1975a: Forms of idealization in the analytic transference. *Journal of the American Psychoanalytic Association* 23:485–505. (F, 1981).

1975b: To Heinz Kohut: on his 60th birthday. *The Annual of Psychoanalysis* 3:313–322. New York: International Universities Press.

1975c: (with E. Wolf), The last introspective psychologist before Freud: Michel de Montaigne. *The Annual of Psychoanalysis* 3:297–310. New York: International Universities Press.

1976a: (editor, with G. Pollock), *Freud: The Fusion of Science and Humanism*. *Psychological Issues*, monograph 34/35. New York: International Universities Press.

1976b: (with E. Wolf), From the history of introspective psychology: the humanist strain. In: J. Gedo and G. Pollock, eds., *Freud: The Fusion of Science and Humanism*. *Psychological Issues*, monograph 34/35. New York: International Universities Press, pp. 11–45.

1976c: (G. Klumpner and J. Gedo), Toward a conceptual index of psychoanalytic terms: a method to develop a psychoanalytic thesaurus. *Journal of the American Psychoanalytic Association* 24:409–424.

1976d: The topographic model. In: *International Encyclopedia of Neurology, Psychiatry, Psychoanalysis, and Psychology*. Ed. B. Wolman.

1977a: Notes on the psychoanalytic management of archaic transferences. *Journal of the American Psychoanalytic Association* 25:787–803.

1977b: Essay on psychoanalytic education. *The Annual of Psychoanalysis* 5:315–325. New York: International Universities Press.

1977c: Sigmund Freud and the Socratic tradition. *Dialogue* 1:2–15.

1977d: Review of G. Klein's *Psychoanalytic Theory* and M. Gill and P. Holzman's *Psychology Versus Metapsychology*. *Psychoanalytic Quarterly* 46:319–325.

1978a: Some contributions of psychoanalysis to a science of man. *The Annual of Psychoanalysis* 6:67–73. New York: International Universities Press.

1978b: A grammar for the humanities. *The Annual of Psychoanalysis* 6:75–102.

1978c: Nietzsche and the psychology of genius. *American Imago* 35:77–91.

1979a: *Beyond Interpretation*. New York: International Universities Press. (I, 1981).

1979b: A psychoanalyst reports at mid-career. *American Journal of Psychiatry* 136:646–649.

1979c: Magna est vis veritatis tuae, et praevalebit! *The Annual of Psychoanalysis* 7:53–82. New York: International Universities Press.

1979d: The psychology of genius revisited. *The Annual of Psychoanalysis* 7:269–283. New York: International Universities Press.

1979e: Theories of object relations: a metapsychological assessment. *Journal of the American Psychoanalytic Association* 27:361–374.

1980a: Reflections on some current controversies in psychoanalysis. *Journal of the American Psychoanalytic Association* 28:363–383.

1980b: The dream in regressed states. In: J. Natterson, ed., *The Dream in Clinical Practice*. New York: Jason Aronson, pp. 193–207.

1981a: *Advances in Clinical Psychoanalysis*. New York: International Universities Press.

1981b: Measure for measure: a response. *Psychoanalytic Inquiry* 1:289–316.

1981c: On van Gogh, Picasso, and the dynamics of creativity. *Dialogue* 5:60–67.

1981d: The air trembles, for demi-gods draw near. *American Imago* 38:61–80.

1982: On black bile and other humours. *Psychoanalytic Inquiry* 2:181–191.

1983a: *Portraits of the Artist*. New York: Guilford. (Paper, 1989).

1983b: Saints and scoundrels and the objectivity of the analyst. *Psychoanalytic Inquiry* 3:609–622.

1984a: (editor, with G. Pollock), *Psychoanalysis: The Vital Issues*, vol. 1. New York: International Universities Press.

1984b: On some dynamics of dissidence within psychoanalysis. In: J. Gedo and G. Pollock, eds., *Psychoanalysis: The Vital Issues* 1:363–375.

1984c: *Psychoanalysis and Its Discontents*. New York: Guilford.

1984d: Discussion of Joseph Lichtenberg's "The Empathic Mode of Perception and Alternative Vantage Points for Psychoanalytic Work." In: J. Lichtenberg, M. Bernstein, and D. Silver, eds., *Empathy II*. Hillsdale, NJ: Analytic Press, pp. 137–142.

1985a: (G. Pollock and J. Gedo, eds.), *Psychoanalysis: The Vital Issues*, vol. 2. New York: International Universities Press.

1985b: On the dawn of experience: the past recaptured. *Psychoanalytic Inquiry* 5:601–620.

1985c: Fluctuat mec mergitur. In: C. Settlage and R. Brockbank, eds., *New Ideas in Psychoanalysis*. Hillsdale, NJ: Analytic Press, pp. 19–28.

1985d: Mourning, perversion, and apotheosis. In: M. Gedo, ed., *Psychoanalytic Perspectives on Art* 1:269–301. Hillsdale, NJ: Analytic Press.

1986a: *Conceptual Issues in Psychoanalysis*. Hillsdale, NJ: Analytic Press.

1986b: La mia posizione nei confronti della tecnica psicoanalitica. In: *Psicoterapia e Scienze Humane: Numero Speciale del Ventesimo Anno*, 20:269–272. (I only).

1986c: Nosology and the therapeutic goals of psychoanalysis. *Sigmund Freud House Bulletin*, 10/special issue: 160–170. (I, 1987).

1986d: On the therapeutic limits of psychoanalysis: delinquent enactments. In: H. Meyers, ed., *Between Analyst and Patient*. Hillsdale, NJ: Analytic Press, pp. 33–48.

1986e: On the origins of the Theban plague: assessments of Sigmund Freud's character. In: P. Stepansky, ed., *Freud: Appraisals and Reappraisals*. Hillsdale, NJ: Analytic Press, pp. 241–259.

1986f: Portrait of the artist as adolescent prodigy: Mozart and *The Magic Flute*. *Medical Problems of Performing Artists* 1:107–111. (H, 1994).

1987a: Paul Cézanne: symbiosis, masochism, and the struggle for perception. In: M. Gedo, ed., *Psychoanalytic Perspectives on Art* 2:187–201. Hillsdale, NJ: Analytic Press.

1987b: Interdisciplinary dialogue as a *lutte d'amour*. In: M. Gedo, ed., *Psychoanalytic Perspectives on Art* 2:223–235. Hillsdale, NJ: Analytic Press.

1987c: (W. Conger, J. Gedo, and M. Gedo), Autobiography, biography, fiction: a symposium. In: G. Moraitis and G. Pollock, eds., *Psychoanalytic Studies of Biography*. Madison, CT: International Universities Press, pp. 349–404.

1987d: Transference neurosis, archaic transference, and the compulsion to repeat. *Psychoanalytic Inquiry* 7:557–567.

1987e: The art of psychoanalysis as a technology of instruction. In: *The Mind in Disorder*. Hillsdale, NJ: Analytic Press, 1988, pp. 211–226. (I, 1987; S, 1991).

1987f: Sometimes a mother is a mother. At other times, she is only someone else. In: B. Cullen, ed., *The Artist's Mother: Portraits and Homages*. Huntington, NY: Hekscher Museum, pp. 17–21.

1988a: *The Mind in Disorder*. Hillsdale, NJ: Analytic Press.

1988b: Character, dyadic enactments, and the need for symbiosis. *Psychoanalytic Inquiry* 8:459–471.

1988c: Masochism and the repetition compulsion. In: R. Glick and D. Meyers, eds., *Masochism: Current Psychoanalytic Perspectives*. Hillsdale, NJ: Analytic Press, pp. 139–147.

1988d: Looking through the third eye. *Art Criticism* 4:64–73.

1989a: Vicissitudes in the psychotherapy of depressive crises. *Psychoanalytic Psychology* 6:1–13.

1989b: Self psychology: a post-Kohutian view. In: D. Detrick and S. Detrick, eds., *Self Psychology: Comparisons and Contrasts*. Hillsdale, NJ: Analytic Press, pp. 415–428. (G, 1991).

1989c: A psychoanalyst's response. In: J. Oremland, *Michelangelo's Sistine Ceiling*. Madison, CT: International Universities Press, pp. 133–151.

1989d: An epistemology of transference. *The Annual of Psychoanalysis* 17:3–15. (I, 1990).

1989e: Review of W. Runyan's *Psychology and Historical Interpretation* and *Life Histories and Psychobiography*. *Biography* 12:332–335.

1989f: Some differences in creativity in performers and other artists. *Medical Problems of Performing Artists* 4:15–19.

1990a: More on creativity and its vicissitudes. In: M. Runco and R. Albert, eds., *Theories of Creativity*. Newbury Park, CA: Sage, pp. 35–45.

1990b: More on the healing powers of art: the case of James Ensor. *Creativity Research Journal* 3:33–57. (S, 1991).

1990c: Position statement on the training analyst question. In: M. Meisels and E. Shapiro, eds., *Tradition and Innovation in Psychoanalytic Education*. Hillsdale, NJ: Erlbaum, pp. 125–129.

1990d: The roots of personality: heredity and environment. *The Harvard Mental Health Letter* 7(1):4–6.

1991a: *The Biology of Clinical Encounters*. Hillsdale, NJ: Analytic Press.

1991b: Ilion besieged: a tenth year report. *Psychoanalytic Inquiry* 11:227–238. (G, 1992).

1991c: Challenge, apraxia, and avoidance. *Psychoanalytic Inquiry* 11:284–295.

1991d: Review of Modell's *Other Voices, Other Realities*. *Contemporary Psychology* 36:845–846.

1991e: The biology of mind: a foreword. In: F. Levin, *Mapping the Mind*. Hillsdale, NJ: Analytic Press, pp. xi–xx.

1991f: Between prolixity and reductionism: psychoanalytic theory and Occam's razor. *Journal of the American Psychoanalytic Association* 39:71–86. (I, 1994).

1991g: The analytic stalemate: discussion. *Contemporary Psychoanalysis* 27:502–511.

1992a: (with M. Gedo), *Perspectives on Creativity: The Biographical Method*. Norwood, NJ: Ablex.

1992b: Discussion of Arnold Modell's "The private self and private space." *The Annual of Psychoanalysis* 20:15–24.

1992c: Art alone endures. *Journal of the American Psychoanalytic Association* 40: 501–516.

1993a: *Beyond Interpretation*. Revised, paperback ed. Hillsdale, NJ: Analytic Press.

1993b: (with M. Gehrie), *Impasse and Innovation in Psychoanalysis*. Hillsdale, NJ: Analytic Press.

1993c: (A. Wilson and J. Gedo, eds.), *Hierarchical Concepts in Psychoanalysis*. New York: Guilford.

1993d: The hierarchical model of mental functioning: Sources and applications. In: A. Wilson and J. Gedo, eds., *Hierarchical Concepts in Psychoanalysis*. New York: Guilford, pp. 129–152.

1993e: (A. Wilson and J. Gedo), Hierarchical concepts in psychoanalysis. In: A. Wilson and J. Gedo, eds., *Hierarchical Concepts in Psychoanalysis*. New York: Guilford, pp. 311–324.

1993f: Una nota sulla esperienza correttiva emozionale. *Psicoterapia e Scienze Umane* 27:81–84. (I only).

1993g: On fastball pitching, astronomical clocks, and self-cognition. In: J. Barron, ed., *Self-Analysis*. Hillsdale, NJ: Analytic Press, pp. 133–146.

1993h: (K. Bacon and J. Gedo), Ferenczi's contributions to psychoanalysis: essays in dialogue. In: C. Aron and A. Harris, eds., *The Legacy of Sándor Ferenczi*. Hillsdale, NJ: Analytic Press, pp. 129–139.

1993i: The creative personality: challenge and opportunity. *Medical Problems of Performing Artists* 8:103–109.

1993j: Creativity, constitution, and childhood: *Psychological Inquiry* 4:193–196.

1993k: Analytic interventions: the question of form. In: A. K. Richards and A. D. Richards, eds., *The Spectrum of Psychoanalysis*. Madison, CT: International Universities Press, 1994, pp. 111–127. (G, 1993).

1993l: Empathy, new beginnings, and analytic cure. *Psychoanalytic Review* 80:507–518.

1994a: Academicism, romanticism, and science in the psychoanalytic enterprise. *Psychoanalytic Inquiry* 14:295–312.

1994b: The inner world of Paul Gauguin. *The Annual of Psychoanalysis* 22:61–109.

1994c: "The anti-classical insurgency": some psychological aspects of Italian mannerist painting. *Revista Argentina de Arte y Psicoanálisis* 3:121–130. (S, 1994).

1995a: Channels of communication and the analytic setup. *Psychoanalytic Inquiry* 15:294–303.

1995b: The pragmatics of empathy. *The Annual of Psychoanalysis* 25:1–13. (F, 1995).

1995c: Working through as metaphor and as a modality of treatment. *Journal of the American Psychoanalytic Association* 43:339–356.

1995d: Encore. *Journal of the American Psychoanalytic Association* 43:384–392.

1995e: On the psychobiology of motivation. *Psychoanalytic Inquiry* 15:470–480.

1995f: Archaic character types, disorders of communication, and the patient-analyst relationship. *Contemporary Psychoanalysis* 31:575–580.

1995g: Interview with John Gedo (ed. E. Piccioli). *Psychoanalytic Review* 84:1–15 (I, 1995).

1996a: *The Artist and the Emotional World: Creativity and Personality*. New York: Columbia University Press.

1996b: *The Languages of Psychoanalysis*. Hillsdale, NJ: Analytic Press.

1996c: Psychoanalysis and nonverbal communication. *Australian Journal of Psychotherapy* 14:45–53.

1996d: In praise of leisure. In: C. Socarides and S. Kramer, eds., *Work and Its Inhibitions*. Madison, CT: International Universities Press, pp. 133–141.

1996e: The reveries of a solitary scribbler. In: E. Piccioli, P.-L. Rossi, and A. Semi, eds., *Writing in Psychoanalysis*. London: Karnac, pp. 1–12. (I, 1996).

1996f: Tribute to a serious man. *The Annual of Psychoanalysis* 26:35–40.

1996g: Creativity: the burden of talent. *The Annual of Psychoanalysis* 26:97–106.

1996h: Epigenesis, regression, and the problem of consciousness. *The Annual of Psychoanalysis* 26:87–95.

1996i: O, patria mia! In: A Bókay, P. Giampieri, and P. Rudnytsky, eds., *Ferenczi's Turn in Psychoanalysis*. New York: New York University Press, pp. 77–88.

1997a: The primitive psyche, communication, and the language of the body. *Psychoanalytic Inquiry* 17:192–203.

1997b: Reflections on metapsychology, theoretical coherence, hermeneutics, and biology. *Journal of the American Psychoanalytic Association* 45.

1997c: On the psychological core of opera: mythic themes in *Don Giovanni* and *Der Rosenkavalier*. *The Annual of Psychoanalysis* 27.

in press, a: On inspiring confidence. In: E. Piccioli, P-L. Rossi, and A. Semi, eds., *The Person of the Analyst*. London: Karnac.

in press, b: Ferenczi as the orthodox Vizier. *Psychoanalytic Inquiry*.

in press, c: Protolinguistic phenomena in psychoanalysis. *Psychiatry and the Humanities*. Baltimore: Johns Hopkins University Press.

in prep., a: *Metamorphosis: A Readers' Guide to Psychoanalytic Books*, 1973–1998. Northvale, NJ: Jason Aronson.

in prep., b: Psychotherapy as applied psychoanalysis. In: D. Silverman and D. Wolitsky, eds., *Festschrift for Merton Gill*. Hillsdale, NJ: Analytic Press.

REFERENCES

Abrams, S., reporter. (1971). Models of the psychic apparatus. *Journal of the American Psychoanalytic Association* 19:131–142.

Alexander, F. (1951). *Psychosomatic Medicine*. New York: Norton.

Alexander, F., French, T., and Pollock, G., eds. (1968). *Psychosomatic Specificity*. Chicago: University of Chicago Press.

Apfelbaum, S. (1972). Psychoanalysis without guilt. *Contemporary Psychology* 17:600–602.

Appelbaum, A. (1981). Beyond Interpretation: a response from beyond psychoanalysis. *Psychoanalytic Inquiry* 1:167–186.

Benedek, T. (1973). *Psychoanalytic Investigations*. New York: Quadrangle.

Benedek, T., and Fleming, J. (1966). *Psychoanalytic Supervision*. New York: Grune & Stratton.

Blum, H., ed. (1981). *Dix Ans de Psychanalyse en Amérique*. Paris: Presses Universitaires de France.

Boehlich, W., ed. (1990). *The Letters of Sigmund Freud to Eduard Silberstein*. Cambridge: Harvard University Press.

Burris, B. (1994). Review of *Impasse and Innovation in Psychoanalysis* by J. Gedo and M. Gehrie. *International Journal of Psycho-Analysis* 75:423–425.

Carlson, D. (1990). Review of *The Mind in Disorder*. *Psychoanalytic Quarterly*, 59:279–283.

Cocks, G., ed. (1994). *The Curve of Life: Correspondence of Heinz Kohut*. Chicago: University of Chicago Press.

Collins, B. (1990). Psychoanalysis and art history. *Art Journal* 49:182–186.

Cross, R. (1982). Inside Chicago's shrink factory. *Chicago Tribune Magazine*, January 31, pp. 18–20, 23, 26.

Dewald, P. (1981). Revision: yes. Improvement: no. *Psychoanalytic Inquiry* 1:187–204.

Druck, A. (1994). Multiple models and the psychoanalytic stance. *Psychoanalytic Inquiry* 14:243–260.

Dupont, J., ed. (1990). *The Clinical Diary of Sándor Ferenczi*. Cambridge, MA: Harvard University Press.

Eissler, K. (1972). *Talent and Genius*. New York: International Universities Press.

Elrod, N. (1988). John Gedo's Auseinandersetzung mit Kohut. *Psyche* 42:1081–1095.

Erle, J. (1979). An approach to the study of analyzability and analyses: the course of forty consecutive cases selected for supervised analysis. *Psychoanalytic Quarterly* 48:198–228.

Erle, J., and Goldberg, D. (1984). Observations on assessment of analyzability by experienced analysts. *Journal of the American Psychoanalytic Association* 32:715–738.

Esman, A. (1986). Review of *Portraits of the Artist*. *Journal of the American Psychoanalytic Association* 34:227–242.

——— (1988). Cézanne's bathers: a psychoanalytic view. *Psychoanalytic Perspectives on Art* 3:225–238. Hillsdale, NJ: Analytic Press.

Fenichel, O. (1946). *The Psychoanalytic Theory of Neurosis*. New York: International Universities Press.

Ferenczi, S. (1933). Confusion of tongues between adults and the child. In *Final Contributions to the Problems and Methods of Psychoanalysis*, pp. 156–167. New York: Basic Books, 1955.

Firestein, S. (1978). *Termination in Psychoanalysis*. New York: International Universities Press.

Frank, A. (1969). The unrememberable and the unforgettable: passive primal repression. *The Psychoanalytic Study of the Child* 24:59–66. New York: International Universities Press.

Freedman, D. (1984). The origins of motivation. In *Psychoanalysis: The Vital Issues*, vol. 1, ed. J. Gedo and G. Pollock, pp. 17–38. New York: International Universities Press.

French, T. (1952/1953/1958). *The Integration of Behavior*, 3 vols. Chicago: University of Chicago Press.

Freud, A. (1965). *Normality and Pathology in Childhood*. New York: International Universities Press.

Freud, S. (1892–94). Preface and footnote to Charcot's *Tuesday Lectures*. *Standard Edition* 1:133–143.

——— (1894). The neuropsychoses of defence. *Standard Edition* 3:45–61.
——— (1900). The interpretation of dreams. *Standard Edition* 4/5:1–626.
——— (1915). The unconscious. *Standard Edition* 14:166–204.
——— (1920). Beyond the pleasure principle. *Standard Edition* 18:3–64.
——— (1923). The ego and the id. *Standard Edition* 19:12–66.
——— (1926). The question of lay analysis. *Standard Edition* 20:179–259.
——— (1927). The future of an illusion. *Standard Edition* 21:3–58.
——— (1970). Jugendbriefe. *Psyche* 24:766–784.

Friedman, H. (1988). Review of *Conceptual Issues in Psychoanalysis*. *International Review of Psycho-Analysis* 15:263–267.

Friedman, L. (1988). *The Anatomy of Psychotherapy*. Hillsdale, NJ: Analytic Press.

Gabbard, G. (1988). Review of *Conceptual Issues in Psychoanalysis*. *Bulletin of the Menninger Clinic* 15:441–449.

Gardner, R. (1983). *Self Inquiry*. Hillsdale, NJ: Analytic Press.
——— (1994). *On Trying to Teach*. Hillsdale, NJ: Analytic Press.
——— (1995). *Hidden Questions, Clinical Meanings*. Hillsdale, NJ: Analytic Press.

Gay, P. (1984). *The Bourgeois Experience, Victoria to Freud, I: The Education of the Senses*. Oxford: Oxford University Press.

Gedo, M. (1972). *Picasso's Self Image*. Unpublished dissertation, Northwestern University.
——— (1980). *Picasso—Art as Autobiography*. Chicago: University of Chicago Press.
———, ed. (1985/1987/1988). *Psychoanalytic Perspectives on Art*, 3 vols. Hillsdale, NJ: Analytic Press.
——— (1988). Introduction. *Psychoanalytic Perspectives on Art* 3:225–238. Hillsdale, NJ: Analytic Press.
——— (1993). *Looking at Art from the Inside Out*. New York: Cambridge University Press.

Gedo, P. (1988). *The Significant Hour in Psychoanalysis*. Unpublished dissertation. Department of Behavioral Sciences, University of Chicago.

Gill, M., ed. (1967). *The Collected Papers of David Rapaport*. New York: Basic Books.
——— (1981). The boundaries of psychoanalytic data and technique: a critique of John Gedo's *Beyond Interpretation*. *Psychoanalytic Inquiry* 1:205–232.
——— (1983). Radical tradition and conservative revolution. *Contemporary Psychology* 28:69–70.
——— (1994). *Psychoanalysis in Transition*. Hillsdale, NJ: Analytic Press.

Gill, M., and Holzman, P., eds. (1976). *Psychology Versus Metapsychology*. *Psychological Issues*, monograph 36. New York: International Universities Press.

Gitelson, M. (1973). *Psychoanalysis: Science and Profession*. New York: International Universities Press.

Goldberg, A., ed. (1978). *The Psychology of the Self: A Casebook*. New York: International Universities Press.

Goldberg, D. (1985). Review of *Advances in Clinical Psychoanalysis*. *Psychoanalytic Quarterly* 54:83–89.

Grand, S., Feiner, K., and Reisner, S. (1993). The level of integrative failure in borderline and schizophrenic pathology. In *Hierarchical Concepts in Psychoanalysis*, ed. A. Wilson and J. Gedo, pp. 48–75. New York: Guilford.

Grand, S., Freedman, N., Feiner, K., and Kiersky, S. (1988). Notes on the progressive and regressive shifts in levels of integrative failure. *Psychoanalysis and Contemporary Thought* 11:705–740.

Grinker, R. (1995). The history of psychoanalysis in Chicago, 1911–1975. *The Annual of Psychoanalysis* 23:155–193.

Grossman, W. (1976). Knightmare in armor: reflections on Wilhelm Reich's contributions to psychoanalysis. *Psychiatry* 39:376–385.

——— (1986). Freud and Horney. In: A. Richards and M. Willick, eds., pp. 65–87. *Psychoanalysis: The Science of Mental Conflict*. Hillsdale, NJ: Analytic Press.

Grünberger, B. (1980). From the "active technique" to the "confusion of tongues." In *Psychoanalysis in France*, ed. S. Lebovici and D. Widlöcher, pp. 127–152. New York: International Universities Press.

Gunther, M. (1981). Biographical note on John E. Gedo: a peculiar conservative. *Psychoanalytic Inquiry* 1:279–288.

Harsch, H. (1994). Freud's Identifizierung mit Männern, die zwei Mütter hatten. *Psyche* 48:124–153.

Hayman, A. (1969). What do we mean by "id"? *Journal of the American Psychoanalytic Association* 7:353–380.

Hunter, V. (1992). An interview with Ernest Wolf, Part II. *Psychoanalytic Review* 79:481–508.

——— (1994). *Psychoanalysts Talk*. New York: Guilford.

Jaffe, D. (1984). Review of *Advances in Clinical Psychoanalysis*. *International Journal of Psycho-Analysis* 65:223–229.

Kapfhämmer, H.-P. (1985). *Psychoanalytische Psychosomatik*. Berlin: Springer.

Kaplan, D. (1981). Review of *Beyond Interpretation*. *Psychoanalytic Review* 68:285–288.

Katz, J. (1981). Review of *Beyond Interpretation*. *Bulletin of the Menninger Clinic* 45:165–167.

Klein, G. (1976). *Psychoanalytic Theory*. New York: International Universities Press.

Kohut, H. (1959). Introspection, empathy, and psychoanalysis: an examination of the relationship between mode of observation and theory. *Journal of the American Psychoanalytic Association* 7:459–483.

——— (1966). Forms and transformations of narcissism. *Journal of the American Psychoanalytic Association* 14:243–272.

——— (1968). The psychoanalytic treatment of narcissistic personality disorders. *The Psychoanalytic Study of the Child* 23:86–113. New York: International Universities Press.

——— (1970). Scientific activities of the American Psychoanalytic Association: an inquiry. *Journal of the American Psychoanalytic Association* 18:462–484.

——— (1971). *The Analysis of the Self*. New York: International Universities Press.

——— (1976). Creativeness, charisma, group psychology: reflections on the self-analysis of Freud. In *Freud: The Fusion of Science and Humanism. Psychological Issues*, monograph 34/35, ed. J. Gedo and G. Pollock, pp. 379–425. New York: International Universities Press.

——— (1977). *The Restoration of the Self*. New York: International Universities Press.

——— (1978). The psychoanalyst in the community of scholars. In *The Search for the Self*, pp. 685–724. New York: International Universities Press.

——— (1984). *How Does Analysis Cure?* Chicago: University of Chicago Press.

——— (1985). Introspection, empathy, and the semicircle of mental health. In *Psychoanalysis: The Vital Issues*, vol. 2, ed. J. Gedo and G. Pollock, pp. 347–375. New York: International Universities Press.

Kramer, C. (1967). Maxwell Gitelson. Analytic aphorisms. *Psychoanalytic Quarterly* 36:260–270.

Kris, E. (1952). *Psychoanalytic Explorations in Art*. New York: International Universities Press.

Levin, F. (1991). *Mapping the Mind*. Hillsdale, NJ: Analytic Press.

Lewin, B., and Ross, H. (1960). *Psychoanalytic Education in the United States*. New York: Norton.

Lichtenberg, J. (1983). *Psychoanalysis and Infant Research*. Hillsdale, NJ: Analytic Press.

——— (1989). *Psychoanalysis and Motivation*. Hillsdale, NJ: Analytic Press.

Liebert, R. (1983). *Michelangelo: A Psychoanalytic Study of his Life and Images*. New Haven: Yale University Press.

——— (1985). Response to John E. Gedo's essay review. *Psychoanalytic Perspectives on Art* 1:307–313. Hillsdale, NJ: Analytic Press.

Lytton, S., reporter. (1984). Value judgments in psychoanalytic theory and practice. *Journal of the American Psychoanalytic Association* 26:599–613.

Mahon, E. (1980). Contribution to the problem of symptom choice. *Bulletin of the Association of Psychoanalytic Medicine* 19:64–67.

Malcolm, J. (1981). *The Impossible Profession*. New York: Knopf.

——— (1984). *In the Freud Archives*. New York: Knopf.

McLaughlin, J. (1983). Review of *Beyond Interpretation*. *Psychoanalytic Quarterly* 52:271–280.

Mehlman, R. (1987). Review of *Psychoanalysis and Its Discontents*. *International Journal of Psycho-Analysis* 68:303–307.

Meissner, W., reporter. (1976). New horizons in metapsychology. *Journal of the American Psychoanalytic Association* 24:161–180.

——— (1981). Notes on the psychoanalytic psychology of the self. *Psychoanalytic Inquiry* 1:233–248.

——— (1989). *Psychoanalysis and Religious Experience*. New Haven: Yale University Press.

——— (1992). Biology and the mind. Gedo revisited. *Contemporary Psychology* 37:181–182.

Meyer, B. (1967). *Joseph Conrad: A Psychoanalytic Biography*. Princeton: Princeton University Press.

Michels, R. (1982). Review of *Beyond Interpretation*. *Journal of the American Psychoanalytic Association* 30:780–782.

Migone, P. (1985). Monografia: John E. Gedo. *Psicoterapia e Scienze Umane* 19:89–102.

Modell, A. (1965). On having the right to a life: an aspect of the superego's development. *International Journal of Psycho-Analysis* 46:323–331.

——— (1988). Review of *Psychoanalysis and Its Discontents*. *Journal of the American Psychoanalytic Association* 36:180–183.

——— (1992). The private self and private space. *The Annual of Psychoanalysis* 20:1–14. Hillsdale, NJ: Analytic Press.

Moore, B. (1981). Review of *The Psychology of the Self*. *Journal of the American Psychoanalytic Association* 29:249–252.

Moraitis, G. (1985). The psychoanalyst's role in the biographer's quest for self-awareness. In *Introspection in Biography*, ed. S. Baron and C. Pletsch, pp. 319–354. Hillsdale, NJ: Analytic Press.

——— (1994). Beyond the blueprints of mental function. *Psychoanalytic Inquiry* 14:261–275.

Orr-Andrewes, A. (1995). Review of *The Biology of Clinical Encounters*. *Psychoanalytic Quarterly* 64:781–784.

Pine, F. (1990). *Drive, Ego, Object, Self*. New York: Basic Books.

Rangell, L. (1981). A view on John Gedo's revision of psychoanalytic theory. *Psychoanalytic Inquiry* 1:249–266.

Reff, T. (1987a). John Gedo and the struggle for perception. *Psychoanalytic Perspectives on Art* 2:202–222. Hillsdale, NJ: Analytic Press.

——— (1987b). The author, the authority, the authoritarian. *Psychoanalytic Perspectives on Art* 2:237–243. Hillsdale, NJ: Analytic Press.

Robbins, W., reporter. (1977). Varieties of oedipal distortions in severe character pathologies. *Journal of the American Psychoanalytic Association* 25:201-218.

Rodgers, T. (1990). Review of *The Mind in Disorder*. *Psychoanalytic Books* 4:192–203.

——— (1994). The clinical theories of John Gedo: a synopsis. *Psychoanalytic Inquiry* 14:235–242.

Rosen, V. (1977). *Style, Character, and Language*. New York: Jason Aronson.

Rosenfeld, H. (1987). *Impasse and Interpretation*. London: Tavistock.

Rothstein, A., reporter. (1983). Interpretation: toward a contemporary understanding of the term. *Journal of the American Psychoanalytic Association* 31:237–245.

Runco, M., and Albert, R., eds. (1990). *Theories of Creativity*. Newbury Park, CA: Sage.

Sajer, G. (1971). *The Forgotten Soldier*. New York: Harper & Row.

Schur, M. (1966). Some additional day residues of the specimen dream of psychoanalysis. In *Psychoanalysis—a General Psychology*, ed. R. Loewenstein, L. Newman, M. Schur, and A. Solnit, pp. 45–85. New York: International Universities Press.

Searles, H. (1986). *My Work with Borderline Patients*. Northvale, NJ: Jason Aronson.

Segal, H., and Britton, R. (1981). Interpretation and primitive psychic processes: a Kleinian view. *Psychoanalytic Inquiry* 1:267–278.

Shane, E., and Shane, M. (1993). Self psychology after Kohut: One theory or many? *Journal of the American Psychoanalytic Association* 41:777–797.

——— (1994). The developmental approach of John Gedo. *Psychoanalytic Inquiry* 1:187–204.

Siegel, S., reporter (1968). "Toward a developmental psychology" by J. Gedo. *Bulletin of the Philadelphia Association of Psychoanalysis* 18:147–152.

Silverman, D., and Silverman, L. (1983). Review of *Advances in Clinical Psychoanalysis*. *Review of Psychoanalytic Books* 2:321–341.

Silverman, M. (1985). Review of *Portraits of the Artist*. *Psychoanalytic Quarterly* 54:637–642.

Skolnikoff, A. (1989). Review of *Conceptual Issues in Psychoanalysis*. *Psychoanalytic Quarterly* 58:116–121.

Skura, M. (1981). *The Literary Use of the Psychoanalytic Process*. New Haven, CT: Yale University Press.

Spear, R. (1992). *La necessità* of Guido Reni. In *Il Luogo ed il Ruolo della Città di Bologna tra Europa Continentale e Mediterranea*, pp. 313–340. Bologna: Nuova Alfa Editoriale.

Spiro, M. (1965). *Children of the Kibbutz*. New York: Schoken.

Spitz, R. (1945). Hospitalism: an inquiry into the genesis of psychiatric conditions in early childhood. *The Psychoanalytic Study of the Child* 1:53–64. New York: International Universities Press.

Spruiell, V., reporter. (1978). Current concepts of object relations theory. *Journal of the American Psychoanalytic Association* 26:599–613.

Steinberg, L. (1984). Review of Robert Liebert's *Michelangelo. New York Review of Books*, June 28.

Stepansky, P., ed. (1988). *The Memoirs of Margaret Mahler*. New York: Free Press.

Sterba, R., and Sterba, E. (1956). The anxieties of Michelangelo Buonarroti. *International Journal of Psycho-Analysis* 37:325–330.

Swanson, D. (1977). A critique of psychic energy as an explanatory concept. *Journal of the American Psychoanalytic Association* 25:603–633.

Swartz, J. (1980). Review of *Beyond Interpretation*. *American Journal of Psychiatry* 137:272–273.

Tähkä, V. (1993). *Mind and Its Treatment*. Madison, CT: International Universities Press.

Terman, D. (1976). *Distortions of the Oedipus complex in severe pathology*. Presented at the American Psychoanalytic Association, December, New York.

——— (1984/85). The self and the Oedipus complex. *The Annual of Psychoanalysis* 12/13:87–104. New York: International Universities Press.

Trosman, H. (1965). Freud and the controversy over Shakespearean authorship. *Journal of the American Psychoanalytic Association* 13:475–498.

——— (1969). The cryptomnesic fragment in the discovery of free association. *Journal of the American Psychoanalytic Association* 17:489–510.

van Gogh, V. (1959). *The Complete Letters of Vincent van Gogh*, 2nd ed., 3 vols. Greenwich, CT: New York Graphic Society.

von Bertalanffy, L. (1968). *General Systems Theory: Foundation, Development, Applications*. New York: George Braziller.

Waelder, R. (1930). The principle of multiple function. In *Psychoanalysis, Observation, Theory, Application*, pp. 68–83. New York: International Universities Press.

——— (1967). *Progress and Revolution*. New York: International Universities Press.

Wallerstein, R. (1986). Review of *Psychoanalysis and Its Discontents* 55:323–334.

Wayne, M. (1991). Review of *The Mind in Disorder*. *Psychoanalysis and Psychotherapy* 9:88–94.

Weich, M., reporter. (1986). Clinical aspects of language. *Journal of the American Psychoanalytic Association* 34:687–698.

Wilson, A., and Passik, S. (1993). Explorations in presubjectivity. In *Hierarchical Concepts in Psychoanalysis*, ed. A. Wilson and J. Gedo, pp. 76–126. New York: Guilford.

Wolf, E. (1971a). Saxa loquuntur: artistic aspects of Freud's "The aetiology of hysteria." *The Psychoanalytic Study of the Child* 26:535–554. New Haven, CT: Yale University Press.

——— (1971b). Sigmund Freud: some adolescent transformations of a future genius. *Adolescent Psychiatry* 1:51–60. New York: Basic Books.

——— (1976). Ambiance and abstinence. *The Annual of Psychoanalysis* 4:101–115. New York: International Universities Press.

Wolf, E., and Trosman, H. (1974). Freud and Popper-Lynkeus. *Journal of the American Psychoanalytic Association* 22:123–141.

Zabarenko, L. (1993). Review of *The Biology of Clinical Encounters*. *Psychoanalytic Books* 7:33–39.

INDEX